THE DIE-HARD SPORTS FAN'S GUIDE TO BOSTON

THE DIE-HARD SPORTS FAN'S GUIDE TO BOSTON

Christopher Klein

Union Park Press • Boston

Union Park Press
Boston, MA 02118
www.unionparkpress.com

Printed in the United States of America
First Edition

© 2009 Christopher Klein

Library of Congress Control Number: 2009926391
ISBN: 1-934598-04-6; 978-1-934598-04-7

Book design by Elizabeth Lawrence / www.elizabethl.com
Cover art © Elizabeth Lawrence
Maps on pages 203, 212, 238, 250 designed by Elizabeth Lawrence;
all maps © Union Park Press.

All rights reserved. No part of this publication may be copied, stored in a retrieval system, or transmitted in any form by any means, electronic, mechanical, recording or otherwise, except brief extractions for the purpose of review; no part of this publication may be sold or hired without the written permission of the publisher.

Although the author and Union Park Press have taken all reasonable care in preparing this book, we make no warranty about the accuracy and completeness of its content and, to the maximum extent permitted, disclaim all liability arising from its use.

All information in this book, including ticket prices, was accurate at the time of publication but is subject to change. For updates on spectator information, ticket prices, and arena and stadium seating maps, visit www.bostonsportsguide.com.

Acknowledgements

This book was a labor of love, and many people have my deep appreciation in helping it come to fruition.

I want to particularly thank Zack Hample, Greg Rybarczyk, Michael Narracci, Maggie Magner, Eddie Andelman, and Peter Leventhal for sharing their insights. My sincere thanks also go to Kelly Mohr of the Boston Bruins, Jack Fleming of the Boston Athletic Association, Kevin Hassett of the Boston Breakers, Kurt Svoboda of Harvard University, Scott Ellis and Brian Kelley of Boston University, Bob Donovan of the Francis Ouimet Scholarship Fund, Gary Roy of NESN, Marieke Van Damme of The Bostonian Society, Jon Shestakofsky of the Boston Red Sox, and Bob Brady, Ralph Evans, and Byron Magrane of the Boston Braves Historical Association.

I'm grateful to Dave Ahouse, Michele Ahouse, Kevin Forbes, Ed Hannan, Dave Hughes, Mick Morrissey, Mark Newhall, Reed Newton, and Marc Selvitelli for their input on the contents of the book and service as valuable sounding boards.

I'm indebted to publisher Nicole Vecchiotti, who believed in the concept of this book from the very start and sharpened it with a keen editorial eye. Her guidance and encouragement, particularly when the game clock was winding down, were invaluable. Jossie Auerbach was an MVP with her research assistance throughout the project. Special thanks to Erin Whinnery and James Duggan at Union Park Press for all their work on the final stages of the manuscript.

Lastly, I'm immensely grateful to my father, who introduced me to the wonderful world of sports, and to my mother, who indulged my passion. Thanks to my wife, Erin, and to Drew, my rookie of the year, for their endless patience and support.

FOREWORD

Sure, Boston is home to incredible historical sites, world-class universities, and amazing cultural institutions. But as any of us who've lived in the city will tell you, Boston is the Green Monster, the parquet floor, and Heartbreak Hill. Boston is Teddy Ballgame, Larry Legend, and Tom Terrific. Boston is the Beanpot, the Head of the Charles, and high school football on Thanksgiving. Boston is "Sweet Caroline" in the middle of the eighth and the chants of "Beat LA" echoing through the Garden.

Boston is the best sports town in America, hands down, and the pulse of this city beats among the frenzied sports fans who live and die with the home teams. While we've been undeniably fortunate in recent years with championship success, Boston sports fans stick with our teams through thick and thin. We've watched our teams raise our hopes and dash our dreams, and we've got the tears of joy and the emotional battle scars to prove it.

In Boston, we'll do whatever it takes to follow our teams, whether it's camping out overnight for tickets or crowding into the sports bar down the street. We've got the courage to proudly sport our team's colors on enemy turf. We know there's nothing better than tailgating before a football game, or spending a lazy summer day soaking up sun in the ballpark, or lining the route of another Duck Boat parade, no matter what time of year.

So Boston fans, use this book to root, root, root for the home teams, and be sure to be loud.

Wicked loud!
—Sean McDonough

CONTENTS

vii	**FOREWORD**	88	**FOOTBALL**
	by Sean McDonough	92	New England Patriots
		93	*Gillette Stadium*
10	**AMERICA'S SPORTING HUB**	100	New England Patriots Training Camp
	An Introduction	101	The Hall at Patriot Place
		103	Boston College
16	**THE TOP TEN THINGS ALL BOSTON FANS MUST DO BEFORE THE FAT LADY SINGS**	108	Harvard
		114	Northeastern
		117	High School Football
18	**BASEBALL**	119	*Where to Watch:* College and Pro Football
23	Boston Red Sox		
24	*Fenway Park*	120	**HOCKEY**
39	Beyond Boston	123	Boston Bruins
39	*Red Sox Spring Training*	129	Beanpot
43	*Pawtucket Red Sox*	130	Hockey East Championship
45	*Portland Sea Dogs*	131	Boston College
48	*Lowell Spinners*	134	Boston University
50	*Brockton Rox*	139	Harvard
53	*Worcester Tornadoes*	143	Northeastern
55	*Cape Cod Baseball League*	145	Super Eight High School Hockey
		146	Beyond Boston
59	**BASKETBALL**	146	*Providence Bruins*
61	Boston Celtics	147	*Lowell Devils*
64	*TD Garden*	147	*Worcester Sharks*
73	Boston College		
74	Boston University	148	**SOCCER**
77	Harvard	150	New England Revolution
80	Northeastern	155	Boston Breakers
84	High School Championships	156	*Where to Watch:* International Soccer Matches
85	Beyond Boston		
85	*Basketball Hall of Fame*		
86	*Where to Watch:* College Basketball		

158 **AUTO RACING**
160 Larz Anderson Auto Museum
161 Beyond Boston
161   *New Hampshire Motor Speedway*
163   *Where to Watch:*
     Formula One

164 **BOXING**
168 Beyond Boston
168   *Brockton Historical Society*
168   *Foxwoods*
170   *Mohegan Sun*
170   *Twin River*

171 **GOLF**
174 Deutsche Bank Championship
177 Massachusetts Golf Museum

178 **HORSE RACING**
181 Suffolk Downs

187 **LACROSSE**
188 Boston Cannons
190 Boston Blazers

200 **ROWING**
202 Head of the Charles Regatta
203   *HOCR Course Map*
207 Beyond Boston
207   *Harvard-Yale Regatta*

208 **RUNNING**
209 Boston Marathon
212   *Marathon Course Map*
216 Boston Indoor Games
218 USA Indoor Track & Field Championships
218 Nike Indoor Nationals

219 **TENNIS**
221 Boston Lobsters
222 Champions Cup Boston
224 Beyond Boston
224   *International Tennis Hall of Fame*

226 **ADDITIONAL SPECTATOR SPORTS**
226 Australian Rules Football
227 Bay State Games
227 Cricket
229 Cycling
230 Equestrian
230 Gaelic Sports
232 Polo
233 Rugby
233 Sailing
234 Skiing
235 Squash
235 Swimming

237 **THE BOSTON SPORTS TRAIL**
     A Sports-Themed Walking Tour of the Hub
238   *Sports Trail Map*

246 **THE SPORTS MUSEUM**

249 **WHERE TO WATCH (& DRINK)**
249 Boston's Best Sports Bars
250   *Sports Bars Map*
261 Boston Sports Bars Around the World

262 **BOSTON SPORTS PILGRIMAGES**
     Road Trips for the Die-Hard Fan

266 **RESOURCES**

AMERICA'S SPORTING HUB
AN INTRODUCTION

When the Puritans sailed to Boston's shores to create a society founded on their religious ideals, one of the secular vices they were hoping to escape was organized sports. Surely, Boston's forbearers would be shocked to discover the descendants of their "city upon a hill" worshiping a pantheon of athletic gods in sporting shrines throughout the region.

Sports are intricately woven into the fabric of Boston and are an essential part of the daily lives and psyches of its citizens. For Bostonians, sports are a constant

Courtesy Boston Public Library, Print Department.

source of intense ecstasy and—on more occasions than most fans would care to remember—heartbreak. The vibe of the city is often dictated by whether the home team won or lost the night before. On mornings after Boston teams play on the West Coast, you can count on seeing bleary-eyed commuters on the T. Sports stories routinely make the front pages of the city's newspapers, a sports station dominates drive-time radio, and television ratings for Red Sox games trounce network programs. How sports crazy is Boston? Well, when it came time to christen the new tunnel under Boston Harbor, the city chose to honor not a politician, military hero, or Founding Father, but Ted Williams, a baseball legend who hadn't donned a Red Sox uniform in thirty-five years.

And while Boston has a reputation as being a professional sports town, tickets to minor league baseball games and college hockey games regularly sell out, fans pack high school football fields on Thanksgiving mornings, and tens of thousands line the banks of the Charles River to cheer amateur rowers. Basically, if you put up a scoreboard, Bostonians will come.

Boston has always been America's sporting capital, but with the recent championships of the Red Sox, Patriots, and Celtics, the title has never been more deserved. That success has of course brought with it the fair weather fans, but the majority of Boston sports fans are die-hards who stick with their teams through thick and thin, through Duck Boat parades and mind-numbing futility.

The relationships between die-hard Boston sports fans and their teams are lifelong love affairs—and as with all affairs of the heart, there are giddy highs and rocky lows. Fans invest their precious time and treasure into these relationships—purchasing tickets, merchandise, and plane fares to hit the road to cheer on their teams. Stomachs churn during big games, making the victories that much sweeter, but if championship dreams are suddenly snuffed out, a true fan feels as if he or she has been punched in the gut and will start to exhibit the five stages of grief.

Boston sports fans idolize superstars who deliver championships and stay loyal to the home teams. But this intensity cuts both ways, and Boston fans are known to react like jilted lovers when one of their heroes skips town to take up with the enemy. (You haven't been the only one, Johnny Damon.)

It shouldn't be a surprise that a city known as the Athens of America shares with the ancient Greeks a love of sports and an appreciation of the role they play, along with intellectualism and spirituality, in the formation of a well-rounded person. And perhaps sports are treated with zeal in Boston because they are the city's guilty little pleasure, a chance for normally staid Bostonians to shed their austere past and let loose. Or perhaps it's because sports are quintessential meritocracies, where success and failure is based on individual talent and tenacity rather than social and economic background, a democratic concept that still resounds in the city that launched the American Revolution.

The reason for Boston's sports obsession could also be a little more evident. Quite simply, the city has been blessed with some of sports' most-storied franchises, brightest stars, and memorable moments. Iconic settings such as the Green

Boston University and Harvard University play in the Beanpot at Boston Garden.
Courtesy Boston Public Library, Special Collections Department.

Monster, parquet floor, Citgo sign, and Heartbreak Hill are familiar to sports fans around the world. Some of sports' greatest legends—Ruth, Russell, Orr, Bird, Flutie, Yaz, Brady, Williams—have thrilled the hometown fans. Just mention the jersey numbers 4, 9, 12, and 33, and sports fans instantly nod in recognition.

There have been some incredible chapters of sports history written by Boston's teams too. Etched into the memories of fans across the country are moments such as Carlton Fisk furiously waving his extra-inning blast fair during the 1975 World Series, Bobby Orr flying through the air after clinching the 1970 Stanley Cup, John Havlicek stealing the ball, Adam Vinatieri booting a pair of Super Bowl winners, and the Red Sox cowboying up after their backs were against a pinstriped wall in the 2004 American League Championship Series.

Despite all that history, Boston was certainly never predestined to be a great sports town. While the Puritans weren't necessarily the monolithic spoilsports that they are often portrayed to be, they didn't embrace athletic pursuits either. The Puritans tolerated hunting and fishing, but they drew the line at ball games and popular Elizabethan blood sports, such as bear baiting and cockfighting.

It seems the Puritans packed their contempt of ball games and blood sports with them on the *Arbella* and brought them to Boston from the motherland. The city's forefathers believed that spectator sports were incubators of morally corrupt behaviors such as gambling and frivolous activity that profaned the Sabbath. (The latter objection remained firmly entrenched in Boston for centuries with the blue laws prohibiting some Sunday sporting events well into the 1900s.) They also shunned sports such as tennis for their popish origins; other sports, such as horse racing and football, were equally rebuffed for their perceived risks to public safety.

While spectator sports gained popularity in other American colonies in the early 1700s, strong opposition remained in New England. Bowling and swimming were among the few sporting activities to be found in colonial Boston, and horse racing was about the only organized spectator sport tolerated in the city during the eighteenth century because it promoted military training. And even then, horse racing was forbidden within four miles of any town center.

The city's sporting fervor didn't come of age until the middle of the nineteenth century. During the latter half of the 1800s, the Industrial Revolution gave rise to a wealthy merchant class and, in turn, a greater amount of leisure time. Flush in time and fortune, Boston Brahmins baptized tennis, golf, and yachting. Their sons who played on the fields of Boston Common became the pioneers of baseball and football.

On the other end of the social strata, immigrants who poured into Boston in the 1800s brought along their own pastimes, such as cricket, soccer, and hurling. But they also joined with the social elite in patronizing sports already entrenched in the American consciousness, and they saw the opportunity that sports provided for social mobility. Heavyweight champion John L. Sullivan, the son of immigrants from the Emerald Isle, became an idol among the Boston Irish. Francis Ouimet, another product of immigrant parents, captured the city's attention along with the 1913 U.S. Open golf tournament at The Country Club. Even today Rocky Marciano is beloved by Italian-Americans in his hometown of Brockton, nearly forty years after his passing.

Just like today, Boston in the early 1900s offered a smorgasbord of choices for the die-hard sports fan. For instance, Bostonians who picked up *The Boston Globe* on Bunker Hill Day in 1902 could scan the day's sporting program and find a wealth of choices on land and water. Baseball fans could head to the Huntington Avenue Grounds to watch the city's American League team take on Cleveland in the morning and then cross the tracks to watch the National League nine square off against New York in the afternoon. Racing fans could attend steeplechases at The Country Club in Brookline, follow motorcycles circling the track at Cambridge's Charles River Park, or watch the Dorchester Gentlemen's Driving Club race their trotters in a matinee at Readville Trotting Park. Golf clubs staged match play competitions, and the Longwood Cricket Club hosted the Massachusetts state championship tennis tournament. Cricket matches and amateur boxing were also on the docket. Meanwhile, mariners could watch any number of yacht races in Boston Harbor, and crews from around the metropolitan area took to the Charles River for a rowing regatta. Even devotees of the new horseless carriages

Boston College basketball fans sit in silence as the Eagles lose to Temple in the NIT final, March 1969.
Courtesy Boston Public Library, Print Department.

could join in the fun and watch the Massachusetts Automobile Club on a run from Boston to Cohasset.

It's clear that today's die-hard Boston fans are just the latest custodians of a rich sporting heritage that spans generations. And the Hub is a city that deeply honors its traditions. Sports are no exception. The Boston Marathon, Harvard-Yale football, and the Beanpot are quintessential Boston events that are not just athletic competitions, but celebrations of the city's past.

Boston sports fans may have a reputation for provincialism, but they are anything but an insular community. Travel to any part of the country wearing a Patriots hat or Celtics jacket and you'll quickly discover kindred spirits. You can even travel to the far side of the world and find fans in a Red Sox bar. You may not share a language or a culture with the locals, but you have a more important bond—a love of the Sox.

Sports are the great equalizer—crossing not only linguistic and cultural boundaries, but those of ethnicity, power, and economics. The fates of the local sports teams are fodder for conversation from the halls of power in the State House to the lines at city soup kitchens, from the Italian cafés of the North End to the Irish pubs of Brighton and the taquerias of East Boston. In stadiums, bars, and living rooms, Bostonians come together to cheer on the home teams with a singular voice.

In this most historic American city, sports connect Bostonians not only to people around the city and around the world but to distant ancestors and family. After all, Boston is a city where season tickets are birthrights passed down from generation to generation. Fans can go to a baseball game at Fenway Park and sit in the same exact seats as their great-great-great grandparents.

When the Red Sox broke their 86-year championship drought in 2004, thousands of fans made intensely personal pilgrimages to the gravesites of family and friends to share the good news. That's because at its most basic form, being a die-hard sports fan in Boston is about joy, it's about heartbreak, it's about honoring the traditions of the past, and it's about unbreakable bonds with our families and our community. In a sense, it's an experience of the faithful. And for that, hopefully the Puritans can see some virtue and forgive us our trespasses.

Lolly Hopkins, one of Boston's original die-hard fans, was a fixture at Braves home games.
Courtesy Boston Public Library, Print Department.

THE TOP TEN THINGS ALL BOSTON FANS MUST DO BEFORE THE FAT LADY SINGS

Just about every sports fan has a wish list of the games he or she wants to witness at least once in a lifetime. What die-hard Boston sports fans wouldn't want to be in the stands when the Patriots win the Super Bowl or a Red Sox pitcher hurls a no-hitter? But the unscripted moments and unpredictable results that make sports so great—and sometimes so frustrating—also mean there's no certainty they will ever happen again. So keeping to just those dates written in stone on the region's sporting calendar, here's a subjective list of ten events that all die-hard Boston sports fans should experience firsthand at least once. This bucket list includes events that are quintessentially Boston, the hottest tickets in town, and combustible rivalries steeped in history.

❶ Marathon Monday

Patriots Day officially commemorates the Battles of Lexington and Concord. Unofficially, it's a celebration of Boston sports. Set your alarm early and head to Fenway Park for the traditional morning start of the Red Sox game. After the game, make the short walk to the course of the Boston Marathon and cheer on the weary runners in the final stretch to the finish line.

❷ Opening Day

It's amazing how Red Sox Opening Day always coincides with a city-wide epidemic of the 24-hour flu. Go ahead and call in sick; your boss is probably playing hooky too. Not only are World Series dreams renewed on Opening Day, but after a long hibernation, so are the senses. At first sight, Fenway's Technicolor explosion of green almost blinds eyes dulled by wintertime.

❸ Celtics-Lakers

Just how dominant have the Celtics and Lakers been in NBA history? Through 2008 these two franchises had won as many NBA championships as the league's twenty-eight other franchises combined. The rivalry between the teams was renewed in the 2008 NBA Finals, and now—as before—"Beat LA" reverberates throughout the Garden when the Lakers make their one regular-season trip to Boston.

❹ The Beanpot

Bragging rights in office buildings and classrooms all around Boston are on the line each February when Boston College, Boston University, Harvard, and Northeastern take to the ice for the Beanpot. The four schools and their fans prove the old adage that familiarity breeds contempt. Students, alumni, and pep bands infuse the sold-out Garden with boundless school spirit.

❺ Red Sox-Yankees

Every game at the Fens is full of electricity, but a matchup against the Evil Empire takes it to a whole new level. Each season seems to bring new plotlines to the rivalry between the Red Sox and Yankees, baseball's version of the Hundred Years' War. For a truly special experience, watch the Sox and the Bronx Bombers from one of the Monster seats.

❻ Head of the Charles Regatta

Every October a small armada fills the Charles River for the world's largest two-day regatta. Three hundred thousand spectators line the banks of the Charles to watch eight thousand rowers navigate the snaking course, headwinds, and seven bridges. The colorful foliage and crisp weather make this an autumnal Boston tradition.

❼ Harvard-Yale Football

It's known simply as "The Game." Harvard and Yale have battled it out on the gridiron since 1875; in even-numbered years the tilt takes place in historic Harvard Stadium. The Game is always the season finale for both teams, and on numerous occasions, it has decided the Ivy League title. Fans dressed in raccoon coats and waving felt pennants are seriously old school.

❽ Bruins-Canadiens

When the Bruins and Habs meet on the ice, the gloves come off—literally and figuratively. These bitter division foes have battled for more than eighty years, including many intense faceoffs in the Stanley Cup Playoffs. The roar of the Garden crowd right after those final notes of the Canadian and American anthems is deafening.

❾ Cape Cod Baseball League

The amateur Cape Cod Baseball League is a baseball purist's dream. There's no better way to savor the summer than to head to one of the Cape's intimate ball fields, spread out a blanket, munch on a hot dog, and listen to the thwack of the mitt and the crack of the bat under the setting sun.

❿ Thanksgiving High School Football

Along with turkey, stuffing, and pumpkin pie, pigskin is on the Thanksgiving menu for many Massachusetts residents. Sure, going to a Patriots game can be a fantastic (and an all-day) experience, but gathering around high school football fields on Thanksgiving morning to watch timeless rivalries is as much of a communal experience in Boston as the postgame family feast.

BASEBALL

In 1954, French-born historian Jacques Barzun wrote: "Whoever wants to know the heart and mind of America had better learn baseball." Well, the same sentiment holds true for Boston.

Since the sport's inception, Boston has had a love affair with baseball, and in particular with its beloved boys of summer, the **Boston Red Sox**. It's perfectly logical, of course, that the city where America was born would have an enduring attachment to this quintessential American sport.

Television ratings for Red Sox games consistently outdraw network programs, blockbuster trades are front-page news for the city's papers, and playoff games dominate local television newscasts. Between April and September (and hopefully October), Red Sox games provide the soundtrack to everyday life in Boston. You could wander Boston on a summer day and not miss a pitch. The crackle of the radio play-by-play emanates from taxi cabs and variety stores. Even during the winter, the Hot Stove League draws more attention in Boston than the regular season does in many other cities.

It's not just the Sox who have a hold over Bostonians and New Englanders—but the very sport itself. From big cities to small towns, from storied Fenway Park to small high school fields on Cape Cod, fans across New England spend their summers packed around baseball diamonds. Old men diligently score each pitch in their programs while young children scoop ice cream out of their helmet sundaes. Perhaps it's the bitter winters that draw the region to baseball. Fans relish each one of those precious summer days and savor the sport that matches the pace of the season. By focusing on each individual pitch, each relay throw, each bunt, or each lazy fly ball before the days grow short and the weather turns cold, New Englanders live the baseball season deliberately, in the finest tradition of Henry David Thoreau.

The region's intense attachment to baseball and its unceasing fixation on the fortunes of its beloved teams is nothing new. Boston is the only city that has had a major league baseball team continuously since 1871, and even in the nineteenth century, legions of fans were obsessed with Boston's local nines. From the cheering "cranks" (the old terminology for baseball fans) who formed the Royal Rooters at the turn of the twentieth century to today's Red Sox Nation, which is actually a global phenomenon, Boston is crazy about baseball.

The sport of baseball has its roots in cricket and similar games that were brought to America by English immigrants. Even back in the early 1600s, the first European arrivals to New England played some form of bat-and-ball game called stool ball that was popular in the west of England. William Bradford, the governor of Plymouth Colony, confiscated balls and bats as the merriment didn't sync with the Pilgrims' way of life.

By the 1850s, baseball as we know it began to emerge, and in 1854, the Boston Olympics formed the first baseball club in the city. Games were played across New England in village greens and city parks, including Boston Common. Even in the 1850s, it was not unusual for the ballgames on Boston Common to draw thousands of spectators.

When baseball began to come of age before the Civil War, two sets of rules emerged: the "Massachusetts game," which was popular in Boston, and the "New York game." Under the rules of the Massachusetts game, the batter stood halfway between home plate and first base, there was no foul territory, and fielders could get a runner out by hitting him with a thrown ball. The New York game, which was first played on Boston Common in 1858 by the Tri-Mountain Club, ultimately won out, even in Boston. The modern sport developed from the New York game although elements from the Massachusetts game, such as catching a ball for an out and overhand pitching, also found their way into today's rules. Unfortunately, the triumph of the New York game wouldn't be the last time that the Big Apple would prevail over Boston on diamond-related issues. (Vintage baseball games played under nineteenth-century rules are regularly played throughout the summer on Georges Island, part of the Boston Harbor Islands national park area.)

Boston was home to the first professional team and the first baseball dynasty— the Red Stockings—who won four of five National Association pennants between 1871 and 1875 with stars George and Harry Wright and Albert Spalding. The Red Stockings played their games at the South End Grounds, located at the present site of the MBTA's Ruggles Station in Roxbury. Over the years, the team's name changed from Beaneaters to Red Caps to Doves before it officially became the Boston Braves. The Braves played at the South End Grounds until 1914. Between 1888 and 1894, the ballpark featured a grand pavilion that looked like a fairytale castle with its medieval-style turrets. It was Boston's only double-decked ballpark. Unfortunately, the Great Roxbury Fire of 1894, which started in the right-field bleachers during a game, destroyed the pavilion and 177 surrounding buildings.

While the South End Grounds was being rebuilt, the team played their games at the Congress Street Grounds, located on a site crossed by Thompson Place and Stillings Street in the Fort Point Channel area of Boston. (The Dartmouth Street Grounds, located at the present-day site of Copley Place, was also home to baseball teams in the 1880s.)

> ### ★ The Babe in Boston
>
> Between 1922 and 1926, Babe Ruth owned Home Plate Farm, a 155-acre farmstead in Sudbury. Although technically a Yankee ballplayer at that time, it's not surprising that the Babe was ill-suited to be a Yankee farmer. All that remains of **Home Plate Farm** is the old farmhouse at 558 Dutton Road. Believe it or not, the Curse of the Bambino is strangely related to this private residence. During a 2004 game at Fenway a Manny Ramirez foul ball struck the face of Lee Gavin, who lived in Ruth's old Sudbury farmhouse, perhaps marking the start of the exorcism.

The Braves moved in 1915 to Braves Field, which was built on the site of the Allston Golf Links, a little more than a mile away from Fenway Park. (The South End Grounds would endure until 1929.) The home of the Braves was the largest baseball stadium in the country when it opened, and the Red Sox actually played their home games in the 1915 and 1916 World Series at Braves Field because the stadium had a larger crowd capacity than Fenway Park. (The Red Sox also played Sunday games at Braves Field between 1929 and 1932 as the blue laws prevented them from using Fenway Park because of its proximity to a church.)

By the time the Braves slinked out of town and moved to Milwaukee on March 13, 1953—right before the start of the season—the Red Sox had played in one more World Series in the Braves' ballpark than the home team had. Today, the site of Braves Field has been converted into Boston University's Nickerson Field, but some vestiges remain. The right-field bleachers were incorporated into the grandstand of Nickerson Field, and a portion of the exterior right-field wall still stands along Harry Agganis Way. The stucco ticket office down the right-field line is now a child-care center and campus security office, and a plaque behind the building commemorates Braves Field.

Of course most fans know that Babe Ruth's major league debut was with the Red Sox, but many forget that the Sultan of Swat ended his career in the Hub as well, this time with the Braves. Ruth only played a handful of home games at Braves Field before retiring in 1935. Earlier in his career he pitched a 14-inning gem there during Game 2 of the 1916 World Series. The game ended in a victory for the Red Sox.

From 1901 to 1911, before the Bambino showed up in the Hub and the Red Sox moved to Fenway Park, Boston's American League franchise played at the Huntington Avenue Grounds, just a tape-measure shot from the South End Grounds. Today it is the site of Northeastern University, but back in 1903 it was the site of the first World Series between Boston, the American League champion, and Pittsburgh, the National League champion. Boston won the inaugural fall classic in eight games (it was best of nine at the time) and ushered in baseball's modern era.

Along a footpath named World Series Way, a bronze statue of Cy Young, crouching down with his five-fingered glove resting on his left knee, stands outside Northeastern's Churchill Hall. The statue marks the spot of the ballyard's old mound. A home plate marker is embedded in the grass, sixty feet and six inches away from the flamethrower, at the same spot where home plate rested in the old ballpark.

A plaque on the exterior of Northeastern's **Cabot Physical Education Center** (400 Huntington Avenue. 617-373-2672) commemorates the 1903 World Series and is located approximately on what was the stadium's left-field foul line. A display case on the center's second floor houses a small collection of artifacts, including old photographs and wool jerseys.

When the Huntington Avenue Grounds closed in 1912, the infield dirt and grass was moved to the team's new ballyard, **Fenway Park**. Boston baseball fans are absolutely blessed to have such a jewel of a ballpark in their midst, and they know it. No other baseball stadium in the majors is so intimate and filled with such history. Since Fenway Park opened, the Red Sox have won six World Series titles and experienced consistent championship success—well, with the exception of that one 86-year drought between 1918 and 2004.

The one downside of the team's recent championship success for Red Sox fans has been that tickets are as tough to find as ever. The team set a major league record for consecutive sellouts, beginning in May 2003. And even if you're lucky enough

★ Royal Rooters: The Founding Fathers of Red Sox Nation

Boston's Royal Rooters—a group of baseball "cranks," as fans were known at the turn of the twentieth century—were the founding fathers of today's Red Sox Nation. Those cranks were as passionate as today's rabid baseball fan base, even if the dress code has changed slightly. With their buttons, signs, and chants, the Royal Rooters, who followed both the city's National and American League franchises, were the original die-hards. They even hit the rails to take in road games and spring training, and their exploits were breathlessly covered in newspapers of the day.

Headquarters for the Royal Rooters was the saloon owned by Michael McGreevey. The mustachioed son of Irish immigrants earned the nickname "Nuf Ced" for the words he would shout to end arguments in the tavern. McGreevey's bar became known as the Third Base Saloon. (It advertised itself as "the last stop before you go home.") Baseball players such as Babe Ruth, politicians such as John "Honey Fitz" Fitzgerald, gamblers, and cranks all hung out at the saloon, which might have been America's first sports bar. Its walls were plastered with baseball photographs and memorabilia. Game bats from stars such as Nap Lajoie, King Kelly, and Cy Young were transformed into electrical fixtures attached to frosted glass spheres that resembled baseballs.

McGreevey's saloons were strategically located near the South End and Huntington Avenue Grounds at **940 Columbus Avenue** and then **1153 Tremont Street**. Alas, the enactment of Prohibition in the 1920s brought about the demise of McGreevey's business. However, the spirit of "Nuf Ced" was revived in 2008 when Dropkick Murphys' lead vocalist Ken Casey and other investors opened **McGreevy's Third Base Saloon** on Boylston Street.

to score a ticket, the amount you'd spend on tickets, parking, Fenway Franks, and watered-down beer may match the payroll of the Tampa Bay Rays.

A great alternative to Fenway are the three minor league affiliates of the Red Sox, all within easy driving distance of Boston: the Single A **Lowell Spinners**, the Double A **Portland Sea Dogs**, and the Triple A **Pawtucket Red Sox**. You might be lucky enough to see a Sox player on a rehabilitation assignment, or just consider it a scouting trip to see future Red Sox stars on the road to Fenway. The minor league teams provide affordable and family-friendly entertainment, and additional teams in the area include the **Brockton Rox** and **Worcester Tornadoes**. But in this baseball-crazy area of the country, even minor league games can sell out.

Not only do the pros pack the fans into ballparks around New England, but the amateurs do as well. The **Cape Cod Baseball League**, the premier summer collegiate league in U.S., draws hundreds and, sometimes, thousands of fans to games. Closer to Boston, the **North Shore Navigators** (365 Western Avenue, Lynn, MA 01904. 339-440-8201; www.nsnavs.com) field a collegiate team that plays summertime games in Lynn's historic Fraser Field. The area's colleges and universities also field teams that play in what passes for springtime weather in this part of the world.

Let's play ball!

Michael McGreevey, owner of the Third Base Saloon, and Red Sox players at spring training in Hot Springs, Arkansas, in 1912. Courtesy Boston Public Library, Print Department.

BOSTON RED SOX

Boston may be America's premier sports city, but more than anything else, the Hub is a Red Sox town. Boston is a city painted red. Fans of the Olde Town Team are the most loyal, knowledgeable, and passionate supporters in American sport.

The familiar blue baseball cap with the bright red "B" has always been ubiquitous around Boston and New England, but now, with the team's recent championships, it's almost impossible to travel around the country or around the world and not spot other Red Sox fans declaring their loyalties with Red Sox gear. The population of Red Sox Nation now dwarfs that of many countries around the world. (The Red Sox payroll also outranks the GNP of several small countries.) Fans drive to games from all across New England, and many even fly in from cities around the country or around the world to catch a game or two at historic Fenway Park.

The popularity and recent success of the team, the size of its fan base, and its diminutive ballyard have all contributed to the longest sellout streak in Major League Baseball, which dates back to May 2003. Tickets to Fenway Park are cherished possessions, clutched firmly like winning lottery tickets, and many a fan has lost an entire Saturday staring at a computer screen, trapped in a virtual waiting room when tickets go on sale. Some fans may feel as if they need to win the lottery to pay for their tickets, as the Red Sox have the priciest entrance fee in baseball, with the average ticket costing about $50.

As a result, fans hit the road along with the team in order to get a ticket to a Sox game. Red Sox fans regularly have a large presence at road games, and in some cases outnumber supporters of the home team. The Red Sox have even launched a travel service called Red Sox Destinations that sells ticket packages to road games.

While there are undoubtedly a fair share of fans who have jumped on the bandwagon with the team's recent success, as a whole, citizens of Red Sox Nation have lived and died with the team all their lives. Being a Red Sox fan is a birthright handed down from generation to generation, and today's fans are the current custodians of the flame. True Sox fans know where they were when the ball dribbled through Buckner's legs, when Fisk waved a ball fair in the early morning darkness, when Teddy Ballgame bowed out with a home run in his final at bat, when an Impossible Dream came true, and when an epic curse was finally foiled with a world championship.

Die-hard fans follow every game between April and September, and if the team is fortunate enough to play in the chilled air of October, crimson-hose supporters will hang on every, stomach-turning pitch, bouncing between hope and dread. It's hardly an easy existence. Not even Stephen King, New England's resident horror expert and ardent Sox fan, could have dreamt up the countless storylines of disappointment that plagued the team over the decades. At times, the crimson "B" on Boston's ball cap has felt like a scarlet letter. But the championships of 2004 and 2007 have removed a millstone around the neck of Sox fans, and their fatalistic approach to the team has begun to temper.

What hasn't faded—in fact it has only been augmented—is the city's passion for the Red Sox. When Daisuke Matsuzaka first arrived in Boston in 2007, tens of thousands of fans followed the progress of his plane online. Talk radio lines seem to be forever jammed with fans who want to dissect the latest win or loss. It's even a known fact that traffic is always lighter on mornings following the team's West Coast games, as local die-hards catch some shut-eye. The truth is, every Red Sox game is an event. The atmosphere at each contest has an electric intensity of a playoff game, and if the game is against the dreaded Yankees, it's taken to a whole other level.

Baseball purists will love that cowbells and rally towels are shunned in Boston. There are no exploding fireworks or blaring rock music. The sounds you'll hear before games are of sausages sizzling on the grills, the shouts of street vendors hawking programs, and the call of ticket scalpers searching for prey. Inside Fenway, you'll hear the buzz of the crowd, the dulcet organ tunes, the crack of the bat, and the fans singing "Take Me Out to the Ballgame" in the middle of the seventh and "Sweet Caroline" in the middle of the eighth. And if the Sox prevail and the die-hards get their wish, you'll hear the distinctive sounds of "Dirty Water" celebrating another victory.

Fenway Park

"Ladies and gentlemen, boys and girls, welcome to Fenway Park."

In a city that treats its sports like religion and worships its sporting heroes like gods, Fenway Park is its most hallowed piece of turf. It is only fitting that Boston's baseball team has such a historic edifice. Since the first of the acolytes entered the park's turnstiles in 1912, such venerable sporting shrines as Boston Garden and Yankee Stadium have come and gone. Indeed, Fenway Park is a piece of America, and countless literary giants—including the likes of Updike, Angell, and Halberstam—have paid tribute to the ballpark and its team.

Yankee fans grumble, but Fenway is touted as "America's Most Beloved Ballpark," and although it looks like a nondescript brick warehouse outside, a trip inside is always a nostalgic journey. Die-hards never forget that first time they walked up the ramp from the bowels of the stadium and glimpsed the verdant field and its mighty wall. The first trip to Fenway is as much of a rite of passage to New Englanders as a first kiss. And while there have been some changes to Fenway over the years, the field that was once patrolled by Ruth, Williams, and Yastrzemski looks about the same as it has for decades.

At its core, Fenway Park is the same ballpark visited by the great-grandparents of today's Sox fans, as evidenced by some of the park's 15-inch-wide wooden seats and cramped concourses. Those idiosyncrasies and the crowd's proximity to the field bestow Fenway with an undeniable charm—although the park seems infinitely less charming if you are unlucky enough to have an obstructed view behind a pesky pole (not to be confused with *the* Pesky Pole).

Still, a game at Fenway Park will have you feeling like you're ten years old again. Partly because of childhood memories, but mostly because the stadium is caught in a perpetual time warp. The Wave, which had its heyday in the 1980s, is still a fan favorite. And the organ playlist tilts heavily toward the hits of the 1960s with Motown favorites such as "I Second That Emotion," Beatles' tunes like "With a Little Help From My Friends," and the Monkees' "Pleasant Valley Sunday." Jock jams and pounding rock anthems, these are not.

Fenway Park opened in April 1912—the same week in which the Titanic met its watery demise. Boston won the inaugural game against New York's American League

> ### Fenway's Other Tenants
>
> While it's known as a baseball cathedral, Fenway Park has hosted a wide variety of sporting and entertainment events. The Patriots played in Fenway between 1963 and 1968, and Boston College and Boston University took to the gridiron there as well. Other football teams that called Fenway home were the Boston Bears, the Boston Shamrocks, the NFL's Boston Redskins in the 1930s, and the Boston Yanks in the 1940s. (Can you imagine a team nicknamed the Yanks allowed to play home games in Fenway?) Fenway was home to the Boston Beacons soccer team in 1968, and it even hosted a basketball game in July 1954 between the Harlem Globetrotters and George Mikan's all-stars. The park has been used for rallies for Irish independence and one of Franklin Roosevelt's final campaign speeches in 1944, and summer concerts with acts such as Bruce Springsteen and the Rolling Stones have now become annual traditions.

franchise, then known as the Highlanders. The Red Sox won the World Series in that first season, followed by titles in 1915, 1916, 1918, 2004, and 2007. In 1914, while a new stadium was being built, the Boston Braves actually celebrated a World Series title in Fenway Park as well.

The most distinctive feature of Fenway Park is the Green Monster; after the Great Wall of China, this might be the most famous wall in the world. When the park first opened, it featured a shorter wall, twenty-five feet high, in left field that was fronted by a 10-foot embankment, which served double-duty as seats for fans who sat in front of the wall. The 37-foot-high Green Monster was built in 1934, although it wasn't painted green until 1947. Until then, the wall was plastered with advertisements for products such as soap, shaving cream, cigarettes, and alcohol.

The job of painting the Formica-like surface of the Green Monster appropriately falls to Fenway Painters of Wilmington, Massachusetts. (A Red Sox executive found them in the Yellow Pages and thought their name was appropriate for the job.) The paint color is "field green," and it's a customized blend created by California Paints solely for the Red Sox. Approximately twenty-two gallons are sprayed on the Monster every few years for upkeep. It takes about five hours to spray a single coat on the 8,547-square-foot wall.

The Monster's manual scoreboard is another throwback. The line score and out-of-town scores are still posted by hand, although these days, the scorekeepers lurking inside are assisted by a wireless Internet connection. The scoreboard offers another nod to history; on two vertical white stripes, written in Morse code are the initials of the team's former owners, Thomas A. and Jean R. Yawkey.

The ladder above the scoreboard is an anachronistic feature since the team added seats on top of the Green Monster in 2003. It once allowed workers to scale the wall and retrieve the baseballs that collected in the screen that topped the Monster beginning in 1936. The ladder, although rarely hit, is in fair territory and can cause crazy bounces.

Another landmark associated with the Green Monster isn't even inside Fenway Park. Overlooking Beacon Street in Kenmore Square, the Citgo sign has the distinct privilege of always being in the televised shots of home runs over the Green Monster—in fact, it's almost as if the sign's pulsing light patterns practically induce home runs toward its red, white, and blue display. It is an even more appropriate backdrop if you break down the company name to C-IT-GO.

If you can manage to draw your eyes away from the Citgo sign to the right-field grandstand, you'll see the team's seven retired numbers on display. They include 1 (Bobby Doerr), 4 (Joe Cronin), 6 (Johnny Pesky), 8 (Carl Yastrzemski), 9 (Ted Williams), and 27 (Carlton Fisk). Jackie Robinson's 42, which was retired by all teams, is also on display. Pesky's number was added on the last day of the 2008 regular season, and it's a happy coincidence that it overlooks the right-field foul pole that has been nicknamed the "Pesky Pole" in his honor. Several of Pesky's infrequent home runs curved around that pole, which stands a mere 302 feet from home plate.

Pesky may not have been a power hitter, but the Splendid Splinter, Ted Williams, was. In fact, Teddy Ballgame hit such a mighty shot on June 9, 1946, that it traveled 502 feet before smashing the straw hat of Joseph Boucher, who was sitting in the bleachers in section 42, row 37, seat 21. It was the longest home run ever hit into the bleachers, and it's rare to see a dinger even come close to that distance. The Red Sox memorialized that titanic blast by painting the bleacher seat red. It's the lone island of crimson in a sea of green.

The current ownership has done a fantastic job of making enhancements to Fenway Park and the game day experience. The Sox have added the seats on top of the Green Monster and a rooftop pavilion in right field, above the retired numbers. They have created more spacious concourses in right field and along the third-base line and significantly upgraded the food and beverage concessions. The team has also increased access to the stadium and field with events such as the Picnic in the Park and Father's Day Catch, both held on the field. Plus, they have closed down Yawkey Way to vehicle traffic before games, which has created a festival-like atmosphere with food stands, Dixieland bands, and entertainers. (It's also a popular spot for smokers to congregate, so beware the second-hand smoke.) All the additions have raised the capacity of Fenway Park to just under 37,000 for day games and 37,400 for night games.

And despite squeezing all they can from the hulk of baseball's grand dame, the historical nature of Fenway Park has been well preserved. This is still the place where "Smoky" Joe Wood outpitched Walter Johnson in an epic 1-0 showdown in 1912, where Babe Ruth made his big-league debut in 1914, where Ted Williams homered in his final at bat, where Yaz hit for the Triple Crown in 1967, where Bucky Dent crushed Sox hopes in 1978, and where Curt Schilling, bloody sock and all, led Boston to its first world championship in eighty-six years.

Still, with all the history that has occurred on the field, the memories that endure for die-hard Sox fans are often the intensely personal ones—holding your father's hand while walking into Fenway for the first time, biting into a Fenway Frank and scoring the game on a warm summer day, hanging out with buddies in the bleachers on a cold night, or taking your own children and grandchildren to the ballpark for the first time. That's why Fenway isn't just home to the Red Sox—it's home to all of us.

WHEN: The Red Sox regular season runs from April to September.

GETTING THERE: Everyone knows how much fun Boston traffic is; well it's even more of a joy right around Fenway Park at game time.

View of the outfield and stands at the Huntington Avenue Grounds during a game between the Boston Red Sox and the Detroit Tigers. Courtesy Boston Public Library, Print Department.

If you're going to drive to the ballpark, be prepared to get there early or shell out a lot of money for parking.

There are **parking** lots off Beacon Street or Brookline Avenue near the ballpark or at businesses along Boylston Street, but the prices range from $25 to $40. Just remember that it may take a while to exit the lots after a game. There are cheaper parking options, some as low as $6 for night and weekend games, around Boston University and the Longwood Medical Area, which are about a fifteen minute walk to Fenway.

If you're lucky, you might be able to find on-street parking at metered spots along the major roads in the Fenway area and Brookline.

Try Commonwealth Avenue and Beacon and Boylston streets. On-street parking is the easiest on Sunday when meters are not in effect. For weekday night games try to find an open metered spot just after 4 PM and fill it until 6 PM when the meters are no longer in effect. The cost is twenty-five cents for fifteen minutes. If you park in Brookline, be aware that overnight parking is not allowed and cars will be towed after 2 AM.

Discount parking is available at the Prudential Center parking garage, about a mile from Fenway and directly accessible from Exit 22 off the eastbound Massachusetts Turnpike. Discount parking is also available

> ### ★ Getting on TV
>
> Want to make your trip to Fenway extra-memorable by getting your mug on TV? Michael Narracci, director of Boston Red Sox baseball telecasts at NESN, offers some tips for improving your odds of getting on camera. "We look for energetic and loyal fans, those who show some type of emotion depending on the game situation. Virtually all of Fenway Park's seats are in camera range except the blue grandstand seats behind the screen and the last few rows of the grandstand in other sections. Just about all cameras shoot fans at some point during the game, but during an exciting moment, high first base, left field, mid-first base, and the dugout cameras may shoot fans.
>
> "Most sign shots are recorded between innings and played back as a 'look-live.' Fans should look at the cameras and hold the sign up for thirty seconds or more. Signs must have a few ingredients: Don Orsillo's name, Jerry Remy's name, and NESN HD. Everything else is secondary. Of course, 100-year birthdays, new babies, and veterans have a good shot. The sign should look like you put some time into making it; a pizza box with magic marker on it doesn't have a chance."

at the 100 Clarendon Garage in the Back Bay. Keep your ticket stub for the discount. For more information on available parking around Fenway Park, visit www.redsox.com.

If, despite all these warnings, you still want to drive to Fenway Park, take Storrow Drive to the Kenmore exit and turn right onto Beacon Street and then left onto Brookline Avenue in Kenmore Square to get as close as possible to the ballpark. Or take Storrow Drive to the Fenway exit and turn right onto Boylston Street for neighborhood parking.

If possible, take **public transportation** to Fenway. Take any branch of the Green Line, except the "E" branch, to the Kenmore station. It's about a five minute walk from the Kenmore station to Fenway Park. Another option from the suburbs is to take the "D" branch of the Green Line in from Riverside, where there are nearly a thousand parking spaces, and get off at the Fenway stop, which is about a ten minute walk to the ballpark. If you're heading back downtown after the game and want to avoid the crush of humanity on the Green Line, skip Kenmore station and head to either the Fenway, St. Mary's, or Blandford Street stations, west of Fenway Park, and get on there instead. If you're planning on taking the Green Line for only a couple of stops to and from Fenway, particularly during rush hour, bypass the crowded trains and walk. In addition to being more enjoyable, it may actually be quicker.

The Red Sox also offer a **complimentary shuttle bus from the MBTA's Ruggles Station**, which is served by the Orange Line subway, buses, and commuter rail lines from Needham, Franklin, and Providence/Stoughton. Buses run every ten minutes, beginning an hour and a half before game time. Fans are dropped off at Gate B at the corner of Ipswich and Van Ness streets. Return service ends one hour after the end of the game.

By **bus**, the MBTA's numbers 8, 19, 57, 60, and 65 buses also stop at Kenmore station. In addition, the **MBTA commuter line from Worcester** to South Station stops at Yawkey Station, a two minute walk from the ballpark.

TICKETS: There may be no more coveted item in Boston than a ticket to a Red Sox game. It's economics 101: the law of supply and demand. With Red Sox Nation clamoring for tickets and seating at Fenway Park limited, it may seem as if your best bet to catch a home game is to hit the Megabucks numbers or blatantly suck up to any and every season-ticket holder you know. However, there are several ways to get tickets to Fenway—even on game days—and with a little planning, you should be able to catch the Olde Town Team in person.

Generally, the Red Sox put individual tickets for April and May games on sale in the weeks before Christmas. The very popular Sox Pax (packages of tickets to four home games) also go on sale around this time. The team offers about ten different choices of Sox Pax, and they sell out quickly. In January, group tickets are usually put on sale along with individual tickets for the remainder of the season. This excludes tickets for Opening Day, Patriots Day, and Yankees games; right-field roof deck seats; and Green Monster seats, all of which are distributed by an online lottery conducted in February or early March. Playoff tickets tend to be distributed by an online lottery in the weeks before the games.

Go to www.redsox.com and sign up for the team's email newsletter to be kept abreast of ticket sale dates and lotteries. When choosing games, keep in mind that while late September games have the highest potential for drama, there is also the possibility that star players will be resting for the playoffs, or the team is salvaging a lost season by giving minor league players a shot at the big leagues.

You can order tickets online at www.redsox.com, by phone from the ticket office at 877-RED-SOX9, or by phone from the team's 24-hour touchtone ticketing system at 888-327-0100 (617-226-6644 TDD number). Tickets for groups of forty or more people

Fenway is touted as "America's Most Beloved Ballpark."

are available by calling 617-262-1915. The Boston Red Sox ticket office is located at Four Yawkey Way near Gate A. The ticket office is open Monday to Friday between 10 AM and 5 PM (on game days, it stays open until one hour after the start time). Will call windows are available at Gates B, C, and E.

An advantage of ordering tickets by phone or in person from the ticket office as opposed to the website and touchtone ticketing system is the ability to request specific seats and ask for help in avoiding obstructed views. Handling fees are assessed to online and phone orders. If you're seeking to buy tickets the day they first go on sale, try not to make any plans like, say, going to work—even though you should go to work because you're going to need the money.

While most games are sold out before the season begins, additional tickets are usually released on game day or a few days beforehand. Even if the website says a game is sold out, call the ticket office to double check. In addition, a limited number of day-of-game tickets are put on sale at the ticket window at Gate E along Lansdowne Street. They go on sale two hours before the game when gates open, and once you buy a ticket, you are required to go directly into the park. Lines may start forming four or more hours before the game, depending on its importance—so the earlier, the better.

Another way to get your hands on some tickets is to become a card-carrying member of Red Sox Nation, the team's official fan club. Memberships are sold through the team's website, and some membership levels include game tickets or the chance to purchase tickets. The Ultimate Fan Pack Citizenship includes two tickets to the outfield grandstand in the membership cost, and Monster Citizenship includes guaranteed access to purchase two Green Monster tickets.

In addition, there are plenty of ticket brokers legally selling tickets at a markup. You may also want to check online sites such as eBay, Craigslist, and StubHub. You won't be hard-pressed to find ticket scalpers lurking around Fenway Park, but keep in mind that scalping is illegal and, while rare, the police can make arrests. The Red Sox have set up a "scalp-free zone" for supervised ticket sales at face value near the Ted Williams statue on Van Ness Street near Gate B. Buyers must enter the park as soon as they make a purchase.

There is an incredible range of seating choices at Fenway Park. In general, box seats and bleacher seats are uncovered and at the mercy of the elements, while grandstand seats are covered. Here are your ticket options from most expensive to least:

Green Monster ($160) tickets are the most-sought after in Fenway, and possibly in all of sports. There are nearly three hundred seats with countertops that were added atop the famous wall in 2003, and there is a standing room area with countertops that costs $30. These seats give you the best chance of walking away with a home run ball. The Monster seats have their own concession stands and restrooms. The one downside is the limited view of the action in left field and balls hit off the wall, but hey, you can live with it for at least one game in your life. Tickets are available through a lottery system.

Field box ($125) seats are directly behind the dugout boxes and ring the field from the middle of the right-field line to the middle of the left-field line. They are among the few in the park with cup holders and beer vendors. Most of these seats are taken by season-ticket holders.

Right-field roof deck ($115) seats are located above the team's retired numbers and sections 1 to 4 of the grandstand. In the seating section, four swivel chairs flank a table shaped like home plate, and tickets are only sold by the table, so you'll need to buy four at a time ($460). There is wait service at the tables, and the ticket price includes a $25 credit toward food and beverage. Most of the offerings are standard ballpark fare. Standing room tickets are available on the right-field roof deck for $30. If you have a standing room ticket, be sure to get there early to stake out a spot along the countertops or you may find yourself with a poor view of the action. The right-field roof deck includes a bar; the bar tops are actual bowling lanes from the old Kenmore Bowladrome that was located in the basement of Fenway Park. Tickets are available through a lottery system.

Loge box ($90) seats are located between the grandstand seats and field boxes. They run from halfway down the right-field line to just before the Green Monster. Most of these seats are taken by season-ticket holders. Note that row AA in front of sections 30 through 33 isn't as good as it sounds. The row is located directly on a walkway, and there is constant foot traffic blocking your view.

Infield grandstand ($50) seats run between sections 11 and 31, from the middle of the right-field line to the middle of the left-field line. Infield grandstand seats are covered, but the downside of that is you may be seated behind one of the twenty-six poles that hold up the roof. (Visit www.fenwaydata.com to see if your desired seat has an obstructed view.) You'll be

★ Catching Foul Balls & Dingers

When you consider that Red Sox superfan Elizabeth Dooley attended nearly four thousand games between 1944 and 2000 and came away with one foul ball (and two broken fingers for her effort), Zack Hample's haul of 3,800 major league baseballs and counting is pretty impressive. The author of *How to Snag Major League Baseballs* has a few good tips for leaving Fenway with a ball: "Bring a glove. Try camping out on Lansdowne Street before the game and wait for a Red Sox batting-practice home run to sail over the Monster. If you're inside the park, head to the left-field foul line during batting practice. Get as close to home plate as you can; you may be able to scoop up grounders if you lean over the wall. (The front row just before where the ball girl sits is a great spot to catch foul grounders.) Another option is to stay close to the foul pole to get balls tossed to you by the players. The bleacher seats to the right of the batter's eye are also good during BP. Players toss lots of balls to the fans up there. No matter what, be prepared to run." For more tips, visit www.zackhample.com.

If catching a mere foul isn't good enough for you, and you want to snag a home run ball, your best bet is to get a seat above the Green Monster. According to an analysis by Greg Rybarczyk, who compiles home run data at www.hittrackeronline.com, more than half of the home runs landing in Fenway's stands between 2006 and 2008 dropped down into the Monster seats. The next best shot is in the lower bleachers (sections 35 and 40 are the best), where about a quarter of home runs landed. Other good spots are right-field boxes 86, 87, 92, and 93, where nearly as many home runs landed as in the whole of the bleachers.

real cozy with your neighbor sitting in the grandstand's wooden seats, which are fifteen inches wide. They date back to 1934, making them the oldest seats in the majors, and they will give you a sense of how much plumper Americans are these days.

Right-field box ($50) seats are located in front of sections 1 to 10 of the grandstand and straddle the Pesky Pole.

Right-field roof box ($50) seats are located above sections 5 to 10 of the grandstand. The seats are uncovered and have an unfettered view of the field and the bullpens. A bonus of this section is access to a concession stand and restrooms that usually have few lines, so you can grab a hot dog or use the restroom without missing any action.

This section of the ballpark was expanded before the 2009 season. Right-field roof terrace seats ($50) were added. These seats include stools and drink rails similar to the Green Monster seats. Standing room ($30) tickets are also available for the right-field roof box.

Outfield grandstand ($30) seats include sections 1 to 10 in right field and sections 32 and 33 in left field. Without a doubt, sections 32 and 33 provide a vastly superior view than the right-field grandstand seats. (Note that sections 32 and 33 are designated as no-alcohol family sections.) The right-field grandstand seats may be the worst value in Fenway. Many seats are far from the action and face the outfield, so pack some Advil to sooth the neck pain that will develop from constantly craning to see home plate. In addition, the setting sun may be in your eyes for a few innings in sections 1 to 4, although one benefit of sections 3 and 4 is that they have flat-screen televisions mounted from the roof so you can watch the broadcast.

Lower bleacher ($26) seats include sections 34 to 40 behind center field and sections 41 to 43 behind right field and the bullpens. The bleacher seats in dead center field in sections 34, 35, and 36 are among the best in the ballpark as you'll have a good view of balls and strikes from your position behind the pitcher. Seats in sections 34 and 35 are not sold for day games, however, because they are covered with a tarp to provide a hitters' backdrop. During day games, bleacher seats are completely exposed to the sun and on hot days you can feel yourself baking in your seat. Keep in mind that the bleacher section is huge, and you may be as many as forty rows back, and if you are in sections 40 to 43 behind the bullpen, you may have to watch the game through the metal screen that walls the stands off from the bullpen. The setting sun may also be in your eyes during an inning or two if you sit in the right-field bleachers.

Standing room ($20) tickets are not as bad as they sound. You can be in the shade, and a nice breeze occasionally comes through the windows on hot days. Standing room spots are along the walkway behind the grandstand. The walkway is marked with white paint showing you where you can stand and where you can't. The new concourse in left field is a great spot to grab a standing room spot along the countertop. You're close to concessions and bathrooms, you can lean on the counter and put your stuff on it, and you have a pretty good view to boot.

Upper bleacher ($12) seats are the cheapest ticket in Fenway. They are generally the last five to ten rows of bleachers sections 36–39 and 41–43. You're definitely far from the action and you may be sitting underneath the video scoreboard, but hey, at least you're in the ballpark.

In addition to these individual tickets, seats are available in the following premium areas:

Dugout boxes are ultra-premium, field-level seats that comprise the first rows ringing the field from halfway down the left-field line to the Pesky Pole. They are the closest seats to the action. Ticket holders get in-seat wait service and access to the Absolut Clubhouse.

The **EMC Club** provides one of the best views in baseball, from right behind and a story above home plate. The EMC Club has a climate-controlled area with three full-service bars and an upscale restaurant serving dishes such as filet mignon and swordfish. Outside, ticket holders have padded seats, in-seat wait service, and television screens in front of each section. Seats are sold on a season-ticket basis.

The **State Street Pavilion** includes a climate-controlled club lounge and dining area and seats directly above the luxury boxes. The most-expensive tickets on this level are the HP Pavilion Club ($215) and Pavilion Club ($165) options, which are sold on season-ticket basis. These ticket holders have in-game wait service and access to a private lounge with a la carte food options and a buffet. Pavilion Box ($90) seats run from halfway down the right-field line to halfway down the left-field line. Left-Field Pavilion Reserved ($75) seats are located in far left field. In addition, there are standing room tickets available to the Pavilion ($25).

There is a waiting list of nearly six thousand names for season tickets. You can add your name to the wait list for a fee of $50.

DISABILITY ACCESS: Wheelchair spaces are located throughout Fenway Park. A very limited amount of handicap parking is available on Yawkey Way between Van Ness Street and Boylston Street near Gate D and on Ipswich Street near Gate B. While all gates are handicap-accessible, only Gates B and D have elevators. Grandstand wheelchair ticket holders should enter through Gate B or D.

Seating for visually impaired fans is located in the field box, loge box, and grandstand areas. Seating for hearing-impaired fans is located in the loge box and right-field box sections. Hearing-impaired fans can contact the ticket office by calling the TTY phone at 617-226-6644. Listening devices are available at the customer service booths located at Gates D and E and in the Big Concourse near Gate B. Tickets for fans with disabilities must be purchased at least three days in advance.

THE SPLURGE: Of course, a normal day at Fenway Park is a splurge for most fans—not to mention families—since the tickets and concessions are so expensive. But, if you want to drop some crazy money, you could always buy tickets to the EMC Club and State Street Pavilion, park in the lot right across from Fenway Park, stuff yourself silly on filet mignon, and quaff some fine wine at the upscale restaurants.

If that's not good enough and you want to drop *crazy, crazy* money, the Red Sox will be happy to oblige. There are luxury suites, which hold between twenty and twenty-five people with indoor and outdoor seating, available for rental for $7,000 to $8,750. However, if you want to offer your guests something to eat or drink, that will cost extra.

Want some more pampering? Try renting the Legends Suite just behind home plate. For $15,000 ($20,000 for Yankees games), you and twenty guests will get a behind-the-scenes tour of the park, a chance to view batting practice from the Green Monster seats and on the field behind home plate, four Green Monster seats, and two parking passes. Plus, you'll be hosted in the suite by a Red Sox legend such as Dwight Evans or Jim Rice.

Still not crazy enough? Then the Ultimate Monster Package is for you. You get all of section 10 on the Green Monster to impress twenty-seven of your closest friends. (If you don't have twenty-seven friends, that will change as soon as you purchase the package.) There's on-field access during batting practice, a behind-the-scenes tour of the park, Red Sox jerseys for everyone, and unlimited in-game food and beverage. The price? A mere $32,400.

For availability and further information, call 877-RED-SOX9 or email premiumsales@redsox.com.

THE CHEAPSKATE: It's certainly a lot harder to have a cheap day at Fenway Park than it is to splurge, but it's possible to enjoy a day at the ballpark without breaking the bank. For starters, take public transportation or, if you have to drive, find on-street parking and feed the meter. Your cheapest ticket options are the $12 upper bleachers or $20 standing room tickets. Thirsty? You're allowed to bring in one unopened water bottle that is sixteen ounces or less. (It will taste about the same as that watered-down Bud Light anyway and you can refill it at a water fountain.) Smuggle a granola bar or another small foodstuff in your jacket for sustenance.

If the ticket prices are still too rich for your blood, buy a $5 upper bleachers ticket to the annual Futures at Fenway, which features a double-header involving Boston's minor league affiliates. (Tickets for the Green Monster seats and other areas of high demand are $30.)

Shot on September 28, 2008, at Fenway Park. New York Yankees vs. Boston Red Sox.

THE DIE★HARD SPORTS FAN'S GUIDE TO BOSTON

SPECTATOR TIPS: Batting practice is a great opportunity to get some autographs, catch a baseball, or watch players take their hacks at the Green Monster. Gates open two hours before the game, and you can usually catch the last of Boston's power hitters taking their cracks before the visiting team steps in to take their cuts.

If you're not from around here, keep in mind this is New England, so the weather—not unlike the prices—can be crazy. Some days you may have to wear a knit hat and sip on hot chocolate; others you may be down to a tank top and trying to eat your ice cream before it melts in front of your eyes. Check the weather forecast, dress appropriately, and wear sunscreen.

The following items are prohibited in Fenway Park: bags larger than 16"x16"x8", hard-sided coolers, containers, cans, computers, umbrellas, and food. Fans are not permitted to store any prohibited items at the park.

If you're interested in some souvenirs or merchandise to commemorate your day at Fenway, you will find any possible item you could ever imagine in the Official Red Sox Team Store at 19 Yawkey Way. You can also find vendors selling some cheap merchandise, such as $5 hats, around the ballpark, although you can be the judge of whether that is a fair price or not.

SCORING AUTOGRAPHS: Your best chance to get the autograph of your favorite Red Sox player is to show up four to five hours before game time and stake out an area near Gate D at the corner of Yawkey Way and Van Ness Street. That's where the home team arrives for the game. While most players go directly from their luxury cars straight into the ballpark, some may take the opportunity to sign some autographs. If nothing else, you can usually get a few good photographs and admire the players' wheels.

Another tactic is to be at the ballpark right when the gates open and grab a place flanking the dugouts. Occasionally players will sign autographs on their ways in and out of the dugout, but you'll have better luck with the visiting team. Some Red Sox players may sign as well, but they tend to be the players who are not in the lineup for that game. Also be sure to check out Autograph Alley adjacent to Yawkey Way where a former Red Sox player, coach, or personality will sign autographs free of charge before the game.

FOR THE KIDS: Unlike minor league games, there isn't a lot of entertainment specifically for children—although Wally the Green Monster, the team's furry mascot who roams the ballpark during the game, is usually a hit. Children under the age of two do not require a ticket, but you must pay full price for children two and older.

Strollers and diaper bags are allowed provided they can fold up easily and can fit beneath the seats. Strollers may not be checked once inside the ballpark. Changing tables are located in the men's and women's restrooms at Gate E, the men's and women's restrooms at the lower concourse level behind home plate, as well as the family restrooms at Gate E and the Big Concourse. There is also a changing table at the first aid station behind section 12.

There is a no-alcohol family area of the ballpark in sections 32 and 33 of the grandstand. Oh, and it may be a good idea to leave the kids at home for Yankees games, during which the crowd can rival an R-rated movie in its language and potential violence.

STADIUM CONCESSIONS: The concessions at Fenway Park were notoriously limited and of poor quality for many years. That has changed over the last decade to the point that Fenway Park even has an executive chef. But if you're packing your appetite, make sure to bring your wallet too.

Before the game, there are a number of concession stands along Yawkey Way, including **El Tiante's**, which serves Cuban sandwiches, barbeque rib sandwiches, and El Presidente beer. Pitching great Luis Tiant, the stand's namesake, is often there greeting guests and signing autographs. Across the street is **RemDawg's**, run by former Sox second baseman and NESN broadcaster Jerry Remy, which serves various types of hot dogs, Italian sausage, and barbeque chicken skewers. Other Yawkey Way food options are whole pizzas, calzones, steak tip sandwiches, and hot pastrami sandwiches.

Inside the ballpark, the largest concession area is the relatively new Big Concourse, which is behind the bleachers and between Gates B and C. In addition to a wide range of food and beverage options, there are family-style picnic tables and televisions.

The team offers healthy alternatives such as fruit and vegetable cups and yogurt. There is even a vending machine in the Big Concourse that dispenses kosher food. (Another vending machine in Fenway dispenses lottery tickets, so if you're looking for a way to pay for season tickets, that might be your long-shot chance.)

Of course, there is standard ballpark fare such as the signature Fenway Frank ($4.50 at concession stands and $4.75 from vendors), but you'll also find panini, lobster rolls, and—if the recent success of the Sox has you in the mood for Thanksgiving—turkey sandwiches with cranberry and stuffing. But there's also clam chowder from Legal Sea Foods, pizza from Papa Gino's, coffee from Dunkin' Donuts, fried chicken from Popeyes, and steak tip sandwiches from Hilltop Steak House.

Unless you are in a premium seat, you'll need to hit the concession stands if you want beer or wine. In recent years, the team has upgraded its beer options, which now include Heineken, Guinness, Harp, and Smithwicks. A domestic draft costs $7.25 and a foreign draft costs $7.75. Anyone looking to have a brew at the game should remember to bring along a picture ID as the concessionaires card religiously, whether you look like a rookie or a grizzled veteran. There is a limit of two beers per person at a time, and no beer is sold after the seventh inning or two-and-a-half hours after the start of the game.

FOOD AND DRINK AROUND THE BALLPARK: There are a plethora of restaurants and watering holes in Kenmore Square and the neighborhood around Fenway Park. Some fans looking for a pregame meal opt for the street vendors along Lansdowne Street and other streets around the park that serve sausages with onions and peppers, hot dogs, and other grilled meals. Be aware that the bars and restaurants nearest the ballpark begin filling up before game time, and lines may even begin as early as two hours before the first pitch. These spots are within a ten minute walk to Fenway.

Who's on First (19 Yawkey Way, 617-247-3353, www.whosonfirstboston.com) has all the ambiance of a frat house basement, but the Yawkey Way location can't be beat, and beer prices are on the reasonable side. It's still possible to visit the bar through its back entrance off Brookline Avenue when Yawkey Way is closed for a Sox game, but you'll need a ticket to get out of the bar onto Yawkey Way. It's a good spot to head during a rain delay.

★ A Girlsox Guide to Fenway Park

Women baseball fans in Boston are known as "girlsox fans," and they should never be dismissed. These are hard-core, sports-savvy enthusiasts. Here are three tips from Maggie Magner, one of the original girlsox:

1. *Choose your wardrobe carefully.* It is awful, but if you're not in traditional gear, you have one strike against you (so to speak). If you wear a pink "B" hat expect to be glared at. It's important to remember that suffering is part of the psyche of the typical Sox fan, and the new versions of the Boston "B" are signs of new-found commercial success, which post-dates the years of suffering.

2. *Prepare for "the Quiz."* At some point during a Red Sox game, you will get excited. You may shout, "SLIDE, you idiot!" Nearby, a guy will cheer too. He'll probably ask you something like, "You know what Daisuke's ERA is with runners in scoring position, right?" When you tell him you don't, he might say: "Huh? I thought you were a real fan!" I recommend the tried and true girlsox response: Tell Mr. Inquisitor to poll five guys in the vicinity and see if they all know the answer. (Never once have all five men come through.) This is just a gentle reminder that there is no entrance exam to Fenway Park, for men or women.

3. *Be in the know.* Still, the more you know about the team and the game, the more fun it is to be a fan. The lessons of our national pastime are not for men only, nor is the thrill of ending an 86-year-old curse, nor the admiration of a Ted Williams swing. These are the joys that girlsox fans have been claiming as their own, and you should too. *Get in the know at www.girlsoxnation.com.*

Boston Beer Works (61 Brookline Avenue, 617-536-BEER, www.beerworks.net) is a popular pregame option and is located at the foot of Yawkey Way. In addition to a full menu, Boston Beer Works offers more than sixteen microbrews, including a blueberry ale that features real Maine blueberries. If that doesn't float your boat, try the Bambino Ale to get in the baseball spirit.

Game On! (82 Lansdowne Street, 617-351-7001, www.gameonboston.com) is an upscale, and somewhat pricey, sports bar at the corner of Brookline Avenue and Lansdowne Street. On nice days, there are outdoor seats and the windows to the dining room are opened up. It's not an uncommon sight to see one of the Red Sox enjoying a pregame meal at Game On! It's a popular spot even when the Sox are out-of-town because of its bank of televisions above the bar.

Cask'n Flagon (62 Brookline Avenue, 617-536-4840, www.casknflagon.com) has been a Fenway institution for nearly forty years, as evidenced by the presence of a merchandise booth inside. Literally in the shadows of the Green Monster, the Cask gets crowded before and after games, but a recent renovation has added considerable space inside, and outdoor seating is available along Lansdowne Street's sidewalk for a pregame meal. There is an extensive menu and plenty of big-screen televisions along with two large bars and smaller stations selling beer in between.

Bleacher Bar (82A Lansdowne Street, 617-262-2424, www.bleacherbarboston.com)

opened in 2008 inside Fenway Park's old batting cages. The big draw of the Bleacher Bar is its view directly onto Fenway's center field through a converted garage door where you can catch batting practice or part of a game. Like the park itself, the Bleacher Bar has a highly irregular shape, so only a few coveted tables have field views. Those seats are limited to forty-five minutes during games, but you can also stand and get field views or take a trip to the men's room, which has a high window looking out onto the field. A standard food menu is available.

La Verdad (One Lansdowne Street, 617-421-9595) is a Mexican restaurant with an outdoor patio, private dining room, and a take-out taqueria. In addition to standard fare, the menu features super-size margaritas and tequilas. All the food is made fresh daily, including handmade tortillas, and is popular with Dustin Pedroia and other Red Sox.

Jillian's Boston (145 Ipswich Street, 617-437-0300, www.jilliansboston.com), located at the corner of Lansdowne and Ipswich streets, is a vast entertainment complex that includes a bowling alley, a night club, video games, and billiard table after billiard table. Jillian's also features an extensive menu. Note that Jillian's dress code means your Sox hat will have to come off after 8 PM.

The Baseball Tavern (1270 Boylston Street, 617-867-6526, www.thebaseballtavern.com) recently moved into infinitely more spacious accommodations that includes a basement for music acts and two floors with long bars. There are numerous televisions on which to follow the action, and a menu with standard pub fare. If the weather is nice, The Baseball Tavern's roof deck overlooking Fenway Park may be the best place to be before a game. The roof deck's green paint job and miniature light towers will have you thinking you're already in the ballpark.

The Chicken Bone (1260 Boylston Street, 617-267-9464, www.thechickenbone.com) is a newly opened outpost of this popular MetroWest eatery known for its chicken wings, with more than a dozen flavors. In addition to a bar and dining room, The Chicken Bone has an outdoor patio. Try the fried cheesecake for dessert.

Cambridge, 1 (1381 Boylston Street, 617-437-1111, www.cambridge1.us) is an upscale pizza restaurant with more than a dozen choices of toppings such as Italian sausage, roasted onion, grilled steak, and lobster.

Burtons Grill (1363 Boylston Street, 617-236-2236, www.burtonsgrill.com) is a contemporary restaurant serving seafood, steak, burgers, and fine wine. Burtons has an outdoor patio, and you might spy one of the Red Sox players who live in the condominiums above the restaurant.

Chipotle (148 Brookline Avenue, 617-236-4950, www.chipotle.com) is a casual Mexican grill with numerous locations across the country.

Copperfield's Bar (98 Brookline Avenue, 617-247-8605, www.copperfieldsboston.com) is a rather bare-bones watering hole that features live music and an extensive array of draft beers. Reasonably priced, but no food.

There are a number of places where you can grab a bite or hoist a pint in Kenmore Square. Options include *Uno Chicago Grill* (645 Beacon Street, 617-262-4911, www.unos.com) and *Bertucci's* (533 Commonwealth Avenue, 617-236-1030, www.bertuccis.com). The more upscale *Eastern Standard* (528 Commonwealth Avenue, 617-532-9100, www.easternstandardboston.com), which is reminiscent of a Parisian brasserie, has outdoor seating and is known for its world-class cocktails. ***Great Bay*** (500 Commonwealth Avenue, 617-532-5300, www.gbayrestaurant.com) is a pricey seafood restaurant located in the Hotel Commonwealth.

There are also a number of dining options on the other side of Boylston Street from Fenway Park. ***Canestaro*** (16 Peterborough Street, 617-266-8997, www.canestaro.com) is an Italian restaurant with a warm dining room, outdoor patio, and leather-booth pizzeria. ***Sorento's*** (86 Peterborough Street, 617-424-7070, www.sorentos.com) is an Italian restaurant with an extensive menu. ***El Pelon Taqueria*** (92 Peterborough Street, 617-262-9090, www.elpelon.com) is a Mexican restaurant with reasonable prices. ***Thornton's Fenway Grille*** (100 Peterborough Street, 617-421-0104) is a casual restaurant with standard fare and outdoor seating. ***Church*** (69 Kilmarnock Street, 617-236-7600, www.churchofboston.com) has a restaurant serving burgers, seafood, and comfort food such as macaroni and cheese in addition to a live music club.

Try both Brookline Avenue and Boylston Street for additional fast-food options.

TOURS: If you can't get into Fenway Park for a ballgame, you can still get inside on one of the tours offered by the team. Tours include the Green Monster seats, the press box, and the State Street Pavilion Club. Tickets are sold on a first-come, first-serve basis at the ticket office and are subject to availability. During the season, tours are offered between 9 AM and 4 PM or until three-and-a-half hours prior to game time. In the off-season, tours are offered between 9 AM and 3 PM. $12 for adults; $11 for seniors; $10 for children three and older and military. For more information, call 617-226-6666, visit www.redsox.com, or email tours@redsox.com.

CONTACT INFORMATION: Boston Red Sox, Four Yawkey Way, Boston, MA 02215-3496. 617-226-6000; www.redsox.com.

BEYOND BOSTON

Red Sox Spring Training

Each February, a moving van pulls up to Four Yawkey Way. The van's loaded up with bats, gloves, balls, and uniforms and then departs Fenway Park, due south to Florida. Another long winter is entering its final throes, and the boys of summer are gearing up for the season. But the moving van isn't the only thing making the 1,467-mile journey to the southwest Florida city of Fort Myers. Legions of Red Sox fans are heading south as well.

Over the decades, the Red Sox have trained in Virginia, Georgia, Arkansas, California, Texas, Louisiana, Arizona, and Florida. During World War II, they were forced to train in the distinctly colder locales of Atlantic City, New Jersey, and Tufts University in Medford. City of Palms Park in Fort Myers has been their winter home since 1993. The Red Sox have signed an agreement to move into a new Fort Myers spring training complex in 2012, which will combine practice fields with a larger stadium resembling Fenway Park.

There aren't many cultural sights in Fort Myers, with the exception of the wintertime estates of Thomas Edison and Henry Ford. Navigating the seemingly endless string of traffic lights and snowbirds cruising to early-bird specials can be maddening, but hey, you're here for the baseball and the beaches anyway. Fort Myers Beach and the more upscale Captiva and Sanibel Islands are popular bases for vacationers, and there is a whole range of hotel options from budget inns to opulent resorts.

The Red Sox play in the 16-team Grapefruit League and have an exhibition schedule of approximately thirty games throughout March, with half of those being played at City of Palms Park. The Sox generally play five games with the Minnesota Twins, who also play in Fort Myers, with whom they compete for the hallowed Mayor's Cup.

Before the Red Sox start their exhibition season, they spend their first few weeks of spring training doing workouts at the team's minor league facility, which is about two-and-a-half miles east of City of Palms Park at 4301 Edison Avenue. You'll have a much better chance to get close to your favorite Red Sox at the minor league facility than during games at City of Palms Park. While watching the players stretch and do calisthenics may not be the most exciting thing you've ever seen, it gets a little more interesting when they begin batting and fielding practice on the complex's five fields.

There is no charge to attend the workouts, which usually run between 9 AM and noon. Parking is extremely limited around the training complex, and cars will be towed if they are parked illegally. The Red Sox offer a shuttle from the parking lot at City of Palms Park to the training complex. There is a concession stand with limited offerings, but you can bring in a water bottle and food. Bags will be subject to a security inspection. There are tiny sets of bleachers at each practice field, but most people will have to stand the whole time. Wear a hat and sunscreen as there is little shade.

Keep in mind that many schools in the Boston area are on vacation the week of Presidents Day, and many families choose to spend it in Fort Myers and at spring training.

Cy Young played for the Red Sox (1901–1908) and the Boston Braves (1911) before retiring in 1911.
Courtesy Boston Public Library, Print Department.

So if you have some flexibility, it would be better to avoid this week.

STADIUM INFORMATION: The Red Sox play their spring training games at 7,290-seat City of Palms Park (2201 Edison Avenue, Fort Myers, FL 33901). In terms of scale, history, and climate, the Sox's spring training stadium couldn't be any more different from its big-league home. There are some Fenway touches, however, such as a statue of Ted Williams and newspaper boxes for *The Boston Globe* outside the gates, the pennants painted on the façade, and the retired numbers hanging in right field. The swaying palms behind the outfield fence, however, are probably something you won't be seeing at Fenway anytime soon (unless global warming starts to accelerate). A souvenir shop attached to the stadium is open year round.

WHEN: Red Sox players start reporting to camp in the latter half of February. The reporting date for pitchers and catchers is generally a few days before the rest of the team, but it's not unusual for players to arrive a few days in advance of their deadlines. Players practice for about ten days to two weeks before exhibition games begin in March.

GETTING THERE: While you could drive, most Boston fans take to the sky. The nearest airport to Fort Myers is Southwest Florida International Airport, which is served by most major airlines. Delta, AirTran, and JetBlue have direct flights from Boston. Fort Myers is about a two-hour drive south of Tampa and St. Petersburg.

To get to City of Palms Park, take Interstate 75 to Exit 138 and head west on Martin Luther King Boulevard for approximately four miles. Take a left onto Fowler Street and follow it for half a mile to Edison Avenue. Take a right onto Edison, and City of Palms Park is two hundred yards ahead on the right. (To get to the team's minor league complex, take a left on Edison Avenue and follow for more than two miles.) **Parking** is available in lots adjacent to the stadium and at local businesses and homes in the area.

TICKETS: Unfortunately for fans, the worldwide growth of Red Sox Nation has meant that the price and availability of spring training tickets has gone the way of the regular season. Just as at Fenway Park, all spring training games at City of Palms Park have sold out in recent years. With the tremendous demand for tickets, you may need to buy them the day they go on sale to make sure you're not shut out of your desired game. In 2008, the Red Sox sold over twenty-seven thousand tickets for spring training games on the first day of sales.

Home plate box ($46) seats are the best in the house, directly behind home plate.

Dugout box (first row $40, second row $36) seats are field-level, cushioned seats along the left-field line.

Box seats ($26) are the next-closest to the field and run from deep right field to close to the left-field foul pole.

Right-field deck ($26) seats, located behind the right-field wall, are City of Palms Park's version of the Green Monster seats.

Reserved ($23) seats compose the majority of the seats in the ballpark; most reserved seats with the exception of sections 201 and 202 in right field are covered.

> ★ **While You're There**
>
> Former Red Sox left-fielder Mike Greenwell once had a clause in his contract that prohibited him from engaging in one of his favorite hobbies: automobile racing. Now that he's retired, it's fitting that he's opened up **Mike Greenwell's Bat-a-Ball & Family Fun Park** (35 Pine Island Road, Cape Coral, FL 33909. 239-574-4386; www.greenwells familyfunpark.com), an amusement park that features four go-cart tracks. Located just a few miles from Fort Myers, the fun park includes a miniature golf course, video arcade, fish-feeding dock, two paintball fields, and, of course, eight batting cages. The main building is decorated with more than fifty game-used bats signed by other ballplayers.

Bleacher ($15) seats are located in right field and have poorer views than most seats in the park; in addition, the metal bleacher seats under the hot sun can get uncomfortable on sunny days.

Lawn area ($12) tickets allow you to sit on the grassy berm in front of the bleacher seats and provide a cooler alternative to the bleachers.

Standing room ($12 and $10) tickets go on sale when games become sold out, and some could be available on the morning of a game on a first-come, first-serve basis.

Note that seats in left field get less direct sun than those in right, and if you wish to see the entire team, be sure the game for which you are buying tickets isn't a split-squad game. If you are shut out at City of Palms Park, keep in mind that tickets could be available to road games in Florida, including those against the Twins across town in Fort Myers.

Generally, spring training tickets go on sale in early December and are available online at www.redsox.com, by phone at 877-RED SOX9, and at the City of Palms Park box office.

DISABILITY ACCESS: Hearing-impaired devices and seats for physically disabled fans are both available.

THE SPLURGE: Red Sox Destinations arranges trips to spring training in late February and early March. Packages include three nights in a hotel, rental car, tickets to two spring training games, and an exclusive postgame barbeque with three players and coaches. You can drop some more dough and get a VIP tour of City of Palms Park and take batting practice and play catch on the field. Packages have sold out in prior years. For more information, call 617-226-6400 or visit www.redsox.com/springdestinations.

THE CHEAPSKATE: Standing room tickets, bleacher tickets, and lawn area tickets are your cheapest options. You can find some cheaper parking options on the front yards of homes just a five minute walk from City of Palms Park. Buy a bottle of water inside the park and keep refilling it from the water fountains. In addition, the Red Sox generally open Grapefruit League play against collegiate teams from the Boston area, such as Boston College and Northeastern, and tickets for those games have been sold for half-price in previous years.

SPECTATOR TIPS: Gates open two-and-a-half hours prior to game time. No outside food or beverages are allowed. Umbrellas are prohibited as well, and the concourses are open air, making the covered grandstand seats even more attractive. The long winter may have you out of practice, but be sure to don your Red Sox cap and put on some sunscreen to protect yourself from the Florida sun.

SCORING AUTOGRAPHS: Your best bet to get autographs is to attend the workouts at the minor league complex before the exhibition season begins. You'll get much closer to the players than you will during exhibition games, and players are often willing to sign autographs and pose for pictures. Also, there may be some former Sox legends helping the players train, so keep an eye out for them. It's a good idea to get your hands on a roster from the team's website or the souvenir stand since there will undoubtedly be some unfamiliar faces, mostly career minor leaguers, among the dozens vying for a spot on the big-league team.

The area around the clubhouse—from which the players head to the fields—is usually very congested. A better spot to get a player's attention is along the roped-off walkways between the practice fields.

Players will rotate among the fields to do different drills and may be willing to sign in between the fields. They are usually more accommodating when the workouts are done for the day.

At City of Palms Park, players will often sign autographs after batting practice and stretching. The area around the dugouts is a good spot to stake out. Players are more willing to sign autographs before exhibition games than during the regular season, but you definitely have less access than during the workout days.

FOOD AND DRINK: There are no restaurants or vendors adjacent to City of Palms Park; however, there are some options a few blocks west on Cleveland Avenue. Inside the stadium, there are standard concession stands and a tiki bar in right field.

CONTACT INFORMATION: Boston Red Sox, City of Palms Park, 2201 Edison Avenue, Fort Myers, FL 33901. 239-334-4700; www.redsox.com.

Pawtucket Red Sox

Pawtucket, Rhode Island, is only forty-five miles away from Boston, tantalizingly close for members of the Pawtucket Red Sox who want to take the next step up to the big leagues. Still, the PawSox, as they are affectionately known, play in the International League and are one of the top draws in minor league baseball. The team averaged more than nine-thousand fans in 2008, and sellouts are common at 10,000-seat McCoy Stadium, particularly in the summertime.

Pawtucket became an Eastern League affiliate of the Red Sox in 1970 and moved up to the Triple A level in 1973. Owner Ben Mondor bought the team in 1977, and his investments kept the Red Sox in Pawtucket when the future looked bleak. The entrance road to the stadium is named in his honor.

Many Red Sox greats have played for Pawtucket over the years, including Carlton Fisk, Wade Boggs, Jim Rice, Roger Clemens, Tony Conigliaro, Dennis Eckersley, Nomar Garciaparra, Fred Lynn, and Mo Vaughn. However, McCoy Stadium's big claim to fame is that it saw baseball's longest game—a record 33-inning affair between Pawtucket and Rochester in 1981 that ended in a 3-2 PawSox victory. The game began on April 18, 1981, until it was called by curfew and completed on June 23, 1981. The game took more than eight hours and twenty-five minutes to complete. Baseball's Iron Man, Cal Ripken, Jr., naturally played all thirty-three innings for Rochester, and he came to bat eighteen times.

STADIUM INFORMATION: McCoy Stadium is located in the middle of a working-class neighborhood of this blue-collar city five miles north of Providence. It is one of the oldest stadiums in minor league baseball, built under the Depression-era Works Progress Administration and opened in 1942. The stadium, named for the Pawtucket mayor who pushed for its construction, underwent a significant renovation in 1999.

McCoy Stadium is the largest minor league baseball stadium in New England, and it has a big-league feel to it compared to other minor league stadiums in the region. As with Fenway, the grandstand roof of McCoy Stadium is held up by numerous poles, which results in obstructed views. Unlike Fenway, however, the ballpark doesn't exude tremendous charm, although it does go to great lengths to honor the franchise's history. Painted on one of the concourse's walls is the endless box score from that 1981 Pawtucket-Rochester epic, and memorabilia from that game is displayed above it.

There are banners throughout the stadium that celebrate McCoy's greatest moments, such as the perfect games thrown by Tomo Ohka and Bronson Arroyo. Red Sox fans, however, will particularly enjoy the dozens of portraits and photographs ringing the stadium's winding ramps that honor those PawSox alumni who went on to play for Boston. Among the portraits, which look like super-sized baseball cards, are Red Sox legends such as Boggs, Rice, Vaughn, Garciaparra, and Clemens. But it's almost as fun to recall some of the nearly forgotten names of summers yore such as Luis Alicea, Paul Quantrill, Ken Ryan, Brian Rose, Aaron Sele, and Bob Zupcic.

WHEN: Pawtucket's regular season runs from the beginning of April through early September.

GETTING THERE: Pawtucket is forty-five miles from Boston. From Boston, take Interstate 95 south to Exit 2A (1A South/Newport Avenue). Follow Newport Avenue for two miles and take a right onto Columbus Avenue. Follow Columbus Avenue for half a mile. Turn right after the traffic light onto George Bennett Highway. Follow George Bennett Highway for three-tenths of a mile. At the traffic light, turn left onto Division Street and follow signs for parking. From points south, take Interstate 95 north to Exits 27, 28, or 29 and follow signs to McCoy Stadium.

There is limited free **parking**, available on a first-come, first-serve basis, at a small lot adjacent to McCoy Stadium. Free parking is also available at Jenks Junior High School on the corner of Divisions and Ashton streets. Fans may also park for free along either side of Division Street, Ashton Street, and Delta Drive. Fans will need to get to the park early to take advantage of the free parking. When the free parking is filled, there is $2 parking available at Quebecor World on Delta Drive.

TICKETS: *Box* ($10) seats are the reserved green and red seats in McCoy Stadium's grandstand, which spans from just behind first base to halfway down the left-field line. Box seats are covered with the exception of sections 13, 14, and 15 along the left-field line.

General admission ($6 for adults, $4 for children twelve and under and senior citizens) seats are first-come, first-serve and include the upper portion of the grandstand (the stadium's blue seats), the left-field berm, and center-field bleachers. The grandstand seats are covered, but those behind home plate are badly obstructed by the press box and any seats behind row HH could have views obstructed by poles. The bleachers consist of aluminum benches and are in full sun during day games. The left-field berm is a popular spot, and fans bring blankets to sit on and enjoy the game.

Season tickets are $585, and the team offers numerous multi-game packages. Fans can order tickets by phone at 401-724-7300, online at www.pawsox.com, or at the ticket office, which is located near the main entry tower on the left-field side of McCoy Stadium.

DISABILITY ACCESS: Disabled seating is available in sections 2, 3, 6, 7, 10, 11, 13, and 15 of the green seats and 2, 3, 10, 11, and 14 of the blue seats. Handicap parking is available on both sides of McCoy Stadium.

THE SPLURGE: The PawSox rent 20-person luxury suites for $950 and 30-person luxury suites for $1,250. Food and beverages are extra. McCoy Stadium's luxury boxes are unique in that they are located on field level along with the dugouts and tucked underneath the grandstand.

SPECTATOR TIPS: Gates open two hours prior to game time. No food or beverages of any kind are allowed to be brought into McCoy Stadium—unless prior arrangements have been made for medical reasons. No flash photography is allowed. Bags are subject to inspection. If you're planning an event, a set of bleachers on the right-field line is available for group outings.

SCORING AUTOGRAPHS: One of McCoy Stadium's quirks is that the first row of seats is not at ground level but eight feet above the field. That's led to a unique tradition where fans fish for autographs by dangling baseball cards and souvenirs in soda bottles or milk jugs with their sides cut out. If a player bites, he'll tug on the line, and the fan reels in the catch.

FOR THE KIDS: Unlike other minor league ballparks, McCoy Stadium doesn't have a dedicated kids' area, and there are fewer on-field contests between innings. Following every Sunday afternoon home game, kids can take to the field of McCoy Stadium and run the bases. The team's bear mascots, Paws and Sox, are kid favorites.

STADIUM CONCESSIONS: Pawtucket offers a wide variety of food items. The best selection is in the concourse behind the grandstand. Options are more limited near the outfield seats. In addition to the usual ballpark fare such as hot dogs ($2.75), pretzels, popcorn, and peanuts, McCoy Stadium offers Papa Gino's pizza, fried dough, D'Angelo steak and cheese subs, popcorn chicken, and sausage and pepper subs. There is also a concession stand selling salads, veggie trays, vegan hot dogs and burgers, and fruit smoothies. The stadium has a good selection of domestic and foreign beer choices with 16-ounce draft beers ($4.50) and bottled beers ($5.50).

There are umbrella-covered tables in the concourse and picnic tents in both center and right fields next to concession stands, but they all lack views of the field. Tables on the terrace running along the left-field line allow you to eat and watch the game at the same time. There is a barbeque tent down the right-field line.

FOOD AND DRINK AROUND THE BALLPARK: Food and drink options around McCoy Stadium are limited to a take-out Chinese restaurant and an Irish bar, both on South Bend Street. If you're looking for a good meal before or after the game, head to the Federal Hill area of Providence, home to numerous Italian restaurants.

CONTACT INFORMATION: Pawtucket Red Sox, One Ben Mondor Way, Pawtucket, RI 02860. 401-724-7300; www.pawsox.com.

Portland Sea Dogs

In Maine's largest city, the Portland Sea Dogs, the Double A minor league affiliate of the Boston Red Sox, are just as popular as lobster and lighthouses. The Sea Dogs are among the leaders in attendance in Double A baseball, averaging about 6,400 fans a game, and any merchandise featuring the team's logo—a sea dog (a type of seal) gnawing on a baseball bat—is a big seller.

The Sea Dogs play in the Eastern League, but they came upon the scene in 1994 as a minor league affiliate of the Florida Marlins. Since a warm day in Portland can still be chillier than a cold one in Miami, the match always seemed a little odd. In 2003, Portland became part of the Boston farm system. Given the similar climate and the scant 112-mile distance, it is a far better match.

More than Pawtucket, Portland is where you will find Fenway's future stars. In the team's short history, more than one hundred alumni have made it to the big leagues, including Jon Lester, Jonathan Papelbon, Dustin Pedroia, Manny Delcarmen, Kevin Youkilis, Kevin Millar, Hanley Ramirez, Edgar Renteria, and A.J. Burnett.

Fans flock to Sea Dogs games, even in Portland's nippy spring weather. (The only players taking the field on Opening Day 2007 were snowmen, as a blanket of snow cancelled the game.) It's not uncommon for games in June, July, and August to sell out, and the noise is thunderous when Sea Dogs fans stomp the metal stands during a Portland rally.

Fans from Boston can combine a Sea Dogs game with a visit to one of New England's quaint seaside cities. You can hit the bars, restaurants, and shops along the cobblestone streets of the Old Port, browse the gallery of the Portland Museum of Art, or take a boat trip out into Casco Bay.

STADIUM INFORMATION: Hadlock Field, named for long-time Portland High School baseball coach Edson Hadlock, Jr., was opened in 1994 and has a seating capacity of 7,368. The stadium is surrounded by triple-deckers in a residential neighborhood about two miles north of downtown Portland.

Fans are greeted by a statue of the team's popular mascot, Slugger, before they even enter the stadium. But it's once you get a view of the field, however, that you realize how strong the connection between the Sea Dogs and the Red Sox is, evident by the "Maine Monster"—a nearly identical re-creation of Boston's famed Green Monster. The Maine Monster dominates left field and was built when the Sea Dogs switched affiliations from Florida to Boston. Hadlock's Monster is made of wood, not hard plastic, and features an electronic, not a manual, scoreboard, but a miniature Citgo sign and Coke bottle atop the wall provide ample Fenway flavor. And if that wasn't enough to drive the connection home, the jerseys of current Red Sox players who once played for Portland are displayed atop the stadium behind home plate, and the team shows Red Sox highlights on the scoreboard.

For local color, check out the L.L. Bean boot measuring ten feet high in right field, which lends the quintessential Maine touch, as does the lighthouse—complete with fog and foghorn—that rises up beyond the center-field fence after every Portland home run or victory.

WHEN: The Sea Dogs regular season runs from early April to early September.

GETTING THERE: The drive time to Portland is about two hours from Boston. (Amtrak's Downeaster service also runs between Boston and Portland.) From Boston and points south, take Interstate 95 to Interstate 295. Take Exit 5A (Congress Street), merge onto Congress Street, and stay left. Make a left at the first set of lights (St. John Street), stay right, and merge onto Park Avenue. Hadlock Field will be directly in front of you. From the north, take Interstate 295 to Exit 6A (Forest Avenue South) and turn right onto Park Avenue. The stadium is approximately two-thirds of a mile on the right.

Game day **parking** is not available on the neighborhood streets immediately around the ballpark, so you'll need to pay about $5 in one of the surrounding parking lots if you want to be close to the stadium. The city of Portland has small lots at the Fitzpatrick Stadium and Portland Expo/Ice Arena, both adjacent to Hadlock Field, but they fill up quickly. Fans can also park at the Maine Medical Center Parking Garages located at 887 Congress Street and 995 Congress Street, or at various temporary lots set up by area businesses located around Hadlock Field.

TICKETS: Hadlock Field's seats are completely uncovered, so there is no protection from sun or rain.

Box ($9 adults, $8 children/seniors) seats include those closest to the field and run from first base to halfway down the left-field line.

Reserved ($8 adults, $7 children/seniors) seats are located behind the box seats and run from the first-base dugout to halfway down the left-field line.

General admission ($7 adults, $4 children/seniors) is located behind the reserved section between first base and halfway down the left-field line, and there is also a set of bleachers along the left-field line. General admission seats are metal benches.

The U.S. Cellular Pavilion ($9 adults, $8 for children/seniors) in right field opened in 2006 and includes nearly four hundred seats. The U.S. Cellular Pavilion is modeled after the Green Monster seats at Fenway Park, but its steep rows of seating and countertops look a little like a giant PBS telethon from a distance. The Sea Dogs also have a picnic area for groups down the right-field line, which includes seats.

Season tickets to the 71-game home slate cost $461.50 for box seats and $426 for reserved seats. Season-ticket holders also get to take on-field batting practice. The team also offers five- and ten-game packages.

To order tickets, call 207-879-9500 or toll free 800-936-3647, go online to www.seadogs.com, email tickets@seadogs.com, or go to the ticket office.

DISABILITY ACCESS: There is handicap seating between the blue and green seats, and seats can be purchased by calling the ticket office. Wheelchair seating is not sold online, and a maximum of four people are allowed to sit with the person needing wheelchair-accessible seating. The parking lot next to Hadlock Field is for handicap parking only prior to and during the game.

THE SPLURGE: The top of Hadlock Field is ringed with seventeen luxury boxes, each named after a legendary Red Sox great. Each suite accommodates up to twenty-two people and has outdoor seats and a furnished interior equipped with color televisions, refrigerators, and air conditioning and heat, which can be welcome on cold nights. Boxes are available to rent for $594. The price does not include food and beverages. The catering menu includes lobster rolls, shrimp, beef tenderloin, and ballpark fare.

SPECTATOR TIPS: Gates open an hour and a half prior to game time. Bobblehead giveaways are particularly popular promotions, with long lines forming before gates open, so if you want to ensure you get one, it's best to show up when gates open. Fans are not allowed to bring food or drinks into games.

SCORING AUTOGRAPHS: Some players will sign autographs along the field prior to the game, but the Sea Dogs also have a player available in the concourse before the game to sign autographs for approximately twenty minutes. Players will also sign autographs after the game behind the first-base stands.

FOR THE KIDS: Children two and under do not need a ticket if they sit on an adult's lap. Between-innings, on-field contests—such as the "lobster toss," featuring two fans trying to trap rubber lobsters—will entertain kids as will the team's mascot, Slugger the Sea Dog, who roams the stands.

STADIUM CONCESSIONS: Hadlock Field has numerous concession stands in the concourse underneath the stands. Even in raw and chilly weather, the best-selling item with the team's hardy fans is the Sea Dog Biscuit, vanilla ice cream sandwiched between two giant chocolate chip cookies. Another fan favorite is the ballpark's fish sandwich. A beer garden down the left-field line serves up some of Maine's popular microbrews.

FOOD AND DRINK AROUND THE BALLPARK: Most of the sit-down and fast-food restaurants near Hadlock Field are located on St. John Street. *Amato's* (312 St. John Street, 207-828-5978, www.amatos.com) serves pizza, pasta, and Italian sandwiches. *Margaritas* (242 St. John Street, 207-874-6444, www.margs.com) is a Mexican restaurant chain with a full menu, frozen drinks, and (of course) margaritas. There is a McDonald's at the corner of St. John Street and Park Avenue.

CONTACT INFORMATION: Portland Sea Dogs, 271 Park Avenue, Portland, ME 04102. 207-879-9300; www.portlandseadogs.com.

Lowell Spinners

The Lowell Spinners have been a Single A minor league affiliate of the Boston Red Sox since the team's birth in 1996. The Spinners play in the short-season (76-game) New York–Penn League, and the team's players are the rawest of the prospects in the Red Sox farm system. Many players are right out of high school and college, and nearly all are younger than twenty-three years old. Jonathan Papelbon, Jacoby Ellsbury, and Kevin Youkilis are among those who started their professional careers in Lowell.

The team's nickname honors the city's heritage as a textile-manufacturing center, and the Spinners are an integral part of Lowell's fabric. In fact, the legions of "Thread Sox Nation" are just as die-hard as the members of Red Sox Nation. Boston may have had a sellout streak dating to 2003, but the Spinners have sold out every regular season game in LeLacheur Park since 1999.

Along with a chance to see Red Sox prospects, the Spinners draw fans with creative giveaways, in particular their bobbleheads, which in the past have included Paul Revere, Ted Williams in a fighter plane, Boston Pops conductor Keith Lockhart with his baton in hand, and Stephen King (given out on Friday the 13th) standing on top of three of his tomes. The team's most popular bobblehead was that of native son Jack Kerouac dressed in a red flannel and blue jeans, a pen and pad in his hands. Check out the display case on the concourse behind home plate to see these and other bobbleheads.

The team has also sponsored its Yankee Elimination Program, which donates equipment to local youth baseball teams that change their name from the Yankees to the Spinners.

STADIUM INFORMATION: Edward LeLacheur Park, named for a former state representative, is located near the UMass-Lowell campus and about a ten minute walk from downtown Lowell. The ballpark was designed by HOK, the same architects responsible for Coors Field in Denver and Camden Yards in Baltimore, and its construction helped revitalize this old mill city.

LeLacheur Park, which has a capacity of five thousand people, sits on the banks of the Merrimack River, and the distinctive red trusses of the Aiken Street Bridge rise above the right-field fence. In addition, there are views of smokestacks and redeveloped brick mill buildings, a reminder of the city's industrial heritage and reminiscent of the brick warehouse that flanks Camden Yards.

Once fans enter the ballpark through the main gate, they ascend a staircase or elevator that takes them to the concourse ringing the top of the stadium. A great feature of the stadium is that all the concession stands are located on this open concourse, so fans don't have to miss a pitch while grabbing a bite to eat.

There are some obvious (and not-so-obvious) connections to the parent club at LeLacheur Park. A beer stand in right field is topped by a large, neon Budweiser sign, just like right field in Fenway Park, and retired Red Sox numbers are mounted on the right-field wall along with a banner in memory of Tony Conigliaro. If the large Hood milk bottle in center field looks familiar, that's because it's the same one that used to grace the right-field roof of Fenway before the pavilion was built atop it. Throughout the game, the scoreboard scrawls updates of that day's Red Sox game.

WHEN: The regular season runs from mid-June to early September.

GETTING THERE: Lowell is thirty miles north of Boston. From Boston, take Interstate 93 north to Interstate 495 south to the Lowell Connector. From south of Lowell, take Route 128 north to U.S. 3 north to the Lowell Connector. Follow the Lowell Connector to Exit 5B (Thorndike Street). Follow Thorndike Street through the lights and go past City Hall. Take a left onto Father Morrissette Boulevard. At the first set of lights, take a right onto Cabot Street. Follow the road through the stop sign and take a left at the T. LeLacheur Park will be in front of you.

There is limited on-street **parking** available near the stadium. Parking is available at local businesses for $5, and lots are also available at UMass-Lowell and adjacent to the Tsongas Arena.

TICKETS: The Spinners have sold out every regular season home game since 1999, but it's often possible to get tickets on game days. Player, media, and scout tickets often become available about an hour before game time and are sold at the box office.

Premium box ($8) seats are the closest to the field and run from just behind first base to just behind third base.

Box ($7) seats are the remainder of those located behind the premium box seats between the dugouts, and they also run down to field level in right field, which provides a great angle from which to watch.

Reserved ($5) seats are located beyond the dugouts in right and left field and are aluminum bleachers.

Standing room ($4) tickets are available for the concourse. Since LeLacheur Park is so intimate, there are still good views from the standing room area, and countertops are available along the concourse for fans to rest their food and drink while watching the game.

Note that there is no overhead coverage for any of the seats in LeLacheur Park. In addition, the sun sets on the third-base side, so it may be in the eyes of those sitting in right field for an inning or two.

To purchase tickets, phone 978-459-1702, go online to www.lowellspinners.com, or visit the team's box office. In addition, there is a ticket posting page on the team's website where fans can post messages to buy or sell tickets.

Members of the team's Thread Sox Nation fan club (membership costs $25) get pre-sale ticket access in addition to other benefits. Memberships were limited to two hundred fans in 2008 and sold out in just over a month.

Season tickets are available for premium box ($336) and box ($294) seats. Season-ticket holders are invited to a private meet-and-greet team luncheon and entrance into the team's Gator Pit, which features menu items not available elsewhere in the stadium. The season ticket waiting list is nearly five hundred people long.

DISABILITY ACCESS: Handicap seating is available along the concourse at the top of the stadium.

THE SPLURGE: Luxury suites with cable TV, air conditioning, and wait service are available to rent for $500 a game. The rental includes ten tickets, ten programs, and a pregame, all-you-can-eat buffet.

SPECTATOR TIPS: Gates open an hour and a half before game times. Fans are not allowed to bring food or drinks into the game.

SCORING AUTOGRAPHS: Players will often sign autographs for fans along the field prior to games.

FOR THE KIDS: The Lowell Spinners have a kids' area in the left-field corner of the ballpark that includes a giant slide, bounce house, obstacle course, speed pitch game, and more. Tickets for the kids' area games require purchase. The team's three reptilian mascots, Canaligator, Allie-Gator, and Millie-Gator, are favorites. On certain nights during the season, the team screens postgame movies on the scoreboard and families can spread out blankets on the outfield. The team also hosts days where you can play catch on the field or camp overnight in the outfield. Children three years and younger are admitted free of charge.

STADIUM CONCESSIONS: LeLacheur Park offers standard ballpark staples at pretty reasonable prices. Hot dogs cost $1.50, while jumbo hot dogs cost $2.50. In addition, the stadium fare includes steak tip sandwiches, chicken sandwiches, fried dough, and mini doughnuts. If lines are long at the two main concession stands behind the dugouts, the numerous pushcarts are often quicker options. The beer selection ($5.25 for a 20-ounce domestic beer/$5.75 imported) is varied for a small ballpark and includes Stella Artois, Bass Ale, and Redhook.

If you have a group, the Spinners serve an hour and a half, pregame catered meal in its Gator Pit. Ticket prices ($23–$26) include the meal and seating for the game. The picnic-style meals at the Gator Pit include grilled steak tips, ribs, sausages, hot dogs, chicken wings, tossed salad, pasta salad, New England baked beans, corn on the cob, non-alcoholic beverages, and ice cream for dessert. Beer and wine are not included, but available. For reservations, contact the box office at 978-459-1702.

FOOD AND DRINK AROUND THE BALLPARK: There are two good options one block east of LeLacheur Park. **Lowell Beer Works** (203 Cabot Street, 978-937-BEER, www.beerworks.net) is an outpost of the Boston Beer Works located across the street from Fenway Park. In addition to a huge menu, it serves up its own special brews. Outdoor seating is available. Next door is **The Brewery Exchange** (201 Cabot Street, 978-937-2690, www.thebreweryexchange.com), a three-floor complex of bars and restaurants in a huge old mill that features many large-screen televisions, pool tables, and air-hockey tables.

CONTACT INFORMATION: Lowell Spinners, 450 Aiken Street, Lowell, MA 01854. 978-459-2255; www.lowellspinners.com.

Brockton Rox

It's not unusual to see a baseball team's retired numbers adorning the outfield wall. What is unusual, however, is when the retired numbers honor athletes who not only never played for the team, but never even played professional baseball. But it makes perfect sense in Brockton, the "City of Champions," and home to two of the greatest pugilists to don the gloves—former heavyweight champion Rocky Marciano and former middleweight champion "Marvelous" Marvin Hagler. Painted on the center-field wall are Marciano's 49 and Hagler's 62, representing the number of career wins for each native son of Brockton.

The retirement of the numbers also makes sense since the Brockton Rox got their nickname in honor of Marciano, "the Rock," the only heavyweight in boxing history to retire undefeated. His record of forty-nine wins without a loss may never be broken. (As you might have guessed, the spelling is a nod to the Red Sox.) Before dropping out of school and turning to boxing, Marciano played varsity baseball at Brockton High School, which is also well-known as a football powerhouse. The scouting report on the Brockton Blockbuster was that he was a solid slugger, but not fleet of foot. (The Brockton Historical Society's museum has a room dedicated to Rocky Marciano; see page 168.) Also playing on the boxing theme, the team's mascot is a feisty kangaroo named—what else?—K-O. (The team lists K-O's birthplace as Kangaroo Island, Australia.)

The Brockton Rox are a member of the independent Can-Am League, which means they are not affiliated with any major league ballclub. The Rox are a relatively recent addition to the Boston sports scene. They played their first game in 2002. But since then more than one million fans have passed through the turnstiles at Campanelli Stadium. One of the owners of the Rox is actor and comedian Bill Murray, listed in the team's program as "Director of Fun."

STADIUM INFORMATION: Campanelli Stadium has a capacity of 4,750. (The team averaged 3,018 fans in 2008.) Most of the seats are uncovered, and the stadium has twelve luxury suites, a picnic tent in center field, and a beer garden in right field. There are tables with umbrellas right along the top of the wall, providing a great vantage point from which to watch the game. Concession stands ring the open concourse on the top of the stadium so you can follow the game while standing in line.

A manual scoreboard in right field posts the scores of the Red Sox game and another major league game of interest. Attached to the stadium—named for Alfred Campanelli, a developer whose $2 million donation helped finance construction of the ballpark—is The Shaw's Center, a conference facility that also hosts wedding receptions and other functions in its outdoor space along the left-field line. So if you want to cut your wedding cake under stadium floodlights, Brockton is your place.

WHEN: Brockton's regular season runs from the end of May through the end of August.

GETTING THERE: Campanelli Stadium is twenty-five miles south of Boston. Take Massachusetts Route 24 to Exit 17A (Route 123 east/Belmont Street). Follow Belmont Street for approximately one mile. Bear right onto West Street. Turn right onto Lexington Avenue. Campanelli Stadium will be on the right.

Parking is available for $4 near the stadium at Brockton High School and the West Branch of the Brockton Public Library. Other nearby businesses charge $3 for parking.

TICKETS:

Super box ($15) seats are closest to the field and fill the first handful of rows between the dugouts. Super box seats have wait service and individual cup holders.

Box ($9.50) seats fill the rest of the grandstand between the dugouts.

Reserve ($7.50) seats are located just beyond the dugouts from home plate.

Grandstand ($5) seats are located in sections 101 and 102, the furthest seats from home plate down the right-field line. Most seats in Campanelli Stadium are uncovered.

Season tickets are $300 for reserve seats, $400 for box seats, and $540 for super box seats. Season-ticket holders get to have a batting practice session on the field and are invited to a preseason party. Ten-game mini-plans are available for $70.

Order online at www.brocktonrox.com or call the Rox ticket office at 508-559-7070. The ticket office stops taking any phone sales two hours prior to that day's game. Tickets can also be purchased in person at the ticket office, located by Gate B of Campanelli Stadium. Call or visit the Brockton Rox website for the ticket office's hours of operation.

DISABILITY ACCESS: Handicap seating is available in all seating sections of the stadium.

THE SPLURGE: The Brockton Rox have luxury suite packages starting at $950, including indoor and outdoor seating, wait staff, and food and beverages. Most suites hold twenty people, but there is one suite that holds forty people.

Don't want to miss any of the action to wait in line for food and drinks? Get a Super Box seat. Wait staff will come down to your seat, take your order, and deliver your grub so you won't be caught missing the inevitable home run that seems to happen when you leave your seat.

SPECTATOR TIPS: Gates open one hour prior to game time. Cans, bottles, beverages, food, and coolers are prohibited from being brought into the stadium.

SCORING AUTOGRAPHS: Being the minors, you'll have a good shot at getting player autographs near the dugouts before and after the game.

FOR THE KIDS: The Brockton Rox have one of the most family-friendly sports facilities in metropolitan Boston. The team has dedicated one of its luxury suites, dubbed the Rox-a-Bye Baby Suite, for use by parents and toddlers. Parents can use the air-conditioned suite, stocked with diapers and other baby supplies, to feed and change their young sluggers. There are windows and outdoor seats where the rest of the family can keep watching the game. To use the suite, go to the guest services booth near the main entrance and get a pass that's good for half-hour use of the suite. You may get a pass from the guest services booth multiple times during the game.

The Rox also have a kids' zone located behind the right-field grandstand where children can play games, bounce around the jumpy castle, and win prizes. The team also has periodic kids-eat-free days on Mondays throughout the season.

STADIUM CONCESSIONS: Campanelli Stadium offers the usual ballpark fare at two main concession stands and a number of pushcarts. The offerings at the Roadkill Grill on the right-field line include Italian sausage, veggie burgers, and barbeque chicken sandwiches. There are a number of beer choices at the concession stands and in the beer garden located beyond the right-field fence. Beer prices are downright cheap compared to Fenway ($3.50 for a 24-ounce draft of domestic beer and $2 drafts on the team's thirsty Thursdays). Here's another thing you won't find at Fenway: beer vendors roaming the seats. Want to be a little more highbrow? Try the merlot, pinot grigio, and chardonnay.

FOOD AND DRINK AROUND THE BALLPARK: There are numerous fast-food restaurants lining

Belmont Street (Route 123) between Route 24 and Campanelli Stadium. *George's Café* (228 Belmont Street, 508-588-4231, www.georgescafebrockton.com), a mile east of Campanelli Stadium, is an Italian restaurant wallpapered with photographs of Rocky Marciano, including the brawler's third-grade class picture.

CONTACT INFORMATION: Brockton Rox, One Feinberg Way, Brockton, MA 02301. 508-559-7000; www.brocktonrox.com.

Worcester Tornadoes

Hard as it may be to imagine today, at one time Worcester had a franchise in the National League. Showing up in 1880 and gone by 1882, it didn't last too long—but it's an example of the rich baseball tradition of this central Massachusetts city.

Following a drought of seventy years, professional baseball returned to Worcester in 2005 in the form of the Worcester Tornadoes. The team is a member of the independent Can-Am League, which means it is not affiliated with any major league baseball club.

STADIUM INFORMATION: The Worcester Tornadoes play their home games at Hanover Insurance Park at Fitton Field, which has a tremendous baseball history that dates back more than one hundred years. The stadium is on the campus of Holy Cross, and the college's Crusaders play their baseball games at Fitton Field. In 1952, the team was good enough to win a national championship. In the Roaring Twenties, the Holy Cross hardball teams drew tremendous crowds, particularly when they faced off against their fierce rival, Boston College. Holy Cross–Boston College games were known to draw as many as twenty-five thousand fans.

Decades ago, Holy Cross played exhibition games against major league teams at Fitton Field. Babe Ruth played there late in his career, as a member of the Boston Braves. More noteworthy, in 1939 a slender rookie by the name of Ted Williams hit his first home run in a Boston uniform at the ball field.

When the Tornadoes arrived in 2005, Fitton Field was renovated and modernized into a sparkling minor league ball field. Its 3,000-person capacity makes it an intimate venue with good views, and the open concourse ringing the top of the stadium allows for keeping up with the game when heading to the concession stands.

WHEN: Worcester's regular season runs from the end of May through the end of August.

GETTING THERE: Worcester is forty-five miles west of Boston. From the Massachusetts Turnpike, take Exit 10 to Interstate 290 east toward Worcester. Take Exit 11 (College Square/Southbridge Street) off Interstate 290 and take an immediate right onto College Street.

There is extremely limited on-street **parking** on College Street. On-street parking is also permitted on McKeon Road. To access, follow Southbridge Street and turn right onto Riverside Street and then another right onto McKeon Road. There is a parking garage adjacent to the ballpark that can accommodate more than four hundred cars. Parking in the garage costs $3. To park in the garage, after you turn onto College Street from Southbridge Street, take the first left to Fitton Avenue.

TICKETS: Note that there is no coverage over any of the seats in Fitton Field.

Executive ($18) seats are the closest to the field and are located between the dugouts.

> ### ★ Cape Cod Baseball League Hall of Fame & Museum
>
> Even when the Cape League is done for the summer, you can still get a baseball fix at the Cape Cod Baseball League Hall of Fame and Museum, which opened in 2008 in the lower level of the **John F. Kennedy Hyannis Museum** (397 Main Street, Hyannis, MA 02601. 508-790-3077; www.jfkhyannismuseum.org). The museum features plaques honoring the more than eighty members of the Hall of Fame, the original charter of the Cape League, old photographs, and memorabilia from the league and each of the ten teams. There are bats and balls autographed by league alumni who have made it to "The Show." The video room has original seats from Fenway Park (with one painted red like the Ted Williams seat in Fenway's bleachers) and screens movies such as *Summer Catch* and *Touching the Game*. The museum is open 9 AM to 5 PM Monday-Saturday and noon to 5 PM on Sunday. Admission charge is $5 for adults; $2.50 for children ten and older.

VIP ($14) tickets are located between first base and third base, and they are the closest to the field, except for those sections behind home plate where they are located behind the executive section.

Box ($10) seats are the upper part of the stadium seating between first base and third base, and they are in the first few rows of shallow right field.

Grandstand ($6) seats are aluminum benches located in shallow left field and right field.

Season tickets are available for executive ($850), VIP ($690), and box ($490) seats. The team also has mini-plans available. To purchase tickets, call 508-792-2288, go online to www.worcestertornadoes.com, or visit the box office.

DISABILITY ACCESS: There is seating for disabled fans at the stadium. Parking for disabled fans is available opposite the main gate on Fitton Avenue and at the lower gate on College Street. For additional instructions, contact the Tornadoes office at 508-792-2288.

THE SPLURGE: Well, you probably aren't going to be sitting in the front row behind home plate at Fenway Park anytime soon, so spring for the executive-level tickets and see what the view right behind the umpire is like.

SPECTATOR TIPS: Gates open one hour before game time.

SCORING AUTOGRAPHS: Some players will sign autographs around the field prior to games.

FOR THE KIDS: In addition to other perks, members of the Tornadoes Tykes Kids Club get tickets to every Sunday home game and the opportunity to run the bases after those games. Membership costs $15. There is also plenty of in-game entertainment between innings such as pie-eating contests and on-field races against Twister, the team's mascot.

STADIUM CONCESSIONS: The field has two concession stands available to fans in the concourse.

FOOD AND DRINK AROUND THE BALLPARK: If going out to the ballgame has you in the mood for a hot dog before the game, try a Worcester institution, *George's Coney Island Hot Dogs* (158 Southbridge Street, 508-753-4362, www.coneyislandlunch.com). If you're also in the mood for a brew, hoist a pint at the bar at *Hotel Vernon* (One Millbury Street, 508-363-3507) where Babe Ruth is said to have drank many a shot years before he called his famous shot in the World Series. Also visit *Moynagh's Tavern* (25 Exchange Street, 508-753-9686), where the tables and chairs are said to be made from Babe Ruth's bowling alley.

CONTACT INFORMATION: Worcester Tornadoes, 303 Main Street, PO Box 2211, Worcester, MA 01613. 508-792-2288; www.worcestertornadoes.com.

Cape Cod Baseball League

The crack of the bat and the thwack of the mitt are as much a part of the summer sounds on Cape Cod as the chirping crickets and rolling surf. The Cape Cod Baseball League, the premier amateur baseball league in the country, has been a Cape institution since the 1800s. If your only exposure to the Cape League was watching Hollywood's take in the movie *Summer Catch*, spend some time watching the documentary *Touching the Game*, which gives a truer sense of life in the invitation-only amateur baseball league—or better yet, go to a game. For baseball purists who are put off by superstar egos, out-of-control player salaries, and high ticket prices in the major leagues, the Cape League is hardball heaven.

Games are played at intimate ball fields with chain-link backstops in resort towns up and down the Cape. Fans sit on metal bleachers, lawn chairs, and blankets. The constant hum of the ballpark lights are punctuated by shouts of encouragement and the sounds of the game. Aluminum bats are banned, so the annoying metallic ping is replaced by the much more pleasing sound of ash meeting ball. Unlike pampered major leaguers, the college players competing in the league spend summers living with host families and working in local businesses. Plus, there's no admission charge to games (although donations are very much appreciated).

The 10-team league, which is run by a band of dedicated volunteers, has a rich heritage that dates back to 1885. "Pie" Traynor, Thurman Munson, Mike Flanagan, Craig Biggio, Jeff Reardon, Mo Vaughn, Albert Belle, Nomar Garciaparra, Todd Helton, Frank Thomas, Jason Varitek, and Barry Zito are among the baseball stars who once shone in the Cape League. Nearly one out of every seven current major league players are alumni of the Cape League.

Part of the draw of the Cape League is the opportunity to see the next generation of baseball stars. Hundreds of fans attend each game, as do professional scouts looking to size up potential prospects, with allstar and playoff games drawing as many as eight thousand fans. Based on a statistical analysis done by the league, at any given game, fans will likely see six future major leaguers.

The ten teams in the Cape League are the **Bourne Braves** (www.bournebraves.org), **Cotuit Kettleers** (www.kettleers.org), **Falmouth Commodores** (www.falcommodores.org), **Hyannis Mets** (www.hyannismets.org), and **Wareham Gatemen** (www.gatemen.org) in the west division and the **Brewster Whitecaps** (www.brewsterwhitecaps.com), **Chatham Anglers** (www.chathamanglers.com), **Harwich Mariners** (www.harwichmariners.org), **Orleans Firebirds** (www.orleansfirebirds.com), and **Yarmouth-Dennis Red Sox** (www.ydredsox.org) in the east division. Each team plays a 44-game schedule.

Teams play home games within fifty miles of each other, so if you plan your week-long vacation right, you could spend it watching most of the teams in the league play.

WHEN: The Cape Cod Baseball League runs from mid-June to mid-August. There are generally three to five games played every night across Cape Cod. Game times are usually at 7 PM at fields with lights (Bourne,

Most fans know that Babe Ruth debuted with the Red Sox, but many forget that the Sultan of Swat ended his career in the Hub as well, with the Braves. Ruth is seated far left. Courtesy Library of Congress.

Chatham, Falmouth, Harwich, Hyannis, Orleans, and Wareham) and at 5 PM or 5:30 PM at fields that lack lights (Brewster, Cotuit, and Yarmouth-Dennis).

GETTING THERE: The closest Cape League teams to Boston are in Wareham and Bourne, both of which are less than sixty miles away. Orleans is the furthest out on the Cape. With the exception of Wareham, which is actually "off-Cape," ballparks can be approached from Boston by either the Bourne Bridge or the Sagamore Bridge to get on Cape Cod. As you've probably heard (or experienced) traffic is notorious on summer weekends.

The Bourne Braves play at Doran Park, located at 220 Sandwich Road in Bourne at the Upper Cape Technical High School. Doran Park has a capacity of three thousand people.

The Brewster Whitecaps play at Stoney Brook School at 384 Underpass Road in Brewster. The field has a capacity of three thousand.

The Chatham Anglers play at Veteran's Field at 702 Main Street in Chatham. The field has a capacity of eighty-five hundred with bleachers for two thousand people.

The Cotuit Kettleers play at Lowell Park, located at 10 Lowell Avenue in Cotuit. There is a capacity of two thousand people and seating for six hundred.

The Falmouth Commodores play at Arnie Allen Diamond at Guv Fuller Field at 790 Main Street in Falmouth. The field has a capacity of eight thousand people with seating for one thousand.

The Harwich Mariners play at Whitehouse Field, which is located at Harwich High School at 75 Oak Street in Harwich.

The field has a capacity of four thousand people.

The Hyannis Mets play at McKeon Field at 120 High School Road in Hyannis. The field, which is behind Pope John Paul II High School, has seating for seven hundred people and capacity for three thousand fans.

The Orleans Firebirds play at Eldredge Park at 78 Eldredge Park Way in Orleans. The field has seating for three hundred and a capacity of six thousand.

The Wareham Gatemen play at Spillane Field at 54 Marion Road (U.S. 6) at the corner of Viking Drive. The field is behind the parking lot of town hall, and it has bleachers and a capacity of three thousand.

The Yarmouth-Dennis Red Sox play at "Red" Wilson Field at Dennis-Yarmouth Regional High School at 210 Station Avenue in South Yarmouth. The field has a capacity of five thousand people.

Eldredge Park in Orleans has a large berm down the first-base line that feels like the bowl of a stadium. Veteran's Park in Chatham has clapboard seating between first and third base and grassy berms in the outfield. Both are particular favorites of Cape League aficionados. Visit www.capecodbaseball.org for directions to particular fields.

TICKETS: No tickets are necessary to get into games, but donations are greatly appreciated and are usually accepted at the gate or by a pass of the hat during the game.

SPECTATOR TIPS: Print out roster sheets from the team websites at home, or pick up sheets available at some ball fields, so you know who you're watching. It's also fun to check back in a few years and see if any of the players you watched made it to the big leagues. Bring lawn chairs and blankets with you in case bleacher seats are filled up or if you want a different vantage point. You can bring snacks or dinner with you and make a picnic of it. Don't forget sunscreen and a hat for hot summer days and bug spray for night games.

SCORING AUTOGRAPHS: That college player signing an autograph today could be tomorrow's superstar. Be sure to bring a roster with you so you can put a name to a number when you're asking for an autograph, and make a note on the roster sheet of whose autograph you got in case you didn't recognize the player and can't read his chicken scratch.

FOR THE KIDS: Many teams offer week-long baseball clinics for kids during the season, which could provide some additional fun for families spending a week down on the Cape.

STADIUM CONCESSIONS: Fields generally have concession stands with hot dogs, hamburgers, peanuts, soda, and Cracker Jack. You can also bring your own food, and some fields even have picnic tables.

CONTACT INFORMATION: info@capecodbaseball.org; www.capecodbaseball.org

BASKETBALL

GIVEN THAT BASKETBALL WAS born in Springfield, Massachusetts, a mere ninety miles west of Boston, the city's affinity for the sport seems perfectly natural. The rhythmic bouncing of basketballs on hot asphalt playgrounds all around Boston is a daily soundtrack to summer in the city. In the wintertime, the game simply moves indoors. In fact, Boston is a hub of hoops—from the legendary Celtics to shirts-versus-skins pick-up games.

Unlike baseball, football, and hockey—which evolved slowly from other sports into the games fans know today—basketball sprung forth from a singular inventor's imagination: James Naismith, a physical education teacher at Springfield College. Naismith had been under orders to create an indoor game that would provide an "athletic distraction" for students susceptible to highly contagious cases of cabin fever, extremely common to New England. When he first hung up his peach baskets in 1891, little did Naismith know that his brainchild would become the fastest-growing game in the history of sports. Today Springfield is home to the **Basketball Hall of Fame**, which is dedicated in Naismith's honor, as well as the NCAA Division II Men's National Championship each March.

College campuses around the Boston area became incubators of the new sport, and it wasn't just men taking up the game. The women at Wellesley College played basketball as early as 1893. "Pretty college girls are playing basket ball," read one headline in *The Boston Globe*. The paper reported that basketball was a "very fair feminine substitute for football" and a "feminine encroachment on the masculine domain of outdoor sports." The game played by the women of Wellesley more than a century ago was certainly different from the one engaged in by their contemporaries today. There were nine players to a side, and there was no running with the ball or touching another player.

Further west, another all-female school was pioneering the game. Smith College was drawing crowds of a thousand students with games between freshmen and sophomores. The players' navy blue uniforms—blouses and bloomers—were a little more constricting than those worn by today's hoopsters.

Despite its initial popularity among college campuses, the sport's momentum began to wane in the early 1900s. Harvard went so far as to eliminate basketball as a varsity sport in 1909, and Boston College did the same in 1925. The Boston public schools eventually dropped the sport as well.

The city's first professional basketball team, the Boston Whirlwinds, which began in 1925 and played at Boston Arena (today's Matthews Arena) as well as other local halls, was equally doomed. (In the 1950s, a team called the Boston Whirlwinds, like the latter-day Washington Generals, became the foil of the Harlem Globetrotters.) Boston didn't see another pro team until 1934, when the Boston Trojans arrived. But the Trojans only lasted one season as well. The Trojans played

Wellesley women brought basketball to life in its early years. Courtesy Wellesley College Archives.

at the Boston Arena before moving to the Irvington Street Armory, which was built on the outfield of the old Dartmouth Street Grounds, now home to Copley Place.

By the end of World War II, the sport was once again thriving in Boston's high schools and colleges. Basketball fans packed into the old Boston Garden to watch the Tech Tourney, which featured local schoolboy teams, such as Somerville High School and Durfee High School. Holy Cross, which won the 1947 NCAA Tournament and the 1954 National Invitation Tournament, routinely played to sellout crowds at the Garden as well.

The renewed popularity of basketball was a driving force behind the creation of a new professional league with a franchise in Boston. The **Boston Celtics** came of age in 1946 and are one of only two charter members of the NBA still playing in their original city—the other being the New York Knicks.

The Celtics quickly ascended to hoops royalty and established an unparalleled standard of excellence. The fabled franchise has won seventeen NBA titles and, after some lean years, has returned to the league's elite by capturing the crown in 2008. The Celtics now sell out each game and are the biggest basketball draw in Boston—but that wasn't always the case, even during the team's dynastic reign. For most games, fans could walk up to the Garden's ticket office and score some seats. The Celtics even scheduled doubleheaders with Somerville High to boost attendance.

Today the popularity of the Celtics dwarfs that of high school basketball, but the **High School Championships** still pulls in tens of thousands of fans cheering on boys' and girls' teams throughout the month of March. Hoops fans in Boston can also find plenty of college basketball action, and the **TD Garden** occasionally hosts the NCAA Tournament. There are four Division I schools in the area with men's and women's teams—**Boston College, Boston University, Harvard,** and **Northeastern**. There used to be a basketball version of the Beanpot in the 1960s and 1970s, but no such tournament exists today. On occasion, however, the teams schedule games against each other early in the regular season.

While the Division I teams draw the most fans, there are also Division II and Division III teams in the area with strong college basketball programs. One of the teams, the Tufts University Jumbos, has a tradition unique in college athletics. The university was once home to the stuffed remains of its namesake Jumbo the circus elephant, which was given to the university by school trustee P. T. Barnum. Players patted Jumbo for good luck before big games. Unfortunately, the pachyderm was one of the victims of a 1975 fire, and now the players do the next best thing—rub a peanut butter jar said to contain Jumbo's ashes.

BOSTON CELTICS

New York may have its Yankee dynasty and Montreal its Canadiens, but Boston has the Celtics. There is no more storied franchise in the NBA, and the numbers say it all: seventeen world championships, twenty-two retired numbers, and even more hall of famers.

Now that the team has returned to glory by raising another banner to the rafters in 2008, Celtic pride is alive and well in the Hub. Winning a playoff series or two is great, but the Celtics are all about championships. Take a look at the ceiling of the TD Garden, and you won't see flags celebrating division titles or even conference championships—when it comes to the Celts, it's all about being world champions.

The Celtics' success over the decades has been more than just the luck of the Irish. It has been the byproduct of having many of basketball's greatest figures on that famous parquet floor.

Walter Brown, manager of the Boston Garden, was the founder of the Celtics. To Brown, a basketball team was an attractive way to fill open dates between hockey games. During Brown's tenure as president of the Celtics, the franchise captured seven NBA championships. Since then, the Celtics have retired the number 1 in his honor. Brown was also so instrumental in the creation of the NBA that the league championship trophy was named in his honor until 1983, and he was enshrined in the Basketball Hall of Fame. (For his work as president and owner of the Bruins and other hockey-related activities, he's also enshrined in the Hockey Hall of Fame, the only inductee to do a twofer.)

The Celtics first took to the floor in 1946 against the Chicago Stags in front of 4,329 fans at Boston Arena. The Green were inaugural members of the Basketball Association of America, which would merge three years later with the National Basketball League to form the National Basketball Association.

The initial years of the Celtics, who split their time between Boston Arena and Boston Garden until the late 1950s, did not foreshadow greatness. The team missed the playoffs in three of its first four years. The groundwork for dynastic rule began in 1950, however, with the arrival of coach Red Auerbach and point guard Bob Cousy, a Holy Cross graduate whose no-look passes and behind-the-back dribbling brought a flair to the game not seen before. In thirteen seasons together, the pair never missed the playoffs.

With rookie center Bill Russell and another Holy Cross standout, Tom Heinsohn, on board, the Celtics captured the first of their seventeen titles in 1957. They lost in the final the next year but then won eight amazing consecutive titles. (In fact, they won ten titles in eleven years.) When he finally retired, Russell would have needed a third hand to wear all eleven of his championship rings. (Russell also won two NCAA championships and a gold medal at the 1956 Summer Olympics.) But even with the team's on-court success, many games at the Garden were far from sellouts. Professional basketball was still trying to gain a foothold in Boston.

Led by Dave Cowens and John Havlicek, the Celtics captured two more titles in the 1970s. The Green won three more in the 1980s, the last in 1986, with the Big Three of Larry Bird, Robert Parish, and Kevin McHale patrolling the parquet. During the Bird era, the Celtics were the hottest ticket in town. From December 1980 to its close in 1995, the team sold out 662 consecutive games in Boston Garden.

It took twenty-two years, a drought of biblical proportions for a team accustomed to championship success, before the Celtics won another title in 2008. This time it was the new Big Three leading the way. Under the guidance of Paul Pierce, Kevin Garnett, and Ray Allen, another consecutive sellout streak has begun. Once again, it's fashionable to be seen courtside at the Garden—and on any given night you could very well spot Hollywood stars and Pats and Sox players watching the Cs.

Going to a Celtics game today is nothing like it was during the dynasty years—or even in the 1980s for that matter. For one thing, the Celtics now have cheerleaders, a decision that caused the ground of this tradition-laden town to shake just a bit. The cacophony of music and video clips on the scoreboard during timeouts verges on auditory overload. As soon as there's a break in the action, the Celtics Dancers or other troupes perform on the parquet, t-shirts are shot into the crowd, and fans mug for the video scoreboard. A decibel

Of course, when the team is winning, it doesn't matter where the game is being played. The building is loud. And what the fans really want to see is a Celtics victory and the present-day version of Red's victory cigar: Gino, a disco dancer from the old *American Bandstand* show, who boogies down on the screen in his t-shirt and bell bottoms whenever a win is imminent.

While Gino is a new addition, some of the franchise's familiar icons have endured

Arnold "Red" Auerbach chats with three Celtics players in the locker room.
Courtesy Boston Public Library, Print Department.

meter measures crowd noise; with the apex considered "Garden level," the measurement sounds almost like a concession that the new place just doesn't rock like the old one did.

in the new Garden. There's the familiar winking leprechaun logo (designed by Red Auerbach's brother) and the parquet floor—with its alternating wooden panels and the rumored dead spots. The story behind the parquet floor is almost as good as the team's.

Celtics Hall of Famer Bill Russell goes up for a block against longtime rival Wilt Chamberlain.
Courtesy Boston Public Library, Print Department.

The East Boston Lumber Company built the floor in 1946 for a mere $10,000. Due to lumber shortages in the aftermath of World War II, long boards weren't available, and the floor had to be constructed with small scraps of wood pieced together in the untraditional parquet style. The floor was first installed in the Boston Arena but moved to the Garden in 1952. The original floor was retired in 1999 after more than a half-century of service. At the beginning of 2007, the court was dedicated to Auerbach, who had passed away the year before, and Red's autograph now graces the parquet near center court.

The number 2 has been retired in Red's honor, and that digit along with twenty others (the number 18 was retired twice—for Dave Cowens and Jim Loscutoff) hangs from the Garden rafters. All the banners since the team's first title in 1957 have been made locally by New England Flag and Banner. (The company also makes banners for the Bruins and teams across the country, including—*gasp!*—the Los Angeles Lakers.) When the team moved into the TD Garden, larger banners were made, and the originals were moved to the team's practice facility in Waltham. On each banner, a penny stamped with the year of the banner is sewn into the label.

TD Garden

The Celtics play home games at the TD Garden, located on Causeway Street above North Station. The Garden has a capacity of 18,624 for basketball games and features private restaurants, ninety executive suites, eleven hundred premium club seats, and a high-definition video scoreboard.

Like many sports venues around the country, the naming rights to Boston's indoor arena have been sold to corporations, and the name of the arena has gone through various incarnations since it opened in 1995. (For a period in 2005, one-day naming rights to the arena were put up for auction on eBay for individual events.) Before the building even opened, its name was changed from the Shawmut Center to the Fleet Center. When TD Banknorth purchased the naming rights, the bank at least returned the Garden name to the façade. Following the bank's rebranding in 2009, the arena's name changed once again, from TD Banknorth Garden to TD Garden.

Old habits die hard, however, and many Boston sports fans still refer to the building just as the Garden. True—the new joint has definite improvements over the old barn, but die-hards know that this new iteration of the Garden will never, ever be the "Gah-den."

The venerable Boston Garden was the brainchild of George L. "Tex" Rickard, a boxing promoter who had just built Manhattan's Madison Square Garden and planned to construct six similar structures across the country, with the first in Boston. When it opened in 1928, the Boston Madison Square Garden was touted as "New England's greatest sports palace."

For sixty-seven years, Bostonians came to the Garden to watch basketball, hockey, boxing, tennis, track meets, cycling races, concerts, political speeches, and even indoor football, softball, and ski jumping. Fans—including the "gallery gods," who sat in the balcony—entered the smoky hall in the dark shadows of the rickety, elevated Green Line that rattled over Causeway Street. Once through the turnstiles, fans ascended the winding ramps before arriving in the concourses. (Local kids found a different way to get inside—sneaking into the Garden through its fire escapes.)

The new Garden was constructed directly behind the old one, which used to hug Causeway Street. At their closest point, the two buildings were only nine inches apart. That made demolition of the Boston Garden a painstaking task. In some places, the old building was removed brick by brick. For months Bostonians sitting in traffic on the Central Artery—another relic of the city's past—could gawk at a cross section of the Garden as it was sliced open and exposed to the world.

With the new Garden, there are no more dingy bathrooms, no more obstructed views, no more sweltering bodies in an arena without air conditioning—but there's also not nearly the same sightlines, character, or soul. There's little about the new Garden that is distinctive about Boston. Outside of the seats clad in the black-and-gold of the Bruins (the team's owners also own the Garden), the Garden could be in any city. The building's exterior is so sterile that by comparison, the new Garden makes Boston City Hall look warm and inviting.

When the TD Garden opened, the Celtics and Bruins were in the midst of sagging fortunes. The most notable event in the Garden's first decade was the 2004 Democratic National Convention that nominated John Kerry but might be better remembered for propelling Barack Obama onto the national stage. However, the quiet years ended in 2008, when the Garden was finally able to christen a new banner.

In addition to the Bruins, Celtics, and Boston Blazers lacrosse team, the Garden hosts concerts, the Beanpot, the Hockey East Championship, and NCAA tournament action in college hockey and college basketball. It is also home of **The Sports Museum**, which chronicles the history of sports in New England (see page 246).

WHEN: The Boston Celtics regular season runs from late October or early November to April. The Celtics play most home games on Sundays, Mondays, Wednesdays, and Fridays.

GETTING THERE: The TD Garden is located on Causeway Street. From the north on Interstate 93, take Exit 26A (Leverett Circle, Cambridge). Follow the signs toward North Station and turn right at the end of the ramp onto Nashua Street. The Garden is on the left. From the north on U.S. 1, follow signs for Storrow Drive/North Station once across the Tobin Bridge. Follow the signs toward North Station and turn right at the end of the ramp onto Nashua Street. The Garden is on the left.

From the south, take Interstate 93 into Boston and take Exit 26 (Storrow Drive). After exiting, stay left and follow the signs for North Station. After exiting onto Nashua Street, the Garden is on the left.

From the west, take the Mass Pike to Boston, take Exit 24B to Interstate 93 north, and then take Exit 26 (Storrow Drive). After exiting, stay left and follow the signs for North Station. After exiting onto Nashua Street, the Garden is on the left. An alternative route is to take Storrow Drive eastbound. At the end of Storrow Drive, stay in the far right lane and then turn right onto Martha Road toward North Station. The Garden is on the left.

There are numerous **parking** garages around the Garden, and there is limited metered parking on the streets around the arena, such as Cambridge, Staniford, Merrimac, Portland, Friend, Canal, New Chardon, and North Washington streets. Meters with two-hour limits may run until 8 PM, so if you're grabbing a spot before 6 PM, be sure to check. A 1,150-space garage, accessible via Nashua Street, is underneath the Garden. The garage offers the convenience of taking an elevator right up to the concourse and leaving your bulky jacket in the car. It may take a while to exit the garage right after the game, so bring some reading material. And expect to pay about $25. Parking garages within about a five minute walk of the Garden charge upwards of $20, while garages closer to Quincy Market, about a ten minute walk from the Garden, charge $10-$13.

The Garden is extremely convenient to **public transportation** by subway and commuter rail. The Garden is directly atop North Station, the terminus for commuter rail lines north of Boston: Newburyport/Rockport, Haverhill, Lowell, and Fitchburg. The Orange Line and Green Line both stop at North Station. Some fans north of Boston park at lots along the Orange Line, such as Sullivan Square, and take the T for a few stops to North Station. Taxi stands are located on Causeway Street in front of the Garden.

TICKETS: Since the team's revitalization, tickets to most Celtics games sell out. Tickets to individual games go on sale in September. When choosing games, keep in mind that while April games have the highest potential for drama, there is also the possibility that star players will be resting for the playoffs.

Individual tickets to most games range from $10 to $190. Courtside seats go for even higher prices. Loge tickets are for the lower level of the arena, and balcony tickets are for the upper level. Sections 1 and 12 in the loge of the Garden and 301 and 316 in the balcony are at center court. The Celtics bench is located in front of section 22, and the visitor's bench is located in front of section 2. Tickets to the Premium Club level, located between the loge and the balcony, sell for $186.50.

> ★ **Boston Garden Scoreboard**
>
> The old Boston Garden may be no longer, but sports fans can still check out the arena's old scoreboard that used to tally goals and baskets. The board that was once suspended above a basketball court now hangs above the food court of Watertown's **Arsenal Mall** (485 Arsenal Street, 617-923-4700, www.simon.com). When the Garden was dismantled, the mall's owner bought the memento, sixteen feet tall and fourteen feet across, for $40,000.

Loge center (sections 1–3, 10–14, and 21–22) tickets, outside of the front rows, range in price from $115 to $190. Center court tickets in sections 1 and 12 cost $170 to $190. Most, but not all, tickets in loge center sections are between the hoops.

Loge end (sections 4–9 and 15–20) tickets range in price from $75 to $105. Loge end seats are in the corners and behind the baskets. The priciest seats in this portion of the arena are on the floor and in the first rows behind the basket.

Balcony center (sections 301–303, 314–318, and 329–330) tickets are $75 for the lower rows, $55 for the middle rows, and $45 for the upper rows. Most, but not all, tickets in balcony center sections are between the baskets.

Balcony end (sections 304–313 and 319–328) tickets are located in the corners and behind the baskets. The lower rows in the corners cost $55, while the lower rows behind the hoops are $45. Ticket prices for upper rows range from $45 in the corners to $10 behind the basket. The $10 seats are located in sections 308, 309, 323, and 324.

Tickets can be purchased by calling Ticketmaster at 617-931-2000 or going online to www.ticketmaster.com. Tickets are also on sale at the TD Garden box office, located on the main level of North Station. During the basketball season, the box office is open seven days a week between 11 AM and 7 PM.

Even if a Celtics game is sold out, it's still possible to get tickets from brokers and from season-ticket holders on Internet sites such as eBay, Craigslist, and Ticketmaster's TicketExchange, which allows fans to buy directly from season-ticket holders. There are also plenty of scalpers working the streets and bars around the Garden.

Celtics season tickets in the loge and balcony have sold out since the team returned to championship form. Fans who wish to be placed on the season-ticket waiting list must enroll annually in the team's official fan program, Club Green. Members also receive merchandise discounts and information on pre-sale and special offers for individual game tickets.

The Celtics offer varying levels of membership in Club Green. For $39, rookie members receive exclusive pre-sale offers and access to the season-ticket waiting list. For $99, banner members also gain the ability to purchase six tickets, ranging from $10 to $55 per ticket, from a reserved seating area in the corners of the balcony. For $179, parquet members gain access to the waiting list, exclusive pre-sale offers, priority to purchase tickets to the first round of the playoffs, and either two free tickets in the corners of the balcony or the right to purchase tickets in the back of the loge section. For $299, elite members get priority access to purchase tickets to the loge section or four free tickets to the corners of the balcony. Elite members also receive priority to purchase tickets in all rounds of the playoffs and an invitation to an open practice. For more information on Club Green, phone 866-GO-CELTICS or go online to www.celtics.com. For any ticket questions, call 866-4CELTIX.

DISABILITY ACCESS: Spaces for fans with wheelchairs and companions are dispersed vertically and horizontally throughout the Garden in numerous price ranges. Fans requiring handicap-accessible seating should call the ADA phone line at 617-624-1754. Wheelchair escorts are available for disabled guests who may need assistance getting to and/or from their seat. The Garden has two public elevators, one each in the southeast and southwest corners of the building. Both elevators provide access to all levels. Assistive Listening Devices are available from the Garden's customer service office, located outside of section 4 on the loge level.

THE SPLURGE: The Garden's Premium Club, sandwiched between the upper and lower bowls of the Garden, offers many ways for fans to indulge themselves, from luxury boxes to individual club seats. Former Bruins great Ray Bourque is the Premium Club's executive host, so you may see number 77 floating around the club on occasion. An added bonus to checking out a game from the Premium Club is that it houses the collection of The Sports Museum, so fans can check out its wide array of exhibits before, during, and after the game.

The easiest way for fans to see a game from the Premium Club is by getting a ticket to one of the eleven hundred club seats, which provide theater-style seating with extra legroom and in-seat wait service. Some club seats are available for individual Celtics games for $186.50. Fans with a little more disposable income can purchase club-seat memberships in packages with twenty-one to eighty-six games. Packages can be strictly for the Bruins or Celtics or include a combination of both. Memberships start at $5,000 and include golf privileges at private courses and the opportunity to purchase tickets to Garden events before they go on sale to the general public.

The SportsDeck is located behind the basket on the east end of the arena and features three rows of terraced seating in the lower bowl of the Garden, so fans are completely immersed in the energy of the arena. The SportsDeck also offers a fully stocked bar surrounded by swivel seats, in-seat wait service, and complimentary appetizers and soft drinks. Tabletops in the terraced seating have miniature televisions, and the menu includes bar fare and items such as nine-layer chocolate mousse cake. Tickets to the SportsDeck are available in ten- and twenty-game packages, starting at $2,100, and include priority ticket access to Garden events and Celtics playoffs.

The stylish, upscale Boardroom is behind the hoop on the opposite end of the arena from the SportsDeck. The Boardroom features an expansive lounge area, top-shelf liquors and wines, and all-inclusive gourmet cuisine. Memberships to the Boardroom start at $17,160 and guarantee access to every Garden event on demand.

The Premium Club's newest luxury seating area is the Lofts. Each loft hosts four to six people in a nook overlooking the east of the arena. Fans sit on L-shaped couches that are a few steps below a trendy lounge that has a fully stocked bar. Lofts are available in ten-game packages that start at $14,810 and are all-inclusive with a small plated five-course menu and parking.

Executive suites, which hold between eighteen and twenty-one fans, are available to lease for individual games. Suites include theater-style seating on a terrace in the arena, two televisions, and a private restroom. Prices range from $3,500 to $6,000 and do not include food and beverages. You can even arrange for a Celtics legend to drop by the suite for an appearance.

Skybox suites are available on the promenade, which rings the top of the Garden, and the Garden View corporate event suite hosts forty to sixty fans, who can stand in the lounge on the same parquet floor on which former Celtics greats once played.

Fans with tickets to the Premium Club level can find various food stations serving pizza, sandwiches, and ice cream inside the

Premium Club Bistro on level 5. The bistro includes a full bar and open table seating. In addition, Premium Club level fans can eat at the Banners Harbor View restaurant, which offers fine dining on level 6. Reservations are strongly recommended and can be made at 617-624-2501. The restaurant specializes in seafood and steak, and the prices for appetizers start at $6 and entrees start at $23.

Premium Club members receive preferred parking and early entrance into the Garden, access to tickets for all Garden events, tee times at private golf clubs around the country, and invitations to golf outings with Bruins and Celtics players. For more information on the Premium Club for Celtics games, call 617-854-8018. For information on the Premium Club for other Garden events, including Bruins games, call 617-624-CLUB or visit www.tdbanknorthgarden.com/premiumclub. For information on luxury suite rentals to Bruins games, call 617-624-1VIP.

Celtics fans can also get a bite to eat before, during, and after the game at Legends, a members-only bar and restaurant inside the Garden. Memberships in Legends cost $874 for an entire Celtics season or $1,000 for memberships that include both Celtics and Bruins games. The restaurant, which includes buffet stations and a la carte menus, opens two hours before games and remains open one hour after games. In addition to plenty of televisions and Garden memorabilia, fans can find over the long bar the old Boston Garden sign that used to grace the building's exterior. Members may bring three guests into Legends. For more information, call 617-624-1807.

THE CHEAPSKATE: Sports fans would be hard-pressed to find a better deal in town than the $10 seats offered up by the Celtics. The team offered these sawbuck seats for years during some rough seasons, but even after the team returned to glory, the Celtics kept a portion of the Garden's seats at $10. Just forget about paying your $10 and then moving down to empty courtside seats—that might have worked in the lean years, but no more. To receive advanced notification of other ticket deals, register for the free Celtics Beat email newsletter at www.celtics.com.

SPECTATOR TIPS: Gates open one hour before tip-off. Items prohibited from being brought into the Garden include bags, backpacks, coolers, briefcases, cameras with detachable lenses, and video cameras. Food and beverages are not allowed to be brought into the arena, but guests with special dietary needs due to medical conditions or religious requirements should contact the Garden at 617-624-1331. All fans are subject to a search of their person and/or possessions. There is no storage or bag check at the Garden. Smoking is not permitted in the arena.

SCORING AUTOGRAPHS: Autograph hounds stake out the entrance to the players' parking lot on Causeway Street in front of the Garden two to three hours before games in the hope that some players may sign. Your odds of getting an autograph inside the Garden are enhanced if you get there when the doors open and immediately head courtside. Occasionally players will sign after their shootarounds, but the odds drop precipitously if you're after a superstar.

The Celtics have practice sessions during training camp and the regular season at the **Sports Authority Training Center at HealthPoint** at 840 Winter Street in Waltham, but getting close enough to the players for autograph signing can be a challenge. If you're interested in tracking down a player from a visiting team, they sometimes hold closed shootarounds at the Regan Gymnasium at Suffolk University and at Emerson College. In the past, visiting teams have stayed at the Four Seasons, Boston Harbor Hotel, and the Ritz-Carlton.

FOR THE KIDS: How would your kids like to help out the Celtics or the visiting team during warm-ups? The Celtics hold a sweepstakes for children to be honorary ball kids for a game. Sign up at www.celtics.com.

Children under two do not need a ticket to Celtics games, provided they sit on an adult's lap. Strollers are permitted, but they must be collapsible and fit under the seat. Strollers may not be left in walkways or concourses but can be checked at the customer service office near section 4 on the loge level. There are baby changing stations in all restrooms, but there are no family restrooms.

ARENA CONCESSIONS: In addition to the Garden's restaurants that are only open to Premium Club members, there are forty-seven concession stands featuring various themes throughout the Garden. The Frank House features traditional concessions, including Nathan's hot dogs ($4.25), which fans can load with chili, cheese, and jalapenos. The Seaside Shack serves seafood, including shrimp cocktail, fish and chips, and clam rolls. Campione Pizzeria serves pizza, calzones, and chicken parmesan sandwiches. The Links Grill features Italian sausage with peppers and onions, spicy chorizo, and jumbo hot dogs.

Sandwich fans can find corned beef, beef brisket, and hot sandwiches along with Italian pastries at the Pile High Deli. The Boston Pops Stand offers freshly squeezed lemonade, flavored popcorn, and ice cream. Fried-food lovers will find jalapeno poppers, cheese fries, and chicken sandwiches at the Fry Depot. The Sweet Spot offers gelato. Dunkin' Donuts stands sell coffee and drinks.

Beer and other liquor—including hard alcohol such as tequila, rum, and gin—are available at concession stands and pushcarts as well as at the Hub, a full-service bar on the loge level that has panoramic views of Boston Harbor and Charlestown. Expect to pay at least $7 for a 16-ounce beer. The Garden has a wide array of beer choices, from light beers to local brews, such as Sam Adams and Harpoon, to premium imports, such as Guinness and Heineken. Fans who want a brew or a cocktail at the game should remember to bring along a picture ID as vendors card religiously. Out-of-state licenses are only acceptable for fans twenty-five years and older, and another form of ID, such as a credit card, will be required for fans between twenty-five and thirty years old. There is a limit of two drinks per person at a time.

FOOD AND DRINK AROUND THE ARENA: Sports fans who want to have a bite to eat or wet their whistles before a game at the Garden certainly aren't hurting for choices. Fans who want an Italian meal can head to the North End, about a five minute walk east of the Garden, and there are plenty of choices on Cambridge Street, about a five minute walk on the west side of the Garden. Even Quincy Market isn't that far, about a ten minute walk.

There are also a whole range of options in the blocks immediately surrounding the Garden in the Bulfinch Triangle, a wedge of the city bordered by Causeway, Merrimac, and North Washington Streets. In particular, check out the three streets running south of the Garden toward Quincy Market—Portland, Friend, and Canal Streets—which are lined with bars and restaurants.

Three of Boston's best sports bars are near the Garden. *The Four's* (166 Canal Street, 617-720-4455, www.thefours.com) is unusual for a sports bar in that it's acclaimed for its food as well. Spread over two floors, the Four's serves up seafood, buffalo wings, and signature sandwiches named after Boston sporting greats. The house specialty is the Bobby Orr steak sandwich topped with melted American cheese. (See page 249 for more on The Four's.)

The *Sports Grille Boston* (132 Canal Street, 617-367-9302) is nirvana for TV addicts. It's impossible to turn anywhere inside without seeing a game on the tube. There are even televisions in the booths to add to your dining pleasure. (See page 252 for more on the Sports Grille Boston.)

The Greatest Bar (262 Friend Street, 617-367-0544, www.thegreatestbar.com) is a good place for sports fans looking for a doubleheader. The Greatest Bar is a great pregame spot with a dinner menu and a bar sporting a full bank of televisions, including a 14-foot high-def beauty. After the game, the bar has DJs, live music, and dance floors, although there can be a cover charge. (See page 253 for more on The Greatest Bar.)

There's probably not a longer bar in town than *Sullivan's Tap* (168 Canal Street, 617-617-7617). This dive bar is basically a long hallway of drinkers stretching between Canal and Friend streets.

If a trip to the Garden coincides with a date night, a more stylish drinking alternative is the *Ruby Room* (155 Portland Street, 617-557-9950, www.rubyroomboston.com) in the Onyx Hotel. The trendy lounge serves up classic and contemporary libations along with light dinners, tapas, and desserts.

Across the street from the Garden, *The Harp* (85 Causeway Street, 617-742-1010, www.harpboston.com) has a full menu and is a popular pregame spot. If you're looking for a postgame spot on Thursday through Saturday, the bands, DJs, and dancing draw a young singles crowd, which may or may not be to your liking, and there is a cover charge.

Boston Beer Works (112 Canal Street, 617-896-2337, www.beerworks.net) is an outpost of the microbrewery located across from Fenway Park. The burgers, sandwiches, and sweet potato fries are popular choices; if you like your Miller Lite, then the microbrew selection may not be up your alley.

Porters Bar & Grill (173 Portland Street, 617-742-7678, www.portersbar.com) serves pub grub and pizzas and usually offers quick turnaround. It's busy but not obnoxiously crowded before games.

Unlike some faux Irish bars in the downtown area, *McGann's Pub* (197 Portland Street, 617-227-4059, www.mcgannspub-boston.com) is the real deal, from the rich red walls to the traditional music to the soccer and Gaelic games broadcast on the televisions.

The Grand Canal (57 Canal Street, 617-523-1112, www.thegrandcanalboston.com), another Irish pub, has a more extensive menu and offers live music on weekend nights for a $5 cover. The pub's nineteenth-century Victorian décor mixes with twenty-first century plasma televisions.

If you want some of the Creole, Irish, and American-style pub food at *Hurricane O'Reilly's* (150 Canal Street, 617-722-0161, www.irishconnection.com), it's best to go before the game when the atmosphere is chilled. After the game, it's a better place to go for its nightlife, with its multiple bars and dance floor.

If you're looking for an alternative to pub grub, there's the *Flat Iron Tapas Bar & Lounge* (107 Merrimac Street, 617-778-2900,

Shot of the Boston Garden's exterior in 1929. Courtesy Boston Public Library, Print Department.

www.flatironboston.com) in the Bulfinch Hotel, which specializes in small plates and tropical cocktails.

Johnnie's on the Side (138 Portland Street, 617-227-1588, www.johnniesontheside.com) offers full entrees that are on the pricier side. Images from pop culture and sports memorabilia line the walls, and a fantastic giant dining room with windows stretching from the hardwood floors to the super-high ceilings adds to the décor.

DJ's at the Garden (222 Friend Street, 617-723-3222, www.djsatthegarden.com), a new addition to the bar and dining scene, has twenty-five high-def televisions, tons of bottled beer choices, and upscale menu items like fish tacos, Cajun surf and turf, and Guinness braised short ribs. Black-and-white, art deco murals of views of the old Boston Garden painted on the exterior and on the walls inside will have you once again hearing the screech of the long-departed elevated Green Line.

Tastier pizza can be found nearby in the North End, but **Halftime Pizza** (115 Causeway Street, 617-720-4578, www.halftimepizzaboston.com) can fill up before games with fans opting for convenience, reasonably priced slices, and 32-ounce drafts. The plastic booths and video games don't offer much ambiance, but Bruins fans do enjoy watching the highlight reels of classic hockey fights.

If you prefer more upscale pizzerias—without fisticuffs—there's **Nebo** (90 North Washington Street, 617-723-6326, www.nebopizzeria.com), which features pizza as well as antipasti, bruschetta, desserts, and an extensive wine list.

For pizza buffs who want to head to the North End, **Pizzeria Regina** (11½ Thacher Street, 617-227-0765, www.pizzeriaregina.com) is a Boston institution, but if you want a quick (and gigantic) slice, **Ernesto's** (69 Salem Street, 617-523-1373, www.ernestosnorthend.com) is the choice.

CONTACT INFORMATION: Boston Celtics, 226 Causeway Street, Fourth Floor, Boston, MA 02114. 617-854-8000; www.celtics.com.

BOSTON COLLEGE

Boston College is the premier college basketball program in the Boston area. The Eagles have produced some great guards, including John Bagley, Michael Adams, Dana Barros, and Troy Bell. In recent years, the Eagles have produced pros such as Jared Dudley, Craig Smith, and Sean Williams.

Although varsity basketball at the Heights dates back to 1904, the sport was not an instant success. Basketball was discontinued after 1907 due to low attendance and a lack of interest on campus. It returned in fits and starts over the next two decades before it was whacked again in 1925. This time, it was twenty years before basketball returned to Boston College as a varsity sport.

Throughout its formative years, BC basketball players were nomads moving from gym to gym around the Boston area. Boston Garden, Boston Arena (now Matthews Arena), Brandeis University, and even a high school in Cambridge served as home courts for the Eagles before an on-campus facility was finally constructed.

The BC men qualified for their first NCAA Tournament in 1958 and have been regular participants in March Madness in recent years, playing in the tournament seven times between 2001 and 2009. Boston College reached the Elite Eight on three occasions: 1967, 1982, and 1994.

The Boston College women have also experienced success on the hardwood. The team, which began play as a varsity sport in 1972, didn't qualify for their first NCAA Tournament until 1999. They quickly made up for lost time, however, making a total of seven tournament appearances through 2006 and twice reaching the Sweet Sixteen.

Boston College was a charter member of the Big East basketball conference but jumped to the Atlantic Coast Conference (ACC) in 2005. The ACC is one of the premier college basketball conferences in the country for both men and women, and Duke and North Carolina are among the powerhouse teams that are now on the Boston College schedule. The atmosphere inside Conte Forum crackles when Duke and Carolina come to town, and the student section, clad in gold "Boston College Superfan" t-shirts, are always in full throat.

In addition to conference games, the Eagles usually play local schools, such as UMass-Amherst, and a highly ranked team in the first half of their schedule. The season culminates in the ACC Championship, which offers a feast of games over four days in March, with the winner automatically moving on to the NCAA Tournament.

ARENA INFORMATION: The Eagles play on campus at the Conte Forum, which seats 8,606 for basketball. The arena is named for Silvio Conte, a western Massachusetts congressman. For more information on Conte Forum, see page 132.

WHEN: The Boston College men's and women's basketball regular season runs from November to March.

GETTING THERE: See page 133.

TICKETS: Tickets for Boston College men's basketball games sell out against top opponents such as Duke and North Carolina, and they can sell out against other conference opponents or if the team soars in the rankings. Tickets for the women's games sell out only on rare occasions.

Individual tickets for men's games are $20. Individual tickets for women's games are $7 for adults and $4 for youths. Fans can order tickets by phone at 617-552-GOBC, online at www.bceagles.com, or at the ticket office, which is located inside Conte Forum at Gate B. The ticket office is open between 9 AM and 5 PM on weekdays and prior to basketball games. Fans can purchase tickets directly from season-ticket holders through the Ticket Marketplace at www.bceagles.com.

DISABILITY ACCESS: There is wheelchair seating located at center court on both sides of the arena. The wheelchair seating areas are located at the top of the lower level. Handicap parking is available adjacent to Conte Forum.

THE SPLURGE: Major donors to the Flynn Fund—which provides money for scholarships, recruiting, facilities, and operating costs for all varsity sports—are given the option to purchase season tickets on the lower level of Conte Forum along the sidelines. For more information, call 617-552-0772. Flynn Fund donors can also get parking passes to the Beacon Street Garage.

THE CHEAPSKATE: Boston College may offer special $10 ticket deals for men's games during the winter and spring breaks, when the students have vacated campus. If you want to watch the women play for gratis, the team stages periodic promotions where fans can bring canned goods or used tickets stubs to the game and receive free admission.

If you want to bring the family to a game and don't care about the opponent, have one of your kids join the Baldwin's Bunch kids' fan club. (More information below.) In addition to other benefits, members receive free tickets for the whole family to a men's and women's basketball game as well as other Boston College athletic events.

SPECTATOR TIPS: There are standing room areas along the concourse behind each of the baskets that might provide a better view if you have seats in the nosebleed section.

SCORING AUTOGRAPHS: Access to players in uniform before and after games is limited, but the women's basketball team designates a few games during the season where the team signs autographs for all fans after the game.

FOR THE KIDS: Children under twelve can join the Baldwin's Bunch kids' fan club, which includes free BC gear, free tickets to Eagles sporting events, and invitations to special member events. Membership costs $20 a year. During a few Eagles women's games throughout the year, kids can wear their youth jerseys to the game and receive free admission.

ARENA CONCESSIONS: See page 134.

FOOD AND DRINK AROUND THE ARENA: See page 108.

CONTACT INFORMATION: Boston College Men's Basketball, 140 Commonwealth Avenue, Chestnut Hill, MA 02467. 617-552-3006; www.bceagles.com.

Boston College Women's Basketball, 140 Commonwealth Avenue, Chestnut Hill, MA 02467. 617-552-4530; www.bceagles.com.

BOSTON UNIVERSITY

There's no doubt that hockey is the sport of choice at Boston University, but it's the basketball program that has the longer, if not more glorious, history. The Boston University men's basketball program dates back to 1901 but didn't gain official status until 1916. Over its lengthy history, the program has accumulated nearly one thousand wins and made six appearances in the NCAA Tournament, with the last in 2002. BU's best squad was probably the 1959 team that made it to the Elite Eight. The Terriers have had some success in recent years, winning twenty games and making postseason tournament appearances each season between 2002 and 2005.

The Boston University women have played varsity basketball since 1975. The team has made one appearance in the NCAA Tournament, in 2003. In 2007-08, the team won twenty games, including an undefeated mark at home, for the second time in the program's history.

Both the men and women play in the America East conference. In addition to their slate of conference opponents, the men's schedule usually includes some other New England schools along with one mid-major team early in the season.

The men's team divides its season nearly evenly between two on-campus gyms that have completely different vibes: Agganis Arena and the Roof. Agganis Arena is a large, state-of-the-art facility with many concession stands, bathrooms, and fan amenities that provides a big-school feel. The Roof is an intimate gym where you get more of a high school atmosphere. If the crowd is sparse, you can sit right behind the benches and watch coaches draw up plays on white boards and hear their impassioned pleas to the referees about how their squads are being terribly wronged. The pep band and cheerleaders add life to the event, along with the enthusiastic group of students chanting "Go BU."

ARENA INFORMATION: The Boston University basketball teams play the majority of games on campus at the Case Gymnasium, which has been nicknamed the Roof for its location atop the athletic center. The teams also play at Agganis Arena.

The Roof, located inside the Case Center at 285 Babcock Street, has a capacity of 1,800. It's similar in setup to a large high school gym with seating limited to the sidelines, but fans enjoy upholstered theater seats with armrests, rather than bleachers. Fans coming through the turnstiles enter a lobby with concession stands, restrooms, and a trophy case before entering the gym itself. Teams enter the gym through the lobby as well. Sections 1 to 5 are located behind the press table, and sections 6 to 10 are located behind the benches. The pep band sits at the bottom of section 1, and students congregate in section 2. There are approximately twenty rows in each section.

The high school vibe of the Roof, which opened in 1972, isn't limited to the seating arrangement. The gymnasium is tight, with a padded wall just feet behind one basket, while the exit doors to the lobby are directly behind the other. One hard foul going to the hoop and players may find themselves leaving the building altogether. Hanging from the roof of the Roof are banners honoring men's and women's NCAA and NIT appearances, conference championships, and retired numbers.

Agganis Arena is located at 925 Commonwealth Avenue. Seats are sold along the sidelines in the seating bowl as well as on the floor behind the baskets. For more information on Agganis Arena, see page 136.

WHEN: The Boston University men's and women's basketball regular season runs from November to March.

GETTING THERE: The Case Center and Agganis Arena are located about a mile west of Kenmore Square. From north and south of Boston, take Interstate 93 into Boston.

Exit onto Storrow Drive and continue to the Kenmore Square exit. At the first set of lights, turn right onto Beacon Street. Bear right at the far end of Kenmore Square onto Commonwealth Avenue. Agganis Arena is approximately one mile up on the right. For the Case Center, proceed one block past Agganis Arena and take a right on Babcock Street. The Case Center is ahead on the right.

From west of Boston, take the Massachusetts Turnpike east to Exit 18 (Brighton/Cambridge). Follow signs to Cambridge and turn right at the second set of lights onto Storrow Drive. Continue on Storrow Drive to the Kenmore Square exit. At the first set of lights, turn right onto Beacon Street. Bear right at the far end of Kenmore Square onto Commonwealth Avenue. Agganis Arena is approximately one mile up on the right. For the Case Center, proceed one block past Agganis Arena and take a right on Babcock Street. The Case Center is ahead on the right.

For games at the Case Center, there is limited on-street metered parking on Commonwealth Avenue and the surrounding side streets. There is also a **parking** lot on Babcock Street across from the Case Center that costs $5. For games at Agganis Arena, there is an underground garage, which is a nice option on bitterly cold or snowy days. There are also various campus lots within easy walking distance of Agganis arena. The cost of these lots on game day is $10.

If you prefer **public transportation** to the Case Center, take the "B" branch of the Green Line (with a terminus at Boston College) to the Babcock Street stop and walk north on Babcock Street. For Agganis Arena, take the "B" branch of the Green Line to either the St. Paul Street or Pleasant Street stops. Both are approximately one block from the arena. In addition, the 57 bus stops near both arenas.

TICKETS: Tickets to Boston University men's and women's basketball games rarely sell out. Individual tickets for men's games cost $10, and season tickets cost $90. Individual tickets for women's games cost $7, and season tickets cost $48. For more information on season tickets, call 617-353-GOBU.

To purchase tickets through Ticketmaster, call 617-931-2000 or go online to www.ticketmaster.com. Tickets may also be purchased at the Agganis Arena ticket office, which is located on the east side of the arena lobby. The ticket office is open Monday through Friday from 10 AM to 5 PM. For events at Agganis Arena, the ticket office opens at noon on game days. For events at the Case Center, the box office opens ninety minutes before tip-off.

DISABILITY ACCESS: The Agganis Arena offers wheelchair-accessible and companion seating along the concourse at the top of the seating bowl. The accessible drop-off location is located on the corner of Harry Agganis Way and Commonwealth Avenue. There are two elevators serving the underground parking lot and two providing access from the lobby to the concourse. For accessible seating tickets at the Roof or Agganis Arena, call 617-358-7000.

THE SPLURGE: Agganis Arena has suites available to rent for individual games. Suites hold between four and twenty-four people and have granite countertops, sinks, a refrigerator, a private server, and theater-style upholstered seating. Call 617-358-7000 for more information.

THE CHEAPSKATE: Season tickets for men's basketball are pretty reasonable at just $90. For special deals on basketball tickets, sign up for the free Advantage Club email on the

Agganis Arena website at www.agganisarena.com.

SPECTATOR TIPS: Fans who enter the Case Center off the Babcock Street entrance will find the Roof's nickname well deserved. Wandering the maze of doors and staircases to find the Roof can make Boston's street layout seem straightforward. Fans might expect to have to climb a ladder and pop a hatch, like a Beacon Hill roof deck, to finally see the Roof. Enter the Case Center through the entrance behind the back along Nickerson Field, and it's much simpler.

SCORING AUTOGRAPHS: Access to players in uniform before and after games is limited, but you could always try getting them walking through the lobby after the game.

FOR THE KIDS: Occasionally, Boston University offers special family four-packs for basketball games, which include four tickets, four hot dogs or pretzels, and four sodas for just $25. Sign up for the Agganis Arena email Advantage Club to be informed of family four-packs.

ARENA CONCESSIONS: There are two small concession stands at the Roof that serve basic staples such as hot dogs ($2.75), pretzels, popcorn, and soda. Alcohol is not served at games at the Roof. For information on concessions at Agganis Arena, see page 138.

FOOD AND DRINK AROUND THE ARENA: See page 139.

CONTACT INFORMATION: Boston University Men's Basketball, 285 Babcock Street, Boston, MA 02215. 617-358-0749; www.goterriers.com.

Boston University Women's Basketball, 285 Babcock Street, Boston, MA 02215. 617-358-5864; www.goterriers.com.

HARVARD

While Harvard isn't known for turning out NBA stars, the university has produced one famous baller—President Barack Obama. While a student at Harvard Law, Obama was a gym rat who regularly played pick-up games on campus. His secretary of education, Arne Duncan, is a former Harvard basketball co-captain. Former vice president Al Gore played on the freshman team at Harvard as well.

The Harvard men and women compete in the venerable Ivy League conference, which is unique among Division I NCAA basketball programs in that it's the only one without a postseason tournament. Before taking on Ivy League competition after New Year's, the men and women play a number of local colleges in the first half of the season.

While the geometry and physics of putting a ball in the hoop is simple math for these intellectuals, only the women have mastered Ivy League competition so far. The Harvard women's program, which dates to 1974, captured eleven Ivy League titles between 1986 and 2008. The men, on the other hand, have yet to raise an Ivy League championship banner in more than fifty years of league play.

Men's basketball has always had a rough go of it at Harvard compared to the football and hockey teams. Sellouts are the exception, rather than the rule, and the matchup against Yale generates nowhere near the enthusiasm as the football tilt. On the gridiron Harvard-Yale is "The Game;" on the hardwood, it's just another game.

Back in the early 1900s, Harvard's own leaders even abolished basketball as a varsity sport. Harvard president Charles Eliot told *The New York Times* in 1906, "Basket ball is very objectionable. It is too rough, and there are too many chances for cheating. The rules have been stretched so that they spoil the game. It would be a good thing, especially, to have basket ball discontinued." The manager of the 1908-09 squad wasn't much more supportive: "We are being defeated all the time in basketball. It is a poor sport. Therefore, we had better abolish it." And indeed that is was happened in 1909. Perhaps the real reason for the Crimson's antipathy toward basketball was that it was introduced on campus in 1900 by law student John Kirkland Clark, a Yale grad.

Luckily, basketball returned as a varsity sport at Harvard in 1920. Games at Harvard have a bit of a retro feel to them. For starters, the teams play in one of the oldest athletic venues in Boston. The cheerleaders wear classic crimson outfits with a big white "H" on the front; male cheerleaders wear long pants and use megaphones to lead chants. And in one of the stranger entrances into a basketball game, teams take the floor by running down a staircase from the upstairs locker room.

ARENA INFORMATION: The Harvard men's and women's basketball teams play home games at Lavietes Pavilion, located in the Briggs Athletic Center at the campus athletic complex on North Harvard Street in Allston. The 2,050-seat arena, which first opened in 1926, is named in honor of Ray Lavietes, a two-time letterman for Harvard basketball and a major benefactor of the program.

Lavietes Pavilion is tied with the University of Oregon's McArthur Court as the second-oldest building used for basketball among Division I schools. Only Fordham's Rose Hill Gymnasium, built in 1924, is older. Harvard hoopsters played across the river in Cambridge until 1982 when the Briggs Center, which was used by Harvard's indoor track teams and also served as a batting cage for university baseball players and major leaguers such as Ted Williams, was converted to a basketball arena.

Seating inside the pavilion is similar to a high school setup, with two sets of stands flanking the sidelines. Bleachers are about twenty rows deep. Seats are molded plastic bleachers that lack seat backs. Sections 1 to 5 are behind the team benches. Sections 6 to 10, across from the benches, tend to have fewer fans, so if you want more space you may want to request tickets on that side. Fans wishing to go from one stand to another must pass through the pavilion lobby, which has trophy cases and the indoor ticket window. The banners hanging from the rafters of the arena celebrating NCAA appearances and Ivy League titles are all for the women's team.

WHEN: The Harvard men's and women's basketball regular season runs from November to March. Most Ivy League home games are played on Friday and Saturday nights.

GETTING THERE: Lavietes Pavilion is about four miles from downtown Boston. To get to the arena, take the Mass Pike to the Brighton/Cambridge exit (Exit 18 eastbound and Exit 20 westbound). After paying the toll, bear left at the fork toward Allston. Turn right at the second set of lights onto North Harvard Street. The arena is on the athletic complex just beyond Harvard Stadium, approximately one mile ahead on the left.

There is limited on-street **parking** on North Harvard Street. Parking is available next to the arena for $10; enter Gate 6 on the south side of Harvard Stadium. Parking is also available across the street for $5 at the Harvard Business School lot, about a five minute walk from the arena.

Lavietes Pavilion is also accessible by **public transportation.** By subway, take the Red Line to the Harvard station. It's about a ten minute walk from Harvard Square down JFK Street and across the Charles River to the arena, which is on the Soldiers Field Road side of the athletic complex. Several MBTA bus lines also stop at Harvard Square, and bus routes 66 and 86 stop on North Harvard Street outside the athletic complex.

TICKETS: Game day tickets are available for women's and most men's games, although tickets for matchups against Penn, Princeton, and Cornell can sell out and should be purchased in advance. Tickets for men's games are $10 for adults ($12 for games against Penn, Princeton, and Yale) and $5 for youths (ages three to fourteen). Tickets are $5 for Harvard graduate students and free for undergraduates. Season tickets are available for $78 ($52 for Allston-Brighton residents) with discounts for faculty, staff, young alumni, and graduate students.

Tickets for women's games are $8 for adults and $4 for youths and students. Season tickets for women's games are $55 ($44 for Allston-Brighton residents) with discounts for faculty, staff, young alumni, and graduate students.

To purchase tickets, phone 877-GO-HARVARD (877-464-2782), go online to www.gocrimson.com, or visit the ticket office (Monday–Friday, 9 AM–5 PM) in the Murr Center at 65 North Harvard Street. Game day ticket sales are at the ticket window in the lobby of Lavietes Pavilion. It's important to note that only cash or checks are accepted at the arena's ticket window on game days; credit cards are not accepted.

DISABILITY ACCESS: Call 877-GO-HARVARD for information.

THE SPLURGE: The Friends of Harvard Basketball host receptions and events throughout the year with coaches and players. Call 617-495-3535 for more information.

THE CHEAPSKATE: While $78 season tickets won't break the bank, Allston-Brighton residents receive discounts for both men's and women's season tickets.

SPECTATOR TIPS: Game programs are free at all games and available from the athletics table in the arena's lobby.

SCORING AUTOGRAPHS: Access to players in uniform before and after games is limited.

FOR THE KIDS: The university sponsors the Crimson Kids Club for both men's and women's basketball. Members receive tickets to all home games, a membership card, t-shirt, monthly newsletters, and exclusive invites to pizza parties and autograph sessions with Harvard athletes. The club is for kids in eighth grade and below and costs $39 for men's basketball and $22 for women's basketball. Membership applications are available on the Harvard Athletics website.

ARENA CONCESSIONS: Concessions at Harvard basketball are limited. There is just one concession stand inside the arena next to section 1, and the choices are pretty sparse. Beyond the normal hot dogs ($3), pretzels, and soda, the most exotic menu items are Italian sausage and hot cookies. Alcohol is not served at games.

FOOD AND DRINK AROUND THE ARENA: See page 114.

CONTACT INFORMATION: Harvard University Men's Basketball, Murr Center, 65 North Harvard Street, Boston, MA 02163. 617-495-4856; www.gocrimson.com.

Harvard University Women's Basketball, Murr Center, 65 North Harvard Street,

Boston, MA 02163. 617-495-2214; www.gocrimson.com.

NORTHEASTERN

There's no doubt that Matthews Arena is a great ice palace—the popularity of hockey led to its construction after all. But it's not a bad place to watch some hoops either. The arena has fantastic sightlines, and at most games you can grab a seat in the front row of the balcony, where you feel incredibly close to the action. If the crowd is thin, you can be sure that the referee will hear even the mildest catcall.

The Northeastern men and women play in the Colonial Athletic Association (CAA). The Huskies are the only CAA team in New England, so there are few natural rivals that generate great excitement for casual sports fans, although the conference's most notable team is George Mason, the Cinderella that went all the way to the Final Four in 2006. Before getting into the CAA season, Northeastern also takes on some local schools.

The men of Northeastern have been playing basketball since 1920. The team has played in the NCAA Tournament seven times with the last appearance in 1991. Undoubtedly, the golden years for the program were the 1980s. Hall of Fame coach Jim Calhoun guided the Huskies to five of their six trips to the tournament during that decade. Calhoun's star player was Reggie Lewis, the greatest athlete ever to wear a Northeastern uniform and the program's all-time leading scorer. The Huskies won their league title and played in the Big Dance in all four of his years at Northeastern.

Lewis was a first-round draft pick of the Celtics in 1987, and he became the team captain and an All-Star while patrolling the parquet. In one of the saddest moments in Boston sports history, Lewis died in 1993 at the age of twenty-seven after collapsing while practicing at Brandeis University. His funeral at Matthews Arena drew Bostonians from all walks of life. They waited in line for hours to pay their respects to Lewis. His number, 35, was later retired by the Celtics; another 35 hangs in his honor next to the scoreboard in Matthews Arena.

The Northeastern women have been bouncing the ball since 1966; they made their one and only NCAA Tournament appearance in 1999.

ARENA INFORMATION: The Northeastern men's basketball team plays at historic Matthews Arena, located on the university campus at 238 St. Botolph Street. The Northeastern women's basketball team plays at the 2,500-seat Solomon Court inside the Cabot Center at the corner of Huntington Avenue and Forsyth Street.

Matthews Arena was known as Boston Arena when it opened its doors in 1910. (It was renamed in 1982 in honor of former chairman emeritus of Northeastern Board of Trustees George J. Matthews and his wife.) The building is the city's oldest multipurpose arena and the oldest artificial ice arena in the world.

Tremendous history has occurred underneath the gym's barn-like roof. The Bruins played their first game at the arena on December 1, 1924, defeating the Montreal Maroons. Twenty-two years later, the parquet floor was first bolted together inside the Boston Arena. The Celtics took to the floor of the arena for their first game on November 5, 1946. Eager fans had to wait a little longer than they anticipated to catch the new team because the start of the game was delayed by an hour when Celtics center Chuck Connors, who later gained fame as television's

Rifleman, shattered the backboard with a dunk in warm-ups.

The Celtics were not actually the first professional basketball team to play in the Boston Arena. That honor goes to the Boston Whirlwinds of the original American Basketball League back in 1925. Financial constraints, however, forced the team to relocate midway through the inaugural season. Boston College also used the arena as a home court.

The Northeastern men's and women's hockey teams skate at Matthews Arena, and over the years, the New England Whalers and the hockey teams at Boston College, Boston University, and Harvard also skated on the ice. Legendary brawlers Joe Louis, Jack Dempsey, and Gene Tunney all fought under the arena's roof, and presidents such as Teddy Roosevelt, Franklin D. Roosevelt, and John F. Kennedy shook its rafters with soaring oratory. Today, it's also home to university convocations and intramural sports. Special hours are set aside for free skating for those with Northeastern IDs.

The building's original façade was art deco, with twin capped towers flanking a dramatic archway. The towers are gone today, but fans still file in under a large brick arch, albeit more utilitarian and not as ornamental. The gilded Victorian lobby, however, has been polished into a resplendent jewel, with soaring ceilings and flourished columns reminiscent of many of Boston's old theaters.

If you step inside Matthews Arena today, you will likely feel as if you've stepped inside a miniaturized version of the old Boston Garden. Just like the Garden, Matthews Arena, which has a capacity of fifty-nine hundred fans, includes a lower level with an overhanging balcony. Fans get two very different perspectives from these two levels, and if there are empty seats, it's worth it to spend one half watching the action downstairs and the other half watching it from the balcony, particularly from the front row.

The history of Matthews Arena is honored by some of the banners hanging from its rafters. The uninitiated might be surprised to see flags proclaiming that the arena was the "Boston Bruins original home, 1924–1928" and "Site of the Boston Celtics first game and secondary home, 1946–1959." Banners celebrating Northeastern's Beanpot hockey titles, hockey and basketball conference championships, and NCAA Tournament appearances in hockey and basketball also hang from the ceiling.

Sections 8 and 23 of the arena are at mid-court on the lower level, and sections 38 and 52 are at mid-court on the balcony. Sections 21 to 25 on the lower level are between the hoops behind the benches. Sections 6 to 10 on the lower level are between the baskets across from the benches. There are low risers behind the baskets that are used by the band, students, and cheerleaders. While the arena seats have backs, they are anything but comfortable. The balcony is five to six rows deep, and most sections in the lower level have nine rows.

Fans are not going to get pampered at Matthews Arena. In many ways, little has changed from when Matthews Arena first opened its doors a century ago. There is neither a video scoreboard nor are there any luxury suites. Exposed pipes and poles hold up the balcony, and steamy heat emanates from exposed radiators. Nope, this utilitarian structure is all about the game. And that's actually quite charming.

A segment of Boston sports fans decries any little change to Fenway Park and wants to preserve the gem in the Fens as it was when it opened in 1912. The stomachs of the same fans dropped as they watched the Boston Garden come down brick by brick. But little is ever said about Matthews Arena, which has so many of the same great features. At one time, this arena was firmly in the public consciousness as the hub of Boston's wintertime sports. Today, it feels more like a hidden jewel.

WHEN: The Northeastern men's and women's basketball regular season runs from November to early March.

GETTING THERE: Matthews Arena is located on St. Botolph Street, a block west of Massachusetts Avenue and a block south of Huntington Avenue. From west of Boston, take the Mass Pike to Exit 22 (Prudential Center) and proceed west on Huntington Avenue. After the underpass, take a left at the lights onto Gainsborough Street. Take the first left onto St. Botolph Street, and the arena is on the right.

From south of Boston, take the Southeast Expressway to Exit 18 (Mass. Ave.) and follow the ramp onto Frontage Road and take the left onto Melnea Cass Boulevard. Take a right at the lights onto Massachusetts Avenue and follow for about two miles (seven sets of lights). Take a left onto St. Botolph Street and the arena is on the left.

From north of Boston on Interstate 93, take Exit 26 (Storrow Drive) and follow the signs for Storrow Drive west. Take the Fenway exit and follow the signs for Boylston Street inbound by bearing left at the first set of lights. Continue to Boylston Street and take a right onto Massachusetts Avenue. Take the second right past Symphony Hall onto St. Botolph Street, and the arena is on the left.

There is limited on-street metered **parking** around Matthews Arena. Many of the surrounding streets have parking reserved only for those with local parking permits. The Gainsborough Garage offers the closest parking to the arena; be aware that the garage charges exorbitant prices for event parking, nearly twice as much as the ticket price. The Renaissance Parking Garage across Northeastern's campus on Columbus Avenue provides a cheaper alternative but will require a bit of a walk.

Public transportation is a better option to get to Matthews Arena. Take the "E" branch of the Green Line to the Symphony stop. Walk south on Massachusetts Avenue away from Symphony Hall and take a right onto St. Botolph Street. The arena is on the left. Another option is to take the Orange Line to the Massachusetts Avenue stop. Exit the station onto Massachusetts Avenue and take a left. Take the first left onto St. Botolph Street, and the arena is on the left. For directions and transportation options to the Cabot Center, visit www.gonu.com/news/directions.html.

TICKETS: Sellouts for Northeastern basketball are extremely rare. Tickets for men's games cost $10 for adults and $5 for youths. Season tickets cost $90 for adults and $45 for youths. Tickets for women's games cost $5 for adults and $3 for youths. Season tickets for the women's team cost $40 for adults and $25 for youths.

Game day tickets can be purchased at the ticket windows at Matthews Arena. To purchase advance tickets, call the Northeastern University ticket office at 617-373-4700, go online to www.gonu.com/tickets, or visit the ticket office at Ell Hall. The ticket office is open from noon to 6 PM on Monday, Tuesday, Thursday, and Friday and from noon to 8 PM on Wednesday.

DISABILITY ACCESS: There are a limited number of spots at the top of the concourse in the lower level for wheelchair seating.

THE SPLURGE: Fans who purchase a Husky MVP Pass receive free admission to all football, men's and women's hockey, and men's and women's basketball regular-season home games. The cost is $275 for adults, $125 for youth, and $550 for families.

THE CHEAPSKATE: Northeastern basketball is a good option for skinflints. Tickets are just $10. Cheapskates should take the T to the game, however. If you do drive, the parking rates at the nearby Gainsborough Garage will send shivers down your miserly spine.

SPECTATOR TIPS: Crowds for Northeastern basketball are rarely big enough to require tickets to be sold in sections of the lower level behind the baskets, but be aware that those are not good seats for basketball because they are far from the action and behind the nets set up for hockey.

SCORING AUTOGRAPHS: Access to players in uniform before and after games is limited.

FOR THE KIDS: Northeastern sells season tickets for families to men's and women's basketball. A family pack includes tickets for two adults and two youths. A family pack for men's games costs $180, while a family pack for women's games costs $90.

ARENA CONCESSIONS: Concessions in Matthews Arena are extremely limited. There is a single concession stand in the arena's lobby, which can get very crowded at halftime. The menu options are more reminiscent of a college dining hall than fine cuisine. The few choices are hot dogs, bags of chips, bland pizza, and soda. You might as well hit the vending machines in the bowels of the arena behind the basket on the west end. The stand also closes early in the second half. Alcohol is not served at games.

FOOD AND DRINK AROUND THE ARENA: Huntington Avenue is home to some of the best food options for fans going to Matthews Arena. *Betty's Wok and Noodle Diner* (250 Huntington Avenue, 617-424-1950, www.bettyswokandnoodle.com) is a retro eatery serving Asian-Latino inspired noodle and rice-based dishes along with beer, wine, and sake. For something really different from the normal pregame meal, there's *Symphony Sushi* (45 Gainsborough Street, 617-262-3888, www.symphonysushi.com). Pizza lovers have a few options: *Boston House of Pizza* (305 Huntington Avenue, 617-266-4605, www.bhop-online.com), *Cappy's Pizza* (309 Huntington Avenue, 617-236-4461, www.cappyspizza.com), and *Uno Chicago Grill* (280 Huntington Avenue, 617-424-1697, www.unos.com). Fans looking for pub grub can choose either the basement bar *Conor Larkin's Grill & Tap* (329 Huntington Avenue, 617-867-0084) or *Our House East* (52 Gainsborough Street, 617-236-1890, www.ourhouseeast.com), which serves wings, salads, sandwiches, and burgers.

Closer to the Cabot Center are Mexican chains *Qdoba* (393 Huntington Avenue, 617-450-0910, www.qdoba.com) and *Boloco* (359-369 Huntington Avenue, 617-536-6814, www.boloco.com). *Chicken Lou's* (50 Forsyth Street, 617-859-7017), a small sandwich shop, is a perennial Northeastern favorite. Chicken Lou's most popular sandwich is the TKO—baked chicken, bacon, Swiss cheese, and honey mustard.

CONTACT INFORMATION: Northeastern University Men's Basketball, 219 Cabot Center, 360 Huntington Avenue, Boston, MA 02115. 617-373-7590; www.gonu.com/mbasketball.

Northeastern University Women's Basketball, 219 Cabot Center, 360 Huntington Avenue, Boston, MA 02115. 617-373-2702; www.gonu.com/wbasketball.

HIGH SCHOOL CHAMPIONSHIPS

While madness sweeps the country each March during the NCAA Tournament, boys and girls across Massachusetts engage in some craziness of their own in the MIAA's state high school basketball tournament. The postseason tourney may not whip fans into the same frenzy as March Madness or state championships in Hoosiers country in Indiana, but for a three-week period, Boston sports fans crowd into small, sweaty gyms as well as the state's biggest venues to cheer on hometown teams.

Brackets are formed among teams in the MIAA's four divisions, with Division I composed of the largest high schools in the state. Charlestown High School and Boston College High School are among the city schools that have captured boys' titles in recent years.

The tournament begins in late February, and early rounds are played at the home gyms of top seeded teams before moving to neutral sites at high school gyms around the area. In eastern Massachusetts, teams are divided into north and south regions.

View of the TD Garden and its famous parquet floor.

The north regional final is usually held at the Tsongas Arena in Lowell, and the south regional final is usually held at UMass-Boston.

Winners of those games move on to the state semifinals at the TD Garden, with the girls playing one night and the boys playing the next. The opportunity to play on the parquet floor is the crowning moment in the basketball career of many scholastic players. Of course, lucky players who emerge from the Garden victorious get the chance to play for the state title against teams from either central or western Massachusetts at the DCU Center in Worcester. (The one exception is in Division IV, where schools are limited to eastern Massachusetts.) Championship Saturday at the DCU Center is a hoops feast with six title games played from morning to night.

In a sense, the tournament represents basketball in its purest form. Cheerleaders and student sections chanting, "Warm up the bus," infuse games with school spirit. There are no television timeouts, corporate crowds, or t-shirt tosses. Players are playing for pride, not salary, and often demonstrate hustle that isn't seen at the professional level. Games move quickly and may be over in ninety minutes. Tickets for early-round games at high schools are usually around $7. Tickets for the Tsongas Arena, TD Garden, and DCU Center are around $12.

CONTACT INFORMATION: Massachusetts Interscholastic Athletic Association, 33 Forge Parkway, Franklin, MA 02038. 508-541-7997; www.miaa.net.

BEYOND BOSTON

Basketball Hall of Fame

Boston sports fans are fortunate that the Basketball Hall of Fame is only ninety miles west of the city in Springfield, Massachusetts—the birthplace of basketball.

With its basketball-inspired architecture, the building on the banks of the Connecticut River is hard to miss. The bulk of the Basketball Hall of Fame, dedicated to James Naismith, is housed in a giant 120-foot-high dome that looks like a basketball dribbled into the ground. The current building, which opened in 2002, is the hall's third location in Springfield. In front is a 136-foot spire supporting a 13-foot illuminated basketball. There are also retail outlets and restaurants at the museum.

Unlike other halls of fame, the Basketball Hall of Fame is hardly limited to the professional ranks. Enshrinees and exhibits are focused on the game on every level, including high school, college, and even international. Another difference from other halls of fame is that women are well represented throughout the building.

Visitors begin their tour by ascending in a glass elevator to the Honor Ring dedicated to the members of the Basketball Hall of Fame. Just as with a planetarium, stars shine overhead. In the case of the Basketball Hall of Fame, however, the stars gazing down from the dome ceiling are photographs of the enshrinees—including coaches, contributors, referees, players, and teams. Visitors can read biographies of all the greats.

The galleries themselves are filled with artifacts from the history of the game. The gallery focusing on the pioneer years of basketball is particularly interesting. There is an old 1915 uniform from Smith College, ancient basketballs, and old-time peach baskets. Naismith's original rules of the game, confined to two simple typewritten pages, are enclosed in glass. Visitors can even see a small handwritten edit he made to the rules.

Other galleries focus on players, media, coaches, and teams. Theaters show basketball films, and interactive exhibits allow fans to play one-on-one virtual hoops against superstars of today or try their hands at calling play-by-play of game action. There is audio and video from famous moments in basketball history. Celtics fans will enjoy listening to Johnny Most, the team's longtime radio voice who always saw the world through green-colored glasses, making his famous raspy call of "Havlicek stole the ball!"

Since the franchise played such an important role in the history of the NBA, the Celtics are a constant presence throughout the hall and are well represented among more than 130 enshrinees. A display case devoted to the Celtics has sneakers, autographed basketballs, and the jerseys of Hall of Famers Tom Heinsohn, Frank Ramsey, Dave Cowens, and Larry Bird. Visitors will also see a statue of Larry Bird ready to shoot a free throw. There are now new additions from the latest team to author a championship story. There is a Kevin Garnett jersey, a bottle of champagne from the locker room victory celebration, and a version of Paul Pierce's locker.

After seeing all the exhibits, you'll probably be inspired to take the ball to the hoop, and fans can do just that on the hall's regulation basketball court. The hall stages clinics, skill challenges, and shooting competitions at the court, and kids can shoot at baskets placed at lower heights. Like any basketball arena, there is a giant scoreboard hovering above the court, but this one plays highlights from basketball history. The hall's members also keep a constant vigil on the court from the Honor Ring, and visitors can't help but feel a little intimidated pulling up for a jumper under their eyes.

A new class of members is enshrined each September, and there is a gala and induction celebration on enshrinement weekend.

GETTING THERE: Springfield is ninety miles west of Boston. From Boston, take the Mass Pike west to Exit 6 (Interstate 291 west). Take Interstate 291 west to Exit 1A (Interstate 91 south). Take Interstate 91 to Exit 6 (Union Street). Proceed down the exit ramp onto West Columbus Avenue. Continue straight on West Columbus through one set of lights, and the Hall of Fame is on the right.

HOURS: Tuesday–Friday, 10 AM–4 PM; Saturday, 10 AM–5 PM; Sunday, 10 AM–4 PM; closed on select Mondays.

ADMISSION: Adults $16.99; seniors $13.99; youth $11.99; children under four free. Discounts for AAA members. Admission tickets may be purchased by phone at 866-468-7619 and online at www.hoophall.com.

CONTACT INFORMATION: Naismith Memorial Basketball Hall of Fame, 1000 West Columbus Avenue, Springfield, MA 01105. 413-781-6500; www.hoophall.com.

Where to Watch: College Basketball

Watching a game with die-hard hoops fans or college alumni can definitely provide a welcome dose of school spirit no matter what your alma mater may be. This fact is never more evident than during the three glorious weeks of the NCAA Tournament fondly known as March Madness. If you want to make your March even crazier—or enliven a regular-season game, for that matter—try one of the following locations around the city. Even if you aren't a member of one of the alumni groups listed that frequent a particular bar, it can be fun to watch along with fans who have a definite rooting interest. If your favorite team is not listed below, check social networking websites like Facebook and Meetup—or consult local alumni groups—to find out if a viewing party is scheduled somewhere in the city.

The Baseball Tavern, 1270 Boylston Street, Boston, MA 02215. 617-867-6526; www.thebaseballtavern.com. *College teams: Cal Golden Bears, LSU Tigers, Oregon Ducks.*

Champions, Boston Marriott Copley Place, 110 Huntington Avenue, Boston, MA 02116. 617-236-5800 x6936; www.marriott.com. *College team: Gonzaga Bulldogs.*

Game On!, 82 Lansdowne Street, Boston, MA 02215. 617-351-7001; www.gameonboston.com. *College teams: Indiana Hoosiers, Wisconsin Badgers.*

The Greatest Bar, 262 Friend Street, Boston, MA 02114. 617-367-0544; www.thegreatestbar.com. *College teams: Kansas Jayhawks, Michigan State Spartans, Ohio State Buckeyes.*

The Joshua Tree, 1316 Commonwealth Avenue, Brighton, MA 02134. 617-566-6699; www.joshuatreeallston.com. *College teams: Florida Gators, Maryland Terrapins, Miami Hurricanes, Notre Dame Fighting Irish.*

McFadden's, 148 State Street, Boston, MA 02109. 617-227-5100; www.mcfaddensboston.com. *College team: Florida Gators.*

The Place, 2 Broad Street, Boston, MA 02109. 617-523-2081; www.theplaceboston.com. *College teams: Duke Blue Devils, Michigan Wolverines, UCLA Bruins, USC Trojans.*

The Pour House, 907 Boylston Street, Boston, MA 02115. 617-236-1767; www.pourhouseboston.com. *College team: Syracuse Orange.*

Sports Depot, 353 Cambridge Street, Allston, MA 02134. 617-783-2300; www.sportsdepotboston.com. *College teams: Alabama Crimson Tide, Auburn Tigers, Miami Hurricanes, Oregon State Beavers, Virginia Tech Hokies.*

Sports Grille Boston, 132 Canal Street, Boston, MA 02114. 617-367-9302. *College teams: Colorado Buffaloes, North Carolina State Wolfpack, UCLA Bruins, USC Trojans, Virginia Tech Hokies.*

Tavern in the Square, 730 Massachusetts Avenue, Cambridge, MA 02139. 617-868-8800; www.taverninthesquare.com. *College team: Duke Blue Devils.*

Tavern in the Square, 1815 Massachusetts Avenue, Cambridge, MA 02140. 617-354-7766; www.taverninthesquare.com. *College team: Michigan Wolverines.*

Tommy Doyle's, 96 Winthrop Street, Cambridge, MA 02138. 617-864-0655; www.tommydoyles.com. *College team: North Carolina Tar Heels.*

★ Tips for Autograph Collectors

It's no surprise that collecting autographs is a popular pastime in the hometown of John Hancock, the founding father who inked the most famous signature in American history. If you want to collect players' John Hancocks, you can try to catch them at games, entering and leaving practices, and around visiting teams' hotels such as the Ritz-Carlton, Four Seasons, Boston Harbor Hotel, and Westin and Marriott in Copley Square.

When autograph hunting, always be respectful and scan team photographs so you can put a face with a name. Peter Leventhal, owner of **Kenmore Collectibles** (466 Commonwealth Avenue, 617-482-5705, www.kenmorecollectibles.com), offers some additional pointers:

"Sharpies are great for most items being signed, but ballpoint pens are best for baseballs because they won't spread over time. Blue pens are good because they show up better on darker objects.

"An athlete may be more apt to sign if you want the autograph personalized, but for resale value it's best to have just a single athlete's signature on a particular item. One secret I heard from an autograph hound for getting noticed in a throng is to 'accidentally' drop your item onto the field so that the athlete will pick it up and sign it."

FOOTBALL

AUTUMN IN NEW ENGLAND is a feast for the senses. Colorful foliage dazzles the eyes, mulled apple cider warms the taste buds, and crisp morning air tickles the nose. For Boston sports fans, autumn weekends also mean gathering with friends and family to enjoy another sensory feast: the smell of charcoal embers from the pregame tailgate, the taste of burgers and hot dogs grilled to perfection, and the sounds of roaring crowds.

Sure, Boston isn't as football crazy as other parts of the country. This isn't SEC country in the South or Big Ten country in the Midwest. High school football isn't the focal point of small-town life as it is in Texas, and the city itself isn't *defined* by its pro football team like Pittsburgh and Green Bay. But football is an important part of the sporting life of Boston. The three-time Super Bowl champion New England Patriots sell out every game and may be second only to the Red Sox in fan popularity. Fall Saturdays bring with them an incredible range of college football choices, from a local school that plays at the sport's highest level to small colleges barely big enough to field a team. Then there are high school teams that draw thousands of fans each weekend, playing just for the love of the game.

Boston has played an important role in the evolution of football since the nineteenth century. Football was born on the fields of New England, and there is a proud pigskin tradition around the region, from the oldest schoolboy football matchups in the country to grand college rivalries such as Harvard and Yale to touch football games on the lawn of the Kennedy compound.

The historical legacy of football in Boston dates back to the time of the Civil War. The version of football played in postbellum Boston bore little resemblance to today's game, where warriors clad in suits of armor throw long bombs downfield, huddle up between plays, and celebrate with choreographed end zone dances. This early version of football—the "Boston game," as it was known—was more of a mix of soccer and rugby, played with a ball more spherical than it was oblong.

The grassy expanse of Boston Common was the city's proving grounds not only in the early years of baseball but also in the annals of football. Schoolboys from Boston Latin played football on the Common as early as 1860, and it was on the parade ground that the Oneida Football Club first took the field in 1862. The Oneida Football Club, made up of schoolboys from Boston Latin, Boston English, and Mr. Dixwell's Latin School, is considered the first organized football club in the United States. For four years they never lost a game against teams of high school and college students, and more amazingly, no opponent ever crossed their goal. A granite tablet, dedicated by the surviving members of the team in 1925, sits in the northwest corner of the Common.

Under the rules of the Boston game, there was no gridiron, no touchdowns, and no stoppage in play except when the ball went out of bounds or someone scored. Red handkerchiefs knotted around players' heads sufficed for uniforms. The ball was kicked and dribbled—but in a critical difference from other football codes being played in the 1860s, which were more akin to soccer, the ball could be *carried*. This simple distinction is a key component of the sport as we know it today. The Boston game played by those football pioneers in the 1860s was so different that James D'Wolf Lovett, one of the Oneida players, wrote in his memoirs that the modern game of football being played in 1908 bared little resemblance to the game he once played. Imagine what Lovett and his teammates would think today if they took in a Patriots game?

The Boston area's wealth of college campuses and boarding schools made it the prime incubator for the nascent sport. Some claim that **Harvard University** played the first college football game, using the rules of the Boston game, when

Harvard-Yale game at Harvard Stadium during the 1910s. Courtesy Boston Public Library, Print Department.

it squared off against McGill University in 1874. Two years later, Harvard, Yale, Princeton, and Columbia met in Springfield, Massachusetts, to standardize a new code of rules, many of which were based on the football code being played by the Crimson.

In the first half of the 1900s, Boston sports fans were more interested in college football than the pros. By the turn of the twentieth century, Harvard was a national football power with eight national titles between 1875 and 1919. The Crimson drew as many as sixty thousand fans to games at Harvard Stadium, with no tilt bigger than "The Game" against arch-rival Yale, a matchup dating back to 1875.

Crowds as big as fifty thousand also packed into venues such as Fenway Park and Braves Field to watch the annual rivalry between **Boston College** and Holy Cross, which dated back to 1896. Both Jesuit schools were big draws in the 1940s, with the Eagles playing in the 1941 Sugar Bowl and 1943 Orange Bowl and the Crusaders competing in the 1946 Orange Bowl.

Decades before the dawn of arena football, even Boston Garden was used as a football venue. In 1935 a group of local college all-stars played a group of Notre Dame alumni on a gridiron seventy yards long and thirty feet wide that was built with left over rodeo loam, which made the running game a hard slog.

With so much attention being paid to the collegiate teams, it was difficult for professionals to get any traction in Boston in the 1920s, '30s, and '40s. Professional teams also had to compete against the thoroughbreds and—at least on Sundays—the Almighty. Boston, with its Puritanical roots, had only recently abandoned centuries-old blue laws that prevented games on Sunday, but many of the sports fans who ventured out tended to be lured by the ponies at Suffolk Downs.

Long before the **New England Patriots** came upon the scene, the National Football League (NFL) made its first foray into the Hub in 1929 when the Boston Bulldogs debuted in front of one thousand fans at Braves Field. The Bulldogs lasted only one season, but three years later, the league returned to Braves Field with a football team called the Boston Braves (not to be confused with the baseball team that played between 1871 and 1952). When they moved to Fenway Park for the 1933 season, team owner George Preston Marshall changed the team's name to the Redskins. Marshall was perpetually unhappy with the crowds he drew compared to Harvard and Boston College. He finally moved the team to the nation's capital, where they are known today as the Washington Redskins. During World War II, the NFL returned to Boston with the Yanks, who played for five seasons in Fenway Park. The Yanks left Fenway for New York—where a team with that name belonged anyway—and the holdings of the franchise eventually became today's Indianapolis Colts.

Other professional leagues tried to place teams in Braves Field and Fenway Park before World War II, but they met with little success. Boston wouldn't get another professional team until the Boston Patriots of the American Football League (AFL) came on the scene in 1960. The Patriots played their first game at Boston University's Nickerson Field and bounced around to Fenway Park, Boston College's

Alumni Stadium, and Harvard Stadium. The Patriots were merged into the NFL in 1970. A year later they finally moved into a permanent home in Foxborough and changed their name to the New England Patriots.

The Patriots had some decent seasons in Foxboro Stadium, but playoff appearances were few and far between until the team reached its first Super Bowl in 1985. Still, the stadium was subpar, not unlike many of their seasons in the early 1990s. There was the very real possibility that the Patriots would move out of town until Robert Kraft bought them in 1994.

Since then there has been a remarkable transformation. Behind the foot of Adam Vinatieri, the golden arm of Tom Brady, and the expert coaching of Bill Belichick, the Patriots have become a perennial presence in the playoffs, recording a perfect regular season in 2007 and capturing three Super Bowl titles in 2001, 2003, and 2004. There has been an incredible change off the field in Foxborough as well. The Patriots moved into a gleaming new gridiron, **Gillette Stadium**, and have built Patriot Place next door. The centerpiece of this massive retail and entertainment complex is a new museum devoted to the football team, **The Hall at Patriot Place**.

Unlike the mid-1900s, it's the city's professional football team that gets the bulk of the attention these days. Boston University dropped its football program in the 1990s, and Holy Cross and Harvard no longer compete on the highest levels. While they are not considered prime-time, these universities, along with **Northeastern**, still play Division I football, and there are plenty of other collegiate teams in lower divisions that take the field each Saturday as well. They play for the love of the game, just like the boys of the Oneida Football Club and the dozens of **high school football** teams across metropolitan Boston who strap on their helmets and pads each Thanksgiving in one of the region's best sporting traditions.

★ Tailgating Tips

Tailgating before football games is a time-honored sporting tradition. To make the most of your tailgating experience, be sure to prepare beforehand. Don't hit the stores at the last minute to try and get everything you need. If you have more than one carload of fans coming to your tailgate, find a meeting place such as a rest area or supermarket miles away from the stadium so you can get your convoy together and park side-by-side at the lot. That way you don't have to lug supplies around and you can stake out more space for your tailgate. The New England football season can last from the summer heat of early September to the icy chill of dead winter, which means that a tent is a valuable investment to protect you—and your food—from the elements. Be sure to get a tent with sides to block the wind. If you're going old-school with a charcoal grill (and you've had a couple of beers), be sure to let the grill cool down before putting it back in the car when you head into the game. And just because the game is over doesn't mean the party has to end. Instead of sitting in parking lot traffic, fire up the grill again and keep the party going!

NEW ENGLAND PATRIOTS

It's hard to imagine today, but it wasn't that long ago that the New England Patriots failed to capture true fan affection. As recently as the 1990s, the team played to less-than-capacity crowds in a spartan stadium, and it was on the verge of moving out of New England altogether.

When Robert Kraft, a former Patriots ticket holder, bought the team in 1994, the Patriots experienced a dramatic turnaround—both on and off the field. The Pats have sold out more than 150 consecutive home games dating back to the 1994 regular-season opener. The team has gone from having just seventeen thousand season-ticket holders in 1991 to having a waiting list three times that size. Most important for fans, the team has become a constant winner, capturing three Super Bowl titles in a four-season span between 2001 and 2004.

It's been a long road to the top for the Patriots. The team had very shallow roots in the Boston area, and like so many of Boston's previous professional football teams, it struggled during its first decade in the American Football League. Many football fans were still more interested in the NFL's New York Giants, whose televised games were beamed into New England households for years. The Patriots even played their home games on Fridays to avoid conflicts with the Giants!

During the 1960s, the Patriots were football's ultimate nomads, unable to afford a field to call home. The Pats spent their AFL days bouncing from one college stadium to another and even playing home games in California and Alabama. After joining the NFL in 1970, the Patriots were finally able to scrape up the money to afford a place of their own.

Their no-frills starter home was in Foxborough, a good thirty miles south of Boston and a true monument to Yankee frugality. Foxboro Stadium (which used the shorter spelling of the town's name) had few amenities. Fans endured dusty tailgates on the racetrack next door and complained of frozen backsides on the stadium's notorious aluminum benches. Some seasons fans suffered through games that could have been confused as episodes of *Football Follies*. The Patriots managed to capture two AFC championships (in 1985 and 1996), but over its thirty-one seasons in Foxboro Stadium, they only hosted five playoff games.

The crowning moment for Foxboro Stadium was its last—the "Snow Bowl" overtime playoff victory over Oakland that launched the team to its first title in Super Bowl XXXVI. After that inaugural championship, the Patriots moved into Gillette Stadium, a pigskin McMansion replete with luxurious amenities.

One thing that hasn't changed much with the new stadium is the glacial pace of traffic getting to and from the games. Vehicles festooned with Patriots paraphernalia make the slow crawl down U.S. 1 past strip malls, warehouses, and rundown motor inns until Gillette Stadium suddenly emerges like the Emerald City towering on the horizon.

The caravan stretching along the highway may look like the final scene from *Field of Dreams*, but this game day traffic is an absolute nightmare. The traffic makes a Patriots game an all-day commitment, and since it takes so long to get in and out of the parking lots, New England fans have extra incentive to tailgate both before and *after* games.

On game days, Gillette Stadium's parking lots become a veritable tent city—particularly during the winter, when fans dressed in Brady, Bruschi, and Moss jerseys huddle around charcoal fires to brave the cold. Some fans even set up makeshift living rooms right on the asphalt with furniture and televisions to watch other games.

License plates from all six New England states are a testament to the Patriots' regional draw. Many Patriots fans get up before daybreak to make the drive to Foxborough. Clearly, the team made the right move in changing its name from the ill-fated Bay State Patriots, which it initially chose upon moving to Foxborough. Not only has it fostered regional affection for the team, but it has also put an end to bad jokes about the "B.S. Patriots."

In another sign of how much the fortunes of the Patriots have changed, the team has built Patriot Place next to the stadium. The team hopes that this retail and entertainment complex will transform Foxborough into a year-round destination. Hard-core tailgaters probably won't skip the pregame grilling to browse the aisles of Bath & Body Works, and some complain that they feel as if they're now tailgating in a mall parking lot, but the shops, movie theaters, and restaurants provide an alternative that might appeal to some.

Of course, the tailgate is only the first act. The main event begins when the Pats run onto the field to Ozzy Osbourne's "Crazy Train" and the mighty roars of the sellout crowd packing the stadium. The End Zone Militia, a band of minutemen dressed in colonial garb behind the end zone, fire a salute. The militia stands at the ready to fire off a volley after each field goal and touchdown. And if the hometown fans are lucky, their gridiron greats will walk off the field victoriously as a final congratulatory salute rings through the air.

Gillette Stadium

If Foxboro Stadium was little more than a glorified high school stadium, then Gillette Stadium is a pigskin mecca. Gone

Patriots training camp is a great place to score autographs and see how the season is going to shape up.

are the days of tailgating in dusty parking lots, bathrooms actually work, and the cold aluminum benches are a thing of the past. All ticket holders at Gillette Stadium, which opened in 2002, get an individual seat with armrests and cup holders. The seats, between nineteen and twenty-one inches wide, are each angled toward the fifty-yard line.

Gillette Stadium, which is also home to the New England Revolution soccer team, consists of three seating decks. The lower section of seats encircles the field, while the club and upper levels of seating are on both sides of the gridiron. The open concourses are a great feature of the stadium; there are plenty of places to stand and watch the game, which can be an attractive option for fans with seats in the nosebleeds or while you're waiting in the concessions line. Either way, with over one thousand television monitors around the stadium you won't miss a down.

Architecturally, the designers incorporated numerous elements to give Gillette Stadium a New England motif. On the north side of the stadium is a faux lighthouse and a replica of the Longfellow Bridge. A seascape with rocks and ornamental grasses complements the bridge and lighthouse and flanks the players' entrance. A granite map of New England constructed of stone from each of the six states in the region is located near the lighthouse.

Known as "the Razor," Gillette Stadium is certainly not as revered as other gridiron coliseums—and it's certainly not hallowed ground like Fenway Park—but it has seen considerable success in a very short time. In just its first six seasons, Gillette Stadium hosted seven playoff games—two more than Foxboro Stadium saw in its 31-season run. Banners honoring the team's three Super Bowl championships fly in one corner of the stadium, and another banner commemorating the team's perfect 16-0 regular season in 2007 flies in another.

Like all modern stadia, Gillette Stadium is filled with amenities, including more than eighty luxury suites and over six thousand club seats—but not all Patriots fans think that's a good thing. Just as America has been divided into red states and blue states, the Gillette Stadium crowd has a division of its own: red seats and blue seats. The red seats belong to the club level ticketholders, who pay premium prices for a great view of the field and access to preferred parking and a climate-controlled lounge. This doesn't sit well with a number of die-hard fans in the blue seats, who point to the sea of empty red seats when the cold weather comes and those in the luxury sections have retreated to the warmth of the lounge. Of course, there probably wouldn't be a new stadium without those red seats. Gillette Stadium's $325 million price tag was paid entirely with private money, and those high-end club seats contributed to the project financing.

There are even some Patriots fans who preferred the old stadium because they felt the lack of amenities ensured that only die-hard football fans showed up. These fans complain that Gillette Stadium is not nearly as noisy as Foxboro Stadium and that they are further from the action—not to mention that the ticket prices have increased to such a point that some fans are being priced out. On the flip side, there have been fewer problems with rowdy behavior in the new stadium, and every one of its 68,759 seats have sold out since Gillette Stadium opened its doors.

WHEN: The Patriots regular season runs from September to late December or early January.

GETTING THERE: Foxborough is thirty miles south of Boston. The most important piece of information you need to know is this: *leave early*. U.S. 1 is the only road in and out of Gillette Stadium, so traffic backups, while improved in recent years, can still be monstrous.

From Boston and points north, take U.S. 1 south (Exit 9 off Interstate 95). Gillette Stadium is three miles from the exit off Interstate 95. As you approach the stadium, use the left lane to enter the P2 **parking** lot or the right lane to enter P10 north. From points south, take U.S. 1 north (Exit 14A off Interstate 495). Gillette Stadium is four miles from the exit off Interstate 495. As you approach the stadium, stay to the right to enter P8 and P7 or stay to the left to enter P10 south or P11. Lines may be shorter for the P10 and P11 lots, which are across U.S. 1 from the stadium. Like the tickets, the price of stadium parking is steep—$40 per car.

For RV parking, enter P10 (from the north) or P11 (from the south). RV parking costs $125. Club level or suite parking pass holders should follow signs for Reserved Parking and enter P1 (from the north) or P8 (from the south) and then follow signs for either the east or west clubhouse/suite lot.

Watch signs and overhead message boards for the latest traffic conditions and information on when driving in the breakdown lane of U.S. 1 is permitted. Print out a map of the stadium parking lots from the Patriots website to make sure you're in the correct lanes for your desired parking lot. Stadium lots open four hours before kickoff and close within two hours after each game.

Fans also have the option of parking in satellite lots operated by local businesses. The satellite lots may be quicker to clear out but are a further walk to the stadium. Some nearby satellite lots cost a few dollars more than the stadium lots, while those farther from the stadium may cost a few dollars less.

The MBTA operates **commuter rail** service to and from Boston and Providence to all Patriots home games. Trains from Boston leave from South Station and stop at Back Bay, Dedham Corp., and Norwood Central. Trains from Providence stop at South Attleboro, Attleboro, and Mansfield. Trains depart approximately two hours before kickoff and arrive at the stadium an hour before game time. Round-trip tickets are $12 and may be purchased with cash only. Coolers and backpacks are prohibited on board. Trains depart thirty minutes after the conclusion of the game. For more information, visit www.mbta.com or call the MBTA information line at 617-222-3200.

TICKETS: Even though they play in the biggest stadium in metropolitan Boston, the Patriots have fewer tickets on sale than any of the city's major sports teams because they only play eight home dates. With every game sold out, the team is able to charge a premium for tickets, and the Pats have the highest average ticket price in the NFL. Note: most seats in Gillette Stadium are completely uncovered and exposed to the elements.

Lower level sideline ($169) seats are the closest to the action, running the length of the sideline and thirty-eight rows deep. Seats in sections 105–114 are behind the Patriots sideline and seats in sections 127–136 are behind the visitors' sideline.

Lower level corner/End zone ($117) seats encircle each end zone and run thirty-eight rows deep. Seats in sections 101–104 and 137–143 are located in the north end zone, and seats in sections 115–126 are in the south end zone.

Mezzanine level corner/End zone ($117) seats are located on the stadium's second level, flanking the club seats in the four end zone corners. Seats are located in sections 201–205, 214–218, 223–227, and 236–240, and sections are twenty-seven rows deep. Sections 225 and 238 are alcohol-free.

Upper level sideline ($89) seats run the length of the sideline and are twenty-six rows deep. Seats in sections 305–314 are on the Patriots sideline, and seats in sections 327–336 are on the visitors' sideline.

Upper level corner/End zone ($89) seats are located in the four end zone corners and include sections 301, 303, 304, 315, 316, 318–323, 325, 326, 337, 338, and 340. Seats are located in the seven lowest rows of the upper level.

Upper level corner/End zone ($65) seats are located in the four end zone corners and include rows eight to twenty-six in sections 301–304, 315–318, 323–326, and 337–340.

Standing room only ($49) areas are located throughout the stadium—including the open concourses, pedestrian ramps, and end zone plaza—and some of them offer great sightlines. Standing room areas are delineated by the red lines on concourse level. The better standing room areas are located on the lower level and along the walkways in the south side of the stadium near the championship banners (although it can be windy there on breezy days) and the pedestrian ramp in the northwest corner. Good spots fill up early, however, so don't wait until just before kickoff to snag one.

The season-ticket base is capped at 61,759 so that the team can put a limited number of individual game tickets on sale each spring. Tickets are solely available through Ticketmaster at www.ticketmaster.com or by phone (617-931-2000 in the Boston area). Visa credit or debit cards are the only acceptable form of payment for phone and online orders. Individual game tickets sell out in a matter of minutes, so get that finger ready to dial or click.

An application to join the season-ticket waiting list is available on the Patriots website. A deposit of $100 is required for each seat requested, and all deposits will be applied toward account balances once seats are purchased. Don't hold your breath on getting season tickets anytime soon, since more than fifty thousand fans are on the waiting list. However, one benefit of being on the waiting list is getting the opportunity to purchase Patriots, New England Revolution, and concert tickets before they go on sale to the general public.

Even with all Patriots games sold out, it's still possible to get tickets from brokers and from season-ticket holders online; try sites such as eBay, Craigslist, StubHub, and Ticketmaster's TicketExchange—the only NFL-authorized online ticket marketplace. It may be possible to find game day tickets on TicketExchange for night games or for games with poor weather forecasts. And there should be no problem finding tickets to exhibition (sorry, *preseason*) games from season-ticket holders. Just note that the Patriots have cracked down on fan behavior in the last decade; they are known to revoke seats from season-ticket holders who misbehave. So be on your best behavior if you have someone else's ticket—or more important, make sure the buddy you give *your* tickets to is on his!

The Patriots ticket office is located on the north side of the stadium. It is open weekdays between 10 AM and 5 PM (on game days, it opens four hours before kickoff and closes at the end of the second quarter). The ticket office phone number is 508-543-1776.

DISABILITY ACCESS: The Patriots offer wheelchair and companion seating along the concourses on all stadium levels. For wheelchair-accessible seating, call 508-384-9191. There are two elevators located in each EMC Suites entrance, and there are three code-compliant ramps to upper levels. Handicap parking is located adjacent to the stadium and can be accessed by the P2 entrance from the north and the P6 entrance from the south.

Headsets and receivers for Assistive Listening Systems are available at no charge at Guest Services stands located at midfield on the main and upper concourse levels. A driver's license, credit card, or some form of identification will be required as a deposit. Guests who choose to bring their own headset and receiver may access the system on a standard FM broadcast. Hearing-impaired fans can call the stadium ticket office at 508-384-4389.

THE SPLURGE: Sure, those six thousand red seats in Gillette Stadium may be scorned by many fans because they're cushy, but few would turn down the chance to watch the game from them. Situated between the goal lines and above the lower level of the stadium, these club level seats come with exclusive access to the Fidelity Investment Clubhouse. The Clubhouse features a climate-controlled area that includes fully stocked bars, premium food service, carving and sauté stations, fireplaces, dozens of televisions, and floor-to-ceiling glass windows that look out on the field. The clubhouses are available to members year-round, and club seat holders also get to park adjacent to the stadium and get express lanes for exiting. The seats require a multi-year commitment that costs tens of thousands of dollars.

Gillette Stadium also has more than eighty luxury suites with capacities ranging from sixteen to thirty-two people. In addition, there are two super suites that can hold up to seventy people. Call 508-384-4372 for information on premium seating.

If you're part of the masses in the blue seats and want a one-time splurge, the **All-Pro Celebrity Tailgate** (877-PATS-FAN, www.patriotstailgate.com) offers packages ranging from $250 (which includes parking, food, and drinks) to $789 (which also includes a game ticket).

THE CHEAPSKATE: If you're determined to make a day at the football game as cheap as possible, leave the car at home and save the $40 parking fee (or find a bunch of people to pile in the car to split the cost). The commuter rail is the more affordable way to get to the game. And even if you bypass concessions, you'll still need to pay for the ticket. Unfortunately, your cheapest option is a $49 standing room ticket. Bottom line: make friends with someone who'll give you a free ticket and drive you to the game. Good luck!

SPECTATOR TIPS: Stadium gates typically open two hours prior to kickoff. Even if you're not sitting in the upper levels of the stadium, you may want to bring a pair of binoculars to follow the action. The only designated smoking areas in the stadium are on the stadium ramps.

The following items are prohibited at Patriots games: food or beverages (unless a fan has a letter signed by stadium security), coolers or containers, umbrellas, strollers, chairs, noisemakers, bullhorns, air horns, video cameras, and beach balls. The only bags admitted are small purses (no larger than 8.5"x11"x6") and plastic bags carrying only purchases made at the stadium ProShop. Small portable radios and televisions are permitted as long as fans listen to them with an earpiece or headphones. Flags with poles less than two feet in length may be allowed into the stadium after inspection, and banners may be prohibited due to size or message content.

All bags are subject to inspection, and stadium security will generally pat down fans entering the stadium. (Entry points are identified for male or female entry for inspections.) That means that lines to enter the stadium can be sizable near kickoff, so head over to the stadium early to give yourself ample time if you don't want to miss a second of the action. Beware of long lines for restrooms and concession stands at halftime as well. If the game allows, consider making a run at the two-minute warning.

SCORING AUTOGRAPHS: Don't get your heart set on getting autographs at a Patriots game. Access to the players is limited inside the stadium, and security and fences generally keep fans away from players outside the stadium as well. If you want to collect signatures from your favorite player, training camp (see page 100) is a much better option.

FOR THE KIDS: Since going to a game is an all-day affair and the crowd can get a little boisterous, a Patriots game may not be the best destination for small children. If you want to bring older children to the game, the commuter train to the stadium is a good alternative to driving and dealing with the traffic.

Even small children require a ticket for Patriots games, and strollers are prohibited. There are two family restrooms behind the

View of Gillette Stadium.

end zones on the main concourse and four family restrooms along the sidelines of the upper concourse. Sections 225 and 238 are designated as no-alcohol sections.

STADIUM CONCESSIONS: Patriots fans don't have to go far to get a bite to eat or something to quench their thirst during the game. Gillette Stadium has nearly fifty permanent concession stands and sixty portable food and beverage carts throughout the main and upper concourses.

Most concession stands offer the basics such as soda, popcorn, peanuts, pretzels, and candy. Many have a New England theme, offering different specialties in addition to the staples. Boston Common stands offer standard fare as well as draft beers, hot chocolate, coffee, junior Papa Gino's pizzas, and hot dogs ($3.75). Berkshire Grill stands offer grilled Italian sausages, smoked Polish sausages, and kosher hot dogs. The BBQ Blitz stands feature barbeque ribs, beef brisket, pulled pork, and chicken.

If you like fried foods, head to the Freeport Fryer stands, which serve chicken tenders, french fries, and buckets of barbeque or spicy buffalo wings (although you may want to skip these if the Pats are playing the Bills). The Granite State stands feature hamburgers, grilled cheese steaks, and chicken sandwiches. The Nantucket Sound stands offer fish and chips, clam strips, deep fried shrimp, and New England clam chowder. And if you are having a Big Mac attack, McDonald's stands are behind each end zone on the main concourse as well as at two locations on the upper level.

In addition to concession stands, there are portable carts that serve bottled and draft beers. Beer vendors also roam the stadium. The stadium features beers from regional brewers such as Harpoon, Magic Hat, and Sam Adams; imports such as Guinness, Bass, Heineken, and Amstel Light; and standard domestic beers. Sixteen-ounce beers sell for $7.50, and 22-ounce cups cost $10. Margaritas and Bloody Marys are also on tap for $9.50. If you want an alcoholic beverage at the game, remember to bring your ID as vendors card religiously. There is a limit of two beers per person at a time, and all alcohol sales are discontinued fifteen minutes (in real time, not on the game clock) after the second half starts.

FOOD AND DRINK AROUND THE STADIUM: Patriots fans used to have little choice of restaurants and bars within walking distance of the stadium until the arrival of Patriot Place. Now Pats fans have more than a dozen choices, from fast food to casual eateries to upscale dining.

Just beyond the north end zone of Gillette Stadium is the mammoth **CBS Scene** (200 Patriot Place, 508-203-2200, www.cbsscene.com). Each booth in the restaurant is equipped with 19-inch televisions that play classic episodes of Tiffany Network shows such as *I Love Lucy* and *Star Trek*, news programs such as *60 Minutes*, and Patriots highlights. The bar area on the top floor features a 36-foot wraparound high-definition screen that's usually tuned to a game. If you'd rather not watch any of the 130 televisions or eat under the gaze of Gilligan and Archie Bunker, the restaurant's two outdoor terraces overlook the stadium. Food options range from bar snacks to filet mignon.

Davio's (236 Patriot Place, 508-339-4810, www.davios.com) is a 350-seat Northern Italian steakhouse. The bar menu features panini and pizzas. **Tastings Wine Bar & Bistro** (201 Patriot Place, 508-203-9463, www.tastingswinebarandbistro.com) features an extensive wine list and small plate choices designed to be shared. *Skipjack's* (226 Patriot

Place, 508-543-2200, www.skipjacks.com) is a local seafood chain that also serves steak and sushi. **Bar Louie** (232 Patriot Place, 508-623-1195, www.barlouieamerica.com) is a national restaurant and bar chain that specializes in oversized sandwiches and jumbo martinis. **Red Robin** (290 Patriot Place, 508-698-0030, www.redrobin.com) is an affordable, family-friendly chain specializing in gourmet burgers. For a full list of restaurants at Patriot Place, go online to www.patriot-place.com.

CONTACT INFORMATION: New England Patriots, One Patriot Place, Foxborough, MA 02035. 508-543-8200; www.patriots.com.

NEW ENGLAND PATRIOTS TRAINING CAMP

Your best chance to get up close and personal with your favorite Patriots is to attend training camp. The good news for Boston sports fans is that, unlike Red Sox spring training, you don't have to fly to Florida to watch the Patriots get in shape for the season; you can just drive down to Foxborough.

The Patriots hold training camp on the pair of practice fields adjacent to Gillette Stadium, and many sessions are open to the public. Aluminum bleachers with room for three thousand fans flank the sideline of one of the practice fields. An additional two thousand fans can fit on the hillside behind the end zones of the two gridirons.

Training camp offers the first opportunity for fans to catch a glimpse of new draft picks and free-agent signings. Coach Bill Belichick also keeps a close eye on the players as he and the other coaches will need to decide which players will make the active roster. Training camp is as close as most fans will get to front-row seats at a Pats game. Bring along your camera, as you can get some great action shots of your favorite stars. Autograph hounds should be able to get John Hancocks from at least a few of the players as well.

With music blaring from the loudspeakers, players spend part of the practice with their individual position groups and coaches and part of the time with the offense facing off against the defense. Watching the mundane stretching and running drills at training camp will not be the most exciting spectator experience, but some practices feature more entertaining scrimmages and two-minute drills with Tom Brady throwing the ball around to Randy Moss, Wes Welker, and other receivers.

Practice sessions usually last no longer than two hours, and some days coaches will schedule morning and afternoon sessions. Training camp schedules are subject to change, so check the latest schedule on the Patriots website or call the information hotline (508-549-0001) before making the trip to Foxborough.

WHEN: New England Patriots training camp usually runs in the latter half of July and the first half of August.

GETTING THERE: Foxborough is thirty miles south of Boston. See page 95 for directions from Boston. Fans coming from the north should enter the P6 entrance and fans coming from the south should enter the P8 entrance. Parking is free. Lots open one hour before sessions and close one hour after their conclusion.

TICKETS: Tickets are not necessary for training camp; general admission is free.

DISABILITY ACCESS: For those requiring special access, enter the stadium parking lots as directed and follow signs for handicap parking. Seating at the practice fields will be available in all bleacher sections. For more information, call the Gillette Stadium ADA coordinator at 508-384-9191. TTD/TTY is also available by calling 508-384-4389.

SPECTATOR TIPS: With as many as eighty players on the field, plenty of new faces, and uniforms without names on the back, you may not know who you're looking at. Print out a roster from the Patriots website before you leave or pick up a complimentary roster at the *Patriots Football Weekly* tent at the practice fields. Fans can bring their own food and drinks into training camp.

SCORING AUTOGRAPHS: A different group of position players is designated to sign autographs at the end of each practice session, so it's a bit of a crapshoot as to who will be signing. When practice ends, there's a rush of kids toward the ropes, but with a little patience, you should be able to pick up some signatures. Other players not in the designated group may sign as they come on and off the practice fields in the corner nearest the stadium.

FOR THE KIDS: While taking little kids to a Patriots game may not be a good idea, a visit to training camp is definitely family friendly. Kids will enjoy the Patriots Experience, which runs in conjunction with training camp and includes football-themed activities, face painting, and cheerleader appearances. There are also inflatable games that let kids test their running and throwing skills. The Patriots Experience is located on the west side of Gillette Stadium, although its hours don't always coincide with practices, so call ahead.

STADIUM CONCESSIONS: There are concession stands behind the bleachers at training camp, so you can pick up hamburgers, hot dogs, pizza, cotton candy, ice cream, and cold beverages. Vendors even sell concessions in the bleachers. Beer is available from the concession stands. While parking may be free, you'll pay the full stadium prices for food and drink.

FOOD AND DRINK AROUND THE STADIUM: See page 99.

CONTACT INFORMATION: For the latest training camp schedules and information, call the hotline at 508-549-0001 or log on to www.patriots.com/trainingcamp.

THE HALL AT PATRIOT PLACE

For decades the only things surrounding the Patriots' home in Foxborough were barren parking lots and a harness racing track. Now, Patriot Place has sprung up in the shadows of Gillette Stadium. Set among the development's storefronts, eateries, and theaters is its crown jewel—The Hall at Patriot Place.

The Hall is both a massive trophy case for the Patriots' hardware and a museum where fans can trace the franchise's rocky road to championship success. While Patriots devotees no doubt will get goose bumps reliving recent moments of glory, any football fan could spend hours immersed in The Hall's artifacts and fantastic interactive exhibits.

Memorabilia on display in The Hall, which opened in 2008, includes coach Bill Belichick's signature gray hooded sweatshirt, an autographed *Saturday Night Live* script from quarterback Tom Brady's 2005 appearance, an old "Berry the Bears" t-shirt from Super Bowl XX (referring to erstwhile coach Raymond Berry), and a metal bleacher from the defunct Foxboro Stadium, which looks as uncomfortable as ever.

The Hall's quirkiest artifact, hanging from the rafters like a retired number, is the infamous John Deere tractor driven by work-release convict Mark Henderson. That tractor cleared the path on the snow-covered field for the Patriots game-winning field goal against the Dolphins in December 1982. The winning kick marked the only points scored in what is now known as the "Snowplow Game."

Pats fans can now look back with some fondness and chuckle at the team's humble origins in the fledgling American Football League. Inside display cases are the team's initial uniform and helmet, which used to feature the image of a tricorn hat above the player's number, and a program and ticket from the franchise's first game at Boston University. To its credit, the museum pulls no punches in recalling what seemed a never-ending episode of football follies: the nomadic team's quest to find a permanent home in Boston, the 1969 electrical shock of coach Clive Rush at a news conference, a 1970 fire in Boston College's wooden bleachers during a preseason loss, and the unfortunate, albeit brief, name change to the Bay State ("B.S.") Patriots.

The museum also dedicates a wing to New England's rich and often overlooked football heritage and traditions. The jerseys of reigning New England high school champions are on display along with artifacts such as a football from the 1876 Harvard-Yale game, old leather helmets, tickets from the Boston Shamrocks and Boston Redskins, and a pennant from the NFL's Boston Yanks.

The Hall is a highly interactive experience. Visitors hear the sound of cleats on the floor, the roar of the crowd, and the distinctive chords of Ozzy Osbourne's "Crazy Train" from the moment they cross the threshold. You can climb aboard the back of a Duck Boat and envision yourself in a victory parade, try on Richard Seymour's helmet and Super Bowl ring, and go under the hood of an instant replay booth to test your skills as a referee. You can even watch Bill Belichick break down game film, get in the middle of a huddle with life-size mannequins in Patriots jerseys, and listen as Brady barks out plays from his wristband. Another neat thing is trying to replicate Adam Vinatieri's two clutch Snow Bowl field goals by kicking a football off crunchy, white turf against a video screen.

Touch screens throughout the museum allow visitors to scan a timeline of the team's history, watch game highlights, and learn more about the members of the Patriots Hall of Fame. And don't miss the short movie on the team's history. Shown on a huge, panoramic screen, the film has the feel of a sweeping epic with its booming narration and pulse-pounding orchestral score. The sound system is so sharp you can feel the ground shake as Jets linebacker Mo Lewis lays the crippling hit on Drew Bledsoe that led to Brady's ascendancy. The movie has a take worthy of the Athens of America; it's interspersed with Revolutionary War re-enactments and quotes from Ralph Waldo Emerson. (Let's see them try to match *that* in Indianapolis.)

All of the team's championship hardware is on display at The Hall. There are the team's six AFC Championship trophies, a seemingly endless line of game balls from the Patriots' NFL-record 21-game winning streak—including three postseason victories in 2003 and 2004—and an entire wall is devoted to the bounty of league records set by the team. The last room in The Hall houses the team's most prized silver: its three Vince Lombardi trophies. The trophies, bathed in spotlights, proudly stand alone in the middle of the chamber.

Patriots fans should count the blessings of the team's recent good fortune. After all, the region came very close to losing their NFL franchise in the early 1990s. If you need any proof, check out the museum display case with a ball cap emblazoned with the logo of the Saint Louis Stallions. It was created to market a potential move of the Patriots to the banks of the Mississippi. Now it offers a stark reminder of how close the franchise came to skipping town.

GETTING THERE: For directions, see page 95. Enter Patriot Place at the P1 (north) entrance. Turn right at the cinema entrance and bear left at the fork in the road. The Hall is at the end of the road.

HOURS: The Hall at Patriot Place opens at 10 AM. It is open until 5 PM on weekdays (9 PM on weekdays from May to August), 9 PM on Saturdays, and 7 PM on Sundays. Closed Thanksgiving, Christmas, and during all Patriots home games.

ADMISSION: Adults $10; seniors and active military with ID $7; children between five and twelve years of age $5; children four and younger are free. Advanced tickets purchases are available.

CONTACT INFORMATION: The Hall at Patriot Place, Two Patriot Place, Foxborough, MA 02035. 508-698-4800; www.patriot-place.com/thehall.

BOSTON COLLEGE

Local schools such as Holy Cross and Harvard may no longer compete at the highest levels, but Boston College still plays big-time college football; without exception, every tilt at the Heights has a big-game feel to it.

The party starts hours before the game, beginning with the grand entrance of the entire football squad. Led by the Screaming Eagles marching band, color guard, and cheerleaders, the team makes a procession among the fans into Alumni Stadium. During the hour before kickoff, the band continues its pregame performance outside the Conte Forum, kids delight in the FanFest at the campus recreation center, and older folk enjoy plenty of tailgating.

Shea Field on the east side of Alumni Stadium is the best tailgating location. It has a scenic location next to the Chestnut Hill Reservoir with the Boston skyline looming in the distance. Fans can also tailgate in the parking garages adjacent to the stadium, but with low ceilings, dank atmosphere, and flickering fluorescent lights, it's akin to tailgating in your parents' basement. Plus, grills aren't permitted in the parking garages, so sandwiches and chips are generally the food of choice.

As game time approaches, more than forty-four thousand fans file into Alumni Stadium. When the Eagles take to the field, a roar goes up from the students packed into the southwest corner of the stadium, all clad in gold "Boston College Superfan" t-shirts. Throughout the game, the band, cheerleaders, and mascot—Baldwin the Eagle—help to keep this irrepressible spirit going.

If you scan the crowd you'll see plenty of football jerseys with the number 22, worn by the mobile, diminutive quarterback Doug Flutie, the 1984 Heisman Trophy winner. More than twenty years after leaving the Heights, this boy from Natick—who received one of the last scholarships on the team his freshman year and led BC to national prominence—is still beatified by Eagles fans.

In 2008 BC unveiled a statue outside Gate D of Alumni Stadium that immortalizes the singular moment that defined Flutie's career: the Hail Mary pass against Miami in 1984. The bronzed quarterback's right hand grips the football as he plants all his weight on his right leg and rears his arm back as

Boston College "Superfans" show team spirit at a home game.

far as possible, looking to the heavens for some divine intervention. The Hail Mary was answered as the ball fell into the arms of Gerard Phelan to win the game. On the base of the statue is the radio play-by-play: "Touchdown! Touchdown! Touchdown! Touchdown, Boston College! He did it! He did it! Flutie did it!"

Even though Boston College football dates back to 1893, BC didn't appear in a bowl game until New Year's Day in 1940 when it played in the Cotton Bowl. The following year it capped off an undefeated season—including a huge victory over Georgetown in front of forty thousand fans at Fenway Park—by beating Tennessee in the Sugar Bowl.

For years there was no bigger game on the schedule than the annual tilt against Holy Cross. This rivalry dated back to 1896 and drew some of the largest sports crowds in New England. The 1942 matchup between the two Jesuit schools was perhaps the most famous. Holy Cross scored a massive upset by throttling BC 55-12. The defeat turned out to be a blessing in disguise for many of the Eagles, who canceled their planned victory celebration at the Cocoanut Grove nightclub. That night the club went up in flames; the fire killed nearly five hundred people. (For more, see page 242.)

BC ended its rivalry with Holy Cross in 1986, and today its primary opponent is Notre Dame. The Eagles have scored some big victories over the Irish in recent editions of the "Holy War." Unfortunately, the series between these two Catholic schools is scheduled to end after 2010 because Notre Dame wants to include other teams (perhaps some that give them a better chance at victory?) on its schedule. Since 2005, Boston College has played in the Atlantic Coast Conference (ACC) against teams along the Atlantic seaboard. BC usually plays six or seven home games a year against ACC rivals and other squads.

In recent years Boston College has produced some great quarterbacks, such as Matt Hasselbeck and Matt Ryan, and has become known for turning out some great NFL offensive and defensive linemen. It shouldn't be a surprise then that the Eagles make perennial appearances in bowl games. While the Eagles haven't appeared in a major bowl game since Flutie left the Heights, they have had tremendous success in winning games such as the Motor City Bowl, Music City Bowl, and Diamond Walnut San Francisco Bowl. The Eagles have appeared in a bowl game every year since the turn of the millennium, winning eight straight between 2000 and 2007. They've also appeared in a pair of ACC Championship games since making the jump from the Big East. Plus, the Eagles have achieved on-field success without sacrificing academics; indeed, BC football players have a graduation rate consistently above ninety percent, one of the finest in college football.

STADIUM INFORMATION: Boston College plays their games in Alumni Stadium, an on-campus venue located adjacent to Conte Forum and near the Chestnut Hill Reservoir. The stadium, which opened in 1957 and was home to the Patriots in 1969, has grown over the years along with the stature of BC's football program. Luxury boxes and upper decks along the sides of the stadium were added in 1988. The last expansion in 1995 grew the stadium to its present capacity of 44,500. Two-tiered stands surround all sides of the gridiron.

The first Alumni Stadium opened in 1915, two years after the college moved from the South End to Chestnut Hill, and was located on the site of today's campus green. When Boston College enjoyed success in the 1930s and 1940s, it moved a majority of its games to Fenway Park and Braves Field.

WHEN: The Boston College regular season runs from late August or early September to late November. The ACC Championship game is held on the first Saturday in December, and bowl games are played throughout December and early January.

GETTING THERE: Alumni Stadium is located in the Chestnut Hill section of Newton, about six miles west of downtown Boston. Traffic in the streets around Alumni Stadium can be very heavy before and after games. On-campus **parking** is reserved for donors to the Flynn Fund, and on-street parking in local neighborhoods is not permitted. (For directions directly to the stadium and Conte Forum, see page 133.)

Anyone without an on-campus parking pass is required to park at a satellite parking lot in Needham or take public transportation. A complimentary shuttle system takes fans from the satellite lot to the Beacon Street side of campus, about a twenty minute ride. The buses run continuously, starting two-and-a-half hours prior to the kickoff and ending two hours after the game is finished. To reach the Needham satellite lot, take Route 128 to Exit 19A (Highland Avenue/Newton Highlands), merge onto Highland Avenue, take a right onto Second Avenue, and follow the signs to the designated parking area.

If possible, take **public transportation** to Alumni Stadium. Several branches of the Green Line stop near the stadium. From downtown Boston, take the "B" branch to the end of the line at the Boston College stop, which is about a six minute walk to the stadium, or take the "C" branch to the end of the line at Cleveland Circle, which is about a fifteen minute walk. Another option is for fans to park at Riverside station and take the "D" branch to either the Chestnut Hill or Reservoir stops, both of which are about a fifteen minute walk to the stadium.

Taxis to Boston are available following the game in front of More Hall; taxis to Newton are available in front of Saint Mary's Hall.

TICKETS: Tickets for games against top teams sell out, while those against lesser teams tend to be available close to game day. Tickets for individual games are $27 for end zone seats in the upper level and $37 for end zone seats in the lower level. If you'd prefer sideline seats, they are $45 for the upper level and $50 for the lower level. Student tickets are available for Boston College students with a valid student ID card. Student tickets are located in sections E through J in the southwest corner of the lower concourse.

Season tickets are available for $175 for upper end zone seats, $245 for lower end zone seats, and $315 for upper sideline seats. Season tickets for lower sideline seats require a donation to the Flynn Fund.

Note that seats in the upper concourses behind the end zones have limited concessions and no bathrooms, requiring a trip to the lower level. Most of the seats in Alumni Stadium are exposed, and some seats on the east side of the stadium look directly into the sun in late afternoon. All of the seats are aluminum bleachers, although the last row of bleachers on the lower level has seat backs.

Fans can order tickets by phone at 617-552-GOBC, online at www.bceagles.com, or at the ticket office, which is located inside Conte Forum at Gate B. The ticket office is open between 9 AM and 5 PM on weekdays and three hours before kickoff. Fans can purchase tickets directly from season-ticket holders through the Ticket Marketplace at www.bceagles.com. Tickets for bowl games and the ACC Championship can be purchased through the ticket office.

DISABILITY ACCESS: Alumni Stadium has disability seating along the concourse at the top of the lower level of seating. Disability seating may be purchased with one adjacent companion seat through the ticket office. Elevators are located in the corner of each end zone. Handicap parking is available on the second level of the Beacon Street Garage for season-ticket holders and requires a permit issued by Boston College. A handicap shuttle is also available at the satellite lot in Needham for ticket holders who are in wheelchairs or need assistance. The drop-off and pick-up location for the shuttle is outside Gate A. For more information on handicap parking, call 617-552-2628.

THE SPLURGE: The ultimate splurge for Eagles fans would be to get admitted to Boston College and pony up the $50,000 annual tuition. Hey, in addition to getting student tickets, you'll get a great education as well.

If that's a little rich for your blood, you can still splurge a little for some extra game day amenities. Donors to the Flynn Fund—which provides money for scholarships, recruiting, facilities, and operating costs for all varsity sports—who give $500 or more and have season tickets are eligible for a pass for preferred parking on campus. Major donors to the Flynn Fund are given the option to purchase season tickets around the fifty-yard line in sections C and D on the lower level and sections CC and DD on the upper level on the west side of the stadium, as well as in sections Q, R, and S on the lower level and sections QQ, RR, and SS on the upper level on the east side of the stadium. For more information, call 617-552-0772.

THE CHEAPSKATE: If you want to bring the family to a game and don't care about the opponent, have one of your kids join the Baldwin's Bunch kids' fan club. (More information below.) In addition to other benefits, members receive free tickets for the whole family to a football game as well as other Boston College athletic events.

SPECTATOR TIPS: Gates open ninety minutes before kickoff. If you need to warm up or get out of the sun, note that Conte Forum, attached to the west side of Alumni Stadium, is open during games. The concession stands, merchandise stands, and restrooms in Conte Forum may have shorter lines, and you can wander around and check out the trophy cases and the Varsity Club Hall of Fame.

Tailgating on campus is only allowed in Flynn Fund parking lots. Lots around Alumni Stadium open two hours before kickoff for noontime games and three hours before kickoff for all other games. Shea Field opens to pedestrians thirty minutes after the parking areas have opened, and a game day ticket is required to gain entry. While cars parking at Shea Field may bring in alcohol, pedestrians may not. Glass containers are prohibited on Shea Field. No grills of any kind are allowed in parking garages, and charcoal grills and tents are prohibited on campus.

The following items are prohibited at Boston College football games: alcoholic beverages, banners and signs, cameras with lenses that are detachable or more than four inches in length, coolers and containers, whistles, horns, strollers, umbrellas, and video cameras. Small bags may be brought into the stadium but are subject to search.

Note that game times are often dictated by television and may not be determined until only a few weeks in advance. Kickoff times can range from noon to 8 PM. Boston College has a game day hotline at 617-552-2886 with information on game times, parking, tailgating, and public transportation.

SCORING AUTOGRAPHS: It will be difficult to get player autographs once they're in uniform, but you may be able to get autographs before and after games. Members of the football team will enter the stadium at Gate E approximately two hours and fifteen minutes before the game after making the traditional Eagle Walk down Campanella Way from the Robsham Theater.

FOR THE KIDS: Kids will find plenty to do at Boston College football games. Before the game, check out the free FanFest in the Flynn Recreation Complex, just north of Alumni Stadium. FanFest offers face painting, caricature artists, and balloon animals. There are also inflatable games where kids can run through tackle dummies and kick field goals. In addition to concessions, mascots, cheerleaders, and the marching band make appearances. FanFest opens two hours before game time and closes fifteen minutes before kickoff.

Before kickoff, kids will also enjoy standing outside the Boston College locker room near Gate E and high-fiving the Eagles as they emerge to take the field. Note that all children must have a ticket for the game and strollers are prohibited. Restrooms offer changing stations.

Children under twelve can join the Baldwin's Bunch kids' fan club, which includes free BC gear, free tickets to Eagles sporting events, and invitations to special member events. Membership costs $20 a year. Membership applications are available on the Boston College website at www.bceagles.com.

STADIUM CONCESSIONS: Concession stands and carts are located throughout Alumni Stadium and Conte Forum. The concession stands are all inside the concourses, but if you don't want to miss any of the action, try the two concession carts on the east side of the stadium behind the visitors' sideline.

The food options at Boston College football games are pretty straightforward, with the exception of some pulled pork sandwiches, grilled Italian sausage, Papa Gino's personal pizzas, and chicken Caesar wraps. A hot

★ Hajjar Family Football Museum

Want to learn more about Boston College football? Check out the Hajjar Family Football Museum, located in the Yawkey Athletics Center on the north side of Alumni Stadium. You can watch incredible moments in BC history and bios of great players on video screens. Yes, Doug Flutie's Hail Mary is one of them, but the grainy black-and-white film from the undefeated 1940 season is more of a treat. Display cases feature individual and team trophies and memorabilia from the program's history. Also on display are the bowl game trophies won by the team, from the prestigious (Sugar Bowl) to the silly (Carquest Bowl). The highlight though is Flutie's Heisman Trophy, which greets you as soon as you enter the museum. (One was awarded to BC as well as Flutie.) With its throwback leatherhead clutching the ball under his left arm as he delivers a textbook stiff-arm with his right, this may be the most iconic trophy in American sport. The museum is free, but it's closed on Saturday, so it requires a trip separate from game day. Monday–Thursday, 8:30 AM–5 PM; Friday, 9 AM–7 PM; Sunday, noon–5 PM.

---

citysidebarandgrille.com) has a downstairs bar with ten televisions to catch the other college games, an upstairs restaurant, and an open-air deck in warmer weather. *Eagle's Deli & Restaurant* (1918 Beacon Street, 617-731-3232, www.eaglesdeli.com) is a popular spot for breakfast and burgers. If you're a competitive eater, try the "Challenge Burger," which has ten half-pound patties, twenty slices of cheese, twenty slices of bacon, and five pounds of fries. Finish it by yourself in under an hour, and you'll get the $50 burger for free, and they'll name it after you. Just don't plan on walking to the game afterwards. And then there's *Mary Ann's* (1937 Beacon Street). This dive bar of all dive bars is so infamous for underage drinking violations and periodic late-night fights that many Boston College teams ban their athletes from setting foot through its doors.

CONTACT INFORMATION: Boston College Football, 140 Commonwealth Avenue, Chestnut Hill, MA 02467. 617-552-3010; www.bceagles.com.

---

dog costs $4, with jumbo hot dogs a couple dollars more. Bottles of water and soda cost $3.50. There is coffee, hot chocolate, and clam chowder for those cold days. No alcohol is served at games.

FOOD AND DRINK AROUND THE STADIUM: The best places to grab a bite to eat or have a few beers before or after the game are in Cleveland Circle, about a mile walk east from the stadium on Beacon Street around the Chestnut Hill Reservoir. *Roggie's Brew & Grille* (356 Chestnut Hill Avenue, 617-566-1880, www.roggies.com) has more than fifty beers on tap, an extensive menu that includes vegetarian and Mexican choices, and a pizzeria. *CitySide Bar & Grille* (1960 Beacon Street, 617-566-1002, www.

HARVARD

It's hard to imagine today, but at one time Harvard was big-time college football, comparable to today's Florida, Ohio State, and USC. The Crimson won eight national championships, including four between 1910 and 1919. They even took a cross-country train trip to upset the University of Oregon in the 1920 New Year's Day Rose Bowl, their last national championship. The team regularly played in front of full stadiums with crowds of greater than sixty thousand people. Preseason practices and roster cuts were daily fodder for the city newspapers.

Today Harvard plays other Ivy League opponents but chooses not to participate in the football playoffs. The university emphasizes football as part of a well-rounded student athlete, and players are more likely to go on to be titans of business, political leaders, or Rhodes Scholars than NFL draft picks.

Still, Harvard football was a pioneer in the sport, and its colossal stadium helped to shape the rules of the game that fans are familiar with today. The first Harvard football game occurred in 1874 when the school squared off against Montreal's McGill University at Cambridge's Jarvis Field, now the site of Harvard Law School. Some believe this was the first intercollegiate football game in history. The following year, Harvard hosted Tufts, and this time the team was clad in formal white uniforms trimmed in crimson, the newly chosen school color.

A more notable event in Harvard history would occur later that year when Harvard traveled to Yale for a battle on the football field. The game was played with modified rugby rules and fifteen men on each team. Despite the evolution of the sport, the fierce rivalry, simply known today as The Game, continues to endure. Perhaps the most memorable moment in this rivalry occurred in 1968, when both teams entered The Game undefeated. With the Ivy League title on the line, Harvard overcame a 16-point deficit in the final forty-two seconds, which led to the memorable headline in the *Harvard Crimson*: "Harvard Wins 29-29." The Game is always the season finale, and for many players it marks their final snaps in competitive football. (Sometimes those nutty pranksters from MIT like to crash the party. In 1982 a black weather balloon marked "MIT" suddenly rose from the stadium turf and inflated at midfield after Harvard scored. Then it exploded with a cloud of talcum powder over the field.) The teams have played each other 125 times in the third most-played rivalry in college football.

There is a timeless quality about the atmosphere at The Game—you may even think you're having a flashback to those championship years from nearly a century ago when fans dressed in raccoon coats and waved pennants declaring their allegiances. Since the 1884 edition of The Game, the "little red flag" has been waved each time the Crimson scores against the Elis. The Harvard alumnus who is considered to be the team's most loyal fan is given the honor of bringing the pennant to every Harvard-Yale game.

As one might imagine, tailgating at Harvard football games is quite different than at Patriots games. There are *a capella* groups, tote bags, candelabras, and brie. Wine is a popular beverage, so bring your own corkscrew. Some tailgaters even turn their trunks into fully stocked bars.

Harvard generally plays five home games every year against Ivy League schools and other opponents such as Holy Cross, Lehigh, and Lafayette, with one night game. If you go to one of the home games, stay in your seat at halftime long enough to watch the Harvard band's show. More than just a bunch of random songs, the halftime show is scripted, with humor in the tradition of the *Harvard Lampoon* that takes not-so-subtle shots at the opposing university. This is particularly true against Yale, or what the band refers to as "New Haven Junior College." Harvard may be the only college in America that taunts an opponent for "tasteless Gothic architecture." "Yankees suck" this is not. You also won't get too many bands featuring a fight song—"Ten

Thousand Men of Harvard"—that has an entire verse in Latin. After the game, you can follow the band as it processes across the Charles River from the stadium to the campus.

STADIUM INFORMATION: At most universities, trees or scholarship money are typical class gifts. Not at Harvard. When the Class of 1879 gave a twenty-fifth anniversary gift, it settled on a massive football stadium. Before Harvard Stadium opened its doors in 1903, the Crimson football team played elsewhere on campus, as well as several seasons at the South End Grounds.

While most of Harvard is on the Cambridge side of the Charles River, the stadium sits in the Allston section of Boston. Befitting a college that emphasizes the classics, Harvard Stadium incorporates architectural elements from amphitheaters and stadia of ancient Rome and Greece. The stadium's horseshoe shape is similar to Roman circuses that staged chariot races, its arches evoke the Roman Colosseum, and the colonnades along the top of the stadium are reminiscent of the Parthenon and other columned ancient Greek structures. Even today, when players take the field in their suits of armor, they appear like gladiators entering the arena. Given the architectural backdrop, the Harvard Classics Department has staged productions of Greek dramas on the field with patrons sitting in the horseshoe end of the stadium.

Harvard Stadium was a marvel of engineering when it opened. It was the first permanent reinforced concrete stadium of its kind in the country. Some skeptics believed it would crumble in the cold weather, but the old structure still stands as a National Historic Landmark and the oldest stadium of its kind in the United States. The structure has been around for so long, the locals just refer to it as "the stadium."

Because the stadium was built of concrete, its dimensions were set in stone, so to speak, and helped shape the development of the sport of football. By 1905 there was considerable debate about the future of the sport after forty college players died in a two-year span. President Theodore Roosevelt, a Harvard alum and football enthusiast, was so concerned that he convened leaders of college football at the White House and called for something to be done about the violent nature of the game. When the football rules committee met to propose changes, its secretary, the great Walter Camp, proposed widening the field by as much as forty feet to open up the game. That wasn't possible given Harvard Stadium's layout, so the measure was rejected and proposals to introduce the forward pass, increase first down distances to ten yards, and ban mass formations were approved instead. Those measures revolutionized the sport, so the shape of Harvard Stadium indeed shaped the game we know today.

Over the years, the stadium on the banks of the Charles has hosted rugby matches, track meets, and even a few ice hockey games. The New England Patriots called the stadium home in 1970 while its stadium in Foxborough was being built. (The Pats actually played their first game—an August 1960 exhibition against the Dallas Texans—in Harvard Stadium as well.) 1984 Olympic soccer matches were played on the stadium's pitch, and today it's home to the Boston Breakers soccer team and Boston Cannons lacrosse team.

Banners in the horseshoe end of the stadium celebrate the team's national championships, and behind the north end zone is another banner with the Rose Bowl logo, celebrating Harvard's 1920 victory. While history surrounds you at Harvard Stadium, some twenty-first century touches have been added in recent years. Artificial turf replaced the grass field, and they unveiled a new high-resolution videoboard displaying replays and in-game statistics on top of the Murr Center. The biggest change, however, was the addition of a discrete bank of lights along the colonnade. The old concrete horseshoe, which dates back to the days of leather helmets, held its first night game in 2007. It was the beginning of what might be a new tradition in such an historic venue.

Seating capacity in Harvard Stadium is just more than thirty thousand. The stadium has good sightlines for football, but it lacks the creature comforts that are expected by today's modern fan. Fans sit on the stadium's concrete tiers. There are no cup holders or luxury boxes here: this is old-school football, people.

WHEN: The Harvard football season runs from September to November.

GETTING THERE: Harvard Stadium is about four miles from downtown Boston. To get to the stadium, take the Mass Pike to the Brighton/Cambridge exit (Exit 18 eastbound and Exit 20 westbound). After paying the toll, bear left at the fork toward Allston. Turn right at the second set of lights onto North Harvard Street. Harvard Stadium is approximately one mile ahead on the left.

On-street **parking** around the stadium is very limited. Fans with a Gate 6 parking pass, mostly university donors, can enter from North Harvard Street. There is also $5 parking at Harvard Business School across the street from the stadium, accessible from North Harvard Street and Western Avenue, but note that tailgating is not permitted in that lot.

Harvard also has general admission parking on the playing fields around the stadium, accessible at Gate 14 off Soldiers Field Road, for $10 per vehicle. Tailgating is permitted in this lot. (The only way to park within the athletic complex for the Yale game, however, is to be a season-ticket holder with a parking pass or a $1,000 contributor to Harvard Athletics.) In addition, there is usually free parking across from the stadium at the lots at Herter and Artesani parks along the Charles River. Note that the police often close the ramps between Soldiers Field Road and North Harvard Street before games. To get to Soldiers Field Road, follow the directions as above from the Mass Pike, but before getting to the stadium, turn left off North Harvard Street onto Western Avenue, follow for nearly a mile, and take a right down the ramp onto Soldiers Field Road.

Harvard Stadium is also accessible by **public transportation**. By subway, take the Red Line to the Harvard station. It's about a ten minute walk from Harvard Square down JFK Street and across the Charles River to the stadium. Several MBTA bus lines also stop at Harvard Square, and bus routes 66 and 86 stop on North Harvard Street outside the stadium.

TICKETS: With the exception of games against Yale, which are held at Harvard in even-numbered years, sellouts are rare. It's wise to purchase tickets to the Harvard-Yale game in advance. Game day tickets can be purchased at the ticket office in the Murr Center, adjacent to the stadium on North Harvard Street, and at the Bright Hockey Center on the northwest side of the stadium. (Note that ticket sales at the Bright Hockey Center are cash only.)

Except for the Yale game, there are usually open seats throughout the stadium if you want to move around. The western stands, behind the Harvard bench, are usually more popular than the eastern stands. Seats in the horseshoe end zone are usually in the shade during the afternoon, which can be a blessing early in the season or a curse later in the year. Most of the seats at Harvard Stadium are uncovered, with the exception of wooden risers at the top of each section that are underneath the stadium's circling colonnade. Except for those wooden risers, the seating in Harvard Stadium is on the edifice's concrete slabs, which can make for an uncomfortable, and on some days frigid, underside after a few hours.

Single-game tickets are $15 for adults, $8 for youths (ages three to fourteen), $8 for Harvard graduate students, and free for Harvard undergraduates. For Yale games, adult and youth tickets cost $30.

Season tickets cost $90, but there are discounts for Harvard faculty and staff, young alumni, graduate students, and Allston-Brighton residents. Season-ticket holders can also purchase passes to park within the athletic complex. Season tickets are available between sections 27 and 32 on the Harvard sideline and between sections 7 and 10 on the visitor sideline. The Harvard band sits in the lower rows of section 33, and sections 34 through 37 in the northwest corner of the stadium is the student section.

To purchase tickets, phone 617-495-2211 or 877-GO-HARVARD, go online to www.gocrimson.com, or visit the ticket office in the Murr Center at 65 North Harvard Street, which is open weekdays between 9 AM and 5 PM.

DISABILITY ACCESS: Handicap seating is available at the bottom of sections 35, 36, and 37 in the northwest corner of Harvard Stadium. Handicap parking is available through the Gate 6 entrance off North Harvard Street, and the handicap entrance is on the northwest corner of the stadium.

THE SPLURGE: Want a few extra perks at the game? Spend at least $500 and join the Friends of Harvard Football. Members receive VIP parking and preferential seating at home events, invitations to special events such as the annual team dinner and

---

★ Dressing for the Cold

Here in New England, if you don't bundle up properly, you may spend more time focused on regaining feeling in your hands and toes than on the intricacies of the 3-4 defense.

The key to dressing for cold-weather games is to wear multiple layers to trap in your body heat. The inner layer in contact with your skin should be made of a material that wicks moisture away and keeps you dry. Your outer layer should be a water-resistant jacket that protects you from rain, snow, and wind. In between, you may need multiple layers of warm clothes.

Stop worrying about hat head and put on a knit cap. Didn't your mother tell you that ninety percent of your body heat can be lost through your noggin? Skip the sneakers and wear insulated shoes or boots. Buy packets of hand and toe warmers and stick them in your gloves and shoes, and your extremities will stay warm for hours. On bitterly cold days, bring in a lap blanket and seat cushion to take the chill off aluminum or concrete benches. And if you're one of the nuts who likes to go shirtless at cold-weather games, just remember: We're not laughing with you, we're laughing *at* you.

lunches with coaches, and the ability to mingle with players and their families at the Friends of Harvard Football tent next to the stadium. Call 617-495-3535 for more information.

THE CHEAPSKATE: If you live in Allston-Brighton and Cambridge, you're in luck. Each season, Harvard designates one game as Allston-Brighton Day and another as Cambridge Day. For those games, the Athletics Department and Harvard's Office of Community Affairs invite Cambridge and Allston-Brighton residents for some neighborly hospitality, including a free ticket to the game and a complimentary pregame lunch. For more information, call 617-495-4955.

SPECTATOR TIPS: Sitting on Harvard Stadium's venerable concrete slabs quickly loses its charm, particularly on cold afternoons. Bring along a seat cushion, and your backside will thank you. Winds can whip around the stadium's horseshoe, so also consider bringing a blanket on particularly frigid days.

Game programs are handed out for free at all games. If you're going to a sold-out game, such as the one against Yale, keep in mind that bathroom facilities for women are limited and lines can get very lengthy at halftime.

If you want to tailgate at Harvard Stadium, parking lots open two hours prior to kickoff and stay open for two hours after the game. Tailgating is not permitted during the game, and charcoal grills are prohibited within the athletic complex.

SCORING AUTOGRAPHS: Access to players in uniform before and after games is limited.

FOR THE KIDS: Children under three are admitted free of charge. There is a fan zone on

Traditions die hard at Harvard, where fans take tailgating to a whole new level.
Courtesy Boston Public Library, Print Department.

the lawn between the Bright Hockey Center and the Murr Center with activities such as face painting, signmaking, coloring, and football, basketball, and hockey games.

Young fans can also sign up for the Crimson Kids Club, which includes a ticket to all home games, special programs, a membership card, t-shirt, monthly newsletters, and exclusive invites to pizza parties and autograph sessions with Harvard athletes. The club is for kids in eighth grade and below and costs $40. Memberships are available on the Harvard Athletics website or email kidsclub@fas.harvard.edu for more information.

STADIUM CONCESSIONS: Concession stands are located along the stadium sidelines under the seating area and include the usual choices of hot dogs, hamburgers, pizza, soda, and pretzels. Hot chocolate and coffee are available to stay warm. You'll also find kettle corn, fried dough, roasted nuts, and Ben & Jerry's. For something out of the ordinary, sample something from Redbones, the popular Somerville barbeque joint. Redbones has a tent and tables in the lawn area beyond the north end zone along with a concession stand inside the stadium on the Harvard sideline. Alcohol is available at the tent area.

FOOD AND DRINK AROUND THE STADIUM: There are some sandwich shops along Western Avenue in Brighton, but there are more food options in Harvard Square across the river in Cambridge. *Mr. Bartley's Gourmet Burgers* (1246 Massachusetts Avenue, 617-354-6559, www.bartleysburgers.com) is a Harvard Square institution with menu items named after local and national celebrities. Sports fans may want to try the "Manny Ramirez" (a real turkey burger with blue cheese, hot sauce, and fries) or "Tedy Bruschi" (a burger with cheddar cheese, guacamole, lettuce, tomato, red onions, and fries). *Border Café* (32 Church Street, 617-864-6100, www.bordercafe.com) is popular for its Tex-Mex and Cajun food at reasonable prices. The patio at *The Red House* (98 Winthrop Street, 617-576-0605, www.theredhouse.com) is a relaxing place to have a drink and a meal on warm days.

CONTACT INFORMATION: Harvard University Football, Murr Center, 65 North Harvard Street, Boston, MA 02163. 617-495-2207; www.gocrimson.com.

NORTHEASTERN

Northeastern's football team may lack the rich history of Harvard and the big-time atmosphere of Boston College, but this local Division I college football team offers an accessible, affordable, and family-friendly option for enjoying a Saturday afternoon watching some pigskin. Northeastern is a member of the NCAA's Football Championship Subdivision, those schools just a half step below the top tier of Division I schools. Northeastern is a member of the Colonial Athletic Association, which has schools stretching from Maine to Virginia. Over its seventy-plus seasons, Northeastern football has made just one bowl appearance (the 1963 Eastern Bowl) and a single postseason tournament appearance (in 2002). Thirteen Huskies have been named All-Americans, and nine have been drafted by the NFL.

STADIUM INFORMATION: Parsons Field is located in the middle of a leafy, residential Brookline neighborhood at 186 Kent Street. Even though the artificial turf and aluminum grandstands surrounding the field look shiny and new, the field dates back to the turn of the twentieth century when it was a public playground. In fact,

Northeastern University squares off on the gridiron against the University of Massachusetts-Amherst.

Kent Street resident Babe Ruth was said to have dropped by the field to play catch with the neighborhood kids. The field, which has a capacity of seven thousand people, was purchased by Northeastern in 1930 and dedicated in 1969 to Edward Parsons, a former athlete, coach, and athletics director at Northeastern. The yellow foul pole mounted in the corner of the north bleachers serves as a reminder that the football field is laid out in the outfield of Northeastern's baseball diamond. The university's soccer team also plays at Parsons Field.

Northeastern generally plays five home games each year at Brookline's Parsons Field. Over a mile away from campus, the atmosphere at Parsons Field during games tends to be more subdued than at other college games in the region.

The most noteworthy aspect of Parsons Field is the long, squat house that runs behind the length of the east end zone, Zabilski Field House, which contains the locker rooms for the football team. Guarding the entrance to the field house is a statue of the university's mascot, King Husky. The school adopted the "Huskies" nickname in 1927, and the first live mascot, "King Husky," appeared on campus on March 4th of that year. The regal name was fitting, since the King was descended from sled dog royalty; his father was the lead dog on Leonhard Seppala's famous team that rushed diphtheria serum across 645 miles of rugged Alaskan land to save the stricken village of Nome, an event that is commemorated by the annual Iditarod Great Sled Race.

Upon their arrival in Boston, more than two thousand students and the university band greeted Seppala and the Siberian husky at the train station. The dog was then given a police escort to campus, where he was presented with a "roads scholarship" for his experience on the Alaskan highways. Unfortunately, given the number of universities in Boston, it's difficult to parade through the city streets and *not* step on enemy turf. According to an account in *The New York Times*, the procession was pelted with eggs, vegetables, and snowballs by seven hundred BU students as it made its way past Boston University.

The first King Husky reigned for fourteen years, and the current incarnation, King Husky VIII, has appeared at Northeastern events since 2005 after receiving extensive training for his responsibilities, such as remaining calm among throngs of fans, greeting the public, and walking in parades. Hopefully, this King doesn't have to dodge any BU students wielding rotten produce.

WHEN: The Northeastern football season runs from late August or early September to November.

GETTING THERE: Parsons Field is located in Brookline near the Longwood Medical Area, about three miles from downtown Boston. To drive to Parsons Field, take Storrow Drive to the exit for Kenmore Square. Take the first right off the exit onto Beacon Street, staying in middle lane. Do not bear right onto Commonwealth Avenue or take a left onto Brookline Avenue. Continue on Beacon Street for one mile and take a left onto Kent Street. Parsons Field is two-tenths of a mile ahead on the right.

An alternative set of directions is to take Route 128 to Exit 20A (Route 9 east). Continue for five miles and take a left onto Brookline Avenue toward Kenmore Square. Take the second left onto Aspinwall Avenue and make a right onto Kent Street at the first set of lights. Parsons Field is immediately on the left.

On-street **parking** around Parsons Field is extremely limited, and the Brookline police will tow cars parked illegally. Your best parking bet is to find a garage in the Longwood Medical Area and make the ten minute walk to the field. Weekend rates at some garages are $6.

Consider taking **public transportation** to Parsons Field. The "D" branch of the Green Line runs to Longwood, just a short walk from the stadium. From the Longwood stop, take a left up the hill on Chapel Street, turn right onto Longwood Avenue, and then take the first left onto Kent Street. The field is one-tenth of a mile ahead on the right. Northeastern also runs free shuttles from the campus to Parsons Field.

TICKETS: Tickets can be purchased at ticket booths at Parsons Field on game days. Seating at Parsons Field is on aluminum bleachers running along the sidelines, most of which lack seat backs. Tickets are for general admission seating.

Single-game tickets are $12 for adults and $6 for youths. Season tickets are available for $70 for adults and $50 for youths, and season-ticket holders receive a padded bleacher seat.

To purchase advance tickets, call the Northeastern University ticket office at 617-373-4700, go online to www.gonu.com/tickets, or visit the ticket office at Ell Hall. The ticket office is open from noon to 6 PM on Monday, Tuesday, Thursday, and Friday and from noon to 8 PM on Wednesday.

DISABILITY ACCESS: Fans in wheelchairs can watch the action along the fence in the east end zone.

THE SPLURGE: Fans who purchase a Husky MVP Pass receive free admission to all football, men's and women's hockey, and men's and women's basketball regular-season home games. The cost is $275 for adults, $125 for youth, and $550 for families. Donors to the Husky Athletics Club are hosted at tailgates at all games during the season. Call 617-373-2582 for more information.

THE CHEAPSKATE: If you don't care about catching the full game, cheapskates can usually get into Parsons Field for free during the second half when tickets are no longer being sold.

SPECTATOR TIPS: The bleachers on the north side behind the Northeastern bench can be in direct sun. The bleachers on the south side behind the visiting team's bench are larger, and spectators have the sun at their backs. There are portable toilets as well as restrooms in the back of the Zabilski Field House.

SCORING AUTOGRAPHS: Access to players in uniform before and after games is limited, but you can take a shot as they enter and leave the Zabilski Field House.

FOR THE KIDS: Northeastern football doesn't have a kids' activity area like Harvard, but it offers the easiest logistics for families with small children. You can wheel your strollers to areas behind the east end zone or the field in front of the south bleachers. On nice days you'll find a number of strollers parked at the base of the bleachers.

STADIUM CONCESSIONS: Concessions at Northeastern football are limited. There is one concession tent, which can get crowded at halftime but is very reasonable. (Hot dogs only cost $2.50.) There are typical options such as hamburgers, chicken sandwiches, pretzels, and sodas. No alcohol is served.

FOOD AND DRINK AROUND THE STADIUM: You'll have to walk a bit to the Longwood Medical Area, Brookline Village, or Coolidge Corner to find any restaurants or bars around Parsons Field. The ***Longwood Galleria*** (350 Longwood Avenue), near the hospitals, has a food court with a bunch of fast-food options. If you want something more substantial than Orange Julius, make the three-quarter mile walk to Coolidge Corner. There you'll find the ***Coolidge Corner Clubhouse*** (307 Harvard Street, 617-566-4948), a sports bar with plenty of televisions and a huge menu. (See page 259.)

CONTACT INFORMATION: Northeastern University Football, 219 Cabot Center, 360 Huntington Avenue, Boston, MA 02115. 617-373-5549; www.gonu.com/football.

HIGH SCHOOL FOOTBALL

While the Patriots and local college teams seem to get all the media's attention, high school football also draws tens of thousands of fans across metropolitan Boston on fall weekends. Massachusetts high school football may not rise to the level of *Friday Night Lights*, but it has a distinguished tradition and may be the purest form of the sport that Boston sports fans can find.

Boys in public and private schools helped grow the sport of football in the 1800s. The Oneida Football Club, the first organized football club in the United States, played games on Boston Common during the Civil War. The team—composed of Beacon Hill schoolboys with familiar Brahmin surnames such as Bowditch, Forbes, Lawrence, and Peabody—played against teams of students from Boston Latin, Boston English, and Dorchester High School. Prep schools were also breeding grounds for the emerging sport.

Thanksgiving in Massachusetts isn't just about Pilgrims, stuffing, and turkey. It's also about high school football. Thanksgiving is by far the biggest day on the high school football calendar. It's a day when kids across the region take to the gridiron to play traditional rivals in front of thousands of family, friends, and alumni. It's a chance for some teams to clinch Super Bowl berths and for others to turn around a terrible season with just one victory. For some seniors, it's also a special game because it will be the last time they strap on the shoulder pads and helmets.

On a typical Thanksgiving, more than one hundred thousand fans across metropolitan Boston pack bleachers and stand two or three deep behind roped-off end zones in the morning chill to carry on this proud Boston sports tradition. Pep bands try to stay in tune, high school students gossip, and cheerleaders keep a perpetual smile even if the game isn't going as hoped. Most games kick off around 10 AM and are over around noon, giving everyone plenty of time to carve the turkey.

One of the most storied Turkey Day matchups takes place at Harvard Stadium when Boston Latin and Boston English take the field. These two high schools have such a rich history that Boston English, which was founded in 1821, is really a newcomer when it is compared to Boston Latin, America's oldest school, founded in 1635. The two schools first butted heads on November 25, 1887, on Boston Common, and they haven't stopped since, making the annual battle the longest uninterrupted high school football rivalry in the country. Latin took that first game, and it has dominated English in recent years. The game no longer draws twenty thousand fans as it did decades ago, but it is still part of the fabric of the city's history.

Another fierce rivalry is the Thanksgiving tilt between Needham and Wellesley. The Rockets and the Raiders first played in 1882, and the matchup is the oldest public high school rivalry in the country. The early years of the rivalry were a bit colorful. The 1887 battle was declared a scoreless tie when spectators stormed the field and brought down runners heading toward the end zone. The contest the following year didn't go much better. Wellesley withdrew in protest because Needham's lineup included college and semiprofessional players, including a father of a Needham student. The 1896 tilt got off to an inauspicious start when the opening kickoff landed in the crowd, and the ball vanished. The game was delayed for nearly an hour before another ball could be found.

Thanksgiving matchups between Malden and Medford, Beverly and Salem, Amesbury and Newburyport, Durfee and New Bedford, Fitchburg and Leominster, Newton North and Brookline, and Falmouth versus Barnstable all date back to the 1800s. (Other traditional prep school rivalries, such as Phillips Andover-Phillips Exeter, that date back to the nineteenth century are played earlier in November.) Football fans have plenty of other enticing rivalries to choose from for their Thanksgiving viewing pleasure including East Boston-South Boston, Framingham-Natick, Brockton-Waltham, Lynn Classical-Lynn English, and Everett-Cambridge.

And for some real Thanksgiving flavor, take in the game between Plymouth North and Plymouth South. Football wasn't on the menu at the first Thanksgiving feast in Plymouth Colony, but surely even those dour Pilgrims wouldn't begrudge honoring another New England tradition.

High school teams in eastern Massachusetts that capture their league crowns and win an opening playoff game earn a slot in the Massachusetts Interscholastic Athletic Association's Super Bowls. Since 2007, all Super Bowl games (except for one of the lower divisions) have been played at Gillette Stadium. The games are played on the second Saturday after Thanksgiving, with the slate of games starting at 9 AM. Tickets cost $13 for adults and $10 for children, students, and seniors. Tickets are good for all six games, but re-entry is not allowed. Parking is free, but no tailgating is allowed. The concession stands in the stadium are open, but alcohol is not served.

Where to Watch:
College and Pro Football

Just about every bar in Boston is full of Patriots and local college football fans. But if your team of choice happens to reside out of town, there are some watering holes around the Hub where you might find some kindred spirits.

The Baseball Tavern, 1270 Boylston Street, Boston, MA 02215. 617-867-6526; www.thebaseballtavern.com. *College teams: Cal Golden Bears, LSU Tigers, Oregon Ducks.*

Brighton Beer Garden, 386 Market Street, Brighton, MA 02135. 617-562-6000; www.brightonbeergarden.com. *College team: Buffalo Bulls.*

Dockside Restaurant & Bar, 183 State Street, Boston, MA 02109. 617-723-7050. *College team: Texas Longhorns.*

Game On!, 82 Lansdowne Street, Boston, MA 02215. 617-351-7001; www.gameonboston.com. *NFL teams: Chicago Bears, Green Bay Packers, New York Giants, Philadelphia Eagles. College teams: Northwestern Wildcats, Ohio State Buckeyes, USC Trojans, Wisconsin Badgers.*

The Greatest Bar, 262 Friend Street, Boston, MA 02114. 617-367-0544; www.thegreatestbar.com. *College teams: Arkansas Razorbacks, Kansas Jayhawks, Michigan State Spartans, Penn State Nittany Lions, Tennessee Volunteers.*

The Harp, 85 Causeway Street, Boston, MA 02114. 617-742-1010; www.harpboston.com. *NFL team: Buffalo Bills.*

McFadden's, 148 State Street, Boston, MA 02109. 617-227-5100; www.mcfaddensboston.com. *College team: Florida Gators.*

The Joshua Tree, 1316 Commonwealth Avenue, Allston, MA 02134. 617-566-6699; www.joshuatreeallston.com. *College teams: Florida Gators, Maryland Terrapins, Miami Hurricanes, Notre Dame Fighting Irish.*

The Place, Two Broad Street, Boston, MA 02109. 617-523-2081; www.theplaceboston.com. *College teams: Michigan Wolverines, UCLA Bruins, USC Trojans.*

Roggie's Brew & Grille, 356 Chestnut Hill Avenue, Brighton, MA 02135. 617-566-1880; www.roggies.com. *NFL team: Pittsburgh Steelers.*

Seapoint Restaurant, 367 East Eighth Street, South Boston, MA 02127. 617-268-1476. *College team: Notre Dame Fighting Irish.*

Sports Depot, 353 Cambridge Street, Allston, MA 02134. 617-783-2300; www.sportsdepotboston.com. *College teams: Alabama Crimson Tide, Auburn Tigers, Miami Hurricanes, Oregon State Beavers, Virginia Tech Hokies.*

Sports Grille Boston, 132 Canal Street, Boston, MA 02114. 617-367-9302. *College teams: Colorado Buffaloes, North Carolina State Wolfpack, UCLA Bruins, USC Trojans, Virginia Tech Hokies.*

Tavern in the Square, 1815 Massachusetts Avenue, Cambridge, MA 02140. 617-354-7766; www.taverninthesquare.com. *College team: Michigan Wolverines.*

Uno Chicago Grill, 645 Beacon Street, Kenmore Square, Boston, MA 02215. 617-262-4911; www.unos.com. *NFL team: New York Giants.*

HOCKEY

BOSTONIANS ARE SOME OF the most dedicated hockey fans in the country—and for good reason. Boston has both the climate and the sensibilities for this hard-hitting sport. From local rinks to the Garden, raucous crowds fill hockey barns across the region on cold winter nights to cheer the home teams on as they put the rubber biscuit in the basket.

Hockey's roots in Boston date back to the nineteenth century. Ice polo, a forerunner to hockey, was a popular spectator sport in the city in the late 1800s. Ice polo was played, not with a puck, but with a rubber ball, and the shape of the stick was different from what hockey fans are familiar with today. By the 1890s the modern sport of ice hockey had spread southward from its cradle in Montreal and quickly took hold in Boston among schoolboys, college students, and amateurs. Many players fashioned their own hockey sticks from hickory cut in suburban Boston; the sticks were then steamed or soaked in boiling water and bent to the required curve.

The first ice hockey games in Boston were played in the great outdoors on city skating grounds. The city flooded Franklin Field for teams to practice and play on. Jamaica Pond and the parade ground of Boston Common were popular venues for hockey games too. Even Harvard Stadium was put to use as the home of the Crimson hockey team.

Even though hockey and basketball both emerged in 1890s Boston, hockey became the wintertime sport of choice. In response to this, the Boston Arena opened its doors on St. Botolph Street in 1910. The arena's ice surface was the largest of its time and bigger than most standard rinks today. Hockey fans, known as "bugs" in the early 1900s, were thrilled by the ability to watch games without worrying about the elements, and the arena was soon overrun with bugs watching local colleges and prep schools take to the ice. The men's hockey teams at **Boston College**, **Boston University**, and **Harvard University** all called the Boston Arena home at one point or another before constructing their own on-campus arenas. The Boston Arena, now known as Matthews Arena, still stands, and it's the oldest artificial ice arena in the world. Today the arena is home to the hockey teams of **Northeastern University** and the Wentworth Institute of Technology.

In 1924 the Boston Arena was also the birthplace of the **Boston Bruins**, the first National Hockey League (NHL) franchise in America. The Bruins moved into Boston Garden when it opened its doors in 1928, and for nearly seventy years the "gallery gods" and other Bruins fans filled the old hockey barn to cheer on their beloved black and gold. Through the 1950s, the Garden was also home to various minor league hockey teams, such as the Boston Tigers and Boston Cubs of the Canadian-American Hockey League and the Boston Olympics of the Eastern Hockey League. Today the old Boston Garden is no longer, and the Bruins skate at the TD Garden.

The Boston Bruins, 1931. Courtesy Boston Public Library, Print Department.

The golden years for Boston hockey were in the late 1960s and early 1970s, when Hall of Famer Bobby Orr led the Big Bad Bruins to two Stanley Cup championships. The image of Orr flying through the air after scoring the cup-winning goal in 1970 is seared into the collective memory of all Boston sports fans—even those who weren't alive at the time.

The popularity of the Bruins set off a hockey boom around Boston in the 1970s. Legions of youth teams formed, and the Boston Braves—a new minor league affiliate of the Bruins—played before sellout crowds at Boston Garden and Boston

Arena. A new World Hockey Association (WHA) formed as a rival league to the NHL, and Boston became the home of one of the charter franchises, the New England Whalers. The Whalers played to a capacity crowd for their first game in 1972 and captured the league's first championship. The Whalers played at both Boston Garden and Boston Arena before moving to Hartford in 1975, when the Boston hockey boom began to wane. (The NHL's Carolina Hurricanes are the current incarnation of the old WHA Whalers.)

While hockey began to decline in popularity around Boston in the late 1970s, a byproduct of the youth teams sparked by the Big Bad Bruins was a generation of great Olympic hockey players from the Boston area, including members of America's 1980 gold medal "miracle on ice" team. Captain Mike Eruzione, a Winthrop native, and goalie Jim Craig, a North Easton native, were two valuable players for the miracle workers, who defeated the heavily favored Soviet hockey team at the height of the Cold War on their way to capturing the gold.

In addition to the Bruins, three minor league hockey teams are within easy driving distance of Boston. The **Providence Bruins** of the American Hockey League (AHL) are Boston's minor league affiliate, and its roster includes the organization's rising stars. The **Lowell Devils** and **Worcester Sharks** are also AHL teams that take to the ice in the Boston area.

While Boston is undoubtedly a city that gravitates toward professional sports, the Boston area is also infatuated with collegiate hockey; its quick style of play and lack of mucking and grinding makes it a popular alternative to the pros for many fans.

What makes Boston such a great college hockey town is that its major universities all compete on the same level. The Hub is home to four of college hockey's best programs—Boston College, Boston University, Harvard, and Northeastern—and the city has hosted both the men's and women's Frozen Fours. Adding to the collegiate atmosphere is Boston's collection of wonderful college rinks that range from the old-school, gritty Matthews Arena to the plush, new Agganis Arena, each ringing with fight songs and clinking cowbells on game days.

What makes Boston an *exciting* collegiate hockey town, however, is the proximity of these four schools to each other. The rivalries are combustible, and the mood at a college hockey game in Boston could easily match that of a big-time college football game. In particular, the Green Line rivalry between Boston University and Boston College can be just as fierce as the rivalry between the Red Sox and Yankees. These perennial powers endlessly butt heads for local, conference, and national tournament titles—so much so that even when they are playing different opponents, chants directed at their rival on the other side of Commonwealth Avenue are known to spontaneously erupt from the student body.

In addition to regular-season matchups, BU and BC have a propensity to meet at the **Hockey East Championship** and the **Beanpot**, the annual showcase event for college hockey in Boston. Between the end of the NFL season and the beginning of Red Sox spring training, the Beanpot is the highlight of the Boston sporting calendar. Held the first two Mondays in February, the Beanpot is almost a season unto itself, and even a team having an otherwise terrible season can turn it all around with just two victories. Both the men and women take to the ice in their own Beanpots.

High school hockey is another popular spectator sport in the Boston area. The pinnacle is the **Super Eight** tournament featuring the best teams in the state. Boston was home to the first interscholastic hockey league in the country, and the city's public and private schools still turn out great players, many of whom will star in the city's college and professional arenas for years to come.

BOSTON BRUINS

Die-hard Boston sports fans have bled black and gold since the Boston Bruins first skated onto the ice of the Boston Arena against the Montreal Maroons in the autumn of 1924. For decades now, the Bruins have been the hub of hockey in Boston, and they have a strong following all across New England.

Charles F. Adams, the initial team owner, chose the Bruins' alliterative name, and legend has it that he chose the original brown-and-yellow color scheme because it matched the palette of his grocery store chain. The Adams family owned the team for six decades, during which the Bruins captured five Stanley Cups.

The Bruins moved into Boston Garden in 1928. In front of a sellout crowd, Boston dropped its first game in the building to the Montreal Canadiens. It was a bad omen, as the hated Habs had the upper hand on their Original Six rival for many years to come. In the early years of the NHL, hockey was almost as popular as baseball, and Eddie Shore, best described as Babe Ruth's counterpart, was the greatest player of that time. Fans filled arenas all around the league to watch this Bruins defenseman rush the goal, delivering unforgiving body checks to anyone who got in his way. Shore was named league MVP four times, and he led the Bruins to Stanley Cups in 1929 and 1939. The famous Kraut Line Hall of Famers Milt Schmidt, Woody Dumart, and Bobby Bauer helped to deliver another title in 1941.

The popularity of the team reached a pinnacle in the late 1960s and early 1970s, when the Big Bad Bruins were led by Bobby Orr, Phil Esposito, and Gerry Cheevers. After his arrival in 1966, Orr quickly achieved legendary status in Boston, and the Bruins became the toughest ticket in town. The team's Stanley Cup championships in 1970 and 1972 sparked an explosion in the construction of ice rinks around New England, but the sport's popularity began to wane after Orr left town in 1976.

The Bruins had some great years in the 1980s and early 1990s when Ray Bourque and Cam Neely roamed the ice. In recent years, the closest Lord Stanley's Mug has come to Boston was when Bourque brought it to a rally at City Hall Plaza after capturing it with the Colorado Avalanche in 2001. Until recently, the Bruins may as well have been in hibernation for all but the team's hard-core, loyal followers—especially while Boston's three other professional teams were delivering championship after championship to the Hub.

But the energy is returning. A new generation of players is attempting to add another

Bruins star Eddie Shore autographs a boy's hockey stick as the rest look on.
Courtesy Boston Public Library, Print Department.

title to Boston, and while many Bruins fans still lament the passing of intimate Boston Garden in 1995, whenever the new building sells out or the Bruins are in the Stanley Cup Playoffs, the gusto in the Garden is contagious.

One of the traditions that carried over from the old Garden is Rene Rancourt's rendition of the national anthem (or anthems when the Bruins take on Canadian teams) before big games—which culminates with his signature fist pump. The pregame introductions and video highlights of Bruins past get the crowd going. Fans still go wild watching Bobby Orr dart around opponents, Terry O'Reilly challenge an entire bench to a brawl, and Ray Bourque and Cam Neely score pressure-packed goals. The highlight footage is punctuated by a primal roar of a salivating grizzly—also very popular with the salivating crowd.

But if you really want to see Bruins fans come to their feet, watch as players throw down their gloves and whip the crowd into a frenzy as the jabs and uppercuts are exchanged. At times like these you can't help but wonder if the Garden has been transformed into the Roman Colosseum—that is if the Colosseum had a high-definition video screen with a picture so crisp that you can see the blood trickling down the cheeks of the combatants.

While organ music still plays during the game—with old favorites such as "NutRocker," the team's signature theme song back when games were aired on channel 38—the

Bruins' game presentation definitely goes beyond the "bear" necessities. Music thunders from the public address system, and timeouts bring t-shirt tosses, trivia contests, and the Ice Girls, the Bruins dance team. After the Bruins score a goal, the horn blares as if the *Queen Mary* is leaving port and wrestler Ric Flair leads the crowd in cheer with his signature "*Woooo!*"

ARENA INFORMATION: The Bruins play home games at the TD Garden, located on Causeway Street. The Garden has a capacity of 17,565 for hockey games. The Bruins shoot at the west end goal twice. Sections 1 and 12 in the loge (lower level) and 301 and 316 in the balcony (upper level) are at center ice. Sections 6 and 7 in the loge and 308 and 309 in the balcony are behind the west end goal. Sections 17 and 18 in the loge and 323 and 324 in the balcony are behind the east end goal, which the Bruins shoot at only once a game. For more information on the Garden, see page 64.

WHEN: The Bruins regular season runs from October to April. The Bruins play many home games on Tuesdays, Thursdays, and Saturdays.

GETTING THERE: See page 65.

TICKETS: Tickets to Bruins games—particularly weekend tilts and games against popular opponents or division rivals—can sell out. Tickets to individual games go on sale in September. To get a jump on the general public in buying tickets, sign up for the Cybear Club on the Bruins website at www.bostonbruins.com. Members get exclusive pre-sale opportunities and discount ticket offers.

Individual tickets to most games range from $16.50 to $189.50. However, the Bruins designate certain games against elite opponents and rivals as gold level games and charge an additional $10 per ticket to the prices listed below. In 2008-09, fourteen games were designated as gold level. If you want to get as close to the action as possible, tickets for the front row against the glass cost $189.50.

Loge center (sections 1–3, 10–14, and 21–22) tickets, outside of the front row, range in price from $110.50 to $125.50. Loge center tickets are between the faceoff circles.

Loge end (sections 4–9 and 15–20) tickets, outside of the front row, range in price from $85.50 to $95.50. Loge end seats are in the corners and behind the goals.

Balcony center (sections 301–303, 314–318, and 329–330) tickets are $71.50 for the first two rows, $55.50 for rows three through seven, $45.50 for rows eight through ten, and $37.50 for rows eleven through fifteen. Balcony center tickets are between the faceoff circles.

Balcony end (sections 304–313, 319, 322–325, and 327–328) tickets are $71.50 for the first row, $44.50 for rows two through ten in corner sections, $37.50 for rows eleven through fifteen in corner sections, $34.50 for rows two through ten behind the goals, $26.50 for rows eleven through fifteen behind the west end goal, and $16.50 for rows eleven through fifteen behind the east end goal, which the Bruins shoot at once. Balcony end seats are in the corners and behind the goals.

The Bruins offer season tickets along with 24-game, 12-game, and 6-game plans. Season tickets in the loge center are $6,450 for the first row and either $3,827 or $4,257 for the rest of the rows in the sections. Loge end season tickets cost $6,450 for the first row and between $2,150 and $3,139 for the rest of the seats in the sections. Season tickets in the balcony center are $2,580 for the first two rows and between $1,118 and $1,978 for the rest of the seats in the sections. Balcony end season tickets cost $2,580 for the first row and between $645 and $1,548 for all other seats.

Tickets can be purchased by calling Ticketmaster at 617-931-2000 or going online to www.ticketmaster.com. Tickets are also on sale at the TD Garden box office, located on the main level of North Station. During hockey season, the box office is open seven days a week between 11 AM and 7 PM.

Even if a Bruins game is sold out, it's still possible to get tickets from brokers and from season-ticket holders; try websites such as eBay, StubHub, and Craigslist. There are also plenty of scalpers working the streets and bars around the Garden, but keep in mind that scalping is illegal and, while rare, the police can make arrests.

DISABILITY ACCESS: Spaces for fans with wheelchairs and companions are dispersed vertically and horizontally throughout the Garden in numerous price ranges. Fans requiring handicap-accessible seating should call the Bruins at 617-624-1950. Wheelchair escorts are available for disabled guests who may need assistance getting to and from their seat. For more information, call the ADA phone line at 617-624-1754. The Garden has two public elevators, one each in the southeast and southwest corners of the building. Both elevators provide access to all levels. Assistive Listening Devices are available from the Garden's customer service office, located outside section 4 on the loge level.

THE SPLURGE: Ever wanted to hitch a ride on a Zamboni? The Bruins offer fans the chance to ride shotgun on one of the Zambonis during intermission for a donation of at least $150 to the Boston Bruins Foundation. All riders must be at least fifteen years of age. For more information, call 617-624-1923.

The Garden's Premium Club offers many ways for Bruins fans to indulge themselves. There are eleven hundred club seats, sandwiched between the upper and lower bowls of the arena, which include theater-style seating at mid-ice and in-seat wait service. Club seats sell for $170.50. The Premium Club also has additional luxury seating options—such as the Heineken Boardroom, the SportsDeck, and the Lofts—and fine dining at the Banners restaurant. See page 68 for more information on the Premium Club.

Bruins fans can also get a bite to eat before, during, and after the game at Legends, a members-only bar and restaurant inside the Garden. Memberships in Legends cost $525 for half of the Bruins season and $874 for an entire season. Membership for both Celtics and Bruins games costs $1,000. Members may bring three guests into Legends. For more information, call 617-624-1807.

Executive suites, which hold between eighteen and twenty-one fans, are available to lease for individual games. Prices range from $3,150 to $4,410 but do not include food and beverages.

THE CHEAPSKATE: Cheapskates with a big appetite—for both food and hockey—may want to sign up for the Bruins' Hungry for Hockey ticket package that includes a ticket in sections 327 or 328 in the balcony and all-you-can-eat concessions. Hungry for Hockey tickets are available in five-game plans ($199) and for the entire season ($39 a game). The concessions include hot dogs, nachos, pretzels, peanuts, and sodas. Beer is not included in the package.

The Bruins also have student nights at the Garden for games on Monday through Thursday. Tickets for high school and college students in sections 320 and 321 sell for $23.50 on student nights. To receive notice

★ Bruins Training Camp

September in New England can mean only one thing for puckheads: time for the goalies and wingers to report to training camp. OK, so the start of Bruins training camp isn't exactly circled on the calendar like the day Red Sox pitchers and catchers report to spring training, but many of the team's practice sessions are free and open to fans eager to watch their team return to the ice.

Camp usually opens in mid-September, and many of the sessions are held at the Ristuccia Memorial Arena in Wilmington. Crowds can sometimes be small, so you can get real close to the players. In fact, stand next to the boards and the only thing separating you from the players is a thin sheet of glass and, well, talent. The rink can be freezing, even on a hot day, so bring some warm clothes. There are a few vending machines near the lobby, but that's about it. After practice, some players will sign autographs on their way out of the rink.

The Bruins also have a few practice sessions inside the TD Garden that have more amenities and draw a bigger crowd—not to mention warmer temperatures. There are games and face painting for kids and air hockey tables for those who are skate-phobic. If you ever wanted to sit in the front row and watch the Bruins, this is your chance. Bring your camera for excellent shots through the cuts in the glass along the boards. Roster sheets are usually available at the Garden. To check the training camp schedule, call the fan line at 617-624-1910 or visit www.bostonbruins.com.

---

of special Bruins ticket offers and discounts, sign up for the Cybear Club on the Bruins website at www.bostonbruins.com.

SPECTATOR TIPS: The Garden opens one hour before the puck drops. If you have a seat behind a goal, you'll be watching the game through the protective netting. If you're not behind the netting, stay alert! Bags, backpacks, food, beverages, cameras with detachable lenses, and video cameras are strictly prohibited from the Garden. Smoking is not permitted in the arena.

SCORING AUTOGRAPHS: Of the professional athletes, hockey players have the best reputation for signing autographs. The challenge for some fans is to recognize the players without their helmets. Do a little reconnaissance by checking out players' photographs on the website of the NHL Players' Association (www.nhlpa.com).

During the season, the Bruins and visiting teams may have late morning skates scheduled at the Garden. Autograph hounds stake out the entrance to the players' parking lot on Causeway Street in front of the Garden during morning skates and two to four hours before games in the hope that some players may sign. Hockey cards, photographs, pucks, jerseys, and sticks are all good items to get signed.

The Bruins also have practice sessions during training camp and the regular season at the **Ristuccia Memorial Arena** (190 Main Street, Wilmington, MA), and players may sign before and after practices. If you're interested in visiting teams, they sometimes stay at the Copley Marriott, Westin Copley Place, and Ritz-Carlton hotels.

If you're willing to pay for autographs—and support a good cause—buy a ticket to the annual Boston Bruins Wives' Charity

Carnival at the Garden. Fans can spend time in the Bruins clubhouse and meet the players. Tickets to get autographs and take pictures with the players are in addition to the cost of admission.

FOR THE KIDS: The Bruins have set aside most of section 326 (rows 3 to 15) as the team's discount family section for all home games. Tickets to the family section cost $20 for adults and $10 for children fourteen and under. (Add $10 for gold level games.) The team also stages a handful of kids' days during the season that include giveaways and entertainment targeted at the young fans. Additionally, the Bruins have a sizable slate of Saturday afternoon matinees in the second half of the season with a family-friendly start time of 1 PM.

During intermission, mites and squirts take to the ice for the team's "3 Minutes of Fame" as their names scroll across the scoreboard. The ice sheet is so big compared to the kids that it seems like it may take them three minutes to skate from one end to the other. Longtime Bruins fans will have flashbacks to the days of Mini 1-on-1 during B's telecasts on channel 38.

Children under two do not need a ticket to Bruins games, provided they sit on an adult's lap. Strollers are permitted, but they must be collapsible and fit under the seat. Strollers may not be left in walkways or concourses but can be checked at the

The Boston Bruins practice at Ristuccia Memorial Arena, the team's training center.

customer service office near section 4 on the loge level. There are baby changing stations in all restrooms, but there are no family restrooms.

ARENA CONCESSIONS: See page 70.

FOOD AND DRINK AROUND THE ARENA: See page 70.

CONTACT INFORMATION: Boston Bruins, TD Garden, 100 Legends Way, Boston, MA 02114. 617-624-1900; www.bostonbruins.com.

BEANPOT

College hockey often plays second fiddle to the Bruins among Boston sports fans, but that changes on the first two Monday nights of February when all eyes focus on the Beanpot tournament, a quintessential Boston institution. The Beanpot features the city's quartet of hockey powers—Boston College, Boston University, Harvard, and Northeastern—battling it out for the right to hoist a silver pot-bellied trophy fashioned after those bygone Boston crocks that were once filled with molasses and beans.

The Beanpot is certainly worth more than a hill of beans to the students and alumni of the four participating schools. From Commonwealth Avenue to Harvard Square to Huntington Avenue, bragging rights in offices, schools, and bars across Boston are on the line. No matter how the rest of the year goes, a win at the Beanpot can turn an entire season into a success.

With no campus more than four miles from another, these schools are like kissing cousins. But in the case of the Beanpot, familiarity breeds contempt. The fans of each team bring their school spirit and their patented dislike for one another to the games. But the Beanpot is a special event, not just because the teams are bitter rivals and the atmosphere inside the Garden is electric, but because these storied hockey programs have achieved recent on-ice success as well. All Beanpot schools except Northeastern have won national championships since 1989, and even the Huskies have achieved high national rankings in recent years.

As hard as it is to believe today, the Beanpot certainly wasn't an overnight sensation. The tournament was originally born as a way to fill open dates at the Boston Arena (Matthews Arena today). The first New England Invitational Hockey Tournament, as it was known then, was won by Harvard and played on the two nights after Christmas in 1952. For the next edition of the Beanpot, the event moved to Boston Garden, but only 711 fans turned out for the first game.

It wasn't until the sixth year of the tournament that the current schedule of the first two Mondays in February was adopted. The first sellout wouldn't occur until 1961, but they quickly became a common occurrence. In fact, the Beanpot was such a draw that even during the great blizzard of 1978, more than eleven thousand fans showed up at Boston Garden. Many stayed to the end, by which point they were trapped inside and condemned to spend the night eating lukewarm hot dogs on stale buns. Today the Beanpot is played at the TD Garden. (For information on the Garden, including directions, disability access, and food and drink, see pages 64–73.)

Terriers fans have dubbed the Beanpot the "BU Invitational," since their team has captured twenty-nine pots of beans since the tournament's inception—more than the other three schools combined. Boston College has captured fourteen Beanpot trophies, Harvard has won ten, and Northeastern, the perennial underdog, has only four. The first-round matchups rotate each year, but it seems as if BU and BC, those pesky Green Line rivals, always find some way to meet.

WHEN: The Beanpot is played on the first two Mondays in February. Semifinal games are played at 5 PM and 8 PM on the first Monday in February with the consolation game and final played on the second Monday in February.

TICKETS: Beanpot tickets are some of the hottest in Boston, and games sell out quickly. Tickets go on sale to the general public in November at the Garden and through Ticketmaster. In addition, the four participating schools sell tickets to students, staff, alumni, and season-ticket holders. Occasionally if schools have leftover tickets, they will sell them to the general public. After the semifinals, there are chances to purchase tickets from fans of the losing teams.

Beanpot tickets for loge seats, the lower level of the Garden, cost $38. Seats in the upper level cost $28, $33, or $38. Club seats for the Beanpot also cost $38 and may be the best value, considering it provides access to the Premium Club levels of the Garden. The Garden also offers several VIP packages that include seating in the Premium Club. For more information, call 617-624-1VIP.

Tickets can be purchased by calling Ticketmaster at 617-931-2000 or going online to www.ticketmaster.com. Tickets are also on sale at the TD Garden box office, located on the main level of North Station. During hockey season, the box office is open seven days a week between 11 AM and 7 PM.

CONTACT INFORMATION: www.beanpothockey.com.

HOCKEY EAST CHAMPIONSHIP

Since its formation in 1984, Hockey East has been one of the premier college hockey conferences in America, producing

---

★ The Women's Beanpot

Women's hockey is one of the fastest growing sports in America, and the local colleges field some of the best players in the country. As with the men, the women of Boston College, Boston University, Harvard, and Northeastern square off in a Beanpot tournament of their own. The women's Beanpot, one of the longest-running women's collegiate tournaments in all of sports, is rotated among the campus rinks of the four teams. Northeastern and Harvard have dominated the women's Beanpot, with the Huskies capturing fourteen titles and the Crimson twelve. Boston College only has three championships and Boston University just one. Harvard has seen recent success after Northeastern captured many of the titles in the Beanpot's early years. However, as women's hockey continues to grow in popularity, there is more parity among the four participants. Boston College captured its initial Beanpot in 2006 and followed it up with wins in 2007 and 2009.

The women's Beanpot is played on the first two Tuesdays in February. Semifinal games are played at 5 PM and 8 PM on the first Tuesday in February with the consolation game and final played on the second Tuesday in February. For arena information on BC, BU, Harvard, and Northeastern see pages 132, 136, 140, and 144 respectively. Tickets to the women's Beanpot, which are available through the box office of the host school, cost $8 for adults and $4 for youths. For more information on the women's Beanpot, go to www.beanpothockey.com.

six national champions between 1993 and 2009. More than a million fans every year fill the rinks at member institutions. In addition to Boston University, Boston College, and Northeastern University, the other men's programs in the ten-team Hockey East are UMass-Lowell, UMass-Amherst, Merrimack College, Providence College, the University of Maine, the University of New Hampshire, and the University of Vermont.

The conference's regular season culminates in the Hockey East Championship, featuring the best eight teams in the standings. Teams battle for the Lamoriello Trophy, named in honor of Lou Lamoriello, the first commissioner of Hockey East. Perhaps more important, they also compete for an automatic berth in the NCAA Division I Ice Hockey Championship. After best-of-three quarterfinal series held at the home rinks of the top seeds, the remaining four teams come to Boston to take to ice at the TD Garden. (For information on the Garden see page 64.)

Unlike the Beanpot, Boston College has had the upper hand at the Hockey East Championship, leading the league with eight tournament titles in the first twenty-five years. Boston University is next with seven tournament titles, followed by Maine with five, UNH and Providence with two each, and Northeastern with one.

WHEN: The Hockey East Championship quarterfinals are held on one of the first weekends in March with the action moving to the TD Garden the following weekend. The two semifinals are held on a Friday night with the final on the following night.

TICKETS: While tickets for the on-campus quarterfinals are easy to get through the participating teams, the semifinals and finals at the Garden can sell out, so it may be worth purchasing tickets in advance. After the Friday semifinals, some fans of losing teams will likely sell off their tickets to the finals.

Tickets to the championship matches go on sale at the Garden in December. For both the semifinals and finals, tickets for the loge seats, in the lower level, cost $37 or $39 and seats in the upper level cost $17 or $29. If you've ever wanted to check out the Garden's Premium Club, here's an economical chance. Club seats for the Hockey East Championship cost $39. The Garden also offers several VIP packages that include seating in the Premium Club. For more information, call 617-624-1VIP.

Tickets can be purchased by calling Ticketmaster at 617-931-2000 or going online to www.ticketmaster.com. Tickets are also on sale at the TD Garden box office, located on the main level of North Station. During the hockey season, the box office is open seven days a week between 11 AM and 7 PM. Student tickets in the upper level are available for $10 with a valid student ID, either on campus or at the Garden box office, beginning the Monday before the semifinals.

CONTACT INFORMATION: Hockey East Association, 591 North Avenue #2, Wakefield, MA 01880. 781-245-2122; www.hockeyeastonline.com.

BOSTON COLLEGE

They've been playing hockey at the Heights since the nineteenth century. The first hockey team at Boston College was sanctioned in the 1890s, and the college's successful squad prompted other local universities to begin clubs as well. The Eagles played their first varsity hockey game in 1918, opening with a win over the vaunted Harvard Radio School.

Today Boston College has one of the premier college hockey programs in the country. The Eagles have appeared in the NCAA Tournament twenty-eight times and participated in twenty-one Frozen Fours, second only to the University of Michigan. BC players have hoisted the Beanpot trophy fourteen times, but Terrier fans of their arch-rival down Commonwealth Avenue like to remind the Eagles that their team has won only half as many as Boston University.

Even when judged by such lofty standards, the past decade has been the golden years for the boys in the gold and maroon. The Eagles qualified for the NCAA Tournament every year except one between 1998 and 2008, and during that span BC made eight Frozen Fours, won six Hockey East championships, and captured national titles in 2001 and 2008.

The Boston Arena (Matthews Arena today) served as the primary home rink for the Eagles before the opening of an on-campus facility in 1958. Today the Eagles play in Conte Forum and skate on a rink named in honor of its legendary coach, John "Snooks" Kelley. In thirty-six years at the Heights, Snooks became the first collegiate hockey coach to accumulate more than five hundred wins. The Eagles have been blessed with a lineage of outstanding coaches, from Kelley to Len Ceglarski to current head coach Jerry York, the most successful active coach in college hockey. The program has turned out great professional players such as Joe Mullen and Brian Leetch, and BC players David Emma and Mike Mottau have won the Hobey Baker Award—college hockey's version of the Heisman Trophy.

The Boston College women don't have quite the same history as the men. The first season for the women on a varsity level was 1994-95, but the Eagles celebrated back-to-back Beanpot wins in 2006 and 2007 and added another in 2009. With women's hockey growing at its current rate, it's surely only a matter of time before BC women's hockey makes some history of its own.

Both the men and women play in the Hockey East conference. The men's schedule usually includes some Midwestern powers early in the season in addition to their slate of conference opponents.

ARENA INFORMATION: Opened in 1988, the Eagles play on campus at the Kelley Rink inside the Conte Forum. The building holds 7,884 fans for hockey. Banners honor Frozen Four and NCAA Tournament appearances along with the team's Beanpot, Hockey East, and three national championship titles. In addition, a banner honoring John "Snooks" Kelley, BC's longtime hockey coach, hangs from the rafters.

Conte Forum is a single seating bowl, but there are two levels along the sidelines. Seats in the lower level of Conte Forum have chairs with backs and spacious legroom. Seats in the upper level of the arena are only padded bleachers. In addition, there are skyboxes high above the goal on the east side of the arena.

Most of the seats in the arena are along the length of the ice. There are only about a dozen rows behind the goals. Trophy cases line the walls of the concourse behind the east goal, while the Varsity Club Hall of Fame, honoring outstanding athletes in all Boston College sports, lines the concourse behind the other goal.

WHEN: The Boston College men's ice hockey regular season runs from October to March.

The women's regular season runs from October to February.

GETTING THERE: Conte Forum is located in the Chestnut Hill section of Newton, about six miles from downtown Boston. If driving to the game, be aware that traffic in the streets around the arena can be very heavy before and after games, so give yourself plenty of time.

From points north and south of Boston, take Route 128 to Exit 24 (Route 30). Proceed east on Route 30 (Commonwealth Avenue) for about five miles to the campus. Enter the campus at the second entrance on the right, at Saint Ignatius Church.

From points west of Boston, take Exit 17 (Newton/Watertown) and take a right at the first set of lights onto Centre Street. Follow Centre Street to the fourth set of lights and turn left onto Commonwealth Avenue. Follow for a mile and a half to the second campus entrance on the right at Saint Ignatius Church. From downtown Boston, take Commonwealth Avenue until the first campus entrance on the left, at Saint Ignatius Church.

Once turning on campus at Saint Ignatius Church, take the next right and follow the road to the available free **parking** lots and Conte Forum. Note that one of the options, the Commonwealth Avenue Garage, can take a while to empty after games. Campus parking lots open to fans ninety minutes before the start of the game. There is also limited on-street parking on Commonwealth Avenue and Beacon Street; it may provide a quicker in and out if you can find an open spot. Fans who have university-issued or Flynn Fund permits may also park in the Beacon Street Garage on the east side of Alumni Stadium. Parking rates may apply in garages during weekday and weeknight women's ice hockey games.

For those taking **public transportation**, several branches of the Green Line stop near the arena. From downtown Boston, take the "B" branch to the end of the line at the Boston College stop, which is about a six minute walk to the arena, or take the "C" branch to the end of the line at Cleveland Circle, which is about a fifteen minute walk. The Reservoir station on the "D" branch is also about a fifteen minute walk, but it's served by the Boston College shuttle bus.

TICKETS: Tickets for Boston College men's hockey games can sell out, particularly against local opponents such as Boston University, Maine, and UNH, and should be purchased in advance. Tickets for individual games range from $10 to $25 for adults, depending on the opponent and the date, and are $10 for youths. Student sections are located behind the goals. There is no charge to attend women's hockey games.

Major donors to the Flynn Fund—which provides money for scholarships, recruiting, facilities, and operating costs for all varsity sports—are given the option to purchase season tickets along the sideboards in the lower level of Conte Forum and receive parking passes. For more information, call 617-552-0772.

Fans can order tickets by phone at 617-552-GOBC, online at www.bceagles.com, or at the ticket office, which is located inside Conte Forum at Gate B. The ticket office is open between 9 AM and 5 PM on weekdays and prior to hockey games. Fans can purchase tickets directly from season-ticket holders through the Ticket Marketplace at www.bceagles.com.

DISABILITY ACCESS: There is wheelchair seating located at center ice on both sides of the arena. The wheelchair seating areas are located at the top of the lower level.

Handicap parking is available adjacent to Conte Forum.

THE SPLURGE: For some extra game day perks, join the Pike's Peak Hockey Club, Boston College hockey's booster group. The club derived its name from the famous mountain in Colorado Springs, where the men's team won the 1948-49 national title. Members of the Pike's Peak Hockey Club can attend an annual skate with the Eagles at Kelley Rink and get autographs as well as attend the season-opening mass and brunch and season-ending banquet. On game day, members and their guests can gather before, during, and after games in the Father Joseph Shea Room. Dinner is served before games, and the club remains open for approximately one hour after the final siren. Membership in the Pike's Peak Hockey Club is $250 for the season.

THE CHEAPSKATE: Boston College often offers special $10 ticket deals during the Christmas break and spring break, when the students have vacated campus. If you want to bring the family to a game and don't care about the opponent, have one of your kids join the Baldwin's Bunch kids' fan club. (More information below.) In addition to other benefits, members receive free tickets for the whole family to a men's hockey game as well as other Boston College athletic events.

SPECTATOR TIPS: There are standing room areas along the concourse behind each of the goals that might provide a better view than seats up in the nosebleeds. Speaking of nosebleeds, watch out for stray pucks. If you have a seat behind a goal, you'll be watching the game through the protective netting.

SCORING AUTOGRAPHS: Access to players in uniform before and after games is limited. Kids might get high-fives from players on the way into and out of the locker room.

FOR THE KIDS: Between periods, there are t-shirt tosses and Baldwin, the Boston College mascot, takes to the ice with the Zamboni and slaps high-fives with kids against the glass. Children under twelve can join the Baldwin's Bunch kids' fan club, which includes free BC gear, free tickets to Eagles sporting events, and invitations to special member events. Membership costs $20 a year. Membership applications are available on the Boston College website at www.bceagles.com.

ARENA CONCESSIONS: In addition to concession stands along the sidelines of the Conte Forum, there are a handful of pushcarts in the corner of the arena that may offer shorter lines. A standard hot dog costs $4, and a 20-ounce bottle of soda costs $3.50. If you need to warm up, the arena sells coffee, hot chocolate, and clam chowder. Concession stands and carts also sell grilled Italian sausages, pulled pork sandwiches, chicken wraps, and Papa Gino's personal pizzas. No alcohol is served at games.

FOOD AND DRINK AROUND THE ARENA: See page 108.

CONTACT INFORMATION: Boston College Men's Ice Hockey, 140 Commonwealth Avenue, Chestnut Hill, MA 02467. 617-552-3028; www.bceagles.com.

Boston College Women's Ice Hockey, 140 Commonwealth Avenue, Chestnut Hill, MA 02467. 617-552-6987; www.bceagles.com.

BOSTON UNIVERSITY

Basketball or football may be the must-see sports at many colleges across the country, but not at Boston University—where men's hockey might as well be the only game in town. Since the Terriers first took to the ice in 1918 against—who else?—Boston College, the men's hockey program at Boston University has been one of the most successful in the country. BU has produced twenty-five Olympic hockey players, including Mike Eruzione, Jim Craig, Jack O'Callahan, and Dave Silk, all of whom were members of the 1980 "miracle on ice." Nearly sixty former Terriers have played in the NHL, and BU players Chris Drury and Matt Gilroy have won the Hobey Baker Award.

The Terriers have captured five national championships: two under legendary coach Jack Kelley and three more in 1978, 1995, and 2009 under current head coach Jack Parker, one of the most successful coaches in college hockey history. In addition, the Terriers have appeared twenty-one times in the Frozen Four.

As impressive as that pedigree is, the Terriers have found even greater success at the Beanpot. Terriers fans like to refer to the Beanpot as the "BU Invitational" for good reason. Through 2009, Boston University had won the Beanpot twenty-nine times, one more title than the other three schools combined. The Terriers have won so many Beanpots that you need a magnifying glass to read the years on the school's Beanpot banner hanging in Agganis Arena—they even had to start a second banner to add to its growing list of titles.

BU played home games at Boston Arena (now Matthews Arena) and Boston Garden until the opening of the intimate Walter Brown Arena on campus in 1971. In 2005 the Terriers outgrew Walter Brown and moved into new digs inside the spacious Agganis Arena. The new arena has all the amenities fans would expect at professional arenas, such as luxury boxes, videoboards, large bathrooms, and numerous concession stands with a wide array of food choices. As an added bonus, the arena is convenient to public transportation and has an underground garage. (And oh yeah, beer is available too.) All of that makes Agganis Arena the most comfortable college hockey venue for fans. However, some old-school Terriers fans don't equate comfort with a great game experience and lament the move from the grittier Walter Brown Arena to what they feel is a more soulless, sterile environment.

One thing that wasn't lost in the move from the old arena is the banner that once hung from the balcony of Walter Brown Arena behind the defending goal. When the Terriers were defending the net, the banner read "GOALIE," with three arrows pointing to the goaltender. When the opposing team defended the same net during the second period, the banner was flipped to reveal "SIEVE." Today the banner hangs from the back of section 108 in Agganis Arena.

Students sit in "the Dog Pound," and if that sounds intense, that's because it is. The Dog Pound is not for the faint of heart; it is the section's duty to make noise, chant, and generally support their Terriers in any way possible. For example, after a big save by the BU goaltender, students bow down with arms extended in homage. Most students wear hockey jerseys, although there are those occasional shirtless fans—none more famous than Sasquatch, a cult hero at BU. Sasquatch will get the crowd going by taking off his shirt and waving it overhead, revealing the hirsute body that has garnered him his well-earned nickname.

Unlike the men's team, the Boston University women are relative newcomers to the varsity level; the 2005-06 season was the first for BU women's hockey in the NCAA's Division I. Prior to that, the women were a club team in existence since 1973. Both the men and women play in the Hockey East conference. The men's schedule usually includes some Midwestern powers early in the season in addition to their slate of conference opponents.

ARENA INFORMATION: The men play their games inside the brand-new Agganis Arena at 925 Commonwealth Avenue. The arena, which opened in 2005, is named in honor of the Golden Greek, former Boston University and Red Sox great Harry Agganis.

The arena's ice sheet has been christened the Jack Parker Rink in honor of the current head coach of the Terriers, who has held his position since 1973 and has amassed the most wins of any college hockey coach at a single institution. Another of BU's legendary coaches, Jack Kelley, is honored with a bust at the top of the west staircase, and murals of the team's greats grace the walls along the staircases. Between periods, fans can pass the time by looking at the photographs of BU players who have made the NHL and members of the BU Hall of Fame. Other displays honor the program's All-Americans and Olympians.

Center ice is occupied by a huge caricature of the team's snarling mascot, Rhett. The Boston Terrier became the university's mascot in 1922 and later received his name from the famous character in *Gone With the Wind* because nobody loves Scarlet (one of the team's colors) more than Rhett. Rhett has left his imprint at center ice. If fans look closely, they'll see little white paw prints dotting the red line.

The capacity of Agganis Arena for hockey is 6,224. All ticketed fans get a seat with upholstered cushions, and the seating is in a single bowl that is about seventeen to eighteen rows deep. The Dog Pound is located behind the goals in sections 107 to 109 and sections 117 to 119. The Terriers attack the goal in front of section 118 twice a game, and the band is located at the top of that section. Sections 101 to 105 are located on the side of the visitors bench, and sections 111 to 115 are located on the side of the Terriers bench. In addition to banners listing the team's league, Beanpot, and national championships, there are ones honoring John Cullen, the program's all-time leading scorer, and Travis Roy, who was tragically paralyzed after crashing into the boards during the first eleven seconds of his premier game for the Terriers.

Those fans who preferred Walter Brown Arena to Agganis Arena can still check it out, as it's home to the women's team. Walter Brown Arena, which has a capacity of just more than thirty-eight hundred people, is located on campus inside the Case Center at 285 Babcock Street. With its low ceilings, Walter Brown has a classic hockey rink's charm. On rare occasions, the women also play inside Agganis Arena.

WHEN: The Boston University men's ice hockey regular season runs from October to March. The women's regular season runs from October to February.

GETTING THERE: Agganis Arena is located about a mile west of Kenmore Square. From north and south of Boston, take Interstate 93 into Boston. Exit onto Storrow Drive and continue to the Kenmore Square exit. At the first set of lights, turn right onto Beacon Street. Bear right at the far end of Kenmore Square onto Commonwealth Avenue. Agganis Arena is approximately one mile up on the right.

From west of Boston, take the Massachusetts Turnpike east to Exit 18 (Brighton/Cambridge). Follow signs to Cambridge and turn right at the second set of lights onto Storrow Drive. Continue on Storrow Drive to the Kenmore Square exit. At the first set of lights, turn right onto Beacon Street. Bear right at the far end of Kenmore Square onto Commonwealth Avenue. Agganis Arena is approximately one mile up on the right.

There is an underground **parking** garage at Agganis Arena and various campus lots within easy walking distance of the arena. The cost of these lots is $10. There is also limited on-street metered parking on Commonwealth Avenue and on some of the side streets around the arena, which could provide a free parking alternative if you're lucky to get a spot. For directions to the Case Center, home of Walter Brown Arena, see page 75.

Consider taking **public transportation** to Agganis Arena, as it is very convenient. Take the "B" branch of the Green Line (with a terminus at Boston College) to either the St. Paul Street or Pleasant Street stops. Both are approximately one block from the arena. In addition, the 57 bus route stops near the arena.

TICKETS: Tickets to Boston University men's hockey games will sell out against top Hockey East rivals such as Boston College, UNH, and Maine, so purchase them in advance. Agganis Arena is a state-of-the art college hockey arena, but the downside is the high ticket prices that come with it. Individual tickets for men's games cost $24 or $26, and season tickets cost $450 ($333 for faculty, staff, and young alumni). Students with Sports Passes from BU can get tickets to the games. Individual tickets for women's games cost $5, and season tickets cost $48. For more information on season tickets, call 617-353-GOBU.

To purchase tickets through Ticketmaster, call 617-931-2000 or go online to www.ticketmaster.com. Tickets may also be purchased at the Agganis Arena ticket office, which is located on the east side of the arena lobby. The ticket office is open Monday through Friday from 10 AM to 5 PM. The ticket office opens two hours before each game. Another ticket option is the Terrier TicketExchange, available through the Ticketmaster website, where season-ticket holders sell unused tickets.

DISABILITY ACCESS: Being a new facility, Agganis Arena offers plenty of wheelchair-accessible and companion seating along the concourse at the top of the seating bowl. Contact the arena ticket office at 617-353-GOBU if you require handicap-accessible and companion seating. The accessible drop-off location is located on the corner of Harry Agganis Way and Commonwealth Avenue. There are two elevators serving the underground parking lot and two providing access from the lobby to the concourse.

THE SPLURGE: Want the VIP treatment? Boston University sells Scarlet Seat VIP packages to men's hockey games for $90. Scarlet seats include some of the best views in the house, a $25 food and beverage card per ticket, and a reserved parking pass in the arena garage for every four tickets purchased. At least two VIP tickets must be purchased.

Agganis Arena also has suites available to rent for individual games. Suites hold between four and twenty-four people and have granite countertops, sinks, a refrigerator, a private server, and theater-style upholstered seating. Call 617-358-7006 for more information on both options.

THE CHEAPSKATE: While the Terriers have the highest college hockey ticket prices in Boston, occasionally tickets are discounted for games during holiday breaks in the university calendar. Sign up for the free Advantage Club email on the Agganis Arena website at www.

agganisarena.com. It includes information on special ticket deals.

SPECTATOR TIPS: Although many fans still wait in long lines at other restrooms, there are enormous men's and women's restrooms behind sections 116 and 120 on the north side of the arena. Skip the lines and head to the spacious restrooms on the north side. If you want to stretch your legs during the game, there's a standing room section overlooking the ice behind section 118. Be aware that some of the rows in Agganis Arena are extremely long, so those with seats in the middle will not have easy access in and out during play. Note that if you have a seat behind a goal, you'll be watching the game through the protective netting.

SCORING AUTOGRAPHS: Access to players in uniform before and after games is limited.

FOR THE KIDS: Boston University doesn't offer any ticket discounts for children, but kids may enjoy cheering on someone their own size. The little kids who take to the ice between periods for a quick game truly look like mites. Rhett comes out in his referee jersey to officiate the game.

ARENA CONCESSIONS: Without a doubt, Agganis Arena offers the best concession choices of any college hockey arena in Boston, and it rivals some of the professional teams' facilities. The arena has six concession stands and several specialty pushcarts selling items such as ice cream and freshly brewed coffee.

Concession stands sell the standard arena fare, such as Nathan's hot dogs ($3.50), pretzels, and soda, but there are some more unusual choices as well, such as onion straws, deli sandwiches, sweet potato fries, buffalo chicken tenders, loaded baked potatoes, and even crab cake sliders. The pizza concession stand on the south side of the arena sells cheese and pepperoni pizza by the slice, chicken parmesan and meatball calzones, and Greek and Caesar salads. The warm cookies are a treat.

What makes Agganis Arena unique among local college rinks is that it sells beer and wine. (Alcohol sales conclude after the second

★ The Legend of Harry Agganis

Long before Bo Jackson and Deion Sanders, Harry Agganis was a two-sport star at football and baseball. Crowds of up to twenty thousand fans came to watch him take the gridiron at Lynn Classical. He passed up a chance to go to Notre Dame to remain near his widowed mother and played both football and baseball at BU. As if that wasn't enough, Agganis was an All-American footballer. He played quarterback, defensive back, and kicker.

Known as the Golden Greek, Agganis signed with the Red Sox and he continued to finish his collegiate degree at BU. On graduation day in 1954, Agganis demonstrated his tremendous multi-tasking skills by hitting a two-run home run to clinch the game for the Red Sox and then rushing down Commonwealth Avenue to get his diploma at Braves Field. His premature death at the age of twenty-six in 1955 was front-page news around the world, and fifty thousand mourners watched the funeral procession.

Today fans file into the Agganis Arena under the watchful eye of the building's namesake. A statue in front of the arena depicts the Golden Greek ready to throw a long pass down the field. Inside the arena, a banner hangs from the rafters with his number 33, and murals, magazine covers, and photographs—including one of the Golden Greek's memorable graduation—featuring Agganis adorn the walls of the arena. In an unfortunate irony, Boston University no longer fields varsity football or baseball teams.

intermission.) Domestic draft beers such as Budweiser, Bud Light, and Miller Lite cost $6. Premium beer choices such as Sam Adams, Harpoon IPA, and Anchor Steam cost a little more.

FOOD AND DRINK AROUND THE ARENA: There are a number of restaurants and bars along Commonwealth Avenue in easy walking distance of Agganis Arena and the Case Center. T's Pub, a popular pre- and postgame spot for BU fans, has been reborn as ***973 Commonwealth*** (973 Commonwealth Avenue, 617-254-0807). The bar and restaurant has numerous televisions tuned into games, including a huge wall-sized screen that is one of the biggest in Boston. For quick bites, there are ***T Anthony's*** (1016 Commonwealth Avenue, 617-734-7708), which serves pizza and sandwiches, and ***Qdoba Mexican Grill*** (961 Commonwealth Avenue, 617-779-9800, www.qdoba.com). For a different pace, try the Thai dishes at the ***Brown Sugar Café*** (1033 Commonwealth Avenue, 617-787-4242, www.brownsugarcafe.com).

There are a couple of choices east of Agganis Arena as well. ***Sunset Cantina*** (916 Commonwealth Avenue, 617-731-8646, www.allstonsfinest.com) features thirty-eight beers on tap and sixty-nine tequilas in addition to pub grub. Closer to Kenmore Square is BU students' favorite subterranean watering hole, the ***Dugout Café*** (722 Commonwealth Avenue, 617-247-8656). The Dugout has been called the campus study hall. Ted Williams hoisted some pints here, and legend has it that the Brink's robbery was hatched inside the dark bar.

CONTACT INFORMATION: Boston University Men's Ice Hockey, 285 Babcock Street, Boston, MA 02215. 617-353-4639; www.goterriers.com.

Boston University Women's Ice Hockey, 285 Babcock Street, Boston, MA 02215. 617-358-3880; www.goterriers.com.

HARVARD

Unlike its Beanpot brethren, Harvard competes in the ECAC hockey conference. While it plays occasional home games against local institutions, most of the teams on the Harvard schedule are ECAC opponents, which include some Ivy League schools such as Cornell and Yale along with other universities in upstate New York such as RPI and Saint Lawrence.

Harvard men have been playing hockey for more than a century, and the university has had an important role in the development of the game. In terms of innovation, it was at Harvard that the shift change was first tried in 1923. The varsity team has accumulated more than twelve hundred victories, and is only the second program in college hockey to hit the 1,000-win mark. If that's not proof enough of their longevity, the rivalry between Harvard and Brown is the oldest continuing hockey series in the country.

The Harvard men have won eight ECAC hockey championships, twenty-one Ivy League titles, and ten Beanpots. The Crimson have appeared more than twenty times in the NCAA Tournament and captured the national championship in 1989. The Harvard men have had considerable success in recent years, appearing in the NCAA Tournament each year between 2002 and 2006. The Crimson have produced numerous Olympians, NHL stars, and three Hobey Baker Award winners: Lane MacDonald and brothers Mark and Scott Fusco.

Before moving into their current home at the Bright Hockey Center, the Crimson played at many different venues around Boston, both indoors and out. Their first intercollegiate hockey game in 1898 was played against Brown at Franklin Field in Dorchester. After Harvard Stadium opened in 1903, it hosted the Crimson hockey team as well as the football team. Two hockey rinks were constructed inside Harvard Stadium, bleachers were moved to the side of the rinks, and admission was charged to some of the more important tilts. Harvard also played home games in front of thousands of fans at Boston Arena (Matthews Arena today) and Boston Garden. Indeed, fourteen thousand fans filled Boston Garden in 1930 to watch Harvard take on Yale in the final tilt of a three-game series to decide the intercollegiate title. Unfortunately, due to Boston's blue laws the game was called at midnight with the score tied at two. These arch-rivals were forced to split the championship.

The Harvard women have been playing varsity hockey since 1978 and are one of the top women's hockey programs in the country. Since the program's inception, Harvard has chalked up nearly five hundred wins along with nine ECAC hockey championships, eight Ivy League titles, and one national championship in 1999. The Crimson are perennial participants in the NCAA Tournament and have captured local bragging rights in recent years by winning twelve Beanpot titles, including seven in a row between 1999 and 2005. Numerous Olympians have passed through the gates of Harvard, and Crimson players have dominated the ranks of the winners of the Patty Kazmaier Award, which is given to the best women's collegiate player in the country. Crimson women took home the award six times in its first eleven years of existence.

ARENA INFORMATION: The Harvard men and women both play home games at the Bright Hockey Center, located in the campus athletic complex on North Harvard Street in Allston. The 2,776-seat rink has standing-room capacity for another six hundred fans. The arena—named after former Harvard hockey player Alec Bright, a 1919 graduate—has the smallest capacity of any of Boston's Division I hockey arenas. The Bright Hockey Center dates back to 1956, but a massive renovation in 1979 created the facility seen today. The arena is very squat. Just eight rows surround most of the ice sheet, although there are a few more in the corner, so every seat is close to the action. The wooden ceiling above the ice looks like it came right out of the pages of *Architectural Digest*, and the pattern of asterisk-shaped lights adds another decorative flair. A new videoboard, which shows game action and replays, was installed in the arena in 2008.

Trophy cases and photographs of the program's All-Americans hang in the front of the arena. Draped from the ceiling are large banners celebrating the men's and women's national championships and ECAC, Ivy League, and Beanpot titles. NCAA Tournament and Frozen Four appearances are also commemorated for both squads. Additional banners celebrate the Harvard winners of the Hobey Baker and Patty Kazmaier awards. A crimson 4—the retired number of former player, hockey coach, and athletic director Bill Cleary—is displayed. Cleary's number is the only one in any of the university's forty-one varsity sports to ever be taken out of circulation.

Sections 1 through 8 of the Bright Hockey Center are behind the Harvard bench; opposing fans generally sit in sections 14 through 20 behind their team's bench. The

A Harvard University player hoists the Beanpot trophy at Boston Garden.
Courtesy Boston Public Library, Special Collections.

pep band sits in section 10, and sections 11 and 12 are student seating behind one goal. Sections 22 through 24 are behind the other goal and nearest the concession stands. All arena seats are on benches with seat backs. Front-row seats provide a unique perspective since they are slightly elevated. The boards come up to the knees of spectators, so fans are at eye level with the players. Try not to duck when the puck makes a beeline for your nose.

WHEN: The Harvard hockey regular season for the men and women usually runs from late October to early March. Most home games are played on Friday and Saturday nights.

GETTING THERE: The Bright Hockey Center is about four miles from downtown Boston. To get to the arena, take the Mass Pike to the Brighton/Cambridge exit (Exit 18 eastbound and Exit 20 westbound). After paying the toll, bear left at the fork toward Allston. Turn right at the second set of lights onto North Harvard Street. The arena is adjacent to Harvard Stadium, approximately one mile ahead on the left.

There is limited on-street **parking** on North Harvard Street. Parking is available next to the arena for $10; enter Gate 6 on the south side of Harvard Stadium. Parking is also available across the street for $5 at the Harvard Business School lot, about a five minute walk from the arena.

The Bright Hockey Center is also accessible by **public transportation**. By subway, take the Red Line to the Harvard station. It's about a ten minute walk from Harvard Square down JFK Street and across the

Charles River to the arena. Several MBTA bus lines also stop at Harvard Square, and bus routes 66 and 86 stop on North Harvard Street outside the athletic complex.

TICKETS: Game day tickets are available for most men's games, although tickets for matchups against local colleges and rival Cornell can sell out and should be purchased in advance. Tickets for men's games are $15–$18 for adults and $8–$10 for youth (ages three to fourteen) depending on the opponent. Tickets are $8 for Harvard graduate students and free for undergraduates.

Season tickets are available for $182 with discounts for faculty, staff, young alumni, graduate students, and Allston-Brighton residents. Season-ticket holders receive guaranteed access to Beanpot tickets and priority to purchase additional tickets to all regular season and playoff games.

Tickets for women's games are $8 for adults and $4 for youth and students. Season tickets for women's games are $55 with discounts for faculty, staff, young alumni, graduate students, and Allston-Brighton residents.

To purchase tickets, phone 877-GO-HARVARD, go online to www.gocrimson.com, or visit the ticket office (Monday–Friday, 9 AM–5 PM) in the Murr Center at 65 North Harvard Street. Game day ticket sales are at the window in front of Bright Hockey Center. It's important to note that only cash or checks are accepted at the arena's ticket window on game days; credit cards are not accepted.

DISABILITY ACCESS: Handicap seating is available at the top of the concourse behind sections 2 and 20 near the arena entrances.

THE SPLURGE: Passes for parking and admission to the Blue Line Room may be obtained with a $1,000 gift to any Friends of Harvard Athletics group. The Blue Line Room offers alcoholic and non-alcoholic drinks and light refreshments during the game, but it doesn't have a view of the ice. Call 617-495-3535 for more information.

THE CHEAPSKATE: Allston-Brighton residents receive discounts on both men's and women's season tickets.

SPECTATOR TIPS: The bathrooms in the Bright Hockey Arena are tighter quarters than a penalty box, so expect long lines between periods. The rink can be particularly cold, so be prepared. Game programs are handed out for free at all games. If you have a seat behind a goal, you'll be watching the game through the protective netting.

SCORING AUTOGRAPHS: Access to players in uniform before and after games is limited.

FOR THE KIDS: The university sponsors the Crimson Kids Club for both men's and women's hockey. Members receive discounted season tickets, a membership card, t-shirt, monthly newsletters, and exclusive invites to pizza parties and autograph sessions with Harvard athletes. The club is for kids in eighth grade and below and costs $52 for men's hockey and $33 for women's hockey. Membership applications are available on the Harvard Athletics website or email kidsclub@fas.harvard.edu for more information. There are no specific activities for kids at games, but Harvard hockey offers a family-friendly environment.

ARENA CONCESSIONS: The Bright Hockey Center has two concession stands behind the goal near the front entrance. The self-service concession stand is the quicker option and offers most of the same items as the regular concession stand. Pizza, cheeseburgers, Italian sausages, candy, churros, pretzels, and hot dogs ($3) are on sale. Hot chocolate and coffee are popular in the cold rink, and the hot cookies are a special treat. Bottles of water and soda are available; small and large fountain sodas are too. No alcohol is sold at games.

FOOD AND DRINK AROUND THE ARENA: See page 114.

CONTACT INFORMATION: Harvard University Men's Ice Hockey, Murr Center, 65 North Harvard Street, Boston, MA 02163. 617-495-2609; www.gocrimson.com.

Harvard University Women's Ice Hockey, Murr Center, 65 North Harvard Street, Boston, MA 02163. 617-495-2609; www.gocrimson.com.

NORTHEASTERN

If you're one of those Bruins fans that laments the passing of the old Boston Garden, longing for its great sightlines, gritty interior, and intimate atmosphere, stop pining and head to a Northeastern hockey game at Matthews Arena. Stepping from the arena's magnificent Victorian lobby into the ice rink, you may feel as if you've been transported back in time to a miniaturized Boston Garden. There's the similar overhanging balcony, the same poles, the same low headroom on the lower level, the same fantastic views, the same cramped bathrooms, and the same staircases leading to the bowels of the building.

Matthews Arena is as old-school as hockey gets in Boston. It couldn't be any different from some of today's modern rinks. There is no videoboard, no luxury suites, no executive chef, no cup holders, and no annoying kiss cam.

Formerly known as Boston Arena, the building opened in 1910 and is the oldest artificial ice arena in the world. Think about it: Fenway Park opened its doors two years *after* Matthews Arena. Not only does the arena interior have a similar look to the old Boston Garden, but it also hosted the inaugural games for both the Bruins and the Celtics. In addition, it was the cradle of high school and college hockey in the Hub. The Beanpot, Boston College, Boston University, Harvard, MIT, Tufts, and Wentworth Institute of Technology have all called the arena home at one time.

Since 1929 the arena has been the home of Northeastern hockey as well. The Huskies have not had as much success as their Beanpot brothers over the years. The Huntington Hounds have made only four appearances in the NCAA Tournament, and they have captured only four Beanpots. The Huskies have been revitalized in recent years, however, achieving rankings in the top five in the country.

No matter what their record, however, Northeastern's student section, "the DogHouse," can make life very uncomfortable for visiting teams. In the intimate confines of Matthews Arena, denizens of the DogHouse can feel like a pack of canines going for the opponent's jugular. The pep band and student section, dressed in black t-shirts and Northeastern hockey jerseys, is headquartered in sections 43 to 45 in the balcony, hovering over the shoulder of the visiting team's goalie just to give him a little extra to worry about. If the Huskies score while he has the misfortune to be tending the net below the DogHouse, the visiting goalie can look up and see hundreds of fingers pointing at him as chants of "Sieve!" rain down from the balcony just feet away. (Talk about a scolding!) After a Huskies player checks an opponent, the DogHouse is also known to start singing the Village People hit "Macho Man."

The Northeastern women have had more luck than their male counterparts at the

Beanpot. Since their inception as a varsity sport in 1980, the women have won the Beanpot fourteen times. The women have also captured three ECAC crowns and produced six Olympians and one winner of the Patty Kazmaier Award, Brooke Whitney. The men and women both compete in the Hockey East conference.

ARENA INFORMATION: The Northeastern men's and women's hockey teams play at Matthews Arena, located on the university campus at 238 St. Botolph Street. Matthews Arena has a capacity of fifty-nine hundred people and includes a lower level and an overhanging balcony, which has fantastic sightlines for hockey. For more information on Matthews Arena, see page 80.

WHEN: The Northeastern men's ice hockey regular season runs from October to March. The women's regular season runs from October to February.

GETTING THERE: See page 82.

TICKETS: Even in down years, large crowds turn out for Northeastern men's hockey, and games against Hockey East rivals and national powers can sell out on occasion. Tickets for men's games cost $16 for adults and $12 for youths. Season tickets for the lower level of Matthews Arena cost $175 for adults and $100 for youths while balcony seats cost $140 for adults and $80 for youths. Season-ticket holders receive priority access to purchase Beanpot and Hockey East Championship tickets.

The Northeastern men's hockey team huddles up.

Tickets for women's games cost $5 for adults and $3 for youths. Season tickets for the women's team cost $40 for adults and $25 for youths.

Northeastern sells season tickets for families to both the men's and women's hockey teams. A family pack includes tickets for two adults and two youths. A family pack to men's games costs $400 for the lower level and $320 for the balcony, while a family pack for the women's games costs $90.

Northeastern also sells a Husky MVP Pass, which includes admission to all football, men's and women's hockey, and men's and women's basketball regular-season home games. The cost is $275 for adults, $125 for youth, and $550 for families.

Game day tickets can be purchased at the ticket windows at Matthews Arena. To purchase advance tickets, call the Northeastern University ticket office at 617-373-4700, go online to www.gonu.com/tickets, or visit the ticket office at Ell Hall. The ticket office is open from noon to 6 PM on Monday, Tuesday, Thursday, and Friday and from noon to 8 PM on Wednesday.

DISABILITY ACCESS: See page 82.

THE SPLURGE: Donors who give at least $500 to the Husky Athletics Club receive the opportunity to purchase Beanpot tickets, invites to receptions with athletic directors and coaches, and access to the Varsity Club, which offers a theater-style viewing box of the rink. Call 617-373-2582 or visit www.gonu.com/huskyathleticsclub for more information.

THE CHEAPSKATE: Cheapskates should definitely take public transportation to Matthews Arena. On-street parking is limited near the arena, and some local garages charge exorbitant prices.

SPECTATOR TIPS: If you have a seat behind a goal, be aware that you'll be watching the game through the protective netting.

SCORING AUTOGRAPHS: Access to players in uniform before and after games is limited.

FOR THE KIDS: There are no specific activities for kids at games.

ARENA CONCESSIONS: See page 83.

FOOD AND DRINK AROUND THE ARENA: See page 83.

CONTACT INFORMATION: Northeastern University Men's Ice Hockey, Matthews Arena Annex, 238 St. Botolph Street, Boston, MA 02115. 617-373-2631; www.gonu.com/mhockey.

Northeastern University Women's Ice Hockey, Matthews Arena Annex, 238 St. Botolph Street, Boston, MA 02115. 617-373-2631; www.gonu.com/whockey.

SUPER EIGHT HIGH SCHOOL HOCKEY

Hockey is one of the most popular varsity sports at high schools across Massachusetts, and the pinnacle of schoolboy hockey in the state is the Division IA Boys Ice Hockey Championship, also known as the Super Eight tournament. The tournament, which started in 1991, pits the eight best Division I teams against each other in a round-robin tournament. The field is divided into two brackets of four teams. Each team plays three games against the teams in their bracket, and the top two teams in each bracket advance to the semifinals, with the winners of those games meeting up at the TD Garden for the state championship.

Since 2001 the tournament field has actually expanded to ten teams with the bottom four teams skating in play-in games. The two losers of the play-in games return to the field of the Division I tournament, which is a level below Division IA.

Both public and private schools compete in the Super Eight, but it wasn't until the eighteenth year of the tournament that a public high school, Reading High, captured the championship. A major reason for the public-school drought is that since its inception, the Super Eight tourney has been dominated by two teams from Boston: Catholic Memorial and its bitter rival Boston College High School. CM won twelve of the first eighteen Super Eight tournaments with BC High taking four others. These two Catholic school rivals from West Roxbury and Dorchester frequently square off in the Super Eight, oftentimes in the championship game. The quality of play and the intensity of the fans—"God's on our side" is one of the chants from the CM faithful—is little seen in Massachusetts high school hockey.

Play-in, round-robin, and semifinals games are held at various locations around Massachusetts, including the DCU Center in Worcester, the Tsongas Arena in Lowell, the Chelmsford Forum in Billerica, and the Bright Hockey Center in Cambridge. Tickets are available at the arena box offices. Most games are held as part of doubleheaders, and ticket prices are around $12. In addition to the Super Eight, the Massachusetts Interscholastic Athletic Association hosts tournaments for boys and girls in Divisions I and II and for boys in Division III.

CONTACT INFORMATION: Massachusetts Interscholastic Athletic Association, 33 Forge Parkway, Franklin, MA 02038. 508-541-7997; www.miaa.net.

BEYOND BOSTON

Providence Bruins

If you want to scout out the Bruins' stars of tomorrow, head fifty miles south of Boston to Providence, Rhode Island. Since 1992 the Rhode Island state capital has been home to the Providence Bruins, Boston's American Hockey League (AHL) affiliate. The P-Bruins sport black-and-gold uniforms that are nearly identical to the parent club, and even the team's spoked logo looks familiar, with only the "B" changed to a "P."

The names of the new draft picks and rising stars on the Providence roster may not be as familiar as the uniforms, but some players may be recognizable from previous stints with the parent club. On occasion, Boston Bruins stars rehabbing from injury may also take the ice with the minor league squad.

The Baby Bs play between October and April in the 11,000-seat Dunkin' Donuts Center. Many of Providence's games are held on Friday night and Sunday afternoon, which is a family-friendly starting time. Tickets cost $25 for the lower level of the arena and $18 for the upper level. Select games during the season are designated as family games with tickets between $16 and $20 that include one hot dog and one soda. Tickets can be purchased online at www.providencebruins.com, by phone through Ticketmaster at 401-331-2211, and in person at the Dunkin' Donuts Center box office.

CONTACT INFORMATION: Providence Bruins, Dunkin' Donuts Center, One La Salle Square, Providence, RI 02903. 401-273-5000; www.providencebruins.com.

Lowell Devils

The Lowell Devils are the AHL affiliate of the New Jersey Devils. Lowell takes to the ice between October and April at the 6,500-seat Tsongas Arena, thirty miles north of Boston. The Devils play many home games on weekends throughout the season and provide a family-friendly hockey option. The team has a Kids Zone with face painting, Xbox 360 games, and inflatable whiffle ball and skeeball games. Team autograph sessions are held after a handful of games throughout the year, and if you go to a game on Sunday afternoon, bring your skates. The team opens up the ice for postgame skates after Sunday games.

Tickets are $19 for adults, $15 for military personnel and students, and $11 for children and seniors. Tickets can be purchased by calling the Devils at 978-458-PUCK or by visiting the Tsongas Arena box office. Tickets are also available through Ticketmaster by phone at 617-931-2000 or online at www.ticketmaster.com.

CONTACT INFORMATION: Lowell Devils, Tsongas Arena, 300 Martin Luther King Jr. Way, Lowell, MA 01852. 978-458-PUCK; www.lowelldevilshockey.com.

Worcester Sharks

The Worcester Sharks are the AHL affiliate of the San Jose Sharks. While three thousand miles separate Worcester from its parent club, the good news for Boston sports fans is the city is only forty-five miles west of the Hub. The Sharks skate from October to April at the DCU Center, which has a capacity of nearly fifteen thousand. The Sharks play many games on the weekend, including 4 PM games on Sunday afternoons. If you're looking to collect some signatures, Sharks players are available for autographs in the arena lobby during the second intermission of Saturday night games.

Tickets are $17.25 for the lower level and $14.25 for the upper level. Tickets for children and seniors are $10.75. Tickets can be purchased by calling the Sharks at 508-929-0500 or by visiting the DCU Center box office. Tickets are also available through Ticketmaster by phone at 617-931-2000 or online at www.ticketmaster.com.

CONTACT INFORMATION: Worcester Sharks, DCU Center, 50 Foster Street, Worcester, MA 01608. 508-929-0500; www.sharksahl.com.

★ Singing the National Anthem

Want to take to the field, hardwood, and the ice along with your sporting heroes? Well, unless you magically develop some mad athletic skills, your best bet may be to work on your vocals. The Sox, Bruins, and Celtics have open calls for singers to perform the national anthem before games. You won't make millions like the players, but you'll have a full house giving you their rapt attention. Here's how you can apply to sing "The Star-Spangled Banner" with three local teams:

Red Sox: Send biographical information and a CD of you or your group performing the anthem a cappella in ninety seconds or less. Put your name and phone number on the CD itself and mail to Boston Red Sox, Attn: Anthem, Four Yawkey Way, Boston, MA 02215.

Bruins: Send a musical resume and an example of a singing performance on tape, CD, or video to Attn: National Anthem Application, Boston Bruins, 100 Legends Way, Boston, MA 02114.

Celtics: Forward a musical resume, current photograph, and tape or CD of your performance of the national anthem to the Boston Celtics, Attn: National Anthem Request, 226 Causeway Street, Fourth Floor, Boston, MA 02114.

SOCCER

SOCCER LOVERS ARE AMONG the most passionate and fervent fans in the world, and like many Boston sports fans, they treat their chosen sport like a religion. In fact, it is telling that the 2005 movie *Fever Pitch*, starring Jimmy Fallon as an obsessed Red Sox fan, is actually adapted from British author Nick Hornby's novel about an obsessed soccer fan.

For better or worse, soccer has never gained the same foothold in the United States as it has in most parts of the world, but Boston is one of the stronger American markets for the sport: the city has hosted World Cup and international matches. Additionally, the city boasts two major professional soccer teams.

That said, soccer hasn't been as recent an addition to the Boston sporting scene as some might think. In fact, there are claims that Boston's 1860s Oneida Football Club, the first organized team to play any kind of football in the United States, was the country's first soccer team too. It is a debatable claim, however, as official rules of soccer didn't actually exist at that time, and the Oneida Football Club played a form of football that had elements of soccer as well as rugby and American football in it.

Professional soccer was played in Boston as early as 1894, when the Boston Beaneaters played a handful of games in the South End Grounds. The league was formed by the owners of the Boston Braves baseball team, who were trying to put their dormant stadiums to better use in the off-season. While that league was short lived, industrial league teams—composed of blue-collar players such as shipyard workers and bricklayers—sprung up across New England, with several of them capturing national championships. Mill towns became the hubs for such soccer teams, as their ranks were filled with immigrants seeking work in the region's textile industry.

Soccer flourished as a spectator sport during the 1920s. Throughout the Roaring Twenties, the American Soccer League was the nation's second most popular sports league, just behind Major League Baseball. Many of the league's teams were owned by major industrial corporations, such as Bethlehem Steel, and their squads were made up of players from the British Isles who had immigrated to the United States in the aftermath of World War I. The Boston Wonder Workers, who played their games at the South End Grounds until the old ballyard shut its doors in 1929, was one of the league's elite teams; they captured the title in 1928. The Wonder Workers were considered to be one of the top soccer teams in the Americas and were prestigious enough to take on the Uruguayan national team and Scottish powers Glasgow Rangers and Glasgow Celtic.

Other teams in the American Soccer League were based in Fall River, New Bedford, and Andover, Massachusetts. The Fall River Marksmen were the league's version of the Boston Celtics, capturing seven of the league's fifteen titles before it collapsed with the onset of the Great Depression in 1932. The Marksmen even held the Glasgow Rangers to a scoreless tie in 1928 in front of more than fifteen thousand hometown fans.

Today, Boston sports fans may not be able to think of Fenway Park as anything other than a baseball diamond, but at one time the stadium also hosted soccer matches. In 1931, eight thousand fans came to Fenway to watch the New York Yankees of the American Soccer League defeat Glasgow Celtic. (Incidentally, Johnny Reder, the Yankees goalkeeper that day, returned to Fenway the following year to take the field with the Red Sox.) Soccer returned to Fenway in 1968, when the ballpark served as the home of the Boston Beacons, charter members of the North American Soccer League (NASL).

Professional teams Boston Beacons and Houston Stars battle at Fenway Park, 1968.
Courtesy Boston Public Library, Print Department.

The Beacons folded after just one season, but the NASL returned to Boston in the 1970s with the Boston Minutemen and then the New England Tea Men, who played at various venues around the city, including Nickerson Field, Alumni Stadium, and Foxboro Stadium.

Foxboro Stadium was a popular venue for the U.S. national soccer teams, who enjoyed considerable success on the stadium's pitch and drew sizable crowds. Foxboro Stadium garnered worldwide attention when it hosted matches in the 1994 World Cup and the 1999 Women's World Cup. Gillette Stadium continues to be New England's premier soccer venue. It hosted the Women's World Cup in 2003; friendlies between premier European clubs such as FC Barcelona, Juventus, Chelsea, and AC Milan; and international matchups such as a 2007 match between Brazil and Mexico that drew 67,684 fans, the largest-recorded soccer crowd in New England.

The real impetus to revive professional soccer in North America, however, can be pinpointed to the 1994 World Cup. By 1996, Major League Soccer was born and among the initial teams was the **New England Revolution**, which became Boston's newest addition to the major professional sports scene.

Women's soccer also received a tremendous boost after the American women captured the 1999 Women's World Cup. Unfortunately, a short-lived women's soccer league, which included a franchise in Boston, folded after three seasons. In 2009, however, a new women's soccer league was launched, and the **Boston Breakers** have been revived. Another local women's team, the **Boston Renegades** (85 Central Street, Suite 204, Waltham, MA 02453. 781-891-6900; www.mpsbr.com), plays on a lower level in the W-League.

In addition to the pros, there's plenty of collegiate soccer action around Boston. College soccer in the Boston area has a rich history, starting with the first intercollegiate soccer game in the United States, played in 1905 between Harvard and Haverford at Soldiers Field. Boston College, Boston University, Harvard, and Northeastern all field men's and women's squads.

While there's plenty of school spirit at work during collegiate matches, Boston's most passionate soccer fans can generally be found in the city's diverse tapestry of ethnic neighborhoods. In many of these enclaves, immigrants to Boston have brought their passion for the "beautiful game" with them to American shores. During the World Cup and other major international competitions, these neighborhoods come alive with the sounds of flag-waving soccer fans supporting their homeland squads. It's a lot of fun to get in the spirit and catch an Italy game in the North End or a Brazil game in Allston.

You don't need to wait for the World Cup to come around to catch a match though. Each week ex-pats and local soccer fans gather in bars, cafés, and restaurants across the city to watch their favorite teams from countries around the world. If you're willing to get up early on the weekends, it's a great way to get your kicks.

NEW ENGLAND REVOLUTION

The New England Revolution are one of the charter members of Major League Soccer (MLS). Since the first Revolution game in 1996, the team has developed a loyal core of followers and has become a regular fixture in the playoffs.

The Revolution share Gillette Stadium with the New England Patriots, but the experience of game day couldn't be more different. Besides the price point, the family-friendly atmosphere, and the sport itself, the biggest difference between Revolution and Patriots games at Gillette Stadium is that seating is usually limited to half of the lower bowl. That can make decent-sized crowds still seem a little sparse. On the plus side, fewer fans means no crazy backups on U.S. 1 getting in and out of games.

The Kraft family owns both the Revs and the Pats, and the stadium owners do their best to make the Revs feel that Gillette is as much their home as the Pats. The teams' nicknames both play into the region's rich

The New England Revolution vs. the Houston Dynamo.

history in the American Revolution. The End Zone Militia, those guys dressed in tricorn hats and colonial garb who fire their muskets in a salute after every Patriots score, do the same at Revolution matches. The Patriots' championship banners are all rolled up and out-of-sight, the goal posts are gone, and the Patriots' name is taken off the pitch. But the sheer size of the stadium is a constant reminder that the Revolution are just using the football team's home when they are away.

To rectify this, there has been some discussion about building a soccer-only stadium with about twenty thousand seats in a location closer to the city, such as in Somerville. A smaller stadium in a new location would greatly improve the game day atmosphere and allow supporters to take public transportation to games.

The Revolution typically average about sixteen thousand fans per match. The team draws its biggest crowds for doubleheaders that include either international teams or popular club teams from around the world. The Los Angeles Galaxy and superstar David Beckham are another big attraction, drawing crowds approaching forty thousand.

If they finish high in the MLS standings the previous year, the Revolution play additional home games as part of the SuperLiga (a competition with teams from Mexico's Primera Division); the CONCACAF Champions League (an international club championship for teams in North America, Central America, and the Caribbean); and the U.S. Open Cup (an open tournament of amateur and professional teams that dates back nearly a hundred years). These postseason games supplement the fifteen MLS home games each year.

For a real die-hard experience, sit with the Midnight Riders in the Fort.

The Revolution did not achieve much success on the field in their early years, but they captured four conference titles between 2002 and 2007. Additionally, the Revolution won the U.S. Open Cup in 2007 and the SuperLiga in 2008. Despite reaching four finals of the MLS Cup, including the 2002 game in Gillette Stadium that drew more than sixty thousand fans, so far a title has proved elusive.

The Revolution have a core group of die-hard fans, including two big groups—the Midnight Riders and the Rev Army. These supporters tailgate before home games, travel to some road games with the Revolution, discuss the team in online forums, and have a voice with Revolution management about the game day experience and team.

Members of the Midnight Riders have their own parking lot at the stadium for tailgating and receive parking passes to gain entrance. In addition, Midnight Riders receive a membership card, discounts on bus trips to Revolution road games, and can participate in a members-only chat session with the coach. For membership information, visit www.midnightriders.com.

Many members of the Midnight Riders and the Rev Army populate "the Fort"—sections 142 and 143 behind the goal in the north end zone. The denizens of the Fort spend the game exuberantly cheering on the Revs—some pound drums; others wave flags. The view from the Fort may not be the best, but it's certainly the place to be if you want to be immersed in vocal and enthusiastic fans.

STADIUM INFORMATION: If you want to impress your buddies with some obscure Boston sports trivia, ask them who scored the first points in the history of Gillette Stadium. Many might guess Tom Brady, Kevin Faulk, or Troy Brown, but the correct answer is Taylor Twellman of the Revolution. While Gillette Stadium is best known as the home of the Patriots, it was the Revolution who opened the stadium on May 11, 2002, against the Dallas Burn.

The Revolution are following in the footsteps of the NASL's Boston Minutemen and the New England Tea Men, each of whom played in Foxborough. One of the former Minutemen, Portuguese great Eusebio, is honored in the stadium's picnic area with a statue that was commissioned by the soccer superstar's local fans. For more information on Gillette Stadium, see page 93.

WHEN: The New England Revolution regular season runs from late March or early April through October.

GETTING THERE: Foxborough is thirty miles south of Boston. There is no public transportation to Gillette Stadium for Revolution games, so driving to the game is the only option. With capacity for Revolution games one-third of that for Patriots games, fans won't encounter the same volume of traffic getting to Gillette Stadium.

From Boston and points north, take U.S. 1 south (Exit 9 off Interstate 95). Gillette Stadium is three miles from the exit off Interstate 95. From points south, take U.S. 1 north (Exit 14A off Interstate 495). Gillette Stadium is four miles from the exit off Interstate 495.

For stand-alone Revolution matches **parking** is free. (Yes, Patriots fans—*free*.) Season-ticket holders with VIP East parking passes should enter at the P1 entrance. Season-ticket holders with VIP West parking passes should enter at the P8 entrance. Tailgating is not permitted on the stadium side of U.S. 1 except in season-ticket holder lots and parking-pass holder lots. If you want to tailgate but you aren't a season-ticket holder and don't have a parking pass, park in the P10 lot across the street from the stadium. Parking lots open two hours prior to kickoff.

TICKETS: The Revolution only sell tickets to half of the lower bowl of Gillette Stadium: behind the goal in the north end zone and behind the benches on the sideline. In addition, the team sells tickets to the Fidelity Investment Clubhouse on the east side of the stadium.

The Revs sell tickets in three categories:

Category 1 ($40) seats are in the middle of the pitch in sections 107 through 112.

Category 2 ($30) seats are toward the corners of the pitch in sections 104 through 106 and sections 113 through 115.

Category 3 ($20) seats include reserved seating in the corners of the pitch in sections 101 through 103 and sections 116, 117, and 141. Category 3 seats also include general admission seating in sections 118 through 120 behind the goal on the south side of the stadium and sections 142 and 143 behind the goal on the north side. (Note that fans in the Fort in sections 142 and 143 will stand throughout the game.)

Prices may vary for special matches, doubleheaders, international matches, or any other special soccer event. Most of the seats on the lower level are uncovered but come complete with seat backs and cup holders.

Purchases of five or fewer tickets can be made at the Gillette Stadium ticket office—which is open weekdays between 10 AM and 5 PM and before games—or through Ticketmaster at 617-931-2000 or www.ticketmaster.com. Orders of six or more tickets and special packages are available by calling 877-GET-REVS.

Season tickets are available for Category 1 ($500), Category 2 ($400), and Category 3 ($300) seats. Season tickets are also available for general admission seating in the Fort for $200. Season-ticket holders receive exclusive reserved parking with tailgating privileges, invitations to a private event to meet the team, special pre-sale opportunities for major soccer and stadium events, and access to Patriots TicketExchange. To order season tickets, call 877-GET-REVS.

DISABILITY ACCESS: The Revolution offer wheelchair and companion seating along the concourses. For wheelchair-accessible seating, call 508-384-9191 or TDD/TTY at 508-384-4389. If an elevator is required, enter through the E2 lobby on the east side of the stadium. Handicap parking is located adjacent to the stadium and can be accessed by the P2 entrance from the north and the P6 entrance from the south.

THE SPLURGE: The Revolution have suites available to rent if you're looking for a group outing, but if you're just looking to pamper yourself, the team sells tickets to the Fidelity Investment Clubhouse (those red club seats in the stadium's middle deck) for $65 for individual games and $900 for the complete season. The clubhouse includes extra-wide, cushioned outdoor seats, and if it's too warm or too cold for your taste, head inside to the climate-controlled area that includes a fully stocked bar, concession stands, dozens of televisions, and floor-to-ceiling glass windows that look out on the pitch.

If you really want to be in the front row, become a member of the Presidents Club. Members sit in exclusive pitch-side seats along the west sideline. You'll be so close to the action, you might be able to tell if a player is sincerely writhing in agony or just gunning for an Academy Award. The cost is $1,200 per seat and includes a ticket, concierge service, private access to concessions and bar service, and a complimentary game program and game notes. For all special soccer events, members receive seats in the Fidelity Investment Clubhouse.

THE CHEAPSKATE: Cheapskates—and Patriots fans, who normally shell out $40 for a parking space at Gillette Stadium—might want to come to a Revolution game just to luxuriate in its free parking. The cheapest ticket option is $20, although you may find some ticket holders selling off extras below face value.

SPECTATOR TIPS: Stadium gates open one hour prior to each match. Smoking is permitted on the public ramps of Gillette Stadium. Banners are permitted, but leave any flagpoles more than two feet in length at home. Outside food and beverages are not permitted inside the stadium unless a prior signed letter is obtained from team security. Bags of any kind, excluding small handheld purses and plastic carrier bags from the ProShop, chairs, coolers, video cameras, and umbrellas are also prohibited.

SCORING AUTOGRAPHS: Players will occasionally sign autographs after the game. A good place to try is along the barricades on field level near the players' locker rooms underneath the lighthouse and bridge.

FOR THE KIDS: Since youth soccer is such a popular activity in New England, it probably should be no surprise that the Revolution provide the most kid-friendly environment of Boston's major sports teams. Hooliganism is not a problem at Revolution games as it can be at soccer matches around the world.

Soccer moms and dads can bring their kids to Soccer Celebration, an interactive theme park that includes face painting; sign making; a chance to meet Slyde the Fox, the Revolution mascot; and inflatable games where kids can test their dribbling, passing, goaltending, and shooting skills. Before entering Soccer Celebration, children need to have a signed liability waiver, which can be downloaded off the Revolution website or completed in person. Soccer Celebration opens two hours prior to every stand-alone Revolution match and is located in the picnic area behind the north end zone.

The Revolution offer youths between the ages of twelve and seventeen the opportunity to become ball kids. Ball kids are selected from groups who purchase fifty or more tickets. Kids with group tickets between the ages of eight and fourteen may also be eligible to walk onto the pitch alongside the starting lineups from the Revolution and their opponent.

Children under the age of two do not require a ticket to stand-alone, regular-season Revolution games, but they do for all other soccer events at Gillette Stadium. Strollers are permitted for Revolution games, but the rules may differ for other soccer events.

STADIUM CONCESSIONS: Concession stands are open behind the goal on the lighthouse side of the stadium as well as along the sideline behind the benches. For concession options in Gillette Stadium, see page 99. The Revolution also offer a family-value menu that includes small pretzels, small popcorn, small cotton candy, and medium sodas for $2; a hot dog, pizza slice, and small fries for $2.25; and chicken tenders and fries for $3.75.

FOOD AND DRINK AROUND THE STADIUM: See page 99.

CONTACT INFORMATION: New England Revolution, Gillette Stadium, One Patriot Place, Foxborough, MA 02036. 508-543-8200; www.revolutionsoccer.net.

BOSTON BREAKERS

Just as the 1994 World Cup gave rise to MLS and the New England Revolution, the success of the 1999 Women's World Cup led to the launch of the eight-team Women's United Soccer Association (WUSA). The WUSA included a local franchise, the Boston Breakers, who played at Nickerson Field between 2001 and 2003.

The WUSA folded following the 2003 season, but women's soccer returned in 2009 with a new league—Women's Professional Soccer (WPS)—and a familiar face. The reincarnated Boston Breakers are among the seven franchises playing in the WPS in 2009, and there are plans to have ten franchises in 2010. The Breakers have eleven home dates scheduled for the 2009 season in their new digs.

STADIUM INFORMATION: Unlike the previous incarnation of the Breakers who played at Nickerson Field, the Boston Breakers play their home games at Harvard Stadium in the Allston section of Boston. For more information on Harvard Stadium, see page 110.

WHEN: The Boston Breakers regular season is scheduled to run from April through August.

GETTING THERE: Harvard Stadium is about four miles from downtown Boston. To get to the stadium, take the Mass Pike to the Brighton/Cambridge exit (Exit 18 eastbound and Exit 20 westbound). After paying the toll, bear left at the fork toward Allston. Turn right at the second set of lights onto North Harvard Street. Harvard Stadium is approximately one mile ahead on the left. On-street **parking** around the stadium is very limited, but parking is available at stadium lots for $10.

Harvard Stadium is also accessible by **public transportation**. By subway, take the Red Line to the Harvard station. It's about a ten minute walk from Harvard Square down JFK Street and across the Charles River to the stadium. Several MBTA bus lines also stop at Harvard Square, and bus routes 66 and 86 stop on North Harvard Street outside the stadium.

TICKETS: The Breakers sell tickets for the east side of Harvard Stadium, behind the team benches. Most of the seats at Harvard Stadium are uncovered, with the exception of wooden risers at the top of each section that are underneath the stadium's colonnade. Except for those wooden risers, the seating in Harvard Stadium is on concrete slabs and lacks any seat backs.

The Breakers sell tickets in three categories:

Category 1 ($25) seating is in sections 6 through 8 at the middle of the pitch.

Category 2 ($18) seating is in sections 3 through 5 behind the Breakers bench and sections 9 through 11 behind the visitor bench.

Category 3 ($13) seating is in the corners of the pitch in sections 1 and 2 and sections 12 through 14.

Season tickets are available for Category 1 ($250), Category 2 ($180), and Category 3 ($130) seats. Category 1 and 2 season-ticket holders receive a free Breakers seat cushion, which is definitely a valuable commodity in this stadium. All season-ticket holders receive an invitation to a meet the team event, a members-only inaugural season lapel pin, and game notes prior to each match. The Breakers also sell season tickets to their pitch-side seats ($675) that are on the far sideline from the team benches.

To purchase tickets, call 781-251-2100 or go online to www.womensprosoccer.com/boston. Game day tickets can be purchased at the box office at the adjacent Bright Hockey Center.

DISABILITY ACCESS: There is wheelchair-accessible seating in front of sections 35–37 on the opposite side of the field from the traditional seating areas for Breakers games. Handicap parking near the stadium is available.

THE SPLURGE: The pitch-side premium seats are as close as you can get to the action. Seats are on the field with an eye-level view of the game. Season-ticket holders who pay the $675 for the pitch-side seats also receive a free parking pass for the year, a pregame catered buffet, and a meet and greet with selected Breakers players.

THE CHEAPSKATE: Take the Red Line or an MBTA bus out to Harvard Stadium. The cheapest ticket option is $13, and you might luck out and find a season-ticket holder selling an extra ducat for less than face value.

SPECTATOR TIPS: Harvard Stadium's concrete seats aren't too comfortable, so bring a cushion. The stadium can also be chilly on April nights, so bundle up or bring a blanket.

SCORING AUTOGRAPHS: Players are made available after the game for autographs in a designated area.

FOR THE KIDS: Breakers games draw lots of kids and have a family-friendly environment. The Breakers have a Fan Zone, located on the north side of the stadium in the quad area between the Murr Center and the Bright Center, which has an assortment of kids' activities. The Fan Zone opens two hours before the start of each game.

STADIUM CONCESSIONS: Concession stands are located underneath the seats along the stadium sidelines and include the usual choices of hot dogs, hamburgers, pizza, soda, and pretzels. There are also specialty vendors, such as Redbones, the popular Somerville barbeque joint. Alcohol is available at Breakers games.

FOOD AND DRINK AROUND THE STADIUM: See page 114.

CONTACT INFORMATION: Boston Breakers, 400 Blue Hill Drive, Suite 302, Westwood, MA 02090. 781-251-2100; www.womensprosoccer.com/boston.

Where to Watch:
International Soccer Matches

All throughout the Boston area—from the North End to Cambridge to Allston—soccer fans gather around televisions in bars, cafés, and restaurants to watch their national teams and favorite clubs. Fans don't just congregate for the big events on the soccer calendar—the World Cup, the European Football Championship, or UEFA Champions League—but for regular-season games as well.

Oftentimes, fans gather in early mornings on weekends to watch games broadcast live from England, Italy, and other countries around the world. While many Bostonians are prying the sleep from their eyes, these supporters, clad in their team's uniforms and scarves, are chanting, singing, and rooting their squads on from thousands of miles away.

Even if you aren't partial to a particular team or country, gathering among the die-hards just to soak up the atmosphere is a worthwhile sports experience. Think of it as a way to travel to sporting events around the world without leaving the confines of Boston. Listed below are some of the best places in and around Boston to follow the world's most popular spectator sport. For some matches, there is a cover charge of up to $20.

Café Brazil, 421 Cambridge Street, Allston, MA 02134. 617-789-5980; www.cafebrazilrestaurant.com.

Lir Irish Pub & Restaurant, 903 Boylston Street, Boston, MA 02115. 617-778-0089; www.lironboylston.com.

The Green Briar, 304 Washington Street, Brighton, MA 02135. 617-789-4100; www.greenbriarpub.com.

Porter Belly's Pub, 338 Washington Street, Brighton, MA 02135. 617-254-3300; www.porterbellyspub.com.

Midwest Grill, 1124 Cambridge Street, Cambridge, MA 02139. 617-354-7536; www.midwestgrillrestaurant.com.

Phoenix Landing, 512 Massachusetts Avenue, Cambridge, MA 02139. 617-576-6260.

The Banshee, 934 Dorchester Avenue, Dorchester, MA 02125. 617-436-9747; www.bansheeboston.com.

Kristine Lilly, Angela Hucles, and Heather Mitts of the Boston Breakers with head coach Tony DiCicco and Women's Professional Soccer Commissioner Tonya Antonucci.

McGann's, 197 Portland Street, Boston, MA 02116. 617-227-4059; www.mcgannspubboston.com.

Caffé dello Sport, 308 Hanover Street, Boston, MA 02113. 617-523-5063; www.caffedellosport.us.

Caffé Graffiti, One Cross Street, Boston, MA 02113. 617-367-3016; www.caffegraffiti.com.

Caffé Paradiso, 255 Hanover Street, Boston, MA 02113. 617-742-1768; www.caffeparadiso.com.

Bad Abbots, 1546 Hancock Street, Quincy, MA 02169. 617-774-1434; www.badabbots.com.

Clash of the Ash, 1464 Hancock Street, Quincy, MA 02169. 617-376-0030.

The Irish Pub, 51 Billings Road, Quincy, MA 02171. 617-774-0222; www.theirishpub.org.

PJ Ryan's, 239 Holland Street, Somerville, MA 02143. 617-625-8200; www.pjryans.com.

Blackthorn Pub, 471 W. Broadway, Boston, MA 02127. 617-269-5510.

AUTO RACING

AFTER SPENDING ALL WEEK stuck in traffic on the Southeast Expressway or Route 128, your average Greater Boston resident may not find the idea of watching cars roar around a track very appealing. Sports fans in Boston may not get as revved up about auto racing as fans from other parts of the country, but devotees only have to travel an hour or so to the **New Hampshire Motor Speedway** to watch the world's premier speed machines.

At the dawn of the automobile age, Boston had a number of racing venues. The city's wealthiest residents who could afford the new-fangled contraptions formed automobile clubs that staged speed, obstacle course, and hill climbing competitions on roads around the city. Because Boston streets were stymied by speed limits as low as eight miles an hour, the horse and bicycle tracks around the area became natural venues for automobile club members to test the velocity of their horseless carriages.

The horse track at The Country Club in Brookline was the site of the first race and meeting of the Massachusetts Automobile Club in 1901. It attracted some of the city's most prominent residents, such as Larz Anderson. Visitors to Brookline's **Larz Anderson Auto Museum** can still see the car he raced that day more than one hundred years ago.

The Charles River Park Velodrome in Cambridge also did double duty as an automobile track. In 1898, velodrome crowds were awed by the demonstration of the Stanley Steamer—the brainchild of entrepreneurial twins Freelan and Francis Stanley—which sped around the track at twenty-seven miles per hour. Five years later, Albert Champion thrilled fans at the velodrome by setting a world motorcycle record by completing a mile in under a minute. (Champion would invent his famous A.C. spark plug at the Cyclorama in the South End a few years after the race.)

After the Stanley brothers' sensation at Charles River Park, their business took off. The Stanley Motor Carriage Company's factory at 44 Hunt Street in Watertown, a building that still stands today, produced about eleven thousand of the legendary vehicles before closing in 1924. Stanley Steamer aficionados may want to check out the **Stanley Museum** (207-265-2729; www.stanleymuseum.org) in Kingfield, Maine—birthplace of the twins—which displays memorabilia and a pair of their original cars.

The Stanley Steamer continued to make automotive history after its coming-out party in Cambridge. In 1899, Freelan Stanley and his wife scaled to the summit of Mount Washington in a steamer in just over two hours. Unfortunately, since his car was the first to scale the 6,288-foot peak, Stanley didn't get one of those neat "This car climbed Mt. Washington" bumper stickers. Five years later, the **Climb to the Clouds** (www.climbtotheclouds.com) automobile race was staged on the winding road to the top of New England's tallest mountain. A modified version of the race is still held today on the Mount Washington Auto Road.

Francis Stanley made a splash in New England auto racing circles as well when he raced a Stanley Steamer at Hyde Park's Readville Race Track in 1903. In front of fifteen thousand spectators, Stanley set a speed record for the mile, covering it in just over a minute, leaving a trail of steam, dust, and the defunct record in his wake.

Readville, which came to fame as the Readville Trotting Park (see page 180) for horses, was the most notable automobile racing oval in Boston. In the early

First held in 1904, a modified version of the Climb to the Clouds is still held today.
Courtesy Fred Vytal, Mt. Washington Auto Road Archives.

1930s, a new track was laid using fill from the Sumner Tunnel. Top drivers came to the track until the middle of the 1930s, and the last official race at Readville was in 1937. These days the closest major racetrack to Boston is the New Hampshire Motor Speedway in Loudon, New Hampshire. It's a bit of a drive, but racing fans tend to like that sort of thing.

LARZ ANDERSON AUTO MUSEUM

Boston gearheads may have to hit the road for live racing action, but they certainly don't have to drive far to see America's oldest car collection. Occupying an 1888 carriage house modeled after a French chateau, Brookline's Larz Anderson Auto Museum features a portion of the collection of thirty-two motorcars acquired between 1899 and 1948 by Larz and Isabel Anderson, the first woman to hold a Massachusetts driver's license. Vehicles from other owners, vintage bicycles, and memorabilia are also on display.

Among the antique cars in the museum is the 1901 Winton car raced by Larz Anderson at The Country Club. The Winton Racer is considered the first production racecar ever offered to the public, and the museum has the only surviving example. Also of note is the Andersons' 1906 CGV limousine coach,

Some pre-race adjustments to the autos at Readville Race Track.
Courtesy Boston Public Library, Print Department.

which is tricked out with a folding bed, electric fans, a sink, and even a toilet. The Andersons bought it for $11,000—equivalent to a whopping $800,000 today.

On weekends throughout the spring, summer, and fall, car buffs proudly display their vehicles on the lawn outside—you can expect to see anything from pristine Corvettes to awe-inspiring Japanese motorcycles and elegant Italian imports. The museum regularly hosts films and lectures on a variety of automotive subjects, including auto racing history. Rotating exhibits sometimes feature racing machines such as Formula One Ferraris and Ducati motorcycles.

GETTING THERE: From Boston, take Route 9 west and take a left onto Lee Street. Follow Lee Street about one-and-a-half miles to its end and take a left at the lights onto Newton Street. Immediately bear right, and the entrance to Larz Anderson Park and the museum is a quarter-mile ahead on the left.

From other points in metropolitan Boston, take Route 128 to Route 9 east. Follow Route 9 for about five miles and take a right onto Lee Street. Follow Lee Street about one-and-a-half miles to its end and take a left at the lights onto Newton Street. Immediately bear right, and the entrance to Larz Anderson Park and the museum is a quarter-mile ahead on the left.

HOURS: Tuesday–Sunday, 10 AM–4 PM (Friday–Sunday only in winter months).

ADMISSION: $10 for adults; $5 for seniors, military, and children.

CONTACT INFORMATION: Larz Anderson Auto Museum, 15 Newton Street, Brookline, MA 02445. 617-522-6547; www.mot.org.

BEYOND BOSTON

New Hampshire Motor Speedway

Twice a year the furious roar of engines shatters the tranquility of the New Hampshire countryside when the NASCAR circuit arrives at the New Hampshire Motor Speedway. On race days the sleepy hamlet of Loudon, New Hampshire—with a population of fewer than five thousand residents—grows by twenty-fold. The one hundred thousand fans gathered around the oval nearly match the population of Manchester, the Granite State's biggest city.

In terms of seating capacity, the New Hampshire Motor Speedway, which opened in 1990, is the largest sports facility in New England. It is the region's only super speedway. Each year the Magic Mile hosts a vintage racing celebration and the Loudon Classic, America's oldest motorcycle meet, but the big days on the racing calendar are two NASCAR Sprint Cup races—the LENOX Industrial Tools 301 in June and the SYLVANIA 300 in September. The LENOX Industrial Tools 301 is the first of ten events in the "Race to the Chase," which determines qualifiers for the Sprint Cup Championship. The SYLVANIA 300 is the first of ten races in the "Chase for the Sprint Cup" playoff that determines the season's top driver.

Caravans of RVs begin to arrive at the track as early as a week before the main races to camp, mingle with other fans, and watch practices and other races that run from Thursday to Sunday. But it is not just fans from New England at the races; there are license plates from all over the United States and Canada as well.

The weekend of NASCAR racing usually kicks off on Thursday with practices and qualifying for modified races and for NASCAR's Camping World Series East, a regional developmental circuit. On Friday the big stars come out for practice runs and qualifying for the Sprint Cup race, the stars of tomorrow drive in the Camping World Series East race, and there is a practice session for either a truck event or an event on the NASCAR Nationwide Series, akin to baseball's Triple A minor league. On Saturday there are Sprint Cup practices in addition to the races for modified vehicles and either trucks or the Nationwide Series. On Sunday full attention is given to the NASCAR Sprint Cup races.

TRACK INFORMATION: The New Hampshire Motor Speedway features a 1.058-mile oval track for stock cars, trucks, and modifieds, along with a 1.6-mile road circuit for motorcycles, sports cars, and carts. There are three grandstands. The main grandstand is located along the start/finish line, and the Concord and Laconia grandstands are located in the corners leading in to and out of the straightaway. The Concord grandstand has fifty-four rows, and the other two have fifty-one. The grandstands, including the thirty-eight suites on top, have a total capacity of 95,491. Along the backstretch is a lawn with seating for fans with RV reservations, bringing the total track capacity to 105,491. Fans on the reserved lawn can bring their own chairs and refreshments.

WHEN: The NASCAR races are generally held in late June and late September.

GETTING THERE: Loudon, New Hampshire, is seventy-five miles north of Boston. From Boston, take Interstate 93 north to Exit 15E. Take Interstate 393 east to Exit 3. Turn left at the end of the ramp onto Route 106 north. The speedway is nine miles ahead on the right. Free **parking** is available. Some lots can be upwards of a mile from the track, but there is shuttle service to the grandstands. Note that it can take a while to get out of the main parking lots after major races. RV and camper parking for NASCAR weekends is available for ticket holders for $100 if reserved beforehand. Parking lots open the Sunday before the NASCAR races and remain open twenty-four hours.

TICKETS: Tickets for the LENOX Industrial Tools 301 and SYLVANIA 300 are the most coveted and should be bought in advance. Tickets for the SYLVANIA 300 are renewable each year. Because of their better views of the track, seats higher up in the grandstand are more desirable and are therefore more expensive. The grandstands have seat backs. Most seats are uncovered, but VIP seating under the suite overhang is available in the main grandstand above the finish line.

Ticket prices vary by event. On NASCAR weekends, general admission tickets are available for $10 on Thursday and $20 on Friday when purchased in advance. Ticket prices on Saturday range from $25 to $55, with half the seats general admission. All seats on Sunday are reserved and range in price from $60 to $110. To purchase tickets, call 603-783-4931 or go online to www.nhms.com. In addition, ticket booths at the track are open on race days.

DISABILITY ACCESS: Wheelchair-accessible viewing areas are available in the Concord and Laconia grandstands. Accompanying individuals are provided companion seats near the wheelchair viewing areas. Handicap parking is available.

THE SPLURGE: Want to watch NASCAR teams up close and personal? Pre-race pit passes ($100 in addition to the grandstand ticket) allow you on pit road between 8 AM and 1 PM to watch the teams get ready. Another option is the Magic Mile Club ($150 in addition to the grandstand ticket), located behind the main grandstand, which offers VIP hospitality such as a continental breakfast, catered lunch, race programs, closed-circuit televisions, and a walking tour of pit road for the NASCAR races.

THE CHEAPSKATE: If you want to catch your favorite NASCAR drivers but don't want to shell out for the top ticket prices, pay the $20 ticket price for the Friday session, which includes practices and pole qualifying for Sunday's race in addition to a race featuring some of the circuit's up-and-coming drivers.

SPECTATOR TIPS: All coolers, bags, and backpacks are subject to searches. Only coolers fourteen inches or under, in all dimensions, are permitted into the grandstand. Umbrellas and glass containers are banned in the grandstand. Bring some binoculars to follow the action around the track, and you may want to purchase a scanner, which is a pair of headphones that allow you to listen in on the communications between the drivers and crews.

SCORING AUTOGRAPHS: Drivers often make appearances at merchandise trailers throughout the weekend.

FOR THE KIDS: Children under eleven are free on Thursdays, Fridays, and Saturdays of NASCAR race weekends, and youth tickets (ages twelve to sixteen) top out at $5 on those days. Discounts are not available on Sunday. Strollers are banned in the grandstands.

TRACK CONCESSIONS: The grandstands have twenty-six concession stands that offer the usual sporting-event fare.

CONTACT INFORMATION: New Hampshire Motor Speedway, 1122 Route 106 North, Loudon, NH 03307. 603-783-4744; www.nhms.com.

Where to Watch: Formula One

While NASCAR and IndyCar dominate the American auto racing scene, Formula One is a more popular choice elsewhere around the world. In the Boston area, Formula One has a small but loyal following composed of ex-pats, immigrants, and gearheads that gather on early weekend mornings to watch European grand prix races, cheering on their favorite drivers and teams, such as Ferrari or McLaren. Not surprisingly, Ferrari is the home team in the Italian neighborhood of the North End. If you want to get up early and watch F1 races with other fans, start your engines with cappuccino and a pastry and head to either of these North End establishments:

Caffé dello Sport, 308 Hanover Street, Boston, MA 02113. 617-523-5063; www.caffedellosport.us.

Caffé Paradiso, 255 Hanover Street, Boston, MA 02113. 617-742-1768; www.caffeparadiso.com.

BOXING

He was America's first sports superstar and the first athlete in the country to earn more than one million dollars. He was the subject of songs and poems. His larger-than-life personality was a godsend to the newspaper industry. He was John L. Sullivan, world heavyweight champion from 1882 to 1892, and he was Boston's own.

Sullivan was the son of Irish immigrants, and his ascendance from a working-class neighborhood to the pinnacle of the sporting world paved the way for many a fighter. The sport of boxing was shunned by proper society in the nineteenth century, particularly in straight-laced Boston. But it was a vehicle for men from immigrant communities and hardscrabble backgrounds to bridge the boundaries of class and ethnicity and rise from the gritty urban streets.

Prior to the Civil War, boxing matches were particularly brutal affairs with few rules. Biting, gouging, kicking, and hitting below the belt were part of the sport; fights lasted until one of the pugilists collapsed. While sparring with gloves was deemed somewhat respectable and legal, bare-knuckle prizefighting was outlawed in many parts of the country, including Boston. The violence, gambling, drinking, and swearing associated with prizefighting ran counter to the values of a Victorian society that emphasized the suppression of man's basest instincts—and it is not surprising that the sport particularly offended the sensibilities of many staid Bostonians.

Bostonians were forced to venture to secluded locations to stage prizefights. One such bout, which the *Boston Democrat* referred to as "one of these disgusting and brutal exhibitions," occurred in 1844 on Outer Brewster Island in Boston Harbor. Under the cover of darkness, two hundred spectators set sail from the city at two in the morning to watch a pair of pugilists duke it out after the sun came up. The *Boston Democrat* was outraged and hoped "the parties to this most disgraceful affair" would be appropriately punished.

The manly art gradually became more respectable as the sport's physical fitness benefits were acknowledged. But it was brawny John L. Sullivan who revolutionized the sport, eventually taking it from the back rooms to the front pages.

Sullivan was born in 1858 at Five East Concord Street, and he grew up along Harrison Avenue in Roxbury and the South End. One night in 1877, Sullivan attended a boxing exhibition at Roxbury's Dudley Street Opera House. A fighter named Scannel challenged anyone in the audience to spar for a few rounds. Sullivan rose to the challenge, laced up his gloves, and proceeded to knock the boxer off the stage and into the orchestra pit. Scannel was the first fighter to feel the wrath of what would become the most famous right hand in America, and the legend of "the Boston Strongboy" was born.

Sullivan's boxing prowess quickly took him from the few square blocks in Boston where he was born and bred. He barnstormed the country, taking on all comers and offering money to anyone who could last four rounds with him. His fists backed up his brash declaration: "My name is John L. Sullivan, and I can beat any sonofabitch alive!" Traveling as far away as England and Australia, Sullivan fought in packed theaters, in back rooms, in rings in front of thousands of fans, even on a barge towed up the Hudson River to elude authorities. He fought legally, sparring with gloves, and illegally, in bare-knuckle brawls—and everywhere he went, the Boston Strongboy carried the city's banner.

After defeating Paddy Ryan in a bare-knuckle fight to become world champion in 1882, Sullivan was idolized by the city's sizable Irish community. Members of proper Boston society who outwardly decried prizefighting were still glad that the hometown boy had won. The citizens of Boston even rose up to defend their native son when New York publisher Richard K. Fox awarded a championship belt to Jake Kilrain after claiming that Sullivan was ducking a fight with his protégé. Proving that nothing unites Bostonians more than an insult from a New Yorker, nearly four thousand people crammed into the Boston Theater on August 8, 1887, as the mayor presented Sullivan with an even grander gold belt, studded with nearly four hundred diamonds. Two years later, the Boston Strongboy proved the belt was richly deserved; he defeated Kilrain in a 75-round prizefight in the backwoods of Mississippi.

Much like Babe Ruth, John L. Sullivan had an insatiable appetite for drinking, eating, nightlife, and women—which provided the newspapers of the day with plenty of copy. He was loud and vulgar, his weight ballooned at times, and he squandered his fortune on his vices. Legend has it that he even chipped the diamonds from his championship belt and pawned them for drinks. In one of his greatest triumphs, the champ, who once owned a saloon on Washington Street, conquered the bottle and became a temperance speaker.

Sullivan helped turn Boston into a boxing breeding ground, and the purses and competition in the city drew up-and-coming fighters from around the country and the world after the turn of the century. During the 1920s, public interest in the "sweet science" surged in America and the Hub, and boxing was never far from the consciousness of the sporting public. There were three to five major boxing cards a week in venues such as the Boston Arena (now Matthews Arena), the Cyclorama in the South End, Mechanics Hall, and Braves Field. The

John L. Sullivan and Jake Kilrain square off in a bare-knuckle prizefight, 1889. Courtesy Library of Congress.

Old Howard burlesque theater in bygone Scollay Square also staged exhibitions by illustrious heavyweight champions such as Jack Dempsey, Gentleman Jim Corbett, Jack Johnson, and Sullivan.

The popularity of boxing—and not hockey or basketball—was the impetus for the construction of Boston Garden. The venerable Garden was the brainchild of George L. "Tex" Rickard, a boxing promoter who had just built Manhattan's Madison Square Garden and planned to construct six similar structures across the country, with the first in Boston. Rickard designed Boston Garden so that spectators would be close enough to the ring to see every expression on the fighters' faces and the beads of sweat on their brows. The Bruins and Celtics were ancillary beneficiaries of the Garden's cozy confines because the proximity to the crowd provided a significant advantage for the home teams.

When it opened in 1928, the Boston Madison Square Garden was touted as "New England's greatest sports palace." Fittingly, the inaugural event in the arena (whose name was quickly changed to Boston Garden) was a boxing card that drew an overflow crowd. In the ensuing years, a number of gyms sprung up in the streets around the Garden to train local fighters.

Perhaps no local fighter is still as beloved as Brockton's Rocky Marciano, the only undefeated heavyweight champion in boxing history. Four decades after his death in an airplane crash, the Rock still has legions of fans in his working-class hometown. Gym rats, Italian-American families, and those who personally knew him stayed loyal to the boxer with the heart of a lion, a chin of steel, and a surprisingly modest build. When Marciano knocked out Jersey Joe Walcott in 1952 to capture the heavyweight crown, it set off wild celebrations around the Shoe City, and tens of thousands turned out when the city threw him a parade. The Brockton Blockbuster held onto his belt until 1956, when he retired with an unblemished 49-0 record.

Sports fans making a trip to Brockton will find a number of sites related to Marciano. The street where Rocco Marchegiano, the boxer's given name, was born is named Rocky Marciano Way in his honor. Around the corner at 168 Dover Street is his boyhood home. There is an historical marker out front, and the home's owner hopes to restore the two-family house to how it looked when the champ lived there and open it as a museum. Across the street is the James Edgar Playground where a young Marciano used to play baseball with neighborhood kids. Mounted on a large rock in the playground is a plaque with a likeness of the Brockton icon that reads, "He beat them all because he refused to lose."

Brockton's minor league baseball team, the Brockton Rox (see page 50), is named in Marciano's honor, as is the post office at 120 Commercial Street and the football stadium at Brockton High School. A giant bronze statue of Marciano, donated to the city by the World Boxing Council, is due to be dedicated at Marciano Stadium (470 Forest Avenue) in 2009. The statue depicts the Rock clad in boxing shorts with his arms outstretched in victory—the only pose he ever struck after a professional bout. The **Brockton Historical Society** also has a museum with an exhibit related to Marciano's life and career.

Nearly twenty-five years after Marciano hung up his gloves, Brockton lived up to its nickname as the "City of Champions" by producing another boxing great—Marvelous Marvin Hagler. The Petronelli Brothers' Gym—a Brockton landmark that stood at 28 Petronelli Way until recently—was a second home to Hagler, who held the world middleweight title for more than six years.

While the tradition of boxers rising from the working-class neighborhoods in and around Boston has continued with fighters such as Lowell's Mickey Ward and Chelsea's John Ruiz, the popularity of boxing as a spectator sport has faded in recent decades. These days there are only periodic bouts at Boston venues such as the TD Garden. Sites around New England host the amateur Golden Gloves competition, but for the most part, the region's boxing fans need to travel to three casinos in southern New England—**Foxwoods**, **Mohegan Sun**, and **Twin River**—to catch any knock-out action.

BEYOND BOSTON

Brockton Historical Society

The affection that the city of Brockton feels for its native son Rocky Marciano hasn't faded with time. The room dedicated to the undefeated world heavyweight champion at the Brockton Historical Society's museum is a clear reminder of this. The exhibit includes the boxing gloves and shoes worn by the Brockton Blockbuster in his 1952 title bout with Jersey Joe Walcott, newspapers and magazine covers, video clips, and photos. While you're there, check out the historical society's Shoe Museum, which celebrates Brockton's heritage as a major American shoe manufacturing center. Marciano, in fact, worked in a shoe factory after dropping out of high school. The museum includes footwear worn by famous figures from Presidents Clinton and Ford to Ted Williams and Marciano himself.

GETTING THERE: Brockton is twenty-five miles south of Boston. Take Route 24 to Exit 18B (Route 27 north). Merge onto Route 27 and turn left at the light onto North Pearl Street. The Historical Society is immediately on the right.

HOURS: Open first and third Sunday of every month from 2 PM to 4 PM or by appointment.

ADMISSION: $2 for adults; children under twelve are free.

CONTACT INFORMATION: 216 North Pearl Street, Brockton, MA 02301. 508-583-1039; www.brocktonhistoricalsociety.org.

Foxwoods

Foxwoods Resort Casino, owned and operated by the Mashantucket Pequot Tribal Nation, is located in the southeastern Connecticut town of Ledyard. The casino, one of the largest in the world, includes thousands of slot machines, hundreds of gaming tables, a bingo hall, and a race book. The complex includes dining, retail, and spa facilities in addition to luxury hotels. Foxwoods has hosted more than one hundred professional and amateur fight cards since its first bout in 1992. In addition to the fights held in its Fox Theater, Foxwoods opened a new 4,000-seat arena in 2008 as part of the MGM

Grand. Much of the seating at the MGM Grand arena is theater style.

GETTING THERE: Foxwoods is approximately one hundred miles southwest of Boston. From Boston, take Interstate 95 south to Exit 92 in Connecticut. Go straight at the light. At the next light, turn right onto Route 2 west. Foxwoods is eight miles west on Route 2.

FOOD AND DRINK: Among the many restaurants at Foxwoods is the ***Stadium Sports Bar & Grill*** (860-312-4263, www.stadiumbars.

Rocky Marciano, local hero, is celebrated by devoted Brockton fans.
Courtesy Stonehill College Archives & Special Collections.

169

com), which serves casual fare and features nearly thirty high-definition televisions. Its Rivalry Bar, which honors the Red Sox and Yankees, features signature drinks such as the "Bronx Bomber" and "Green Monstah."

CONTACT INFORMATION: Foxwoods Resort Casino, 39 Norwich-Westerly Road, Ledyard, CT 06339. 1-800-FOXWOODS; www.foxwoods.com.

Mohegan Sun

Mohegan Sun in the southeast Connecticut town of Uncasville has hosted bouts since it opened in 1996, and the casino generally has a handful of fight cards each year. Like Foxwoods, the casino, controlled by the Mohegan Tribe of Connecticut, is one of the largest in the world with thousands of slot machines, hundreds of gaming tables (with card games ranging from poker to war), and a race book. The complex includes dining, retail, and spa facilities in addition to a 34-story luxury hotel. The casino's 10,000-seat Mohegan Sun Arena—home to the WNBA's Connecticut Sun—hosts boxing events. The ring is located in the center of the arena, and seats on the floor and in the lower and upper levels of the arena are sold around three sides of the ring.

GETTING THERE: Mohegan Sun is approximately one hundred miles southwest of Boston. From Boston, take the Mass Pike to Interstate 395 south. Take Exit 79A onto Route 2A east and then Exit 2 onto Mohegan Sun Boulevard.

FOOD AND DRINK: Among the more than thirty restaurants at Mohegan Sun are a couple owned by basketball great Michael Jordan. *Michael Jordan's Steak House* (860-862-8600, www.mjrestaurants.com) is a pricey, high-end chophouse. If you're more interested in a burger and watching a game, try *Michael Jordan's 23 Sportcafe* (860-862-2300, www.mjrestaurants.com). If you're a die-hard Celtics fan who can't bear patronizing an establishment run by Air Jordan, try *Geno's Pub* (888-226-7711, www.genosfastbreak.com), which is owned by University of Connecticut women's basketball coach Geno Auriemma.

CONTACT INFORMATION: Mohegan Sun, One Mohegan Sun Boulevard, Uncasville, CT 06382. 888-226-7711; www.mohegansun.com.

Twin River

Twin River is a gaming and entertainment complex just over the Massachusetts border in Lincoln, Rhode Island. The casino offers live greyhound racing in addition to simulcast racing, slot machines, and virtual blackjack tables. Twin River is a new entry on the New England boxing scene, having hosted its first boxing card in 2007. Bouts are held in the Twin River Event Center, which includes ringside and floor seats along with bleacher seating that surrounds the ring.

GETTING THERE: Twin River is located approximately fifty miles south of Boston. From Boston, take Interstate 95 south to Interstate 295 south to Route 146 south. Stay on Route 146 south to the Twin River exit. At the end of the exit ramp take a left, proceed through the first set of lights, and Twin River is on the left.

FOOD AND DRINK: In addition to fast-food options, Twin River has *Fred & Steve's Steakhouse* (401-475-8400), owned by former Boston College and New England Patriots players Fred Smerlas and Steve DeOssie.

CONTACT INFORMATION: Twin River, 100 Twin River Road, Lincoln, RI 02865. 877-82-RIVER, www.twinriver.com

GOLF

MARK TWAIN FAMOUSLY DESCRIBED golf as "a good walk spoiled." There's no doubt that a day at the links can quickly turn into a frustrating exercise, but it's a lot harder to have a bad day at the course if you're a spectator watching the best golfers in the world drive for show and putt for dough.

With the region's long, dark winters constantly looming, Bostonians grasp every chance to get in a quick eighteen before the fairways and greens are covered by a blanket of snow. Weekend tee times at public golf courses around Boston are at a premium, and you may even find yourself waiting to hit a bucket of balls at the local driving range.

This obsession has significant regional roots, as Bostonians played an integral role in the evolution of golf from a little-known hobby to a popular national sport. A pioneer of American golf was George Wright, one of baseball's earliest stars with the Boston Red Stockings and proprietor of one of the city's leading sporting goods stores. Wright—who had received a set of golf clubs from Great Britain, birthplace of the sport—successfully petitioned the Boston Parks Commission in 1890 to grant him a permit to play an experimental round of golf in Franklin Park, despite the reluctance of the park's landscape architect, Frederick Law Olmsted. Along with a group of his friends, Wright laid out a small makeshift course with tomato cans as holes and staged the first golf match in an American public park. (Today a city golf course in Hyde Park is named in Wright's honor.)

After six years of battles between golfers and park-goers, the city decided to build a proper golf course in Franklin Park. Behind only the Van Cortlandt Golf Course in New York City, which opened the year before, the **William J. Devine Golf Course** (One Circuit Drive, Dorchester, MA 02121. 617-265-4084), is the second-oldest public golf course in America. (Golf legend Bobby Jones spent endless hours practicing at the course when he attended Harvard in the 1920s.) Even after the course opened in 1896, many city residents were still unfamiliar with the new-fangled sport, which caused potential safety problems. According to an 1899 magazine account, the Franklin Park course had to be closed on public holidays and Saturdays as "experience has shown that there are yet many park visitors who know nothing of the game, and, therefore, fear nothing from standing fifty yards in front of the duffer."

No local club played a more important role in the development of American golf than **The Country Club** (191 Clyde Street, Chestnut Hill, MA 02467. 617-566-0240; www.tcclub.org), one of five charter members of the United States Golf Association (USGA). Pretentious in its utter simplicity, the club's generic, understated name lends it a lofty air that reflects its Brahmin pedigree. The Country Club was established in 1882 by six hundred members of Boston's aristocracy as an equestrian and social club, not as a golf venue. The club leased and purchased a 100-acre horse farm in Brookline that included a half-mile racetrack and a farmhouse once owned by Daniel Webster. (Horse racing continued at The Country Club through 1935.)

The Country Club didn't have a golf course until six holes were opened in 1893. According to legend, Arthur Hunnewell, who had built a course on his Wellesley estate, amazingly christened the course by acing the 100-yard opening hole with his first shot. The crowd, unfamiliar with the new game, figured the feat was nothing special and gave Hunnewell just a smattering of applause. When the other players in the group failed to hit a hole in one, the crowd was less than impressed. The club's equestrians were also less than pleased with the prospect of golf balls whizzing by their heads as they rode around the horse track and steeplechase course, which overlapped the links.

Golf quickly caught on in Boston around the turn of the twentieth century, but it remained a pastime of the social elite. However, that changed during the 1913 U.S. Open at The Country Club, when Francis Ouimet, a skinny twenty-year-old son of immigrants, scored perhaps the greatest upset in sports history. Having grown up in a modest two-story clapboard house at 246 Clyde Street in Brookline, right across the street from The Country Club's seventeenth hole, Ouimet was no stranger to the course. As a youngster, Ouimet caddied at the club and snuck onto the course whenever he could to play a few holes. When the 1913 U.S. Open began, no one gave the amateur Ouimet (who worked as a sales clerk at George Wright's sporting goods store) any shot of winning, particularly as he was up against the two great British pros, Harry Vardon and Ted Ray.

But the ultimate underdog thrilled the local crowds with his play, and Ouimet found himself right in the thick of it. Throngs of Bostonians hung onto crowded streetcars destined for Brookline, and as many as twenty thousand people filled the course to cheer on the local lad, who was assisted by his ten-year-old caddie, Eddie Lowery. It was far and away the largest crowd ever to watch a golf match in the United States. As Francis made his charge on the back nine of the final round, his mother clutched a rosary and rocked nervously in her chair on the front porch of their house across Clyde Street. Each roar of the crowd echoing through the trees must have sounded like an answered prayer to her pious ears.

At the end of the final round, Ouimet found himself in a three-way eighteen-hole playoff with his idols Vardon and Ray. Few expected the skinny amateur to

Francis Ouimet, local underdog, won the 1913 U.S. Open, catapulting the sport into the American spotlight.
Courtesy Library of Congress.

beat the seasoned pros, but more than two centuries after the battles at Lexington and Concord, Ouimet forged another set of shots heard 'round the world as he defeated the British titans and set off an American sports revolution. His victory was front-page news across the country.

It was *the* transformative moment in American golf history. According to the World Golf Hall of Fame, "Ouimet's stunning triumph captured the imagination of sports fans across the globe, sweeping away the notion that golf was a stuffy game for the old and rich." In the decade following Ouimet's monumental upset, the number of American golfers grew nearly seven-fold. The story is a fairytale in the best tradition of Disney—in fact, Disney did make a movie about it—*The Greatest Game Ever Played*, based on the book by Mark Frost.

The Country Club hosted the U.S. Open again in 1963 and 1988. In 1999 it was the site of the Ryder Cup competition between America and Europe. The Americans came back from an almost insurmountable deficit on the final day to win the cup in what has been dubbed the "miracle at Brookline." The spirit of Francis Ouimet seemed to have been at work that day as Justin Leonard's winning 45-foot birdie putt found the bottom of the hole on the seventeenth green, right across the street from Ouimet's childhood home, which still stands as a private residence.

Ouimet's legacy and those of the other Massachusetts golf pioneers are celebrated at the **Massachusetts Golf Museum** in Norton. The museum is located at the Tournament Players Club of Boston, which each year hosts the PGA Tour's **Deutsche Bank Championship**.

In the past, Boston sports fans could also watch the legends of golf when the Champions Tour came to town each summer. The Bank of America Championship, which began in 1981, was the only New England stop on the Champions Tour, the PGA Tour's circuit for golfers age fifty and older. Unfortunately, what was the longest-running 54-hole event on the Champions Tour is in need of new sponsorship. It is uncertain whether the Champions Tour will return to the Greater Boston area.

DEUTSCHE BANK CHAMPIONSHIP

When the inaugural Deutsche Bank Championship teed off in 2003, it marked the return of the PGA Tour to the Boston area after a five-year absence. And what a return it has been. The Deutsche Bank Championship is the second of the four playoff tournaments that determine the PGA Tour's season-long champion and the winner of the coveted FedEx Cup. In addition to getting a leg up on winning the FedEx Cup, the champion walks away with more than $1.3 million.

The championship's inclusion in the playoffs ensures that the tournament always has a stellar field. Most of the world's best golfers are among the one hundred players teeing it up each year. Vijay Singh, Phil Mickelson, and Tiger Woods are among the superstars who have won the tournament in its brief history. The tournament, which concludes on Labor Day, is unique in that it's the only one on tour with a Monday finish.

COURSE INFORMATION: The Deutsche Bank Championship is held at the Tournament Players Club of Boston (TPC of Boston), which opened in 2002. The layout plays to a par seventy-one for the pros and a par seventy-two for mere mortals. The course, located about thirty-five miles south of Boston in the town of Norton, measures over 7,200 yards and was designed by golf legend Arnold Palmer.

WHEN: The tournament is traditionally held on Labor Day weekend, with the four championship rounds running Friday through Monday. Practice rounds are held on the Tuesday and Wednesday before Labor Day weekend with a pro-am on Thursday.

GETTING THERE: Spectator parking is available at the Comcast Center for the Performing Arts in Mansfield, Massachusetts. It's a short shuttle bus ride to the golf course. Parking costs $10 per day, and weeklong parking passes are available for $60.

From Boston, take Interstate 95 south to Interstate 495 south. Take Exit 11 (Route 140 south–Norton). Bear right onto Route 140 south, continue for approximately one-eighth of a mile, and the Comcast Center is on the right.

TICKETS: Spectators can purchase grounds tickets that allow them to wander the course and sit in any of the general admission bleachers. Grounds tickets to the practice rounds and the pro-am round ($25) are cheaper than grounds tickets to the championship rounds ($55). Tickets are day specific. Spectators can also purchase a weekly ticket booklet ($275) that contains one ticket for each day of the championship (Tuesday–Monday) and access to the Deutsche Bank Club, a double-decker pavilion located along the seventeenth fairway that contains a food court and sports bar. Booklets ($175) with tickets for each of the four competition rounds are also available.

If you want to go to a championship round and have your heart set on seeing a specific player, get a ticket for either of the first two rounds (Friday or Saturday). The field is cut to the top seventy players and ties after the first two rounds, so your favorite player may not be around to play on Sunday or Monday. However, crowds are thicker on Sunday and Monday as there are fewer players to follow and the final rounds are more of a draw. Some championship rounds have sold out in prior years.

Tickets to the Deutsche Bank Championship usually go on sale in early June. To purchase tickets, visit www.dbchampionship.com or call 877-TIX-4DBC.

DISABILITY ACCESS: Reserved handicap parking spots are available at the Comcast Center for the Performing Arts. Dedicated wheelchair-accessible buses are available to shuttle disabled persons and their guests to the golf course. At the course, there is a shuttle system that stops at five drop-off and pick-up points for spectators requiring special-needs assistance throughout the grounds.

SPECTATOR TIPS: While golf courses are usually popular places for conducting business, leave your cell phone, pager, and Blackberry at home. They are not permitted at any of the rounds. (If you need to make a call, public phones are located near the clubhouse.) While cameras are permitted during the practice and pro-am rounds, they are not allowed during the championship

Vijay Singh, winner of the 2008 Deutsche Bank Championship.

rounds. Beverages, coolers, radios, televisions, backpacks, items larger than 8"x12" for autographs, and bags larger than 6"x6" are also prohibited. Small lawn chairs are allowed.

Grab a pairings sheet when you enter the course or print one out from the tournament website before you leave home. The pairings sheet will tell you the groupings and their tee times, and there's also a map of the course that details pathways and amenities.

The TPC of Boston is very spread out and has lots of trees, which makes it difficult to pick one spot where you can watch multiple holes. Two of the best spots to watch multiple holes are behind the second green and third tee and behind the fifteenth green and sixteenth tee. Crowds are thinner on the front nine of the course. Also, keep in mind that the hospitality tents on the last four holes make it more difficult to find a good vantage point.

Bleachers are available at the tee box at the first and tenth holes; behind the fourth, ninth, and eighteenth greens; and behind and to the side of the sixteenth green. During the final round, the action all comes down to the eighteenth green, so those bleacher seats are popular, but the fourth hole is also a fun spot to watch from as it's a short par-four that some players may try to drive with their tee shots. There are no bleachers at the par-three eleventh hole, but there's a nice shaded slope behind the green where you can get close to the action, and the refreshment stand and restrooms are right behind the green.

There are also bleachers at the driving range, which is a fun place to sit and watch a bunch of players warm up. You can also stand around the putting green and watch the players' pre-round routines.

Since the TPC of Boston is so expansive, you'll have to do a lot of walking if you want to follow particular players or see most of the holes. Be sure to wear comfortable walking shoes and prepare for the weather. On hot, sunny days, it's important to wear sunscreen and stay hydrated. Unfortunately, spectators are not allowed to bring in water, so you'll need to buy beverages on the course.

One last note: If you want to see Tiger Woods during the practice rounds, set your alarm. Woods likes to hit the course at the break of dawn when there are fewer crowds.

SCORING AUTOGRAPHS: Your best bet to score autographs is to go to one of the practice or pro-am rounds when the atmosphere is more low key and the crowds are much smaller. (If you go during the pro-am round, you might find other stars of sports and entertainment worth asking for an autograph too.)

If there is a particular player whose autograph you want, come up with a game plan for the practice rounds. Head to the practice range and putting green about sixty to ninety minutes before tee time or stake out the first or tenth tee (depending on which one they will tee off from) about ten minutes before tee time. Some players will even sign as they walk from hole to hole. Players may also sign after completing their rounds coming off the ninth or eighteenth holes. The tournament has set up Autograph Alley behind the eighteenth green and adjacent to the scorers' trailer where some players will sign after practice rounds.

During the four championship rounds, your best bet is to hang around Autograph Alley. Always wait until a player completes his round before asking for an autograph; in a sport where etiquette is sacrosanct, it is a major no-no to interrupt a player's round.

FOR THE KIDS: Concession stands offer kids' meals ($7) that include either a peanut butter and jelly sandwich or a hot dog, a carton of milk, and potato chips. Children fifteen and under receive free grounds admission when accompanied by an adult ticket holder.

The tournament has designated specific viewing areas that provide unobstructed views solely for children and parents: at the driving range, at the first and tenth tees, and behind the ninth, fifteenth, and eighteenth greens. There is also an outdoor kids' village near the clubhouse that includes activities such as face painting, video games, golf games, and arts and crafts.

FOOD AND DRINK: Concession tents are located throughout the course, with the biggest tent adjacent to the clubhouse. Breakfast options include muffins, bananas and apples, and Dunkin' Donuts coffee. Lunch choices include cheeseburgers, hot dogs ($4.50), and ham and cheese sandwiches. Beverages include bottles of water, Gatorade, and

16-ounce draft beers ($6). While you can't bring beverages into the course, you can stick a granola bar or small item in your pocket and take it in with you.

CONTACT INFORMATION: Deutsche Bank Championship, 300 Arnold Palmer Boulevard, Norton, MA 02766. 508-285-8333; www.dbchampionship.com.

MASSACHUSETTS GOLF MUSEUM

The Massachusetts Golf Museum is located inside the William F. Connell Golf House and Museum on the grounds of the Tournament Players Club of Boston, which hosts the Deutsche Bank Championship. The small museum, opened in 2002 and run by the Massachusetts Golf Association (MGA), honors the people and the moments that have forged the state's century-old golf tradition.

The museum features interactive kiosks, videos, and a hallway lined with state golfing trophies. Each room has a brief video that highlights key historical moments in the various eras of Massachusetts golf history, ranging from the dawn of the sport to the present day. Timelines along the walls wander from room to room and highlight important historical moments. The exhibits pay tribute to the state's homegrown players who have won MGA titles, both professional and amateur. There are also photographs of some of the game's greats who have won USGA championships on Massachusetts soil, including a sixteen-year-old Tiger Woods at the 1992 U.S. Junior Amateur Championship held at Milton's Wollaston Golf Club.

The highlight of the museum is the Ouimet Room. With its armchairs and couches, it looks like a cozy country club room. It's filled with artifacts connected to the 1913 U.S. Open champion and his caddy, Eddie Lowery. The walls are covered with photographs and newspapers sporting banner headlines about Ouimet's 1913 U.S. Open triumph, and there is a large television screen featuring a short video on Ouimet. Display cases hold golf books and trophies won by Francis Ouimet and the jacket he wore when he captained the American team in the Walker Cup amateur competition for the final time in 1949. There is also a replica of the ballot box used to cast votes for potential captains of the venerable Royal and Ancient Golf Club of Saint Andrews. Ouimet was elected as the club's first American captain.

Hanging above the fireplace is a copy of a portrait of Ouimet in his Royal and Ancient Golf Club red jacket. What's most remarkable about the portrait of the former caddie is that it's a version painted in 1954 by President Dwight Eisenhower, an avid golfer who was also an honorary member of the Royal and Ancient Golf Club and a friend of Ouimet's. Also in the Ouimet Room are items related to Lowery's golfing career, the caddy scholarship that bears Ouimet's name, and mementos from the book and movie *The Greatest Game Ever Played*, including photographs from the movie premier and a copy of the original manuscript.

GETTING THERE: Follow directions to the Tournament Players Club of Boston on page 174, and turn right a half mile past Comcast Center.

HOURS: Monday–Friday, 10 AM–5 PM.
ADMISSION: Free.
CONTACT INFORMATION: Massachusetts Golf Museum, 300 Arnold Palmer Boulevard, Norton, MA 02766. 774-430-9100; www.mgalinks.org/about_mga/museum.html.

HORSE RACING

MASSACHUSETTS CERTAINLY ISN'T THOROUGHBRED country like Kentucky or Maryland, but horse racing has a long history in the Boston area. After all, the most famous—and important—horse race in American history occurred through the streets outside of Boston on an April night in 1775. As soon as two lanterns were hung in the belfry of the Old North Church, Paul Revere and William Dawes (later joined by Samuel Prescott) led their steeds in a race against time to warn the colonists of the imminent arrival of the British regulars.

Today, for the jockeys and horses thundering around the track at **Suffolk Downs** in East Boston, the stakes are richer, though much less dire. When it opened in the midst of the Great Depression, Suffolk Downs regularly drew crowds that were larger than those at Fenway Park, Braves Field, or Boston Garden. Tens of thousands more bettors attended races at tracks across the state on the fairground circuit. No doubt many believed investing their money in the ponies was a safer choice than the stock market. These days the sport of kings has declined in popularity. Suffolk Downs is the only thoroughbred track left in New England, and the fairground circuit is a relic of the past.

The crowds may be sparser, but a day at the races is undoubtedly one of the best sports values in Boston. Plus, track patrons can take pride in the fact that they are carrying on the tradition of one of Boston's oldest spectator sports.

Unlike elsewhere in the colonies, it took time for horse racing to establish itself in Massachusetts. The sport was frowned upon by the colony's Puritan forefathers because of its association with gambling and its potential bodily harm to pedestrians. In 1674 the Plymouth Colony prohibited horse racing in villages, and the Massachusetts Bay Colony followed soon after with a law forbidding horse racing within four miles of a town center. Anyone racing a horse in the street could be fined or sent to the stocks.

During the 1700s, horse racing gradually gained increasing acceptance, due in large part to the military benefit of the sport, and it was pretty much the only organized spectator sport staged around Boston in that time period. Horse races were held outside of town, usually in Cambridge, and advertised in colonial Boston newspapers as early as 1715. Competitors paid an entrance fee at local pubs, such as the famed Green Dragon Tavern in downtown Boston, and winners received prizes such as velvet saddles with silver lace.

During the Victorian era, Boston Brahmins, whose bloodlines could be just as blue as those of champion steeds, enjoyed racing their equines. Racing enthusiasts formed driving clubs and trotting associations all throughout metropolitan Boston, and a host of tracks sprung up where competitors could race horse-drawn vehicles such as buggies, runabouts, and surreys. Crowds as large as fifteen thousand would fill the grandstands and line the rails of these tracks to watch field days,

A day at the track promises to be an exciting event.

interclub races, and national championships. In later years, these tracks would also be used for bicycle and automobile racing. The Charles River Speedway in Brighton, which ran between North Harvard Street and Western Avenue along the Charles River, was even used as a venue for chariot races, perhaps fitting given that the Romanesque structure of Harvard Stadium was adjacent to the track.

One of the more popular tracks in the city was Beacon Park in Allston, which opened in 1864. The track was also used by Buffalo Bill to stage his Wild West Show when it came to town, and he quartered his buffalo and horses between performances in the nearby Brighton Stockyards. The owners of Beacon Park—Eben Jordan and Charles Marsh of Jordan Marsh fame—sold the land in the 1890s to the Boston & Albany Railroad for conversion to a rail yard that still exists on the site along the Mass Pike.

By the end of the 1800s, harness racing was among the most popular sports in the city and the country, and one of America's premier tracks—the Readville Trotting Park—opened in the Hyde Park section of Boston in 1896. The oval at the foot of the Blue Hills and along the banks of the Neponset River was one of the most significant harness tracks in the history of the sport, drawing the country's best owners, trainers, drivers, and horses, including the legendary Dan Patch.

Two of the sport's most important records were set at Readville. In 1897 Star Pointer became the first pacer to break the two-minute mile at the track. As Star Pointer crossed the line, a mighty roar went up from the eight thousand in attendance. Swept up in the excitement, the crowd jumped over the fence and carried the horse's reinsman away on their shoulders as the band played "Hail to the Chief." Six years later, Lou Dillon raced at Readville and became the first trotter to break the two-minute mile. Banner headlines relayed the news of these records from Hyde Park to the rest of the world.

The track was abandoned by the late 1930s, and the site is now occupied by a warehouse. An historical marker unveiled in 2007 commemorating Readville Trotting Park is located at the intersection of Neponset Valley Parkway and Meadow Road. A chain-link fence at the end of Hyde Park Avenue marks the old entrance to the track, which was once graced by a magnificent gate replete with Corinthian columns.

The Dorchester Gentlemen's Driving Club held field days at Readville until a racing oval was built in 1904 at Franklin Field, just off Blue Hill and Talbot Avenues. Two of Boston's legendary politicians and mayors—James Michael Curley and John F. "Honey Fitz" Fitzgerald, grandfather to John F. Kennedy—even participated in trotting races at Franklin Field Speedway.

On Dorchester Day in 1911, Mayor Fitzgerald took to the track and drove his trotter to victory before a crowd of fifteen thousand. After the race, Honey Fitz dedicated the newly expanded track with a short speech, and then he led a rendition of "Sweet Adeline," his campaign theme song. Three years later, Curley, clad in a khaki suit and jockey cap, took a seat in his sulky as nine thousand fans looked on from the grandstand, the infield, and along the fence. The Rascal King, riding in his first race, drove like a veteran, won by a neck, and beat the time of his predecessor.

Even The Country Club in Brookline, best known for hosting the U.S. Open golf tournament, has its roots in horse racing. The club was formed when a group of Boston's most prominent gentlemen leased Clyde Park, a 100-acre horse farm with a half-mile racetrack and a farmhouse once owned by Daniel Webster. The club's equestrians and golfers had an uneasy relationship as the growing golf course eventually overlapped the track. During the 1913 U.S. Open, golfers were forced to play approach shots over the racetrack on the opening and closing holes. The club's annual races continued to be popular social events until the final races were held at the club in 1935.

Actually, 1935 was also the year Massachusetts legalized pari-mutuel betting in an attempt to raise more revenue during the Great Depression. Within months, Suffolk Downs opened its doors. Horse racing was a popular pastime in Boston during the Great Depression, as it was in the country as a whole, rivaling only that of baseball and boxing. In the years leading up to World War II, Sundays were such big days at the track that it diverted crowds from the NFL's Boston Redskins. This failure to capture the public's hearts and wallets led to the Redskins' move to the nation's capital in 1937.

Massachusetts also had a robust racing circuit at fairs across the state. Races at fairs in Topsfield, Marshfield, Great Barrington, Weymouth, Brockton, and Northampton drew crowds as large as twenty-five thousand. The racing circuit slowly fizzled over the last few decades and finally came to an end after the Three County Fair in Northampton, which featured racing of some kind since 1856, announced in 2006 that it would no longer stage a meet.

While the fair circuit is gone, racing enthusiasts in metropolitan Boston have a couple of local harness-racing tracks in addition to Suffolk Downs. (Although there are fears that these tracks may go the way of the fair circuit if they are not permitted to add slot machines or other gambling options to compete with casinos in neighboring states.) The **Plainridge Racecourse** (301 Washington Street, Plainville, MA 02762. 508-643-2500; www.prcharness.com) has live harness racing between March and November as well as year-round simulcasts. Just across the Massachusetts border in New Hampshire, **Rockingham Park** (79 Rockingham Park Boulevard, Salem, NH 03079. 603-898-2311; www.rockinghampark.com) also offers both live harness racing and simulcasting.

SUFFOLK DOWNS

In contrast to today's crowds, Boston sports fans flocked to Suffolk Downs when it opened smack in the middle of the Great Depression. Thirty-five thousand fans came through the turnstiles on the 1935 opening day, and some crowds topped fifty thousand. The track was a marvel of construction; it took just sixty-two days to transform a tract of mudflats straddling East Boston and Revere into a racetrack complete with an enormous grandstand—the first ever built of concrete—two football fields long.

It was at Suffolk Downs on June 29, 1936, that trainer Tom Smith first eyed a gawky three-year-old colt by the name of Seabiscuit. Smith was enraptured with the ragged horse despite his losing record, awkward gallop, and stubby legs, which belied the greatness lurking inside. The trainer helped to transform the also-ran into a champion thoroughbred who became a national sensation. In 1937, Seabiscuit electrified the crowd at Suffolk Downs by capturing the Massachusetts Handicap with jockey Red Pollard, and the horse made eight appearances at the oval. A plaque dedicated to Seabiscuit along with a small lawn jockey statue of Pollard in his red silks and a red-and-white cap stand in front of the clubhouse entrance.

In addition to being a racing venue, Suffolk Downs has been the scene of some of Boston's most notable rock-and-roll concerts. The Beatles played at the track in 1966, and in an odd musical pairing, Aerosmith opened for the retro-fifties group Sha Na Na in 1973. The track is still used for special events such as boxing bouts and Eddie Andelman's annual Hot Dog Safari, a charity event that raises money for cystic fibrosis and draws as many as twenty-five thousand people.

That's an attendance figure that rivals or tops the average attendance for the biggest race held at Suffolk Downs each year—the Massachusetts Handicap (also known as the MassCap). The MassCap was inaugurated the same year Suffolk Downs opened, and it draws a field of horses from around the world. In addition to Seabiscuit, other great winners of the MassCap include Whirlaway, Cigar, and Skip Away.

Perhaps because horse racing has faded in the consciousness of the American sports fan, many Boston sports fans tend to forget about Suffolk Downs as a spectator destination. However, Suffolk Downs is one of the best sports bargains in town; and even if you're not a gambler, odds are you'll have a good time at the track. A typical card has nine races spread over the course of about four hours, and it can be fun to throw down a sawbuck or two on the horse with the can't-miss name like "No Doubt," whether you know anything about the horse game or not. If that doesn't suit you, spend your money on lunch and a beer and sit outside, enjoying the summer sun.

If you prefer to be inside, the huge grandstand offers plenty of enclosed seating and a number of dining options. Banners with the racing silks of famous MassCap champions hang from the grandstand rafters like retired jerseys at the Garden. Right outside the grandstand is the paddock area, where you can give the thoroughbreds a once-over before placing a bet or just admire the strength and beauty of the steeds up close.

Suffolk Downs offers both dirt and turf races. The main dirt track is a one-mile oval with a chute for six-furlong and mile-and-a-quarter races. The turf course is seven furlongs long. In addition to live racing, Suffolk Downs offers year-round simulcast racing that allows gamblers to bet on the action on other tracks throughout the country.

Still, like the worn racing forms discarded on the floor by aging gamblers, Suffolk Downs can feel dated. The track continues to draw decent crowds on weekends and on big calendar days such as the MassCap, Breeders' Cup, Kentucky Derby, Preakness, and Belmont Stakes, but Suffolk Downs has become less of a draw to gamblers because of the growth of state lotteries and casinos.

Track owners have lobbied the state government to allow them to add other gambling options at the track. Without that approval, the glory days of Suffolk Downs will likely remain in the past.

WHEN: The live racing season at Suffolk Downs runs from May to November. Live racing is generally held four or five days a week. The track is also open year-round for simulcast racing.

GETTING THERE: Suffolk Downs is three miles northeast of downtown Boston. General **parking** is free, and preferred and valet parking are both available for a fee on weekends and holidays during the live racing season.

From downtown Boston and most of metropolitan Boston, take the Callahan or Ted Williams tunnels to Route 1A north. Proceed approximately two miles until the first set of lights. Go straight through the lights and turn right at the main entrance two hundred yards up on the right.

From points due north, take U.S. 1 south to the exit for Route 60. Follow the rotary halfway around to Route 60 east. Follow for approximately three miles (the roadway becomes Route 1A south at the Bell Circle rotary), and the Suffolk Downs entrance will be on the left.

Suffolk Downs is also accessible by **public transportation.** Take the Blue Line outbound from downtown to the Suffolk Downs stop. A shuttle bus runs to and from the station to the main clubhouse entrance every ten minutes. Call Suffolk Downs for more information, 617-567-3900.

TICKETS: Admission to Suffolk Downs is $2 for live racing and free on Mondays and Tuesdays, excluding holidays. Admission

★ Eddie Andelman's Guide to Wagering

Eddie Andelman is not only a Boston sports radio legend but an avid lover of horse racing. After fifty years of going to the races, he has some tips for novice bettors.

"The key to the whole thing is managing your money. If you are going to stay for nine races and are prepared to lose no more than $90, don't stray from the plan.

"I suggest buying a program. I'm personally interested in the last two times the horse has run and how they ran in the last quarter mile. Don't make the mistake of looking at the jockey and trainer standings and thinking someone with a bad record is due.

"There's nothing wrong with betting the names you like, and I always play hunches. My theory has always been, 'Have a hunch, bet a bunch.' When it's a rainy day or an off track, always bet on a horse that has a name having to do with water or the Navy. More often than not, it comes out.

"Beginners should stay away from the gimmicks like superfectas and daily doubles until they know the game. Just bet on horses to win and place. Never bet on first-time starters or horses that are shipped in, and stay away from always betting on favorites—they only win thirty percent of the time. Personally, I never bet until seeing the post parade because I don't like betting on horses that are sweating.

"Finally, remember that first-time goers to the track always win; otherwise there would be no race tracks."

The opening day crowd swarms the daily double window at Suffolk Downs.
Courtesy Boston Public Library, Print Department.

is free for days with only simulcast racing. Admission fees may vary for special events such as days of Triple Crown races and the MassCap.

There are several general admission seating options at Suffolk Downs. Grandstand seats and clubhouse reserved box seats, accessible from the second floor, have excellent panoramas of the track. Also on the second floor is a teletheater showing simulcasts on a bank of televisions as well as on personal television sets at each seat. If you prefer to watch the action from outside, there are circular picnic tables, rows of benches, and a large asphalt area with plenty of standing room. Some patrons even bring their own lawn chairs.

DISABILITY ACCESS: All entrances to Suffolk Downs are wheelchair accessible, but for elevator access, use the clubhouse entrance on the far right side of the building.

THE SPLURGE: The Turf Club, on the third floor of the clubhouse, is a private membership area with a bar, dining room, private windows and self-service wagering machines, and a lounge with upholstered sofas and leather chairs. For membership information, call 617-568-3326.

THE CHEAPSKATE: You might not think a gambling venue would be the best place for someone who is tight with a buck, but because Suffolk Downs may be the best sports bargain in Boston, a cheapskate could feel quite at home here. General parking is free, and on most days it's just $2 to get into the track for three to four hours of racing. If $2 is too rich for your blood, there is free admission on Mondays and Tuesdays (excluding holidays). Cheapskates should also keep an eye out for the opening day of live racing when the track owners sometimes give out free season passes to all paid admissions.

Even if you want to place a bet, you can do so for as little as $2, and you can finance it by forgoing the $2 cost of a program by printing out the handicappers' picks off the Suffolk Downs website and ripping the starting odds and race lineup out of the morning newspaper.

SPECTATOR TIPS: Suffolk Downs features pari-mutuel betting, which means bets are pooled and those holding winning tickets divide the total amount bet in proportion to their wagers. Odds are automatically calculated by the amount of money wagered on each horse. The odds in the program and newspapers are the morning line odds established by the track handicapper. Once wagering starts, the odds constantly fluctuate, and the final odds may be different from those when you placed the bet. Watch the tote board on the infield for current odds, the total amount bet to win in the upcoming race and on each horse, post time, results, payoffs, and track conditions.

There are dozens of betting windows and self-service machines around the track. Note that while the track has plenty of machines where you can put your money in, there are none where you can take your money out: by state law there are no ATMs on the premises.

To place a bet at a window, give the clerk the name of the racetrack (since there is simulcast racing as well as live racing) and race number, then the amount of the wager, the type of wager, and the program number of the horse. For example: "Suffolk Downs, race three. I'd like $2 to win on number four." For self-service kiosks, just follow the instructions on the screen. If your horse is a winner, bring your ticket to any window for your payout, or insert the ticket into a self-service wagering terminal and use your winnings for another bet or a credit voucher, which can be redeemed at a betting window. You must be eighteen years or older to place a wager.

The simplest wager is to bet on a single horse to win (finish first), place (finish first or second), or show (finish first, second, or third). Other betting options are daily doubles (choosing the winners of two consecutive races), perfectas/exactas (choosing the two horses finishing first and second in exact order), trifectas (choosing the first three horses in exact order), superfecta (choosing the first four horses in exact order), pick three (choosing the winners of three races in a row), and pick four (choosing the winners of four races in a row).

Racing programs, available for $2, include all sorts of data such as prior results, split times, and meet records for jockeys, trainers, owners, and horses. Handicappers also offer their picks and race analysis. If you're a novice, there's a page in the program that tells you how to decipher it. If you're more of an impulsive bettor and want to go with the horse with the pretty name, buy a program anyway so you can slap it on your thigh as you cheer your horse down the stretch. And if despite all your support, your pick lumbers to the finish line out of the money, get in the true spirit of the event and crumple up your ticket and spike it to the ground in disgust.

Bring a pair of binoculars if you want to keep a close eye on your horse on the backstretch. The track opens daily at 11 AM.

SCORING AUTOGRAPHS: Alas, it might be a bit of a challenge to get the horses to sign anything for you. Jockeys, however, are another story. You might be able to get their autographs along the fence.

FOR THE KIDS: Despite the average age of the fan base, Suffolk Downs can be a fun and affordable day out for the family. Kids can get outside and are generally captivated by the horses. There is a playground on the lawn between the track and the grandstand that is well away from the standing area where many of the cigar- and cigarette-smoking bettors come out to watch the races—and perhaps use some salty language if their thoroughbreds don't behave as hoped. One disappointment is that the playground doesn't have any toy ponies for kids to ride, which would have seemed a natural fit. Children under twelve are admitted without charge.

TRACK CONCESSIONS: There are concession stands throughout the grandstand that serve basic staples such as hot dogs ($2.75), pretzels, peanuts, and hot and cold beverages. Concession stands have both domestic ($4.75 for 16-ounce Budweiser and Bud Light drafts) and imported ($5.25 for a can of Heineken, Corona, or Amstel Light) beer options as well as mixed drinks. The Deli Grill on the first floor of the grandstand also has sandwiches, pizza, ice cream, and soft drinks.

If you're in the mood for a sit-down meal, the Terrace offers tiered seating, reminiscent of Fenway Park's Green Monster seats, above the paddock area and finish line. Unlike the Monster seats, however, the Terrace is completely enclosed. The restaurant serves entrees, seafood, sandwiches, appetizers, and salads, and each table has a television monitor so you can watch all the races. The Terrace is only open on live racing days, and reservations are suggested for most Saturdays and required on MassCap day.

On the second floor above the clubhouse entrance is Legends Bar & Grill, which offers

> ★ **Greyhound Racing**
>
> Just three stops north on the Blue Line from Suffolk Downs is **Wonderland Greyhound Park** (190 VFW Parkway, Revere, MA 02151. 781-284-1300; www.wonderlandgreyhound.com), which stages live greyhound racing and simulcasting of dog and horse races. The track was built on the site of the old Wonderland Amusement Park and Revere Cycle Track and opened a month before Suffolk Downs. On the South Shore, **Raynham Park** (1958 Broadway, Raynham, MA 02767. 508-824-4071; www.raynhamparkfun.com) also features live greyhound racing and simulcasting. For better or worse, the days of greyhound racing in Massachusetts are numbered, however, as voters in 2008 approved a measure to ban dog racing in the state by January 1, 2010.

both table and bar service. The sports bar has a bank of televisions showing races as well as other sporting events.

FOOD AND DRINK AROUND THE TRACK: East Boston is home to a wealth of restaurants—many specializing in Italian, Asian, and South American cuisine—that are just a short drive away from Suffolk Downs. *Santarpio's Pizza* (111 Chelsea Street, 617-567-9871, www.santarpiospizza.com) is considered by some foodies to be the best in Boston. *Kelley's Square Pub* (84 Bennington Street, 617-567-4627, www.kelleyssquarepub.com), with walls filled with photographs of sports figures, is a popular spot for its pub grub and pizzas.

CONTACT INFORMATION: 111 Waldemar Avenue, East Boston, MA 02128. 617-567-3900; www.suffolkdowns.com. (Call 617-568-3216 for information on the simulcast schedule, weather and track conditions, scratches, and live racing results.)

LACROSSE

HUNDREDS OF YEARS BEFORE the Boston Braves took to the baseball diamond, Boston's braves were playing another sport—lacrosse. Native Americans across New England and all over the North American continent played the sport for recreation as well as settling disputes between villages and tribes. Some lacrosse games had hundreds of players to a side, and there were heated matches between villages. In fact, these village rivalries were so fierce they were known to erupt into violent confrontations.

Lacrosse staged a resurgence in Boston in the 1870s and 1880s and often brought thousands of fans to Boston Common's parade ground each Fourth of July for an annual match between Boston's Union Athletic Club and teams from New York City and Canada. Tickets to the inaugural contest in 1872 sold for fifty cents, and newspaper advertisements touted it as "a match of this highly exciting Indian game."

In the decade that followed that first match on the Common, lacrosse became increasingly popular in Boston. Local clubs that formed in city neighborhoods and surrounding towns played matches at the South End Grounds and Franklin Park, among other venues. Harvard students formed a team in the 1870s, and the university won the first-ever intercollegiate lacrosse tournament in 1881.

Although lacrosse didn't have the same staying power as other nascent sports of the time, such as baseball and football, lacrosse is currently experiencing a second renaissance. It is the fastest-growing team sport in America, and its popularity in Boston is spreading beyond its traditional prep-school bastions to public high schools. In particular, younger sports fans are drawn to lacrosse's fast-paced action, physical contact, and high scoring.

Boston lacrosse fans have their chance to watch the sport throughout the year. Local colleges take the field in springtime. (The men and women of Harvard play Division I lacrosse, and the women at Boston University and Boston College also play at the NCAA's highest level.) An added bonus for local fans was the staging of the NCAA Men's Lacrosse Championships at Gillette Stadium in 2008 and 2009, which drew crowds of over forty thousand. During the summer, the **Boston Cannons** draw thousands of fans to Harvard Stadium, and in winter months, the rough and tumble action moves indoors to the TD Garden with the **Boston Blazers**.

BOSTON CANNONS

The Boston Cannons, a charter member of Major League Lacrosse, began play in 2001. The field lacrosse team played in Lowell for three seasons before moving to Nickerson Field at Boston University. Since 2007 the Cannons have called the venerable Harvard Stadium their home.

The Cannons play six home games each year, mostly on Friday or Saturday nights.

A Boston Cannons player evades a defender at Harvard Stadium.

Cannons games, which typically draw an average of eight thousand fans, have a festive, family-friendly atmosphere with fans tailgating and tossing around balls with their lacrosse sticks before games. Games can be high scoring with both teams routinely netting a double-digit number of goals. If for some reason that isn't enough entertainment, there are on-field contests, t-shirt tosses—and cheerleaders too.

STADIUM INFORMATION: The Boston Cannons play their home games at Harvard Stadium in the Allston section of Boston. For more information on Harvard Stadium, see page 110.

WHEN: The Boston Cannons regular season runs from May to August.

GETTING THERE: See page 111.

TICKETS: The Cannons sell tickets for the east side of Harvard Stadium, behind the team benches. Most of the seats at Harvard Stadium are uncovered, with the exception of wooden risers at the top of each section that are underneath the stadium's circling colonnade. Except for those wooden risers, the seating in Harvard Stadium is on concrete slabs and lacks any seat backs.

Season-ticket holders get the best seats in the house at midfield, in sections 6–8 and the lower rows of sections 5 and 9. Season-ticket prices start at $108 and include an exclusive invitation to an event with players and coaches, discounted parking, and a discount on additional individual game tickets.

The Cannons sell individual game tickets in two categories:

Category 1 ($20) seating includes the upper rows of sections 5 and 9 and the lower rows of sections 3, 4, 10, and 11.

Category 2 ($15) seating is toward the corners of the field and includes all of sections 1, 2, 12, and 13 and the upper rows of sections 3, 4, 10, and 11.

To purchase tickets, call 617-746-9933 or go online to www.bostoncannons.com. Game day tickets can be purchased at the stadium box office.

DISABILITY ACCESS: For information, call 617-746-9933.

THE SPLURGE: If you want to get as close to the action as possible, the Sideline Club is for you. The Sideline Club is located right across from the benches on the field. In addition to getting a sideline seat, ticket holders receive private, on-field concessions, a VIP parking pass, a visit from the team's coaches during pregame warm-ups, and a visit from some of the players immediately after the game. A season ticket to the Sideline Club costs $332.

THE CHEAPSKATE: The cheapest seat for a Cannons game is $15, although you may be able to find a season-ticket holder unloading a ticket for less. Take the Red Line to Harvard Square and walk to the stadium to save on parking.

SPECTATOR TIPS: Fans are not permitted to bring food and beverages, coolers, video cameras, and umbrellas into the stadium. Tailgating is limited to three hours before the game and an hour afterwards. Charcoal grills are prohibited within the Harvard athletic complex, and the maximum allowable propane gas cylinder is twenty pounds.

SCORING AUTOGRAPHS: Cannons players will usually sign autographs following the game just beyond the north goal.

FOR THE KIDS: The Boston Cannons draw lots of kids to their games with their family-friendly offerings. The Cannons host a FanZone just outside the stadium with inflatable games and opportunities for kids to test their lacrosse skills. Youth lacrosse teams play on the field before games and at

617-746-9933; www.bostoncannons.com.

BOSTON BLAZERS

The Boston Blazers, who started play in January 2009, may be the city's newest pro team, but the current incarnation of the indoor lacrosse team actually marks the squad's second go-around in the Garden. In their previous stint—after moving from Worcester in 1992—the Blazers played in both the old and new Gardens until they folded in 1997.

The Blazers play on a green carpet placed atop the Bruins' ice rink, and the hard-hitting action of indoor lacrosse—with its cross-checking, penalty box, and fighting—has many features that appeal to New England's numerous hockey fans. As opposed to the ten men on outdoor lacrosse teams, indoor lacrosse teams field six men. The thirty-second shot clock ensures up-and-down action, and each game averages twenty-five goals. The Blazers, one of twelve teams in the National Lacrosse League, play eight home games on Saturday nights. In addition to the action on the field, the Blazers have a dance team, t-shirt tosses, a halftime show, and other in-game entertainment.

halftime, and kids can pal around with the team mascot, Boomer. Note that strollers are not permitted in Harvard Stadium.

STADIUM CONCESSIONS: In addition to the usual stadium concessions, the Cannons have a beer tent behind the goal in the horseshoe end of the stadium. The on-field tent has private concessions and a bar-like atmosphere. The tent is restricted to fans twenty-one years or older, and season tickets cost $90.

FOOD AND DRINK AROUND THE STADIUM: See page 114.

CONTACT INFORMATION: Boston Cannons, 214 Lincoln Street, Suite 320, Allston, MA 02134.

ARENA INFORMATION: The Boston Blazers play at the TD Garden. For more information, see page 64.

WHEN: The Boston Blazers regular season runs from January to April.

GETTING THERE: See page 65.

TICKETS: The Blazers offer numerous ticket options:

Club ($62) seats are situated between the goals on both sides of the field and are on the Garden's club level, located between the upper and lower levels.

VIP glass side ($60) seats are in the first few rows at midfield in sections 1, 2, 11, 12, 13, and 22.

Loge center ($48) seats are in the lower level at midfield and include seats in sections 1, 2, 11, 12, 13, and 22.

VIP glass end ($42) seats are the first few rows in the corners and behind the goals in sections 4–9 and sections 15–20.

Loge corner ($30) seats are located in the corners in the lower level and include seats in sections 3, 4, 9, 10, 14, 15, 20, and 21.

Loge end/Balcony center ($24) seats are located at midfield in the upper deck and includes sections 301, 302, 315, 316, 317, and 330. On the lower level, they include seats behind the goals in sections 5–8 and sections 16–19.

Balcony corner/End ($12) seats comprise most of the Garden's upper level. They include seats in sections 303-314 and sections 318-329.

Season tickets are $72 for balcony corner/end, $160 for loge end/balcony center, $200 for loge corner, $280 for VIP glass end, $320 for loge center, $400 for VIP glass side, and $416 for club seats. To purchase tickets, call 888-BLAZERS or go online to www.ticketmaster.com. Tickets can also be purchased at the Garden box office, which is open daily between 11 AM and 7 PM.

DISABILITY ACCESS: See page 67.

THE SPLURGE: The club seats, sandwiched between the upper and lower bowls of the arena, are the plushest you'll find in the Garden. The theater-style seats have extra legroom and in-seat wait service. The club level also has its own concession stands and bathrooms. They're tough to get—and pricey—for Celtics and Bruins games, but the Blazers offer a more affordable way to get into the club level.

THE CHEAPSKATE: How does $40 for season tickets sound? Pretty good to a cheapskate. The Blazers offer a limited number of seats in the back row of the arena, dubbed the "Ring of Fire," for $40, which amounts to $5 a game. The Blazers offer numerous other ticket deals; sign up for the team's Inferno Fan Club on the website to stay abreast of them.

SPECTATOR TIPS: Bags, backpacks, food, beverages, cameras with detachable lenses, and video cameras are strictly prohibited from the Garden. Smoking is not permitted in the arena.

SCORING AUTOGRAPHS: The Blazers stage autograph sessions after games for fans to get signatures of their favorite players.

FOR THE KIDS: The Blazers host birthday parties with pregame pizza or cake with the team's mascot. Kids are also given the chance to line up on the field and high-five the players as they take the field. Youth teams have the opportunity to play on the same field as the Blazers.

ARENA CONCESSIONS: See page 70.

FOOD AND DRINK AROUND THE ARENA: See page 70.

CONTACT INFORMATION: Boston Blazers, 290 Portland Street, Suite 301, Boston, MA 02114. 888-BLAZERS; www.blazerslacrosse.com

The beloved Cape Cod Baseball League has been a summer tradition since the 1800s.
Courtesy Ted Pappas/pappasproductions.com.

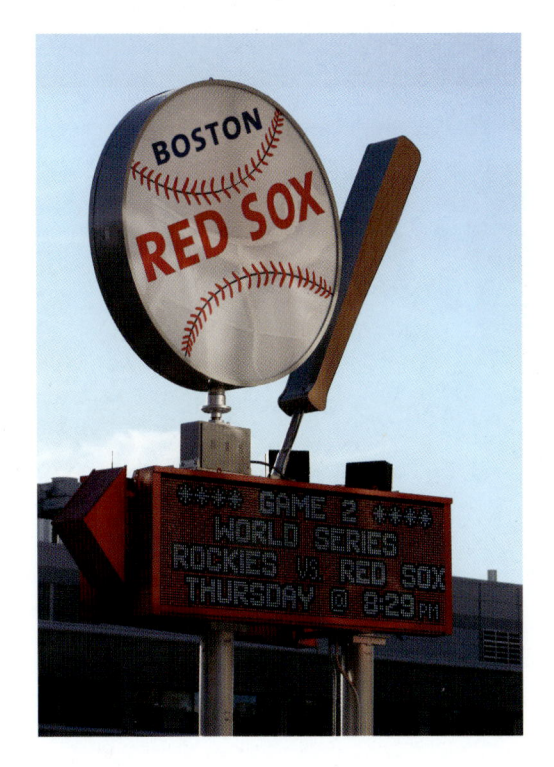

A sign outside Fenway Park previews a 2007 World Series game against the Colorado Rockies.
Courtesy Christopher Klein.

High school football, especially on Thanksgiving, is a proud Boston mainstay. Courtesy Mark Stern.

Patriots players huddle at training camp. Courtesy Christopher Klein.

THE DIE★HARD SPORTS FAN'S GUIDE TO BOSTON

The video scoreboard at the TD Garden shows a nice bird's eye view of the Bruins game.
Courtesy Rozane Velozo.

Excited Celtics fans have a cigar with Red Auerbach's memorial statue at the Faneuil Hall Marketplace.
Courtesy Eric Kilby.

The love for tennis and the Boston Lobsters covers all sizes…and species. Courtesy Karen Draymore.

The State House salutes the Red Sox as world champs! Courtesy Christopher Klein.

THE DIE★HARD SPORTS FAN'S GUIDE TO BOSTON

Signs and fans provide extra (and much needed) support for marathon runners at Heartbreak Hill.
Courtesy Mark Stern.

Even though it's nearly a quarter of a mile from home plate, the Citgo sign feels as if it's part of Fenway Park.
Courtesy Christopher Klein.

Boston University Women's Soccer takes on University of Hartford.
Courtesy Steve McLaughlin.

And they're off! Horse race at Suffolk Downs, East Boston. Courtesy Christopher Klein.

THE DIE★HARD SPORTS FAN'S GUIDE TO BOSTON

Courtesy Allison Fraske/fraskedesigns.com.

If you want a true die-hard experience, head to the Fort for a Revolution game.
Courtesy Keith Nordstrom/New England Revolution.

Rowers cruise by the Cambridge Boat Club during the Head of the Charles Regatta.
Courtesy Christopher Klein.

Two players battle for position at the Major League Lacrosse All-Star Game at Harvard Stadium.
Courtesy Mark Stern.

THE DIE★HARD SPORTS FAN'S GUIDE TO BOSTON

ROWING

THIN WISPS OF EARLY morning fog rise from the Charles River like steam from a cup of morning coffee. The only sounds piercing the noise of city life are the splashes of oars propelling through the placid water and the shouts of coxswains coaxing their crews along. While most Bostonians are still fast asleep, these single sculls and eight-men crews spend the early light dipping their blades in the Charles.

From the time the first Native Americans set foot on the Shawmut Peninsula, the promontory of land on which Boston was built, rowing on the Charles River and Boston Harbor was a primary method of transportation. The popularity of rowing as a recreational pursuit and a spectator sport dates back to around the 1840s, however, when clubs began to form and regattas were organized. Both Brahmin bluebloods and new immigrants from Ireland and England formed clubs, and while the waters on which they battled may have been calm, there was an undercurrent of class warfare just beneath the surface.

Boston is blessed with a perfect rowing venue. The broad expanse of the Charles River has hosted countless regattas and races over the years. Beginning in 1854, the city of Boston staged an annual regatta on the Fourth of July that was as much of an Independence Day tradition as the Boston Pops are today. Another major regatta was staged for years on Bunker Hill Day. These races continued to be major dates on the Boston sporting calendar into the 1900s. Tens of thousands of spectators crowded riverbanks, grandstands, wharves, brownstone rooftops, and boats to follow the races, some of which were as long as six miles. The regatta course ran westward on the Charles from the Braman's Baths at the foot of Chestnut Street. The bathhouse served as the original headquarters of the Union Boat Club, which was organized in 1851 and still exists today on Chestnut Street as one of the oldest boating organizations in the country.

Many of the regattas on the Charles featured students from Harvard, that august institution nestled on its shores. The first Harvard boat club formed in 1844, and two years later it held its first race against an outside opponent on a course on the Charles. In addition to racing their boats, the Harvard crew, in a nineteenth-century take on the designated driver concept, used them to ferry tipsy members back to campus after late nights out in Boston. In 1852 a sober crew of Harvard oarsmen took to the waters of New Hampshire's Lake Winnipesaukee and outraced two boats from Yale. It was the first intercollegiate athletic event in American history, and today the **Harvard-Yale Regatta** is an annual rowing highlight.

The Crimson still take to the Charles today for races in the spring and fall. The river basin offers a fantastic 2,000-meter stretch for standard-distance races and hosts dual and triangular cup races by Boston University, Northeastern, and MIT, all of which have boathouses along its banks. While rowing gained its initial popularity as a manly sport, today it is popular with both male and female athletes. The Charles is home to twenty-two men's and women's college crews, double that of any other body of water, and high school teams race there as well. On a given spring Saturday, there may be as many as fifty races taking place on the Charles.

Of course, the biggest rowing event in Boston—and America—is the **Head of the Charles Regatta**, which has resurrected the tradition of the old Fourth of July and Bunker Hill Day regattas. The October regatta draws more than eight thousand competitors from around the world to the Hub, some coming from as far away as South Africa and China. (Much less known is the Foot of the Charles race, held each November between regional colleges.)

Rowing in metropolitan Boston isn't limited to just the Charles River. Other bodies of water host races, including Lake Quinsigamond in Worcester. Each May the lake is the setting for the Eastern Sprints, the rowing championships for the Eastern Association of Rowing Colleges, which includes Boston University, Harvard, Northeastern, and MIT.

Even when the city's rivers are frozen sheets of ice, Boston is still a center of rowing activity. Each February rowers come to the Hub for the **World Indoor Rowing Championships** (www.crash-b.org), an indoor regatta designed to break up the monotony of winter training. More than two thousand rowers in fifty-eight different categories compete at Agganis Arena on rowing machines in 2,000-meter races. Whether indoors or outdoors, there are plenty of opportunities for Boston sports fans to watch athletes row, row, row their boats.

HEAD OF THE CHARLES REGATTA

Every October the Hub is invaded by an armada of nearly eighteen hundred boats from all over the world competing in the Head of the Charles. The regatta is an autumnal tradition in Boston. It draws as many as three hundred thousand spectators to the banks of the Charles River to watch more than eight thousand male and female rowers who range in age from fourteen to eighty-four.

Members of the Cambridge Boat Club organized the first Head of the Charles Regatta in 1965. About one hundred scullers competed in the inaugural event, but since then it has grown tremendously into the world's largest two-day regatta. There are fifty-seven events split between sculling and crew races with youth, collegiate, master, and veteran age groupings and boats with one, two, four, and eight rowers. In the tradition of "head of the river" races in England, boats race against each other and the clock. Each boat starts sequentially fifteen seconds apart. The winner is the boat that finishes the three-mile course—stretching from Boston University's DeWolfe Boathouse to the Fals/Herter Park along Soldiers Field Road—in the fastest time.

Much like Boston traffic at rush hour, races can be treacherous. The serpentine twists in the river, variable winds, and the seven bridges that span it make the course one of the most challenging in the world to navigate. Fender benders and close-quarter collisions worthy of NASCAR are common, and oar-to-oar combat may break out as faster boats try to pass slower boats and squeeze through the narrow arches of the bridges. A few boats, impaled by another shell or a bridge abutment, have even met a watery demise. All this combines to make the Head of the Charles a test of endurance, strength, and navigation.

WHEN: The Head of the Charles Regatta is held on the weekend of the next to last Sunday in October. Races on both Saturday and Sunday begin at approximately 8 AM and end around 5 PM.

GETTING THERE: There are plenty of places to park near the course, but free **parking** is much easier to find on Cambridge streets on Sunday, when parking permits are not required. Spectators can generally get prime on-street parking spots around Harvard Square before noon on Sunday. Be aware that Memorial Drive and the parking lots along Soldiers Field Road are closed to the public during the regatta.

To reach the Head of the Charles by **public transportation**, take the Red Line subway

HEAD OF THE CHARLES REGATTA *COURSE MAP*

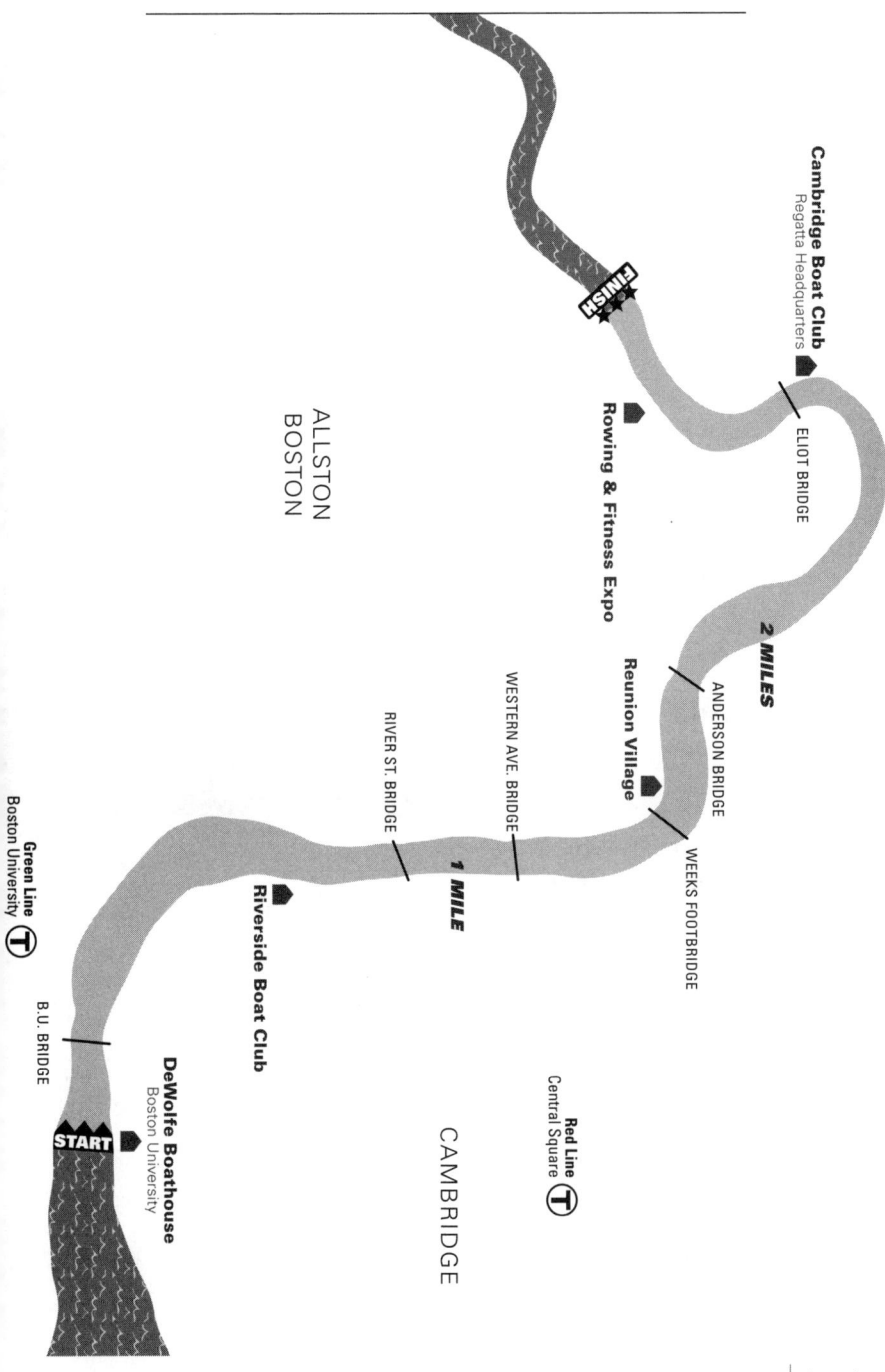

to either the Harvard station, about a five minute walk from the Charles, or the Central station, about a ten minute walk from the river. Another option is to take the "B" branch of the Green Line to either the Boston University West or Boston University Central stations, which are the nearest stops to the starting line. If you want to watch the action from various points along the course and don't want to walk, a shuttle runs between 7 AM and 7 PM.

TICKETS: Tickets are not required to watch the Head of the Charles.

THE SPLURGE: It's certainly not on par with luxury boxes at Fenway Park or Gillette Stadium, but Reunion Village, a hospitality tent area on the south bank of the Charles near Harvard Square, is the place to head if you'd like to watch the races with a cold beer in your hand from the comfort of a seat. Located between the Weeks Footbridge and the Anderson Bridge, Reunion Village offers breakfast and lunch in a dining tent that has seating and hardwood floors, a big-screen television with live racing footage and scrolling results, folding chairs on the riverbank, and commentary from the public address system. Reunion Village is the only place along the route where you can legally get a beer or wine. Beer costs $5; a hamburger costs $7. Many colleges and prep schools, mostly those with teams racing, have alumni reunion events inside Reunion Village, but even if you're not alumni, the village is open to everyone for a $1 admission charge.

THE CHEAPSKATE: The Head of the Charles is a cheapskate's dream. (Heck, even the admission for the splurge costs $1.) There's no charge to watch. There is free parking on surrounding streets on Sunday and a free shuttle to take you to various places on the course. Plus, with exhibitors around the Weeks Footbridge giving out free samples of food and beverages, you may not even have to spring for concessions. Skinflints won't find a better Boston sporting event to attend all year.

SPECTATOR TIPS: Given the winding course and the fact that rowers compete against a clock, watching a race from start to finish is pretty much impossible; it's difficult to even get a sense of who is winning at any point along the course. Instead of following a boat, most spectators stake out a spot and watch the race from a stationary point.

Harvard finishes first in New London, Connecticut, 1908. Courtesy Library of Congress.

To gauge how a particular boat is doing, keep an eye on its bow number—the placard mounted on its front. Boats start the race in sequential order of their bow numbers in 15-second intervals, so if you see a bow with a higher number in front of one with a lower number, it means that boat is racing at least fifteen seconds faster through that point on the course. You'll need to catch a glimpse of one of the race results boards to see who has won a particular race.

There are plenty of spots along the banks of the Charles to watch the action, but bring a blanket or lawn chair and you'll be a lot more comfortable. And if you're a shutterbug, bring your camera. You'll get some great action shots with a telephoto lens, particularly around Harvard where you can get the rowers in front of the university's picturesque brick buildings. There should be a splash of color on the trees as well.

With fifty-seven races and as many as sixty-nine competitors in a race, you definitely need a draw sheet to keep track of who's who. There is a draw on the regatta website, but printing it out will consume reams of paper. A better option is to get a copy of *The Boston Globe* on the Friday before the regatta. It has a map of the course, race schedule, and a list of competitors, which you can easily tear out and take with you.

As far as picking a place to watch the races, most spectators gather around a mile-long swath of shore on the Cambridge side of the Charles River near Harvard University. This section of the course has more vendors, more scenic backdrops, and more action as faster boats begin to make up the time difference against the slower boats in front of them.

The bridges along the course are also popular spots with spectators for their great overhead views of the competitors and the ability to hear the exhortations of the coxswains echoing off the underside of the spans. The Weeks Footbridge and the Anderson and Eliot bridges tend to fill up early, but the BU, River Street, and Western Avenue bridges, closer to the starting line, generally have room at most times of the regatta. The BU Bridge is the best vantage point to watch the start of the race. Beneath the Boston skyline, the flotilla of boats waiting to start looks like a miniature navy.

Sometimes catching the action from the riverbanks next to a bridge offers a better perspective than being on top. On occasion teams have trouble cleanly passing through the bridges, particularly if more than one team is going through at the same time. The bridges are the scenes of the most crashes and oar entanglements. If you're on the bridge, you'll miss the commotion.

Another good spot to watch the races is near the Eliot Bridge and the Cambridge Boat Club, the race headquarters. Spectators can watch the competitors negotiate Dead Man's Curve, a hairpin turn that requires a quick correction to get through the bridge. Inexperienced coxswains on youth, club, and collegiate fours and eights might have trouble navigating their crews through this stretch of the race, and boats tend to be bunched up here as time differences at the start are erased. As an added bonus, race commentary is provided over the public address system at the Cambridge Boat Club, so you can get some analysis on the progress of each race. There are also race announcers at the Riverside Boat Club, Reunion Village, and the finish line.

FOOD AND DRINK: Spectators don't have to wander far to grab a bite to eat. In addition to the food and drink available at the Reunion Village, vendors and pushcarts are concentrated at Magazine Beach near the launch, around the Cambridge Boat Club next to the Eliot Bridge, and at the Rowing and Fitness Expo (which also sells workout and rowing gear) near the finish line. The widest variety of choices, however, can be found on the north bank of the Charles right outside of Harvard Square between the Weld Boathouse and the Weeks Footbridge. Many of these vendors sell fair-like food: think kettle corn, hot chocolate, candied apples, hot cider, burgers, hot dogs, and "chowda" in a bread bowl. If you prefer something more substantial, head to the restaurants in Central Square or Harvard Square (see page 114), just a short walk north of the course.

CONTACT INFORMATION: Head of the Charles, c/o Cambridge Boat Club, Two Gerry's Landing Road, Cambridge, MA 02138. 617-868-6200; www.hocr.org.

BEYOND BOSTON

Harvard-Yale Regatta

Decades before their football teams squared off in The Game, Harvard and Yale staged their first battles on the water. On August 3, 1852, the two ancient universities met on Lake Winnipesaukee for a two-mile crew race, the birth of college athletic competition. The Crimson won the initial contest by defeating two Yale boats, and the rivalry between the men's heavyweight crews is still as fierce as ever.

These days Yale, which formed the first collegiate crew in the United States, and Harvard face off on the Thames River near New London, Connecticut. The Harvard-Yale Regatta, the traditional end to the collegiate rowing season, is staged on a Saturday in June with freshman, junior varsity, and varsity races. The heavyweight varsities eschew the typical race length of two thousand meters for a course more than three times that length—four miles. Only Oxford and Cambridge stage a longer side-by-side rowing event. The freshman race on a two-mile course, and the junior varsity squads cover three miles.

The day before the freshman, junior varsity, and varsity races, there is typically a two-mile combination race composed of second freshman and third varsity rowers. The winner of the combination race gets to paint its school colors on an enormous rock at Bartlett's Cove for the next day's feature races. (Local residents have been known to re-paint the rock in Yale blue after the race if it had been sporting crimson and white.)

Harvard holds a sizable advantage in all three races and has captured twenty-one of twenty-four varsity races between 1985 and 2008. Leading up to the regatta, the Harvard crew prepares at Red Top, its training camp on the east bank of the Thames in Gales Ferry, Connecticut. The Yale crew trains nearby at the Gales Ferry Boathouse.

The 1925 regatta drew a crowd upwards of one hundred thousand spectators; grandstands were even mounted atop flatcars on special 32-car observation trains that rolled along the riverbank following the crews. These days crowds are much smaller. On race day hundreds of Harvard fans picnic and watch the races from Red Top and boats moored along the course.

WHEN: The Harvard-Yale Regatta is held annually on a Saturday in the first half of June.

GETTING THERE: Gales Ferry, Connecticut, home to the Harvard training camp, is approximately 110 miles from Boston. From Boston, take the Mass Pike west to Interstate 395 south. Take Exit 79A off Interstate 395 for Route 2A. Follow Route 2A across the Connecticut River and turn right onto Route 12 south. Follow for just over four miles into Gales Ferry and turn right onto Military Highway Road. Follow for approximately one mile. Red Top is on the right with the road down to the boathouse a quarter mile past the grounds. Signs on race day direct spectators.

CONTACT INFORMATION: Harvard Crew, 65 North Harvard Street, Boston, MA 02163. 617-495-7775; www.gocrimson.com.

RUNNING

THIS MAY BE ONE of the most walkable cities in America, but elite athletes from around the world come to Boston to run. And no road race in the city—or the country—is bigger than the **Boston Marathon**. Every Patriots Day, the world's oldest marathon brings Boston sports fans out in droves.

The marathon is staged by the Boston Athletic Association (BAA), which was founded in 1887 when smaller athletic clubs pooled their resources and finances to form a rival to the New York Athletic Club. The BAA held its first organized track-and-field competition in 1890, and BAA members constituted the majority of the United States team at the first modern Olympiad in Athens in 1896.

In addition to the Boston Marathon, the **BAA Half Marathon** (617-236-1652; www.baa.org/halfmarathon) is held each October on a course stretching from the Fenway to Franklin Park along Frederick Law Olmsted's Emerald Necklace. The BAA also sponsors the **Mayor's Cup** (617-236-1652; www.baa.org/mayorscup) cross-country races each fall in Franklin Park, which has also served as the venue for national world cross-country championships. Another fall running tradition is the **Tufts Health Plan 10K for Women** (888-767-RACE; www.tuftshealthplan.com/tufts10k), which is run on Columbus Day weekend through the streets of the Back Bay and along the Charles River in Cambridge.

Even when winter comes, the runners keep on churning their legs. For decades Boston Garden hosted indoor track meets sponsored by the BAA and the Knights of Columbus. These days the Reggie Lewis Track and Athletic Center is the premier indoor track facility in Boston, and it hosts the **Reebok Boston Indoor Games, USA Track & Field Indoor Championships**, and **Nike Indoor Nationals** in addition to local high school and collegiate track meets. Local colleges also stage indoor and outdoor track-and-field meets and cross-country races at other locations around the city.

BOSTON MARATHON

Every April a sea of twenty-five thousand runners from around the world descends upon the tiny town of Hopkinton; they are filled with carbohydrates and dreams of making the 26-mile trek to the Boston Public Library. About twenty-two thousand runners—leaving a carpet of trampled paper cups in their wake—will complete the Boston Marathon, albeit with exhausted bodies and aching, blistered feet.

The Boston Marathon is not only one of Boston's great sporting traditions but one of the great American sporting traditions as well. Today's marathoners are the trustees of a tradition that dates back to the end of the nineteenth century. Leaders of the Boston Athletic Association were so inspired by the spectacle of the marathon in the first modern Olympic Games in Athens in 1896 that they decided to stage their own race. That starting field of fifteen men in the inaugural Boston Marathon on April 19, 1897, was just a *tad* smaller than today's field of twenty-five thousand. Unlike the present-day course, Metcalfe's Mill in Ashland was the starting point for the 24-mile trek into town. Tom Burke, winner of two sprinting medals in Athens, scraped the heel of his boot across the road to fashion a makeshift starting line, and when he gave the word, the runners were off. Not until 1924 was the starting line moved to Hopkinton, and in 1927 the course was lengthened to its present 26 miles and 385 yards to conform to Olympic standards.

These early marathoners dealt with choking clouds of dust kicked up by the circus of spectators, carriages, wagons, and cyclists who followed them. The finish line for that first race was the city's track-and-field

A couple of young fans high-five runners at the Boston Marathon.

stadium, the Irvington Street Oval, located where Copley Place stands today. Ten of the fifteen runners who started in Ashland crossed the finish line, but none was faster than John J. McDermott, who finished the course in just under three hours in front of a standing-room only crowd that rushed the oval to shake the hand of the victor.

The marathon has been run each year since 1897. That tenure makes it the world's oldest annual marathon. The only year it was modified was 1918, during World War I, when a ten-man relay race with soldiers in full uniform was held instead. Still, there were some hiccups in the early years of the marathon. For instance, in 1907 the race was temporarily interrupted when a train cut across the course in Framingham thereby severing the field and halting all but the lead pack of six runners.

A competitor in the wheelchair division of the Boston Marathon pushes on.

The Boston Marathon has a proud amateur tradition that dates back to its origin. The first winners of the marathon included a student, a blacksmith, a carpenter, and a plumber. Clarence DeMar, who won the race seven times between 1911 and 1930, trained by running from his home in Melrose to his job as a typesetter at the *Boston Herald*. Legend has it that DeMar would go to work after capturing the marathon and set the type that announced his triumph on the front page of the next day's paper.

Johnny Kelley, whose name is synonymous with the Boston Marathon, worked as a florist's assistant in Arlington when he captured the first of his two titles in 1935. Later he worked as a maintenance man for Boston Edison. A working-class product of Medford, Kelley was a hometown hero and a local legend. In addition to his victories in 1935 and 1945, he finished second seven times. Perhaps most remarkable is that Johnny toed the starting line in Hopkinton sixty-one times. He ran his first race in 1928 and his last full marathon in 1992—at the age of eighty-four! (For two more years after that he only ran the last seven miles.) Johnny Kelley's churning legs on Marathon Monday were just as much a rite of spring in Boston as Opening Day at Fenway.

As distance running became a more popular form of exercise in the 1970s, the popularity of the Boston Marathon grew. In 1986 the grandfather of long-distance races began to award prize money in order to draw top runners and compete against other marathons around the world. Runners from Kenya, such as Robert Cheruiyot and Cosmas Ndeti, and other African nations now dominate the marathon. Kenyan runners won all but four of the men's marathons between 1988 and 2008, and Ethiopian men won two others.

Participants in the first Boston Marathon would be stunned by the technology used to track today's runners. Computer chips in runners' sneakers activate when crossing the start line and record exact times at intervals along the race. Friends and family can log on to the marathon website from anywhere in the world and get up-to-the-second split times. Too bad they didn't have those chips back in 1980, when Rosie Ruiz was the first woman to break the tape at the finish line. Oddly, Rosie looked rather refreshed after her twenty-six miles. Her secret? Jumping into the race near the end. Ruiz's ruse wasn't found out until well after the winner's laurel wreath was placed on her head.

For its first seventy-five years, only men were allowed to compete in the Boston Marathon. Female participation was viewed as dangerous to women, given the length of the race. The first official women's race was held in 1972, but in 1966 Roberta Gibb hid in the bushes near the starting line and jumped into the fray. She blended in with the pack and crossed the finish line. "Hub Bride First Gal to Run Marathon" was the newspaper headline the next day. Another breakthrough occurred in 1975 when Bob Hall became the first officially recognized participant to complete the course in a wheelchair. The wheelchair division has now grown to such stature that multiple-winners, such as Jean Driscoll and Ernst van Dyk, have become household names to many Boston sports fans.

The marathon draws a diverse crowd of runners. Elite runners compete against each other, but the rest of the marathoners battle both the punishing course and the limitations of their own bodies. The marathon is unique in that weekend warriors compete alongside the sport's best in the same contest. Imagine if local golfers could take to the links at The Country Club and compete against Tiger Woods and other greats, and you get a sense of how special an event the Boston Marathon is.

The elite runners may garner the headlines and television coverage, but the heart and soul of the Boston Marathon resides among the thousands of amateur runners pounding the pavement. Each runner has his or her own story of motivation, from raising money for charity to overcoming personal challenges. The loudest cheers are often reserved for these runners, such as the father-and-son team of Dick and Rick Hoyt. In addition to competing in triathlons and climbing mountains around the world, the Hoyts have run Boston more than twenty-five times since 1981. What's remarkable about Team Hoyt is that Rick was born with brain damage that left him a quadriplegic. He has never been able to walk or talk. Dick runs the twenty-six miles of the marathon while pushing his son's wheelchair, providing boundless inspiration to all the fans who line the course.

Although snow squalls have fallen on the heads of runners in some years, the Boston Marathon is one of those events that marks the arrival of spring in the city. The race is run on Patriots Day, a provincial public holiday celebrated only in Massachusetts and Maine (which was once part of the Bay State) that commemorates the Battles of Lexington and Concord that launched the American Revolution.

More than half a million fans line the route of the Boston Marathon, watching from the front yards of suburban houses and rooftops of city apartments. The race is the most widely viewed sporting event in New England, and the party starts with bars opening early in the morning. Fans act as a support network, encouraging the anguished and exhausted to the finish line. Of course, this *is* Boston and some spectators embrace the festive atmosphere more than the healthful aspect of the marathon, cheering on the runners while downing cheeseburgers and beers.

The Boston Marathon is considered one of the more difficult courses in the world because of the hills in the latter half of the race. For that reason, don't expect to see too many world records. There are plenty of smiles on the faces of the winners, however, especially when—in the finest tradition of the Greeks—the traditional laurel wreaths are placed upon their heads. The winners' traditional post-race cups of beef stew, however, are a uniquely New England touch.

COURSE INFORMATION: Much like life, the Boston Marathon, which winds through eight towns, is full of ups and downs. After starting at 475 feet above sea level in Hopkinton, the foot race travels through Ashland, Framingham, Natick, Wellesley, Newton, and Brookline before arriving in Boston.

The first half of the Boston Marathon is run on Route 135 before it follows Route 16 through Wellesley. Once in Newton, the course takes a right turn onto Commonwealth Avenue just past the 17-mile mark. This part of the course has the highest dropout rate. Unsurprisingly, the proximity of the Woodland Green Line station tempts those who'd rather avoid the upcoming hills and take public transportation to the finish. A series of three slow, punishing inclines on Commonwealth Avenue, in particular Heartbreak Hill, can take their toll on the weary.

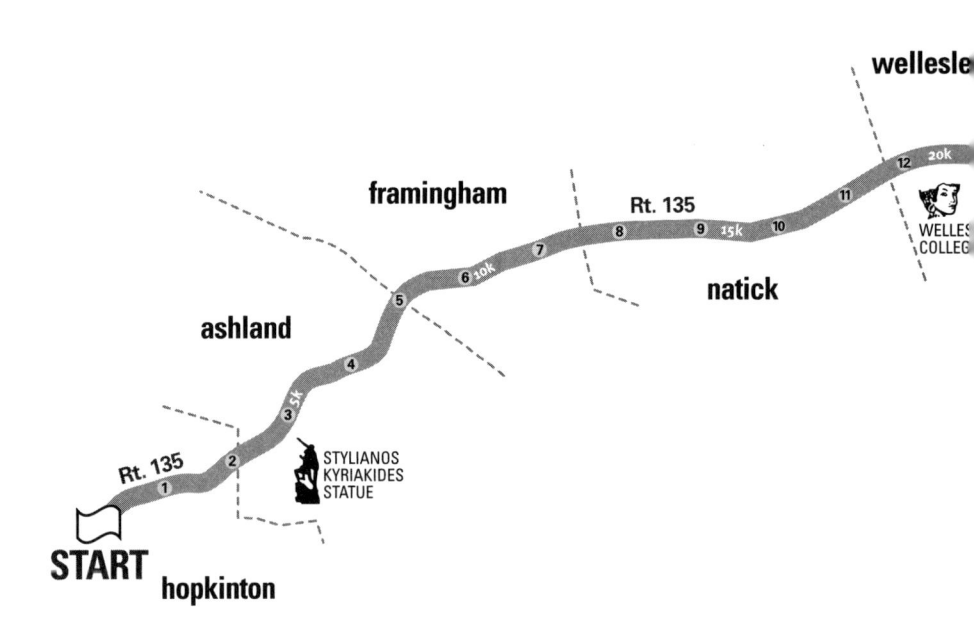

Heartbreak Hill, an 80-foot ascent just more than five miles from the finish line, is the most fabled part of the course. The BAA had wanted a barrier near the end of the race to challenge the runners, and they were successful beyond their wildest dreams. *Boston Globe* reporter Jerry Nason gave the hill its famous moniker after the 1936 race, when favorite Johnny Kelley caught leader Ellison "Tarzan" Brown on the incline and gave him a friendly tap on the shoulder. An incensed Brown responded by regaining the lead and winning the race, and as Nason reported, "breaking Kelley's heart."

Near the 22-mile mark, the course turns right and descends down Chestnut Hill Avenue. After a few hundred yards, the runners arrive in Cleveland Circle and take a left onto Beacon Street. Once in Kenmore Square, near the 25-mile mark, the course returns to Commonwealth Avenue before turning right on Hereford Street and then left onto Boylston Street for the home stretch to the finish line in front of the Boston Public Library between Exeter and Dartmouth streets.

WHEN: The Boston Marathon takes place on Patriots Day, the third Monday in April. The marathon's traditional noon start has

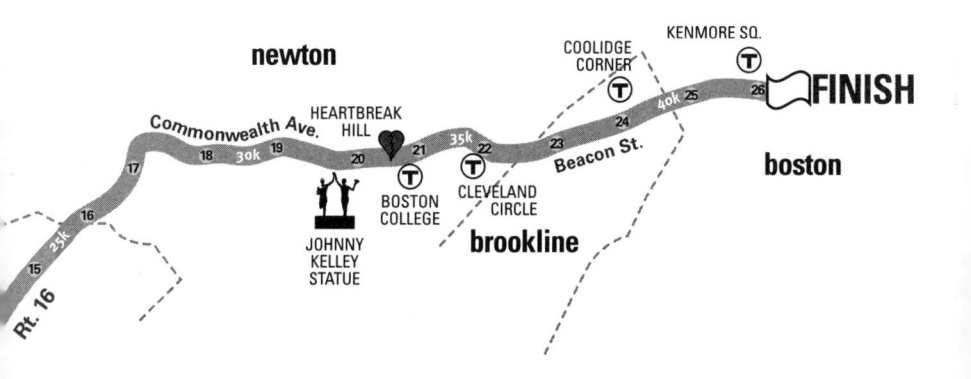

Boston Marathon Course Map

The President's Marathon Challenge fields a team of two hundred Tufts University students, faculty, and alumni from around the country to run the Boston Marathon. It is the largest known collegiate marathon program in the United States.

been replaced by staggered morning start times. Wheelchair racers start a little before 9:30 AM, and the elite women start a short time later. The elite men start at 10 AM. The rest of the field is divided in two, with half starting at 10 AM and half at 10:30 AM. The final band of stragglers stagger to the finish line around 6 PM, filled with equal parts exhilaration and exhaustion.

GETTING THERE: If you're driving to the race, be aware of numerous road closures along the route. You'll have to find **parking** spots on local neighborhood streets and walk to the course. If you're taking **public transportation**, the Green Line is your best bet. Just be ready for the crowds. Many Green Line stops parallel the marathon route: The "C" branch, like the marathoners, runs down Beacon Street. The end of the "B" branch near Boston College also runs along the route. The Green Line's Copley station is the nearest to the finish line, but it's closed on Marathon Monday, so use the Arlington or Hynes Convention Center stations instead. The Back Bay station on the Orange Line is also within walking distance of the finish line. The MBTA commuter rail's Framingham/Worcester line also makes stops along the route in Framingham, West Natick, Natick, Wellesley Square, Wellesley Hills, and Back Bay stations.

SPECTATOR TIPS: Unless your heart is set on it, skip watching the start of the race in Hopkinton. With fleets of school buses transporting runners to the starting line and downtown areas restricted to competitors, it can be a madhouse getting into Hopkinton. If you're set on going, leave early and try to get one of the limited parking spots at the industrial park on South Street or at the Hopkinton State Park on Route 85.

Crowds are thick in the centers of Framingham, Natick, and Wellesley, but it's still not that difficult to find a viewing spot in the suburban portions of the race. There's a lot of energy at Wellesley College around the 10-mile mark, where a boisterous crowd of the all-female students lines Route 135 and encourages the runners in a tradition dating back to the inaugural race. It's one of the loudest areas on the course, so bring earplugs.

Heartbreak Hill can be a turning point in the race for the leaders and the most punishing part of the course for the masses. Crowds at Heartbreak Hill try to perk up the spirits of the runners who may be hitting the wall and puffing up the hills.

Crowds pick up again at the Boston College campus, where the band serenades the runners. Cleveland Circle and Coolidge Corner, both along Beacon Street, are crowded spots due to their numerous watering holes. Avoid the area around Kenmore Square, which can get mobbed after the end of the annual Patriots Day morning game at Fenway Park.

If you want to see the runners in their finishing kick down Boylston Street, get there early or eat your Wheaties and grow a couple of feet taller. Crowds get very deep and unless you're in the front, you won't see anything except the top of the Prudential Center.

If you miss out on the action on Marathon Monday, there are still marathon-related sights to see along the course from Hopkinton to Boston the rest of the year. Feel free to run it if you'd like; most of us will take our cars.

At Hopkinton the starting line is painted across Route 135 at the town green. Nearby is a statue of George V. Brown holding his starter's pistol aloft. Brown was a BAA athletic director and starter of the marathon between 1905 and 1937. He was born and raised in Hopkinton and was instrumental in getting the starting line moved there. Brown's descendants still serve as starters.

At the one-mile mark at Weston Nurseries on Route 135 is a statue honoring Stylianos Kyriakides, whose victory in the 1946 Boston Marathon helped bring worldwide attention and badly needed relief supplies to his war-torn homeland of Greece. Kyriakides himself was so emaciated from the Nazi occupation and the country's civil war that he was advised against running the race by doctors, but he pulled away from Johnny Kelley after hearing a shout from the crowd: "For Greece, for your children!" The statue depicts Kyriakides and Spiridon Louis, his mentor and winner of the 1896 Olympic Marathon. A similar statue is located in Marathon, Greece, a sister city to Hopkinton.

On Pleasant Street in Ashland, about a half-mile north of the current course, is Marathon Park, which commemorates the foot race's original starting line. The park includes a pathway lined with historic stations documenting the marathon.

Even though Johnny Kelley was the marathon's ultimate iron man, you'll find him in bronze these days. At the corner of Commonwealth Avenue and Walnut Street in Newton, near City Hall and just before the inclines leading to Heartbreak Hill, are two likenesses of Kelley. On the left is a 27-year-old Kelley winning the 1935 race, and on the right is an 84-year-old Kelley completing his final marathon in 1992. The two are linked hand in hand, breaking the tape at the finish line.

The painted finish line can be seen outside the Boston Public Library, although it generally fades as the months go by. In 1996 a 15-foot granite medallion was embedded on the Boylston Street side of Copley Square to mark the centennial edition of the race. The medallion includes geographic and topographical maps of the course encircled by the names, countries, and finishing times of previous winners. Four red granite bollards on the medallion's perimeter include bronze reliefs of runners and wheelchair athletes. Also in Copley Square is a three-foot-high tortoise and hare statue, inscribed "in tribute to runners from all over the world." If you crave more, **The Sports Museum** (see page 246) has marathon artifacts on display; the headquarters of the **Boston Athletic Association** does too (see page 242).

SCORING AUTOGRAPHS: Top runners will occasionally sign autographs at the John Hancock Sports & Fitness Expo, held the weekend before the race. On race day runners may be too busy focusing on the marathon beforehand and too tired afterward to sign autographs. And if you really need to be told, don't try and get a signature during the race. Take it from seven-time winner Clarence DeMar, who once remarked, "Once at Auburndale, I was confronted by a youth with a pencil and a book looking for my autograph. Spontaneously, I poked him in the face and ran better for it. Running against time and signing autographs are two feats that cannot be done at the same time."

CONTACT INFORMATION: Boston Athletic Association, 40 Trinity Place, Fourth Floor, Boston, MA 02116. 617-236-1652; www.bostonmarathon.org.

BOSTON INDOOR GAMES

The Reebok Boston Indoor Games, which dates back to 1996, is one of the stops in the USA Track & Field Visa Championship Series. The annual indoor meet attracts elite male and female track-and-field athletes from around the world. Since its start, more than one hundred Olympic and world championship medalists have competed in this one-day event, and six world records have been set in the games staged at Boston's Reggie Lewis Track and Athletic Center. Running events range from 60-meter sprints to 3,000-meter and two-mile middle distance races. Field events include the shot put, long jump, and pole vault. There are also invitational mile events for masters, boys, girls, and a youth relay.

ARENA INFORMATION: The Boston Indoor Games are held at the Reggie Lewis Track and Athletic Center, located at 1350 Tremont Street in Roxbury. The center's field house has permanent seating for thirty-five

---

★ The Connolly Boys

Two of the best track-and-field athletes ever produced in Boston share a common last name—Connolly. James Brendan Connolly, the pride of South Boston, won the first medal of the modern Olympiad by capturing silver (gold medals were not awarded to winners until later) in the hop, skip, and jump (now known as the triple jump) in Athens in 1896. Something of a renaissance man, Connolly also wrote dozens of maritime books and stories. A statue in **Moakley Park** in South Boston along Old Colony Boulevard depicts his winning jump. In 1956 Harold Connolly, the product of Brighton High, won the gold medal in the hammer throw despite a physical disability that left his left arm four inches shorter than his right. A statue of Harold Connolly, frozen in the midst of a hammer throw, graces the lawn of the **Taft School** in Brighton at the corner of Warren and Cambridge streets.

hundred fans, but it can be expanded to five thousand with temporary seating. The field house features a state-of-the-art 200-meter banked track that is considered to be one of the fastest in the country; an eight-lane 60-meter dash runway; and an infield for high jump, long jump and triple jump, and pole vault events. The center, which opened in June 1995 at Roxbury Community College, was named after former Celtic and Northeastern basketball star Reggie Lewis, who tragically passed away in 1993 at the age of twenty-seven.

WHEN: The Boston Indoor Games are usually held on a Saturday in January or February.

GETTING THERE: From north and south of Boston, take the Southeast Expressway to Exit 18 (Mass. Ave.). From the north, follow the ramp onto Melnea Cass Boulevard. From the south, follow the ramp onto Frontage Road and take the left onto Melnea Cass Boulevard. From Melnea Cass Boulevard, take a left onto Tremont Street. The athletic center is a quarter-mile ahead on the left. From west of Boston, take the Mass Pike to Exit 22 (Copley Square) and turn right onto Dartmouth Street. Take Dartmouth Street for about a half-mile and take a right onto Tremont Street. The Reggie Lewis Center is a little more than a mile ahead on the left.

There is very limited free **parking** accessible from Tremont Street at the Reggie Lewis Center. There are also parking spots on neighboring streets as well as parking lots south of the center along Columbus Avenue that can be accessed by New Cedar, New Heath, and Centre streets.

The athletic center is very convenient to **public transportation**. The center is directly across the street from the Roxbury Crossing

Edward "Ned" Gourdin soars through the air as he breaks the world record for the long jump with a leap of 25'-3" at Harvard Stadium in 1921.
Courtesy Boston Public Library, Print Department.

station on the Orange Line. Numerous bus lines also stop at Roxbury Crossing.

TICKETS: Bleachers at the Reggie are located along the two stretches of the track as well as turns one and two. There are generally between eight and ten rows in the bleachers. Tickets to the Boston Indoor Games sell out regularly.

Platinum ($60) seats are located directly above the finish line in sections 7, 8, and 9P. *Gold* ($40) seats are adjacent to the finish line on the home stretch in section 6 and sections 9G to 12. They are also located on the backstretch in sections 15 to 19. *Silver* ($20) seats are general admission on turns one and two and are located in sections 3 to 5 and 20 and 21.

Tickets for children twelve and under can be purchased at a $10 discount. To purchase tickets, call 877-TIX-TRAC, go

online to www.bostonindoorgames.com, or visit the center's ticket window.
CONTACT INFORMATION: Reggie Lewis Track and Athletic Center, 1350 Tremont Street, Boston, MA 02120. 877-TIX-TRAC; www.bostonindoorgames.com.

USA INDOOR TRACK & FIELD CHAMPIONSHIPS

The USA Indoor Track & Field Championships, the final indoor event of the Visa Championship Series, hosts some of the finest American track-and-field athletes. The meet is the world's oldest indoor track championships, dating back to the first event in 1888 in New York. The two-day meet has six to nine hours worth of action each day as men and women compete in heats and finals for events such as the 60-meter dash; 60-meter hurdles; 400-, 800-, and 1,500-meter races; and pole vault.
ARENA INFORMATION: The USA Indoor Track & Field Championships are held at the Reggie Lewis Track and Athletic Center. See page 217 for more information.
WHEN: The USA Indoor Track & Field Championships is usually held on a weekend in February or early March.
GETTING THERE: See page 217.
TICKETS: Bleachers at the Reggie are located along the two stretches of the track as well as turns one and two. Tickets to sessions can sell out.

Gold ($30) seats are located in sections 8 and 9 on the finish line. *Silver* ($20) seats are located near the finish line in sections 10 to 12 and along the back stretch in sections 15 to 19. *Bronze* ($10) seats are located in one of the turns in sections 20 to 22.

USA Track & Field members receive discounts on ticket prices. Tickets for the USA Indoor Track & Field Championships are available by phone at 317-713-4680, online at www.usatf.org, and at the center's ticket window.
CONTACT INFORMATION: USA Track & Field, 132 East Washington Street, Suite 800, Indianapolis, IN 46204. 317-261-0500; www.usatf.org.

NIKE INDOOR NATIONALS

The best high school track-and-field athletes from across the country compete in the Nike Indoor Nationals, owned and operated by the National Scholastic Sports Foundation. After an absence of twelve years, the meet returned to Boston in 2009. There are more than twenty events for both boys and girls. Individual track events range from the 60-meter dash to the 5,000-meter run. There are numerous relay races, a one-mile race walk, and field events such as the high jump, pole vault, triple jump, shot put, and weight throw.
ARENA INFORMATION: The USA Indoor Track & Field Championships are held at the Reggie Lewis Track and Athletic Center. See page 217 for more information.
WHEN: The Nike Indoor Nationals are held annually on a weekend in March.
GETTING THERE: See page 217.
TICKETS: Call 617-541-3535 for information.
CONTACT INFORMATION: Reggie Lewis Track and Athletic Center, 1350 Tremont Street, Boston, MA 02120. 617-541-3535; rltac.com.

TENNIS

Tennis flourished in Boston from the time it was first introduced to America in the 1870s. Lawn tennis quickly became a fashionable pastime among the well-heeled Brahmins of Boston during the Gilded Age. Metropolitan Boston was the location of many of the sport's groundbreaking events, and numerous Bostonians helped to popularize the sport and guide it through its infancy.

In fact, the first tennis match in the United States may have taken place at a seaside estate just north of Boston in the suburb of Nahant. On a summer day in 1874, James Dwight, a Boston physician, and Fred Sears, scion of one of the Hub's wealthiest families, opened up a boxed tennis set newly imported from London, staked out a court, and began to swat the rubber ball with their spoon-shaped rackets.

There are numerous claims as to where the sport was actually introduced, of course, and it's hard to know definitively whether Dwight and Sears were the first players to wield rackets in America. But if you drive down Swallow Cave Road on Nahant's East Point, you'll find a small wooden sign just a short lob from the waters of Massachusetts Bay: "The first game of lawn tennis in the United States was played at this site in August of 1874."

Whether or not that claim is true, it's undeniable that Bostonians were early pioneers and enthusiastic supporters of this new sport, which quickly gained popularity among the genteel denizens of New England's summertime resorts. Dwight, who has been dubbed the Father of American Tennis, organized and won the country's first tennis tournament in Nahant in 1876. He was also a driving force behind the 1881 creation of the United States National Lawn Tennis Association, which he guided for twenty-one years as the organization's president. The association created the U.S. National Lawn Tennis Championships, the forerunner of today's U.S. Open.

The national championships—first held in Newport, Rhode Island—were certainly events for the high-society crowd, a bunch of bluebloods on the green lawns of the Newport Casino. The tournament's early years were dominated by

Bostonian Dick Sears, Fred's brother. Dick Sears was the Roger Federer of his era. He won the first U.S. Championship in 1881 as well as the next six titles before retiring. His seven consecutive wins are a record, although, unlike current greats, defending champions only had to play in the finals to retain their title. Sears also teamed with Dwight for five national doubles championships, and he captured a national amateur title in court tennis.

Eleo Sears, Fred's daughter and Dick's niece, was another Brahmin in the vanguard of the sport. She was also one of Boston's most fascinating personalities and athletes, a four-time winner of the national doubles title, a champion equestrian, and a dogged rambler who was known to walk from Boston to Providence on occasion. Challenging the conventions of the times, Eleo Sears was reputedly the

The national championships—first held in Newport, Rhode Island—were certainly events for the high-society crowd. Courtesy Library of Congress.

first woman to play squash in the United States and one of the first American women to fly in an airplane.

The Sears family has given Boston several landmarks, such as the family mansion at 42 Beacon Street that now houses the Somerset Club and the Sears' Crescent, next to City Hall Plaza, best identified by the oversized, steaming kettle hanging from its front. In addition, a portion of the family's 600-acre estate—named Longwood by David Sears in honor of the house on Saint Helena where his hero Napoleon was exiled—was the original location for the famed **Longwood Cricket Club** (564 Hammond Street, Chestnut Hill, MA 02467. 617-731-2900; www.longwoodcricket. com). Shortly after the club was formed in 1877 (at what are now the grounds of the Winsor School at the corner of Brookline and Longwood avenues) a grass tennis court was added, and in very short order tennis, not cricket, became the club's sport of choice.

In 1900, club member Dwight Davis organized the first international tennis competition between the United States and Great Britain. Davis commissioned the venerable Boston jeweler and silversmith Shreve, Crump & Low to execute a silver punchbowl trophy that now bears his name. Davis and two Harvard classmates, Malcolm Whitman and Holcombe Ward, won the inaugural competition at Longwood Cricket Club, and from those humble beginnings the Davis Cup has grown into an annual global competition with 130 competing countries. In total more than fourteen Davis Cup ties have been played at Longwood, both at its old location and its current site along Route 9 in Chestnut Hill.

Between 1964 and 1999, Longwood was also home to the now-defunct U.S. Pro Tennis Championships, and its roll call of winners includes illustrious names such as Rod Laver, Jimmy Connors, Bjorn Borg, and Ivan Lendl. While the pros have left Longwood, the club still hosts annual national grass court championships for father-son and father-daughter teams as well as for hearty competitors aged eighty-five and older.

While it could have been game, set, and match for Boston tennis fans after the U.S. Pro left town, the sport has staged a revival in recent years. After a nearly two-decade absence, the **Boston Lobsters** returned to the area in 2005, and the **Champions Cup Boston** has been a welcome addition to the local sports scene. The **Sportsmen's Tennis Club** (950 Blue Hill Avenue, Dorchester, MA 02124. 617-288-9092; www.sportsmenstennisclub.org) also hosts an annual USTA Pro Circuit tournament, akin to the minor leagues in team sports, that features women players with world rankings outside of the top fifty.

Boston sports fans are also fortunate to be a short drive away from the **International Tennis Hall of Fame and Museum** in Newport, Rhode Island. In addition to stepping back through the history of the game, Bostonians can pay homage to James Dwight, Dick Sears, Eleo Sears, and Dwight Davis—a group of Brahmins who helped shepherd the sport through its important formative years.

BOSTON LOBSTERS

Long before he ever owned the New England Patriots, Bob Kraft was the owner of another local sports team: the Boston Lobsters of World TeamTennis. The Lobsters were one of the original franchises when the tennis league was launched in 1974, but the team folded in 1978. When the franchise was resurrected in 2005 under a different owner, so was the team's colorful name. (The *Lob*sters ... get it?)

World TeamTennis, co-founded by tennis legend Billie Jean King, features teams of two men and two women, and each match consists of five sets—one set each of men's and women's singles, men's and women's doubles, and mixed doubles. Stars from the past and present—such as Venus and Serena Williams, Martina Navratilova, and John McEnroe—do play, but usually in just one or two of the seven home matches.

VENUE INFORMATION: After spending three seasons at Harvard (two of them indoors at the Bright Center), the Lobsters made the move to the Ferncroft Country Club in Middleton in 2008. This outdoor facility accommodates more than fifteen hundred people.
WHEN: Matches are played throughout July.
GETTING THERE: From Boston, take U.S. 1 north to Interstate 95 north. Take Exit 50 off Interstate 95, bear left to U.S. 1 south, and take first right onto Ferncroft Road, which becomes Village Road. From the north, take Exit 50 off Interstate 95 south, merge onto U.S. 1 south, and take the first right onto Ferncroft Road, which becomes Village Road. The club entrance is on the right of Village Road.

VIP **parking** is at Ferncroft Country Club. All other parking is at a location on Village Road with shuttle service provided to the venue.

TICKETS: Matches that feature one of the sport's headliners can sell out. *Box* ($50) seats are closest to the action ($60 when a marquee player is scheduled). *Reserved* ($25) seats ($30 when a marquee player is scheduled) are further back. Children twelve and under are restricted to reserved seats, and kids' prices are $10 ($15 when a marquee player is scheduled). Season tickets are $300 for box seats, which includes access to the boxholder hospitality area, and $150 for reserved seats.

To order tickets, call 800-514-ETIX (3849) or visit www.bostonlobsters.net.

DISABILITY ACCESS: Contact the Boston Lobsters at 877-617-LOBS for information on disability access.

THE SPLURGE: Get the VIP treatment at the VIP Lounge, which includes a private bar, food, and a chance to meet the players.

SPECTATOR TIPS: Doors open two hours prior to match time. Music and dance performers entertain the crowd before matches and during halftime.
SCORING AUTOGRAPHS: Players are generally accommodating about signing autographs and taking pictures after matches.
FOR THE KIDS: Through its "Ready, Set, Racquet!" program, World TeamTennis distributes a free tennis racquet, tennis ball, and racquet cover to all children between the ages of four and sixteen attending matches. Children under the age of two do not need a ticket.
FOOD AND DRINK: Fans can enjoy concessions and hear live performances in the Woodman's Vendor Village and the VIP Lounge.
CONTACT INFORMATION: Boston Lobsters, 75 Cambridge Parkway, Suite W1206, Cambridge, MA 02142. 877-617-LOBS; www.bostonlobsters.net.

CHAMPIONS CUP BOSTON

While the elimination of the U.S. Pro Tennis Championships has deprived Boston tennis fans of seeing the world's best men's players in their primes, at least they can watch tennis legends compete in the Champions Series, a relatively new competition akin to the senior golf tour. The Champions Cup Boston, first staged in 2006, has included competitors such as Pete Sampras, John McEnroe, Jim Courier, and Todd Martin. Eligible players must be at least thirty years old and have either held a top-five singles ranking, been a Grand Slam singles finalist, or played singles on a Davis Cup championship team.

The event includes six to eight players and has been played in both a round-robin and a single-elimination format. Matches are played in a best-of-three-set format, with the third set consisting of a modified tie-breaker.

The tournament atmosphere is definitely more relaxed than on the regular men's tour, with some players even joking with the crowd. However, the competition can still be intense, particularly if McEnroe is playing. Johnny Mac is still up to his old tricks, arguing and berating the linesmen who consistently miss his calls.

VENUE INFORMATION: The Champions Cup is held at the Agganis Arena on the campus of Boston University at 925 Commonwealth Avenue. (See page 136 for more information.)

WHEN: The Champions Cup has been held at various times from February to May.

GETTING THERE: For directions to Agganis Arena, see page 136. Parking at Agganis Arena and campus lots is $25.

TICKETS: Tickets are available to day and evening sessions, which include two matches. Temporary seating is placed on the floor along the immediate sidelines and behind the baselines. Most of the arena seats sold for tennis are between the baselines (in sections 102–104 and 112–114), so spectators get a good view from most seats.

Platinum ($130) seating is courtside on the floor and closest to the action. ***Gold*** ($90) seating is also on the floor on the sidelines and baselines directly behind the platinum seating. ***Silver*** ($55) seating includes the lower rows of the arena bowl, while the ***bronze*** ($30) seating includes the higher rows of the arena. Tickets can also be bought for the entire tournament.

To order tickets, call Ticketmaster at 617-931-2000 or visit www.ticketmaster.com or www.championsseriestennis.com. Tickets may also be purchased at the Agganis Arena ticket office, which is located on the east side of the arena lobby. The ticket office is open Monday through Friday from 10 AM to 5 PM.

Today, tennis fans can watch marquee tennis greats (Martina Navratilova playing here with Raquel Kops-Jones) with the Boston Lobsters, part of World TeamTennis.

DISABILITY ACCESS: See page 137.

THE SPLURGE: The Champions Series offers VIP packages with options including premium box seats courtside, joining players and sponsors in the Outback Champions Club to enjoy food and open bar, opportunities to play tennis and learn from the players, and meet and greet a player for photographs and autographs. For more information, call 646-367-2770.

SPECTATOR TIPS: Video cameras are not allowed, and flash photography is not permitted during matches.

SCORING AUTOGRAPHS: Players will sometimes sign autographs after matches.

FOOD AND DRINK: See page 139 for details on concessions and nearby restaurants.

CONTACT INFORMATION: www.championsseriestennis.com.

BEYOND BOSTON

International Tennis Hall of Fame

Tennis junkies should definitely make a day trip to the International Tennis Hall of Fame and Museum in Newport, Rhode Island. The hall of fame is located in the historic Newport Casino, which was the site of the national tennis championship before it moved to New York City in 1915.

If you think Wimbledon has a long tennis history, consider that the Newport Casino was built more than forty years before Centre Court opened its doors. In addition to its historical significance, the interior of the building, the first major commission of noted architect Stanford White, is rich in architectural detail.

The International Tennis Hall of Fame and Museum was founded by James Van Alen (also the inventor of the tie-break) in 1954 as "a shrine to the ideals of the game." The museum's galleries chronicle the history of tennis from the first crude rackets used by those Gilded Age pioneers right through the magnificent reign of Roger Federer. The museum includes interactive exhibits, videos, and display items. There are fascinating black-and-white photographs of early competitors clad in knickerbockers, long wool socks, neckties, and caps—a far cry from the fluorescent sleeveless t-shirts and baggy shorts donned by Rafael Nadal. Not surprisingly, the International Tennis Hall of Fame is the world's largest repository of tennis information and memorabilia; the permanent collection alone contains over sixteen thousand objects.

More than two hundred players, coaches, administrators, and writers have been inducted into the International Tennis Hall of Fame, and visitors can see their plaques in the Enshrinee Hall. New to the hall of fame is a 45-minute audio tour of the collections that includes recorded comments of tennis greats and hall of fame enshrinees. New members are inducted into the hall every July in conjunction with the annual Hall of Fame Tennis Championship.

GETTING THERE: The International Tennis Hall of Fame is seventy-five miles south of Boston. From Boston and points north, take Massachusetts Route 24 south through Fall River and into Rhode Island. Take Exit 1 to Route 138 south. Take a left onto Route 138A south. Pass Eaton's Beach on the left, travel to the top of the hill, and take a left onto Bellevue Avenue. The Tennis Hall of Fame will be the first block on your left.

HOURS: The hall of fame is open daily between 9:30 AM and 5 PM, except Thanksgiving and Christmas.

ADMISSION: $10 for adults; $8 for seniors, military, or students with ID; $5 for children sixteen and under; $25 for a family.

WHILE YOU'RE THERE: Whether you're a weekend hacker or a tennis prodigy, you can toss up a serve on the International Tennis Hall of Fame's legendary grass courts. It's an amazing opportunity to play on the same sod that was trodden by Dick Sears in the 1880s and more recent legends such as Martina Navratilova, Bjorn Borg, Billie Jean King, Rod Laver, John McEnroe, and Jimmy Connors.

The courts are open to the public from mid-May through September. Prices start at $80 for the first hour for one to two players. For additional information, call the Hall of Fame's Newport Casino Lawn Tennis Club at 401-846-0642.

HALL OF FAME TENNIS CHAMPIONSHIP: Each July in the week following Wimbledon, the Newport Casino plays host to the Hall of Fame Tennis Championship. Even though the sport was born on grass, the Hall of Fame Championship is the only remaining grass-court stop on the men's ATP tour in North America. Scheduled for the week following Wimbledon, the tournament doesn't attract the elite players, but there are some familiar names and grass-court specialists among the entrants. The Saturday semifinals session traditionally includes a ceremony for the new class of inductees in the hall of fame, and tickets for that session generally sell out months in advance. For tickets, call 866-914-FAME or go online to www.tennisfame.com.

CHAMPIONS CUP NEWPORT: Since 2007 the Newport Casino has also played host to an August stop on the Champions Series, the same tour that visits Boston. Many of the big names, such as John McEnroe and Jim Courier, have played this event in previous years. For tickets, call 866-914-FAME or go online to www.tennisfame.com.

CONTACT INFORMATION: International Tennis Hall of Fame and Museum, 194 Bellevue Avenue, Newport, RI 02840. 401-849-3990; www.tennisfame.com.

★ Court Tennis

Court tennis, dating to the twelfth century, is the original racquet sport from which the modern game of tennis has descended. While the long wooden racquets used to play court tennis are similar to early incarnations of present-day tennis racquets, and players of court tennis hit a ball over a net, that's about where the similarities between the games end. Court tennis is played in concrete chambers one-and-a-half times the length of a tennis court. Players serve balls as hard as baseballs against one of the sloping roofs that line three sides of the court, and players can aim to hit the ball through numerous openings along the court walls.

If the layout is reminiscent of a palace courtyard, well, that's for good reason. Court tennis, also known as real tennis, was a favorite pastime of French and English nobility and royalty. Henry VIII—between dispatching his six wives—built a private court at Hampton Court Palace.

In 1876, the first bona fide court tennis facility in America was opened on Buckingham Street in the Back Bay. Today there are less than a dozen real tennis courts in the United States, but one of them is located at Boston's private **Tennis and Racquet Club** (939 Boylston Street, Boston, MA 02115. 617-536-4630; www.tandr.org). The International Tennis Hall of Fame in Newport has the only public court in the country. The Tennis and Racquet Club periodically hosts national and world championships that draw the sport's best players, and the gallery fits about one hundred spectators.

ADDITIONAL SPECTATOR SPORTS

Sure, squash, polo, and rugby don't draw the same crowds and media attention in Boston as baseball or football, but these less-familiar spectator sports—and others like them—generate just as much passion among their players and hard-core fans. That fervor can be infectious, and even if you aren't familiar with the rules, these less common sports can make for an exhilarating sporting alternative for the adventurous fan.

Some of the spectator sports in this chapter—such as cycling, equestrian, sailing, skiing, and swimming—will be familiar to any fan who has tuned into the Olympics. Others—such as Australian Rules Football or hurling—might be as foreign as the lands in which they were born. But just as you can tour the world without leaving Boston by enjoying the cuisine in neighborhoods such as the North End or Chinatown, sampling some of these imported sports will allow you to be immersed in overseas cultures—without the airfare.

AUSTRALIAN RULES FOOTBALL

If you'd like a more authentic Australian experience in Boston than a trip to the neighborhood Outback Steakhouse, check out a local Australian Rules Football game. Any sports fan who remembers the early days of ESPN probably recalls watching hour after hour of Australian Rules Football when it was one of the few sports broadcast on the fledgling network. Even if you've never seen Aussie Rules before, it's easy to get swept up in its combination of speed and violence.

Aussie Rules is nothing like American football. It's more of a hybrid of rugby, soccer, and basketball. There are no touchdowns; points are only scored by punting the "footy" through the uprights. Despite the sport's vicious tackles and bone-rattling collisions, players don't wear any pads or helmets, so you know they're kind of nuts.

Aussie Rules is played by a number of local teams between April and September, most notably the amateur Boston Demons Australian Football Club. The Demons take on teams from across the Northeast, and players include ex-pats from Down Under and local aficionados. The Demons play games at Magazine Beach, located on Memorial Drive in Cambridge at the base of the BU Bridge, and at the **Irish Cultural Centre of New England** (200 New Boston Drive, Canton, MA 02116). Befitting Aussies' fun-loving reputation, the Demons' social events at local bars, such as Phoenix Landing in Cambridge, are almost as popular as the games. At some of the team's events you can watch the footy action beamed in from Australia as you hoist a few pints with your new mates.

In addition to the Demons, a handful of other teams in the metropolitan area also play footy, usually on Saturday mornings at Magazine Beach. The games are open to all, so if you want to try your foot at Aussie Rules, this is your chance.

CONTACT INFORMATION: Boston Demons; www.bostondemons.com.

BAY STATE GAMES

The Bay State Games are an Olympic-style competition staged by the Massachusetts Amateur Sports Foundation that draws participants from across the state. The Bay State Games began in the early 1980s, and the winter and summer competitions now draw nearly ten thousand athletes ranging in age from six to eighty-six. Previous participants include figure skater Nancy Kerrigan and basketball stars Dana Barros, Rebecca Lobo, and Reggie Lewis.

The Summer Games, which have been held since 1982, are by far the bigger event. They feature over seven thousand athletes in twenty-five different sports, ranging from baseball, basketball, and soccer to swimming, track and field, and fencing. The Summer Games are usually held in July at locations in central Massachusetts and around metropolitan Boston, such as at UMass-Boston and Harvard. The Bay State Winter Games are held in February in western Massachusetts with figure skating, alpine skiing, and ice hockey events.

CONTACT INFORMATION: Massachusetts Amateur Sports Foundation, 55 Sixth Road, Woburn, MA 01801. 781-932-6555; www.baystategames.org.

Even if you've never seen Aussie Rules before, it's easy to get swept up in its combination of speed and violence.

CRICKET

Long before baseball became Boston's bat-and-ball game of choice, the city was crazy for cricket. A cricket club existed in Boston as far back as 1809, but the sport didn't catch on around the city until the 1850s, fueled by the increasing immigration from the British Empire. The Boston Cricket Club, which was active through the turn of the twentieth century, initially played at Boston Common, but the park's hard-baked ground made it ill-suited to cricket, so the club moved to a grounds in East Cambridge.

Before embarking on his hall of fame baseball career, George Wright first took the field in Boston on those East Cambridge grounds in 1863 as a member of New York's Saint George Cricket Club. After retiring

Before baseball became a big hit, cricket was Boston's bat-and-ball game of choice.

from baseball, Wright returned to his native game at the Longwood Cricket Club, which was formed at the corner of Brookline and Longwood avenues in 1877. While the Longwood Cricket Club still exists today, albeit at a different location, tennis long ago supplanted cricket as the sport of choice among club members.

Even back in the 1800s, the pace of cricket matches proved too plodding for Americans, and clubs across Boston disbanded as the new sport of baseball eclipsed its cousin. James D'Wolf Lovett wrote in his 1906 book *Old Boston Boys and the Games They Played*, "There is no doubt that the length of time required for a full two innings match (frequently two days) is a serious handicap for it in this country, and is at variance with the American temperament. The office boy can occasionally get a few hours off in the afternoon to see a baseball game, with the 'grandmother's funeral' plea; but obviously this could not be worked two days running, for a cricket match."

The gentlemanly sport of cricket, with players clad in crisp-white pants and sweater vests, is still played around the city by teams in the Massachusetts State Cricket League. Many of the players are immigrants from cricket-crazy areas of the world such as South Asia, the Caribbean, Australia, and England. League games in Boston are held in Dorchester and Mattapan at Franklin Park, Franklin Field, Almont Park, and Roberts Playground. Suburban teams also host matches at fields throughout metropolitan Boston. Games are usually played each weekend between May and September.

The rules of cricket can definitely be difficult for a neophyte to follow, and the enormous field can make it hard to get a good view of the action, but spectators or players who know the intricacies of the game are happy to share their knowledge.

Most of the action is focused on the dirt rectangle pitch in the center of the field flanked at both ends by wickets. A bowler attempts to hit the wicket with a bounced throw delivered by an overhand windmill action, and a batter tries to hit the ball before it strikes the wicket. Once the batter hits the ball, he runs between the wickets, exchanging ends with a teammate. Runs are scored each time the runners exchange ends or if the hitter strikes the ball past the field's boundary. Games can last for hours on end, so be sure to bring some refreshments.

CONTACT INFORMATION: Massachusetts State Cricket League; www.mscl.org.

CYCLING

After the bicycle was introduced in Boston in the 1870s, the sport of cycling took off like Lance Armstrong on an Alpine mountaintop. The city was the site of the country's first bike race, first bike club, and first collegiate cycling team. Cycling races became an annual feature of Fourth of July celebrations, and the formal opening of the cycling season on Fast Day—a springtime holiday for public fasting and prayer dating back to colonial times—was a major cause for celebration.

At the annual spring meeting of the Harvard Athletic Association on May 24, 1878, a group of Harvard students staged the first recorded bicycle race in America at Allston's Beacon Park, primarily a horse trotting track. The following year, the city of Boston sponsored a bike race on the Fourth of July, and a two-day bike tour, the Wheel Around the Hub, drew forty riders on high wheelers in a 100-mile ride around Boston and the South Shore.

Dozens of bicycle clubs that formed across the city in the 1880s and 1890s staged road races around the metropolitan area. The Boston Bicycle Club, founded in 1878, was America's oldest sporting club dedicated to the bicycle. Club members often met in front of the Museum of Fine Arts and pedaled around the wide avenues to the Chestnut Hill Reservoir in their standard uniform of a gray jacket, shirt, breeches and stockings, and a blue cap.

The popularity of bicycle racing in Boston reached its zenith in the late 1800s when fans poured into velodromes around the city to watch two-wheelers circle the track. One of the area's premier cycling venues was Waltham Bicycle Park, which opened in 1894. The oval was considered the fastest dirt track in the country, and as many as fifteen thousand fans filled the grandstand to watch professional solo and tandem racers. Numerous world records fell at the track, which is now the site of Nipper Maher Park, near Brandeis University.

Cycling fans in the 1890s and early 1900s also filled the bleachers at the Charles River Park Velodrome in Cambridge. The velodrome was bordered by Massachusetts Avenue and Lansdowne, Albany, and Pacific Streets on land that later became home to the old NECCO candy factory. Sprints and endurance races as long as thirty miles were held at the velodrome, and automobiles and motor bikes also raced at the track. The Stanley Steamer made its big public breakthrough at Charles River Park in 1898.

Cycling in Boston began to fall out of vogue around the turn of the twentieth century with the rise of the Stanley Steamer and other automobiles, but professional bicycle racing was still a staple at Revere Beach in the first decades of the 1900s. The Revere Cycle Track opened in 1901 and drew crowds as large as eight thousand. It was replaced by a new track in 1919 on what is today the parking lot for Wonderland Dog Track. Another short-lived track was built in the 1930s, but in short order it was replaced by Suffolk Downs. During the winter, cycling races moved indoors. The Cyclorama in the South End staged cycling races, and Boston Garden also hosted cycling events on a banked track placed on the arena floor.

Today Boston cycling fans have to travel for the premier racing event in the region. The Fitchburg Longsjo Classic, held annually in late June or early July, is the largest pro-am cycling competition in North America. The race was first held in 1960 in memory of Fitchburg native Art Longsjo, who passed away two years prior in an automobile accident. Longsjo was the first person to ever compete in the Summer and Winter Olympics in the same year, appearing in the speed skating and cycling events at the 1956 games.

The Fitchburg Longsjo Classic attracts top male and female cyclists to the Fitchburg area for a four-day stage race that includes a time trial, a road race up Mount Wachusett, a circuit race at Fitchburg State College, and a short-course race through the streets of downtown Fitchburg. Tour de France winners Greg LeMond and Lance Armstrong are among the elite cyclists who have pedaled around Fitchburg in previous editions of the race.

CONTACT INFORMATION: Fitchburg Longsjo Classic; www.longsjo.com.

EQUESTRIAN

Suffolk Downs may be Boston's primary horse track for sports fans, but fans who prefer their horses elegantly airborne rather than thundering down a track head elsewhere. The Jumper Classic in early September is the only grand prix show jumping competition in New England. The five-day event has moved to a new home at the Silver Oak Equestrian Center in Hampton Falls, New Hampshire. The Jumper Classic draws over six hundred horses, Olympic gold medalists, and more than seventeen thousand spectators who watch horses and riders navigate a jumping course. The Jumper Classic is as much of a social event as a sporting contest—filled with gourmet food, champagne luncheons, antique and fine art vendors, and a ladies' best hat contest.

Closer to Boston is the Myopia Horse Show, which has been held for more than one hundred years in Hamilton, Massachusetts. The two-day show, held in late August or early September, is one of the oldest in the country and an annual social event on Boston's North Shore that draws nearly one thousand spectators. The event features show jumping and a team relay race that combines cross-country and stadium jumping, requiring both boldness and precision from horse and rider.

CONTACT INFORMATION: Jumper Classic, 892 Washington Street, Gloucester, MA 01930. 978-283-7708; www.jumperclassic.com.

Myopia Horse Show: 978-468-6146; www.myopiahorseshow.com.

GAELIC SPORTS

No city in America has a stronger connection to the Emerald Isle than Boston. The Hub was the final destination for many Irish immigrants who set sail for America, and by 1900, Boston was the most Irish city outside Dublin. The working-class Irish who came to Boston brought along not only their customs and traditions but their sports as well.

The indigenous sports of hurling and Gaelic football are as much a part of Ireland's national identity as Guinness, James Joyce, and U2. And Gaelic sports are a vehicle for preserving and spreading Irish culture—both in Ireland and among the diaspora in Boston.

Hurling has been described as a mix of field hockey and lacrosse in which players whack a hard leather ball called a sliothar with a long, curved stick called a hurley. Gaelic football is often described as a combination of soccer and basketball in which players carry and bounce the round ball by hand and pass and shoot with their feet. Both sports are played on fields much bigger than American football gridirons. Players shoot at H-shaped goals, and shots through the uprights and over the crossbar are worth one point, while shots into the goal under the crossbar are worth three points. Games are relatively short, consisting of two 30-minute halves, and the exciting, fast pace should appeal to an American audience.

Gaelic sports have a long history in Boston. Hurling matches were held on Boston Common on the Fourth of July in the 1880s and the 1890s, and the first Gaelic football match outside of Ireland was held on the Common in 1886.

Today the Boston branch of the Gaelic Athletic Association (GAA) is the largest member league outside Ireland, with more than forty-five registered teams playing Gaelic football, hurling, and camogie, a women's variant of hurling. Waning Irish immigration to America has had a negative impact on the pipeline of players, however, since teams depend almost exclusively on Irish-born athletes to fill rosters. The GAA stages its games at the **Irish Cultural Centre of New England** (200 New Boston Street, Canton, MA 02116). The Irish Cultural Centre has three pitches and a clubhouse with a pub and snack bar. GAA matches are held between May and August, and as many as ten games a day are played on weekends.

If you can't get to a match in person, many of the city's Irish pubs, such as the ones listed below, beam in live broadcasts of hurling and Gaelic football matches from Ireland on weekend mornings. For some matches, there is a cover charge of up to $20.

Lir Irish Pub & Restaurant, 903 Boylston Street, Boston, MA 02115. 617-778-0089; www.lironboylston.com.

The Green Briar, 304 Washington Street, Brighton, MA 02135. 617-789-4100; www.greenbriarpub.com.

Porter Belly's Pub, 338 Washington Street, Brighton, MA 02135. 617-254-3300; www.porterbellyspub.com.

Phoenix Landing, 512 Massachusetts Avenue, Cambridge, MA 02139. 617-576-6260.

The Banshee, 934 Dorchester Avenue, Dorchester, MA 02125. 617-436-9747; www.bansheeboston.com.

McGann's, 197 Portland Street, Boston, MA 02116. 617-227-4059; www.mcgannspubboston.com.

Bad Abbots, 1546 Hancock Street, Quincy, MA 02169. 617-774-1434; www.badabbots.com.

Clash of the Ash, 1464 Hancock Street, Quincy, MA 02169. 617-376-0030.

PJ Ryan's, 239 Holland Street, Somerville, MA 02144. 617-625-8200; www.pjryans.com.

Blackthorn Pub, 471 W. Broadway, Boston, MA 02127. 617-269-5510.

CONTACT INFORMATION: Boston Gaelic Athletic Association; www.bostongaa.com.

A polo match at the Myopia Polo Club on the North Shore makes for a unique Boston sports outing.

POLO

It's worth going to a polo match just for the sight of seeing a zebra sitting on a horse. OK, so the zebra is a referee in black-and-white stripes, but it's still pretty amusing.

A trip to the Myopia Polo Club on the North Shore offers a refined sporting experience, and the elaborate tailgating scene is definitely more Tanglewood than Patriots. Wine and champagne are the beverages of choice, and strawberries and salads are more likely to be on the pregame menu than nachos. Some fans even bring their own bales of hay for seats. And one thing you'll never be able to do at another sporting event is pull your car right up to the perimeter of the field to tailgate and watch the action!

If you didn't bring a lawn seat—or your own hay—the club has a set of bleachers on one side of the field and tent tables on the other. A typical polo match has four or six chukkers, or periods, that last about seven minutes a piece. Between chukkers, riders switch to a fresh horse. There are four riders on each side with their mounts.

The sport has the feel of field hockey on horseback, and horses thunder up and down the field, working up such a lather that they will sometimes come off the field steaming. Fans are welcome to take the field at halftime, not to mount a steed but to help with the divot stomp by tamping down the torn-up turf to protect the horses from injury. The considerable length of the field, more than three times that of a football gridiron, makes it tough to follow every swing of the mallet, but the commentary from the public address announcer is helpful.

The Myopia Polo Club, founded in 1888, is one of the oldest polo clubs in America.

The club's season runs from Memorial Day to Columbus Day. Gates open at 1:30 PM every Sunday during the season for 3 PM matches. There are approximately forty members of the club team, including men and women. Matches last about ninety minutes, followed by a trophy ceremony and an opportunity to meet the competitors, including the humans. Admission is $10 per person or $20 per car.
CONTACT INFORMATION: Myopia Polo, 435 Bay Road, Hamilton, MA 01982. 978-468-4433; www.myopiapolo.org.

RUGBY

Football is the sport of choice for Bostonians who root for the guys running with the oblong ball, but football has its roots in an older sport full of tackling—rugby. Boston schoolboys and college students played rugby in the 1800s before the evolution of football. Today there are a number of amateur and college rugby teams that play around the city. Boston has two teams that play in the springtime Rugby Super League, the premier rugby union division in the United States: the Boston Rugby Football Club and the Boston Irish Wolfhounds. The teams also take on competition outside the Super League in the fall.

The Boston Rugby Football Club has taken the field for nearly fifty years. The team plays its home games in the spring at Franklin Park on a pitch located behind the Franklin Park Zoo on Pierpont Road. Fall games are played at Moakley Park on William J. Day Boulevard in South Boston.

The Boston Irish Wolfhounds are a more recent addition to the city's rugby scene. The team plays its games at the **Irish Cultural Centre of New England** (200 New Boston Drive, Canton, MA 02116). Despite the team's name, the majority of its players are American, and it boasts an international membership.
CONTACT INFORMATION: Boston Rugby Club, PO Box 52121, Boston, MA 02205. 617-566-BRFC; www.brfc.org.

Boston Irish Wolfhounds RFC, PO Box 35822, Brighton, MA 02135. 617-254-9732; www.biwrfc.com.

SAILING

Boston's commodious harbor not only allowed the city to thrive as a nautical power in colonial times, but it also led to the growth of yachting as a popular city pastime. In the nineteenth century, in addition to a working seaport, Boston Harbor was where city residents spent their leisure time. In the first half of the 1800s, several wealthy city merchants who made their fortunes in the China trade built schooners that they raced in the waters of New England.

The first regatta in the Boston area was held in Nahant in 1845, and the peninsula quickly became a popular sailing center. Yacht clubs, which sprang up around the city and the harbor in the 1860s and 1870s, staged regattas in the waters of Massachusetts Bay and built grand clubhouses with broad verandas from which members could savor cool breezes and harbor views. The Boston Yacht Club, which formed in 1866, is the oldest in the city. The Boston Yacht Club once had a magnificent clubhouse at South Boston's City Point, as did the South Boston Yacht Club, organized two years later. Today the Boston Yacht Club is based in the North Shore town of Marblehead, which continues to be a major yachting center in the metropolitan area.

Glorious yachts owned by wealthy bluebloods and designed by Bostonians such as Edward Burgess captured sailing's holy grail—the America's Cup—in the 1880s. The America's Cup races moved to Newport, Rhode Island, in 1930, and while the races haven't graced the Rhode Island shores since 1983, sailing fans can still visit the Museum of Yachting in Newport and the Herreshoff Marine Museum in Bristol, Rhode Island, home to the America's Cup Hall of Fame.

Today a colorful canvas of billowing sails is a common sight in blue harbors up and down the Massachusetts coast on sunny summer days. Each September, the islands of Boston Harbor are the backdrop for dozens of sailboats competing in the Boston Harbor Islands Sailing Regatta. More than one hundred boats compete for the Massachusetts Bay Pursuit Championship. Pursuit racing awards handicaps up front so boats start at different times and compete to cross the finish line first. Approximately fifteen hundred spectators, who travel from Boston's Long Wharf by ferry, watch the action on Georges Island, home to historic Fort Warren.

CONTACT INFORMATION: Boston Harbor Islands Regatta, 408 Atlantic Avenue, Suite 228, Boston, MA 02110. 617-223-8672; www.bostonharborislandsregatta.org.

The Boston Harbor Islands Regatta is the perfect way to combine a great sports outing with a day at the beach.

Museum of Yachting, Fort Adams State Park, Newport, RI 02840. 401-847-1018; www.moy.org.

Herreshoff Marine Museum, One Burnside Street, Bristol, RI 02809. 401-253-5000; www.herreshoff.org.

SKIING

When the flakes start falling, snow-crazed Bostonians head north to the mounts of Maine, New Hampshire, and Vermont for skiing, snowboarding, and the après ski lounges of resorts. The mountains of northern New England not only attract recreational skiers and snowboarders, but some of the world's best winter sports athletes for international and national competitions.

Northern New England has staged national and international competitions in alpine skiing, cross-country skiing, and ski jumping for decades. In recent years, the region has also become a popular venue for the fast-growing Olympic sports of freestyle skiing and snowboarding, with competitions for halfpipe, snowboardcross, and alpine snowboarding.

In Vermont, Stratton Mountain, Killington, and Mount Snow are among the venues for skiing and snowboarding events. Sunday River and Sugarloaf in Maine have also hosted alpine events. On numerous occasions, Sugarloaf has staged the U.S. Alpine Championships, with America's best skiers competing in the downhill, Super G, slalom, and giant slalom events.

Around the turn of the twentieth century, Scandinavian immigrants who came to New England to work at logging companies and railroads fueled the popularity of alpine and cross-country skiing as a recreational activity. Bostonians took to skis in wintertime at local recreation areas, such as

Middlesex Fells and Blue Hills, and winter carnivals were held all over the region with sports such as tobogganing, skating, and curling in addition to skiing. Ski jumping became a popular spectator sport around New England in the 1920s and 1930s. The ski jump in Berlin, New Hampshire, drew crowds as large as twenty-five thousand. Boston Garden was also turned into a winter wonderland in the 1930s when an annual winter sports exposition and ski tournament drew thousands of fans with sled dog, skiing, and skating exhibitions. There were even ski jumping demonstrations on a jump lined with crushed ice built up to the arena's rafters.

The New England Ski Museum, located about 150 miles north of Boston at the foot of New Hampshire's Cannon Mountain, is filled with artifacts charting the sport's growth in the region. Among the items on display are primitive-looking skis, boots, and bindings that were used in the late 1800s and early 1900s. The museum's theater also shows vintage ski films.

CONTACT INFORMATION: U.S. Ski and Snowboard Association, Box 100, 1500 Kearns Boulevard, Park City, UT 84060. 435-649-9090; www.ussa.org.

New England Ski Museum, Exit 34B, I-93/ Franconia Notch Parkway, Franconia, NH 03580. 603-823-7177; www.skimuseum.org.

SQUASH

The racquet sport of squash has always had a strong foothold among Boston's elite prep schools and colleges. MIT has a men's team; Wellesley has a women's team; and Harvard, Northeastern, and Tufts field men's and women's squads. Harvard has one of the best squash programs in the country, and its teams are consistently at the top of intercollegiate squash rankings. The Crimson play on campus between November and February at the Barnaby Courts inside the Murr Center. There are five feature courts—including a four-wall glass show court that allows viewing from all sides—and room for a thousand spectators. Fans can follow the action from all courts on a high-definition television, and the Murr Center boasts the largest scoreboard in college squash.

The Barnaby Courts are one of the finest college squash facilities in the country, which makes it an attractive venue for national college championships and other squash tournaments throughout the year. The U.S. Open Squash Championship has been held in Boston on numerous occasions at sites as varied as Symphony Hall and John Hancock Hall at the Back Bay Events Center where portable courts have been constructed on stage. Local clubs with squash facilities, such as the Harvard Club and the University Club, also host tournaments from time to time.

CONTACT INFORMATION: Harvard University Squash, Murr Center, 65 North Harvard Street, Boston, MA 02163. 617-495-4851; www.gocrimson.com.

Massachusetts Squash, PO Box 51611, Boston, MA 02205. www.ma-squash.org.

SWIMMING

Benjamin Franklin's accomplishments are well known to every American schoolchild: Founding Father, inventor, member of the International Swimming Hall of Fame. Wait … *what?* Yes, as a boy growing up in bustling Boston, Ben Franklin was an avid swimmer.

At a time when most people didn't know how to swim, Franklin taught himself swimming strokes from a book. Displaying his ingenuity at an early age, young Ben fashioned crude wooden swim paddles for his arms and flippers for his feet. He even experimented with being pulled along the surface of the old Mill Pond by a kite while lying on his back.

It may be surprising in a city known for its dirty water, but Bostonians just like Franklin have been swimming in the Charles River and Boston Harbor for hundreds of years. George Washington tried to forbid his troops from swimming, but it became one of the few recreational outlets for military men during the Revolution. In the 1800s, Boston became the first American city with free public baths. Bathing houses with swimming baths sprung up along the shores of the Charles River in addition to those along the beaches of Boston Harbor.

One of those bathhouses, South Boston's L Street Bathhouse, is home to the L Street Brownies, famous for their tradition of taking a dip in the icy harbor waters every New Year's Day. If the wintry January weather is a little nippy for even *watching* this polar plunge, the annual Boston Light Swim in August promises warmer weather for spectators.

The Boston Light Swim is the "Granddaddy of American Open-Water Swims." The eight-mile swim across the harbor from Boston Light to the L Street Bathhouse dates back to 1909 and draws elite open-water swimmers from countries as far away as Egypt. There's nothing light about the effort required to complete the Boston Light Swim. Swimmers must battle powerful cross-currents, boat traffic, and strong gusts of wind. But it's the frigid water, even in August, that can pose the greatest challenge. While the swimmers must battle the elements, they no longer have to brave a heavily polluted harbor. Depending on weather conditions, most swimmers take between three and six hours to complete the course, although the race record is under two-and-a-half hours. If you prefer a warm pool as a venue for swimming action, Boston College, Boston University, Harvard, and Northeastern all field collegiate swimming teams.

CONTACT INFORMATION: Boston Light Swim; www.bostonlightswim.org.

THE BOSTON SPORTS TRAIL
A SPORTS-THEMED WALKING TOUR OF THE HUB

A veritable rainbow of striped sidewalks weaves through the streets of Boston, leading tourists and locals alike on a tour of some of the city's most noteworthy sites. There's the Black Heritage Trail, the Irish Heritage Trail, the Harborwalk, and of course, the famed Freedom Trail.

In addition to many famous sights that shaped American history, downtown Boston abounds with landmarks related to the city's sporting past and present. So here's a walking tour of the Hub that's dedicated to die-hard fans: the Boston Sports Trail.

Even in a city as walkable as Boston, it would be quite a workout to see all thirty-nine sights on the trail—which stretches from the TD Garden to Nickerson Field—in just one day, so you may want to pick and choose your itinerary. If you want to see the sights in order, the total distance of the walk is about eleven miles—less than *half* the distance of the Boston Marathon—and you're walking, right? So get off that couch and get your blood pumping. And if you still want to be a little lazy and watch some games, you can take a break at one of the city's numerous sports bars along the way (see page 249).

❶ **TD Garden/The Sports Museum.** *100 Legends Way.* Start your tour off at the TD Garden, home of the Celtics, Bruins, Blazers, and the Beanpot. The teams' former home, the old Boston Garden, used to stand along Causeway Street where the players' parking lot is currently located. The Sports Museum (see page 246), which is inside the Garden, chronicles the history of a wide range of sports in the region.

❷ **Mill Pond.** *Rose Fitzgerald Kennedy Greenway between Sudbury and Hanover streets.* In colonial times, the land immediately south of the TD Garden was underwater in the old Mill Pond. Colonists, including a young Benjamin Franklin, swam in the Mill Pond. Swimming was one of the city's few recreational pursuits in the 1700s. The former shoreline of the pond is marked by a strip of granite embedded in the sidewalks and lawn in this parcel of the greenway.

❸ **Bowling Green.** *Six Bowdoin Square.* Long before *Candlepins for Cash* became a Boston television staple, colonial residents bowled on the city turf. A bronze tablet mounted to the side of the art deco Verizon Building near the Bowdoin T stop commemorates the site of one of the city's bowling greens, dating back to 1700. The tablet depicts a scene of colonists bowling. Luckily for them, hideous bowling shirts and shoe rentals had yet to be invented.

❹ **The Green Dragon Tavern.** *11 Marshall Street.* The Green Dragon Tavern, which traces its lineage back to 1654, was a favorite watering hole for the Sons of Liberty and that famous Revolutionary equestrian Paul Revere. Horse racing was one of the few

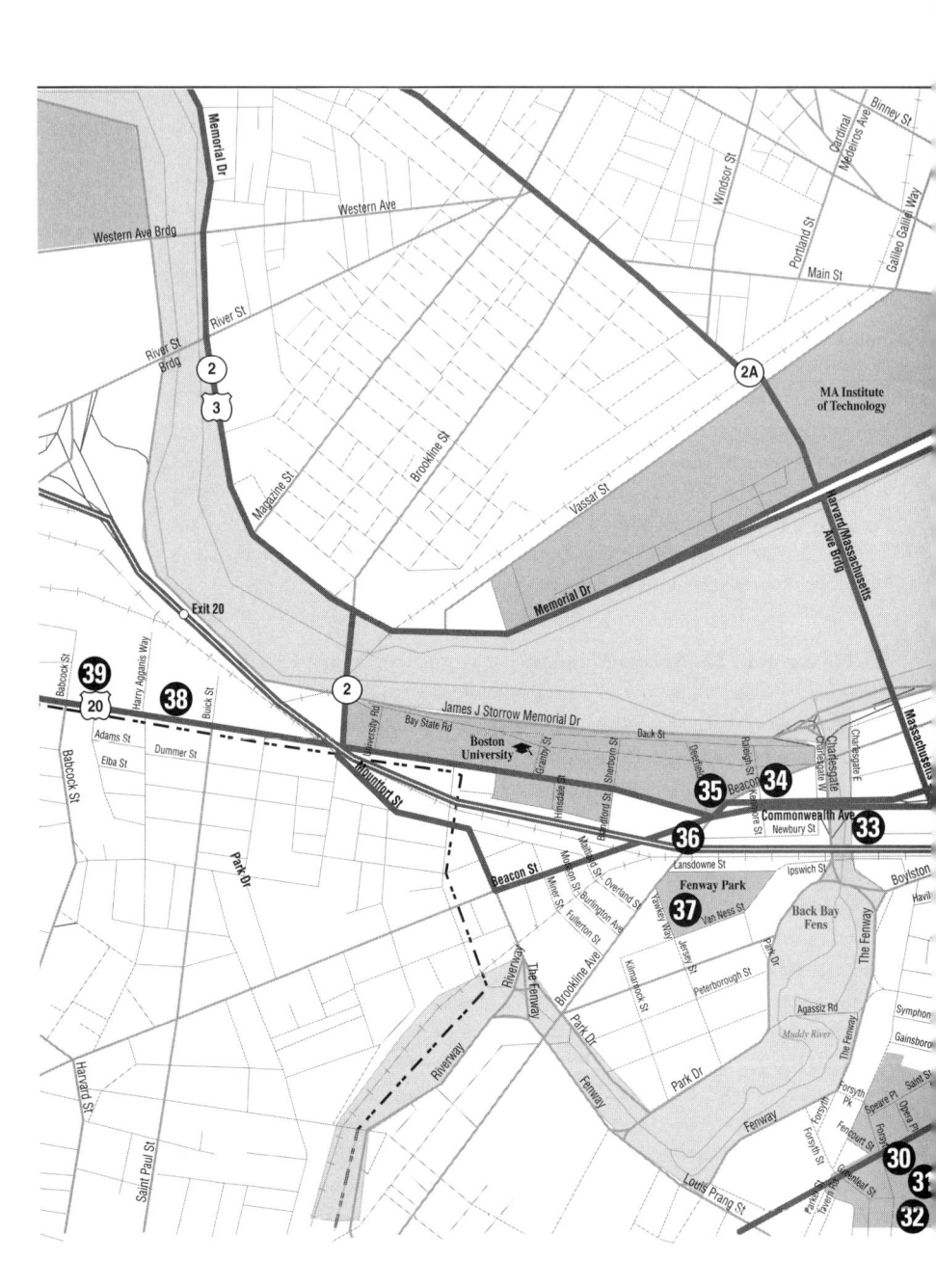

THE BOSTON SPORTS TRAIL
A SPORTS-THEMED WALKING TOUR OF THE HUB

238   THE DIE★HARD SPORTS FAN'S GUIDE TO BOSTON

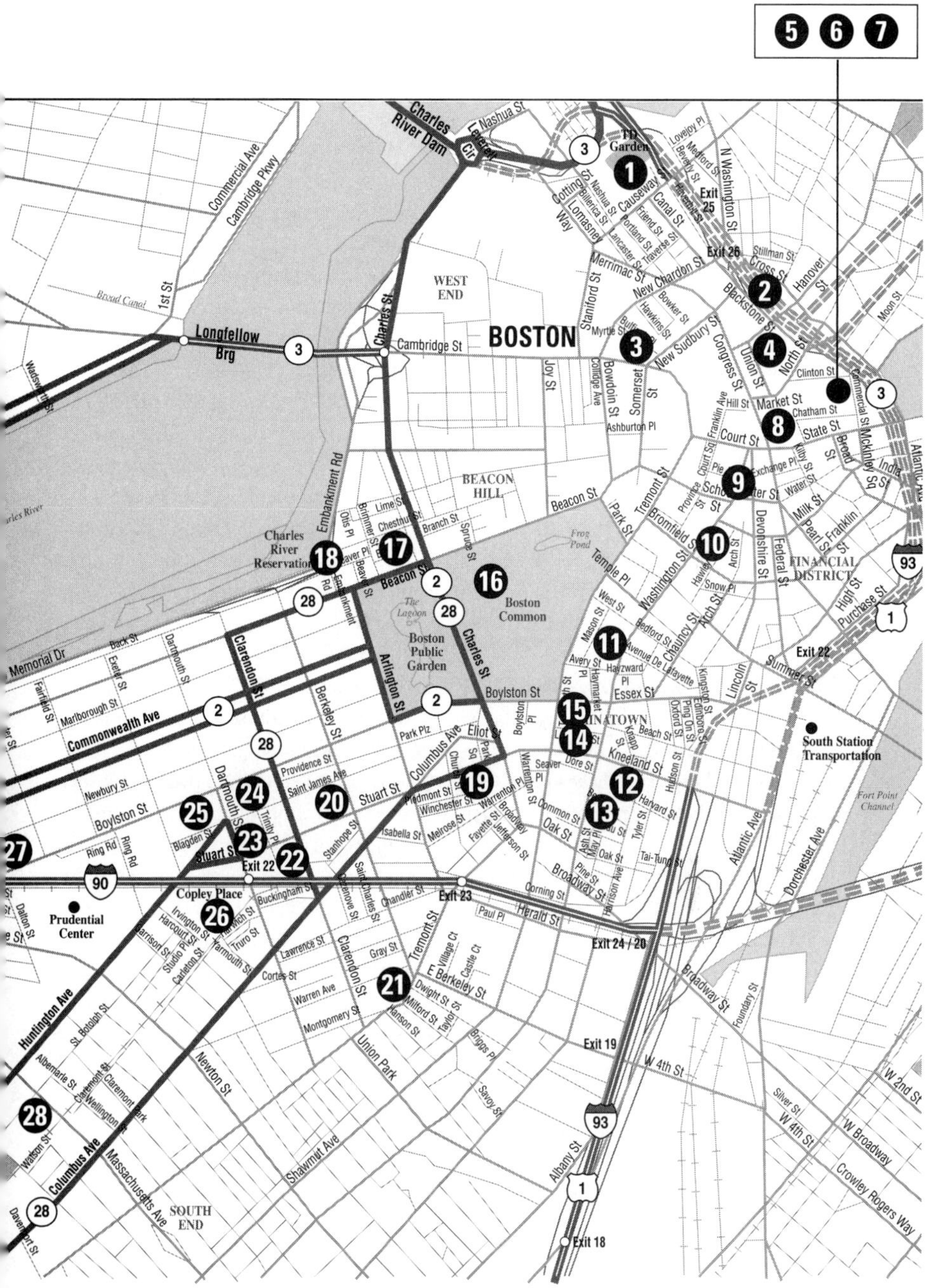
5
6
7
BOSTON
WEST END
BEACON HILL
FINANCIAL DISTRICT
CHINATOWN
SOUTH END
TD Garden
Boston Common
Boston Public Garden
The Lagoon
Frog Pond
Charles River Reservation
Copley Place
Prudential Center
South Station Transportation
Fort Point Channel
Broad Canal
Charles River Dam
Leverett Cir
Longfellow Brg
Nashua St
Causeway St
Canal St
Friend St
Portland St
Traverse St
Lancaster St
Lomasney Way
Billerica St
Lovejoy Pl
Beverly St
Medford St
N Washington St
Stillman St
Cross St
Hanover St
Blackstone St
Merrimac St
New Chardon St
Bowker St
Hawkins St
Staniford St
Myrtle St
New Sudbury St
Congress St
Union St
North St
Clinton St
Commercial St
Moon St
Cambridge St
Charles St
Joy St
Bowdoin St
Somerset St
Ashburton Pl
Hill St
Market St
Chatham St
Court St
State St
Kilby St
Broad St
McKinley Sq
India St
Atlantic Ave
Exchange Pl
Water St
Milk St
Pearl St
Franklin St
School St
Province St
Devonshire St
Federal St
Bromfield St
Arch St
Hawley St
Snow Pl
Tremont St
Park St
Temple Pl
Washington St
West St
Mason St
Bedford St
Chauncy St
Avenue De Lafayette
Avery St
Hayward Pl
Essex St
Kingston St
Lincoln St
Summer St
High St
Purchase St
Exit 22
Exit 25
Exit 26
Beacon St
Branch St
Spruce St
Lime St
Chestnut St
Brimmer St
Otis Pl
Embankment Rd
Back St
Memorial Dr
Dartmouth St
Exeter St
Fairfield St
Marlborough St
Commonwealth Ave
Clarendon St
Berkeley St
Arlington St
Boylston St
Boylston Pl
Park Plz
Columbus Ave
Eliot St
Providence St
Saint James Ave
Newbury St
Stuart St
Church St
Piedmont St
Winchester St
Warrenton Pl
Warrenton St
Broadway
Melrose St
Fayette St
Jefferson St
Isabella St
Stanhope St
Trinity Pl
Blagden St
Ring Rd
Exit 22
Exit 23
Buckingham St
Chandler St
Saint Charles St
Genevieve St
Seaver Pl
Dore St
Kneeland St
Beach St
Knapp St
Edinboro St
Ping On St
Oxford St
Hudson St
Harvard St
Tyler St
Common St
Oak St
Ash St
Pine St
Tai-Tung St
Harrison Ave
Broadway St
Corning St
Herald St
Paul Pl
Exit 24 / 20
Irvington St
Harcourt St
Harwich St
Truro St
Yarmouth St
Studio Pl
Garrison St
Carleton St
Lawrence St
Cortes St
Warren Ave
Gray St
Montgomery St
Village Ct
Castle Ct
E Berkeley St
Dwight St
Milford St
Hanson St
Taylor St
Union Park
Briggs Pl
Savoy St
Huntington Ave
St. Botolph St
Albemarle St
Claremont St
Claremont Park
Wellington St
Watson St
Columbus Ave
Massachusetts Ave
Newton St
Shawmut Ave
Albany St
Davenport St
Dalton St
Exit 19
Exit 18
W 4th St
Broadway St
Foundary St
Dorchester Ave
Silver St
W Broadway
W 2nd St
Crowley Rogers Way
Commercial Ave
Cambridge Pkwy
1st St
Wadsworth St
90
93
1
2
3
28

spectator sports staged around Boston in the early 1700s, and competitors came to taverns such as the Green Dragon in the days leading up to the races to pay the entry fee.

❺ Red Auerbach Statue. *Faneuil Hall Marketplace.* The legendary coach who led the Boston Celtics to nine world championships and played a role in six others as a general manager still holds court from his bench outside the south side of Quincy Market. Red holds a rolled-up program in his left hand and his signature victory cigar in his right. Rub the shamrock on his championship ring for some luck of the Irish.

❻ Bill Rodgers' Sneakers. *Faneuil Hall Marketplace.* To Red's right is a bronzed pair of sneakers worn by four-time Boston Marathon champion Bill Rodgers. "Boston Billy" wore kicks like these in his final kick to the finish line. While at the marketplace, check out the Bill Rodgers Running Center in the North Market Building. The store sells running gear and has walls full of running memorabilia.

❼ Larry Bird's Sneakers. *Faneuil Hall Marketplace.* On the other side of Red's statue are a bronzed pair of Larry Bird's signature Converse sneakers. The three-time NBA Most Valuable Player helped to deliver a hat trick of championship banners to the Celtics. During the 1985 playoffs, Bird was involved in a fistfight about a block away from the sneakers, at the corner of State Street and Merchants Row. The fisticuffs followed an argument that started inside a State Street bar Bird frequented.

❽ Faneuil Hall. So much American history has happened beneath the gilded grasshopper atop the "Cradle of Liberty," but Faneuil Hall has also hosted raucous celebrations of Boston sporting heroes, including Olympic and World Series victors. In 1912, long before the Duck Boats invaded the Hub, the champion Red Sox paraded in Model Ts from Park Square to Faneuil Hall, where they were feted by Mayor John "Honey Fitz" Fitzgerald, grandfather of John F. Kennedy. Fans climbed up fruit stands and through windows just to join in the packed celebration.

❾ Newspaper Row. *Washington Street between State and Milk streets.* Fans at the turn of the twentieth century couldn't punch up the latest Red Sox scores on the Internet or tune into the radio play-by-play. Instead, thousands crammed Newspaper Row, a narrow corridor of Washington Street that was home to eight daily newspapers, for news from major events. They waited with bated breath as the latest results from baseball games, horse races, prizefights, and golf tournaments were telegraphed to the dailies and chalked up on large outdoor blackboards. An historical marker on the side of 226 Washington Street commemorates the former site of *The Boston Globe*. The Transcript Building at the corner of Washington and Milk streets, former home of the *Boston Evening Transcript*, still stands, as does the former home of the *Boston Post*, next door at One Milk Street.

❿ Wright & Ditson. *340 Washington Street.* Near this location stood a retail outlet of Wright & Ditson, one of the first sporting goods stores in America and a household name at the turn of the twentieth century. Bostonians shopped at Wright & Ditson for baseball and cricket equipment, bicycles, tennis racquets, skis, skates, and golf clubs. Baseball Hall of Famer George Wright was one of the store's namesakes, and his importation of tennis, golf, and hockey equipment fueled the growth of those sports in the United States. Francis Ouimet worked at Wright & Ditson when he captured the 1913 U.S. Open at The Country Club.

⓫ Boston Opera House. *539 Washington Street.* The Boston Theater used to stand on the site of the Boston Opera House. Nearly four thousand people crammed into the Boston Theater on August 8, 1887, to watch the city's mayor present a gold belt studded with nearly four hundred diamonds to local heavyweight champion John L. Sullivan. Panels on the belt portrayed Irish and American icons, and the belt's engraving read, "Presented to the champion of champions."

⓬ Saint James the Greater Catholic Church. *125 Harrison Avenue.* Baseball Hall of Famer Michael "King" Kelly was a fan favorite who played in Boston in the 1880s and 1890s. Kelly was a legendary base stealer who was immortalized by the song "Slide, Kelly, Slide." Following his untimely death at age thirty-six from pneumonia, his 1894 funeral was held at this church and was said to have been the biggest Boston had ever seen at the time.

⓭ John L. Sullivan's Tavern. *Washington and Kneeland streets.* The trend of athletes opening up sports bars is not new. This street corner is now home to the New England Medical Center, but near this location in 1883 was a saloon owned by the world heavyweight champion. The tavern at 714 Washington Street featured a mahogany bar, and its walls were filled with fighting scenes. The champ's initials were carved into the frosted glass border on the front windows and etched into each bar glass. The Boston Strongboy held court in a private reception room. Later in life, Sullivan would give up drinking and become a temperance advocate.

⓮ 51 Stuart Street. This Theater District location used to be home to the Buzz Club. On September 25, 2000, Celtics captain and 2008 NBA Finals Most Valuable Player Paul Pierce was inside the pool room in the rear of the nightclub when he was attacked, stabbed eleven times, and hit over the head with a champagne bottle. Pierce was driven by teammate Tony Battie to the nearby New England Medical Center, where he underwent lung surgery. Two men were eventually convicted in the assault.

⓯ Boston Young Men's Christian Union. *48 Boylston Street.* In the 1880s, the Boston Braves exercised during the winter in the clubhouse gymnasium of the Boston Young Men's Christian Union, which was a social, intellectual, and religious organization for men. The union's name is still above the doorway of this Gothic building.

⓰ Boston Common. Boston's historic playground has been a proving ground for some of America's favorite sports. Pioneers of baseball and football who played on the Common's parade ground, which now tops the subterranean parking garage, shaped the development of their sports. The Common was the place where sports such as lacrosse and hurling were introduced to Bostonians, and thousands of spectators came to the Common in the 1800s to watch baseball games and other sporting events. In the northwest corner of the Common along a path leading from Spruce Street toward Frog Pond is a monument to the Oneida Football Club, considered the first organized football club in America. The club played an early version of football—the "Boston game"—that was a mix of soccer and rugby. No opponent ever crossed the Oneida goal in the club's four years of existence between 1862 and 1865.

⓱ Cheers. *84 Beacon Street.* Red Sox reliever Sam "Mayday" Malone once tended bar at this watering hole where everybody knows your name. Unfortunately for Sam's career with the Sox, he was just as proficient at serving up gopher balls to opposing sluggers as he was in serving draft beers to his resident barflies. The Beacon Street bar was the inspiration for the NBC sitcom, although it looks quite different from the Hollywood set familiar to viewers. Kevin McHale and Wade Boggs were among the actual Boston athletes who appeared on the show. Fictional Bruins goalie Eddie LeBec appeared until his untimely demise in a freak Zamboni accident. By the way, the action photograph of Sam in a Red Sox uniform that hung behind the bar on the set was actually that of Cy Young Award winner Jim Lonborg; both hurlers wore number 16.

⑱ Union Boat Club. *144 Chestnut Street.* The Union Boat Club formed in 1851 and is one of the longest continuously operating rowing clubs in the country. The clubhouse, which dates back to the early 1900s, features courts for squash and fives, and the club maintains a boathouse on the Esplanade along the Charles River. The course for Fourth of July regattas, which drew tens of thousands of spectators in the 1800s, ran westward from the Braman's Baths that used to be located at the foot of Chestnut Street.

⑲ Cocoanut Grove Fire Site. *Piedmont Street.* A small historical marker affixed to the back of the Radisson Hotel is one of the only reminders of the Cocoanut Grove nightclub, which was destroyed in an inferno on November 28, 1942, that claimed the lives of 492 people. Earlier that afternoon, the Holy Cross football team scored a monumental upset over Boston College at Fenway Park. The defeat turned out to be a blessing for a group of despondent Eagles who canceled their victory party reservations slated for that night.

⑳ Old John Hancock Building. *200 Berkeley Street.* Who needs the Weather Channel when Boston's got the old John Hancock Building? When rain starts to fall, Red Sox fans look to its spire, which doubles as a weather beacon. If the Red Sox game is postponed because of inclement weather, the colored beacon flashes red. The Back Bay Events Center inside the building has previously hosted the U.S. Open Squash Championship.

㉑ Cyclorama. *539 Tremont Street.* The Cyclorama was built in 1884 in the South End to house a huge panoramic painting of the Battle of Gettysburg, but after the father-in-law of Isabella Stewart Gardner bought the building, it also became a sporting venue. Cycling and roller polo championships were held inside, and John L. Sullivan was among the pugilists who fought under the Cyclorama's tin roof. The building is now home to the Boston Center for the Arts.

㉒ Boston Athletic Association. *40 Trinity Place.* The Boston Athletic Association has an exhibit of historical memorabilia related to the Boston Marathon at its headquarters. Items include photographs, newspaper clippings, trophies, and running shoes. There's even a bronzed pair of two-time winner Johnny Kelley's size eight running shoes. To make an appointment to view the exhibit, call 617-236-1652 x2624.

㉓ The Fairmont Copley Plaza Hotel. *138 St. James Avenue.* This opulent hotel on the south side of Copley Square hosts the awards ceremony for the champions and top finishers of the Boston Marathon a few hours after the conclusion of the race. The hotel has also hosted banquets honoring Boston sporting greats such as Babe Ruth in 1935 and Rural Rube, a greyhound superstar who ran at Wonderland Dog Track in 1939. Fifteen hundred race fans and dignitaries paid to dine with the canine wonder, who sat at the head table devouring a steak dinner.

㉔ Copley Square. There are two landmarks in Copley Square related to the Boston Marathon. A 15-foot granite medallion embedded on the Boylston Street side of Copley Square marks the centennial edition of the race. The medallion includes geographic and topographical maps of the course encircled by the names, countries, and finishing times of previous winners. Four red granite bollards on the medallion's perimeter include bronze reliefs of runners and wheelchair athletes along with the seals of the eight municipalities through which the April foot race is staged. Also in Copley Square is a statue of a tortoise and a hare near Trinity Church that is dedicated to runners from all over the world.

㉕ Boston Public Library. *700 Boylston Street.* Boston's great palace of the written word is also the repository for the collection of Royal Rooter Michael "Nuf Ced" McGreevey. The McGreevey Collection, which is housed in the print department, includes baseball photographs from 1875 to 1916 that were originally on display inside McGreevey's Third Base Saloon. The highlight of the collection are the photographs from the 1903 World Series between Boston and Pittsburgh. Outside the library on Boylston Street is the finish line for the Boston Marathon, but don't take any pictures of yourself crossing it unless you've done the twenty-six miles beforehand.

㉖ Copley Place. *Dartmouth and Stuart streets.* The Copley Place shopping center sits on land occupied in the late 1880s by the Dartmouth Street Grounds. The grounds hosted a couple of Boston baseball teams and even a World Series game in 1887 between the Detroit Wolverines of the National League and the Saint Louis Browns of the American Association. The teams barnstormed the country battling for the championship, and Detroit scored a victory in Boston after arriving on the morning train from Philadelphia. In the next decade, the grounds were converted to the Irvington Street Oval, which served as the finish line for the inaugural Boston Marathon in 1897. Mechanics Hall—which once hosted track meets, basketball games, and boxing matches—used to stand across the street from the Copley Place location at the site of the Prudential Center.

㉗ The Tennis & Racquet Club. *939 Boylston Street.* The red-brick building across from the Prudential Center, which dates back to 1902, is home to the Tennis & Racquet Club. In addition to squash and racquet courts, the club has one of the few court tennis facilities in the United States. The club periodically hosts national and world championships that draw the best court tennis players from around the globe. The first bona fide court tennis facility in America was opened nearby on Buckingham Street in the Back Bay in 1876.

㉘ Matthews Arena. *238 St. Botolph Street.* Matthews Arena, home of Northeastern hockey and men's basketball, has a long and storied history. It first opened its doors in 1910 as the Boston Arena, and it's the oldest artificial ice arena in the world. The Bruins and Celtics both played their inaugural games inside the arena before moving across town to the old Boston Garden. The arena also hosted the first Beanpot in addition to Boston College, Boston University, and Harvard hockey. Both Joe Louis and Jack Dempsey fought inside the arena. On its saddest day, Matthews Arena hosted the 1993 funeral of Reggie Lewis, a Northeastern and Celtics great.

㉙ Boston YMCA. *316 Huntington Avenue.* Boston was home to the first YMCA in the United States, which opened in Boston in 1851 at the intersection of Washington and Summer streets in Downtown Crossing. The Y offered a library, gymnasium, and classes to improve the spiritual, physical, and mental condition of young men. The YMCA's self-improvement lectures were organized into the "Evening Institute for Young Men," which eventually evolved into Northeastern University. The Y's current home was completed in 1912 and dedicated by President William Howard Taft.

㉚ Cabot Center. *Huntington Avenue and Forsyth Street.* A small plaque on the front of the Cabot Center commemorates the Huntington Avenue Grounds, the first home of the Red Sox and the site of the first modern World Series in 1903, which Boston won. The plaque is located approximately on what was then the left-field foul line, and the fence ran along the Huntington Avenue sidewalk. Inside the Cabot Center, which is home to the Northeastern women's basketball team, is a display case on the second floor next to the basketball court that houses a very small collection of artifacts related to the old ballyard, including photographs and replica wool jerseys. Adjoining display cases honor some of the greats of Northeastern athletics. Check in at the front desk to get into the center.

㉛ Cy Young Statue. *Off Forsyth Street behind the Cabot Center.* The small courtyard area on the Northeastern campus looks like a typical college quad except for the singularly focused man, crouched over and staring fiercely ahead with a laser-like gaze. That figure is a statue of former Red Sox flamethrower Cy Young looking toward an imaginary catcher for a sign. Young, who used to go to work on that precise plot of land when it was the mound at the Huntington Avenue Grounds, tallied the most wins of any hurler in baseball history, with 511 victories; he pitched the first perfect game of the twentieth century at the grounds in 1904. Embedded in the ground sixty feet away from Cy Young is a granite marker shaped like home plate that commemorates the first World Series.

㉜ South End Grounds. *Ruggles T Station.* Boston's National League franchise played just across the railroad tracks from the Huntington Avenue Grounds at the South End Grounds. The stadium hosted the city's first professional team, the Red Stockings, beginning in 1871, before becoming the home of the Braves until 1914. At one time, the South End Grounds featured the city's first and only double-decked grandstand, a magnificent edifice with medieval-style turrets. The stadium also hosted the Boston Beaneaters and Boston Wonder Workers soccer teams and the Harvard football team before it closed in 1929. Today an historical marker in the Ruggles T Station is the only connection to the site's baseball past. "Nuf Ced" McGreevey's Third Base Saloon used to be nearby at the corner of Ruggles and Tremont Street.

㉝ Old Somerset Hotel. *Commonwealth Avenue and Charlesgate East.* Now residential housing, this building was once the Somerset Hotel. Ted Williams lived in room 231 for the last half of his career with the Red Sox.

㉞ Myles Standish Hall. *610 Beacon Street.* This dormitory at Boston University was once the Myles Standish Hotel. Visiting baseball teams such as the New York Yankees stayed at the hotel when playing the Red Sox. Babe Ruth requested suite 818 on his stays.

㉟ Citgo Sign. *660 Beacon Street.* Even though it's nearly a quarter of a mile from home plate, the Citgo sign feels as if it's part of Fenway Park. The double-faced sign, sixty feet long and sixty feet wide, has the ultimate bleacher seat for Red Sox games from atop its perch in Kenmore Square. The current sign dates from 1965 and is lit from dusk to midnight. The Citgo sign also serves as a welcome beacon on Beacon Street for runners in the home stretch of the Boston Marathon. Once through Kenmore Square, there is only about a mile left to conquer.

㊱ Hotel Buckminster. *645 Beacon Street.* According to Eliot Asinof's book *Eight Men Out*, the conspiracy to fix the 1919 World Series was first hatched at this hotel in the heart of Kenmore Square. Joseph "Sport" Sullivan, a Royal Rooter who was also a bookmaker and gambler, met Chicago first baseman Chick Gandil in his hotel room when the White Sox were in town and discussed the scheme to fix the upcoming series, which resulted in the infamous Black Sox scandal.

㊲ Fenway Park. *Four Yawkey Way.* Fenway Park has been the home of the Red Sox since 1912. Tours of the ballpark, which include the Green Monster seats and the press box, are given throughout the year, and tickets can be purchased at the ticket office on the corner of Yawkey Way and Brookline Avenue. Even if you don't take a tour, walk around the ballpark and see some of the famous sites—watering holes in the neighborhood, the Green Monster looming over Lansdowne Street, a statue of Ted Williams placing a Red Sox cap on a young Jimmy Fund patient outside Gate B, and a plaque dedicated to former owner Tom Yawkey along the façade on Yawkey Way.

㊳ Agganis Arena. *925 Commonwealth Avenue.* The 6,500-seat Agganis Arena is a new arrival on the Boston sports scene. It is the home of the Boston University Terriers men's hockey team and the Champions Cup tennis tournament. The BU basketball and women's hockey teams occasionally play in the arena as well. The building is named after BU football and baseball great Harry Agganis, "the Golden Greek." In front of the arena is a bronze statue of Agganis in his football uniform getting ready to throw a pass down the field.

㊴ Braves Field/Nickerson Field. *Off Harry Agganis Way.* Nickerson Field on the campus of Boston University is home to the Terriers soccer and lacrosse teams and was where the New England Patriots first took the field. The stadium is also the former site of Braves Field, home of the city's National League franchise from 1915 to 1952. The Red Sox played home games at Braves Field during the 1915 and 1916 World Series as well as Sunday games between 1929 and 1932. Braves Field's right-field bleachers were incorporated into the grandstand of Nickerson Field, and parts of the original exterior right-field wall still stand along Harry Agganis Way. The stucco ticket office down the right-field line is now a child-care center and campus security office, and a plaque behind the building commemorates Braves Field. Boston University's Case Athletic Center, home of Walter Brown Arena and the Roof, occupies the area where the left-field pavilion once stood. The Boston Braves Historical Society offers periodic tours of old Braves Field.

THE SPORTS MUSEUM

Boston has great museums dedicated to science, history, and the arts. And for such a sports-crazed metropolis, it's only natural that Boston has a museum dedicated to its favorite pastimes as well. From the advent of spectator sports right through the recent championship runs of Boston's professional franchises, The Sports Museum tells the story of the development of sports in New England through memorabilia, photographs, and interactive exhibits.

The Sports Museum has led a nomadic existence since its founding in 1977, moving from city to city and location to location, but it has found a stable home inside the TD Garden. The museum's display cases—filled with uniforms, yearbooks, tickets, and other artifacts—ring a half-mile of concourses in the Garden's two Premium Club levels. An added bonus of the museum's current location is getting a peek inside the Garden. Lucky fans might spy a pregame shoot around or a morning skate. (If you have a Premium Club ticket to a Garden event, you can also check out the museum displays while you're at the game.)

Admission to The Sports Museum is at hourly intervals. Once visitors are brought upstairs from the Garden's lobby, there's a brief talk about the history of the Garden and the museum. Then visitors are free to wander the two levels of the museum.

Naturally, there are sections of the museum dedicated to the Red Sox, Patriots, Celtics, and Bruins, but the museum isn't just about the city's four major professional sports teams. Far from it. Displays are devoted to soccer, boxing, golf, horse racing, high school sports, the Bay State Games, the Boston Marathon, and local Olympians. College basketball, college football, college hockey, and the Beanpot are all covered as well. Fans will also be drawn to exhibits on the Boston Braves and Harry Agganis.

Throughout the museum are lockers featuring the uniforms and other keepsakes of Boston superstars. Baseball fans can check out the lockers of Hall of Famers Warren Spahn and Bobby Doerr and present-day stars Dustin Pedroia and David Ortiz, who has a jar of Big Papi Salsa on the top shelf of his locker.

Red Sox fans will particularly enjoy the museum's "Tale of Two Cities" exhibit, displaying the front pages of newspapers from Boston and New York during the epic 2004 American League Championship Series. Covers from the *Boston Herald* celebrating the comeback victory are posted under "It was the best of times…" Front pages from the *New York Post* and *New York Daily News* with headlines such as "Hell freezes over" are posted under "It was the worst of times…" Sox fans will be more sobered, however, looking at the baseball that struck phenom Tony Conigliaro in the eye in 1967 and forever changed his career.

Fans of the old Boston Braves can view the 1915 construction blueprints for Braves Field along with the home plate that was "liberated" from the stadium in 1953 after the Braves bolted for Milwaukee. There's also a locker featuring a blue-and-gold trimmed uniform and pennant of the Boston Bees, as the Braves were known for a few years in the early 1900s.

Patriots fans can view pennants, photographs, and uniforms dating back to the team's early years in the American Football League. The most historically interesting Patriots artifact may be an autographed pair of shoes that were worn by Adam Vinatieri in Super Bowl XXXVI, when he kicked the winning 48-yard field goal as time expired. (The two shoes are actually in different styles. One is for traction, and the other is for kicking.) Museum visitors can also see jerseys from Pats quarterbacks Steve Grogan, Drew Bledsoe, and Tom Brady as well the one worn by hometown hero Doug Flutie in Boston College's 1985 Cotton Bowl victory.

Bruins fans will find items ranging from a horse-drawn Zamboni and an old Eddie Shore hockey stick, sculpted from a single piece of wood, to the lockers of Cam Neely and Ray Bourque. There is even a stuffed bear that was presented to Bruins owner Charles Adams by members of the 1928-29 Stanley Cup championship team. Legend has it that players would rub the bear's forehead for good luck before going into the owner's office to discuss their contracts. After being stuffed by the players, however, the bear may not have been in the right mood to grant them any wishes.

Other hockey-related items in The Sports Museum are pucks and jerseys from the defunct Hartford Whalers franchise, which got its start in Boston, and the Beanpot trophy. There's also memorabilia from the 1960 and 1980 U.S. Olympic hockey teams, which included many players from the Boston area, that both captured gold. The jersey worn by Jim Craig, goalie for the 1980 "miracle on ice" team, is among the items on display.

Hoops fans will find uniforms that run the gamut of fashion from the less-than-aerodynamic flowing robes worn by a member of the 1895 Smith College women's basketball team to the short-shorts worn by Larry Bird nearly one hundred years later. There are lockers belonging to John Havlicek, Bill Russell, and Paul Pierce. Check out their sneakers to see how your feet size up. Other interesting items include one of Red Auerbach's signature cigars and a piece of the parquet floor signed by Celtic Hall of Famers Bob Cousy, Tom Heinsohn, Dave Cowens, Bill Walton, Kevin McHale, Russell, Havlicek, and Bird.

That priceless piece of parquet once resided inside the old Boston Garden. The Sports Museum has other pieces of the old barn on display, including some of the old wooden seats and one of the Garden's hockey goals. Fans can even take a seat in the Garden's old penalty box and feel what it's like to spend five for fighting. The penalty box is on loan from Bruins great Terry O'Reilly, who could have been charged Boston property tax for the record amount of time he resided within its doors.

Among items in the museum are a series of unique Armand LaMontagne wooden sculptures of Boston sporting gods in familiar poses. There's Bobby Orr in his black-and-gold uniform winding up for a slap shot, Larry Bird in his patented free throw stance, and Carl Yastrzemski watching a titanic blast sail toward the fences. The one statue that makes fans do a double-take, though, is that of Ted Williams, clad not in his familiar Red Sox uniform, but in a flannel shirt, tan fishing vest, and waders. Instead of a ball and bat, the Splendid Splinter, an avid fisherman, holds a casting line in his left hand while proudly displaying his latest catch in his right.

Some great pieces of sports-related artwork are hanging from the walls of the museum, including murals filled with images and icons from Boston sports, ranging from Babe Ruth, Francis Ouimet, and a bare-chested John L. Sullivan to Nancy Kerrigan, Pedro Martinez, and Tom Brady. The museum also has a series of autographed caricatures of Boston sports heroes that once hung on the walls of the Sports Depot restaurant in Allston. Don't leave without checking out the cartoon-like depictions of famous moments in Boston sports history—such as Bobby Orr's 1970 cup-clinching goal, Carlton Fisk's Game Six home run in the 1975 World Series, and Doug Flutie's Hail Mary—and relive them by listening to the play-by-play audio. Die-hard Boston sports fans are sure to get chills down their spines, even on a hot summer day.

GETTING THERE: The Sports Museum is located inside the TD Garden. For directions and parking information for the Garden, see page 65.

HOURS: On most days, The Sports Museum opens at 11 AM and closes at either 3 PM or 5 PM. Note that admission into the museum is on the hour: 11 AM, noon, 1 PM, 2 PM, and 3 PM. Miss it by a few minutes, and you'll have to wait nearly an hour to get in, so be sure to plan accordingly. On game days, the last admission is at 2 PM. Museum hours are subject to change due to the Garden's event schedule, and the museum may be closed on certain days as well, so call or check the website to confirm hours.

ADMISSION: $6 for adults; $4 for children ages six to seventeen and seniors; $15 for families; children under six are free. Tickets can be purchased at the TD Garden box office, located on the west side of the arena. The museum's entrance is located at the entrance for the Premium Club, also on the west side of the arena.

CONTACT INFORMATION: The Sports Museum, TD Garden, 100 Legends Way, Boston, MA 02114. 617-624-1234; www.tdbanknorthgarden.com/sportsmuseum.

WHERE TO WATCH (& DRINK)

Even if you can't get a ticket to watch a game in person, that doesn't mean you have to miss out on being part of the crowd cheering on the home teams. There are plenty of watering holes around Boston—and across the world—where Boston sports fans can grab a burger and beer, watch the game, complain about the bad calls, and celebrate the victories with their comrades. And hey, sometimes the view from a barstool beats the one from the upper deck anyway.

BOSTON'S BEST SPORTS BARS

From Irish pubs to colonial taverns to the legendary Cheers franchise, Boston is known around the world for its local alehouses. And even before Michael "Nuf Ced" McGreevey opened his Third Base Saloon and boxer John L. Sullivan became proprietor of a Washington Street drinkery in the late 1800s, Bostonians bellied up to the bar to debate current events, politics, and inevitably, the state of their beloved sports teams.

Today, of course, Boston sports fans not only gather in bars for sports banter and a pint but also for sports on television. Boston is such a sports-crazed town that there's usually no question whether a local bar or restaurant will have the Sox or Pats game on its televisions. It's as much a given as having beer on tap or air to breathe.

But just having the television tuned to ESPN and hanging a few Bruins and Celtics posters on the walls doesn't automatically transform any joint into a sports bar. A sports bar, as opposed to a bar that shows sports, caters to die-hard fans with plenty of televisions, a wide range of games to watch, a variety of beer choices, and a menu that satisfies the appetites of the hungriest of patrons. A sports bar is also a place where fans can come dressed in their team colors and unabashedly cheer on their squads. The fifteen listed here are the best in Boston in catering to die-hards from all walks of life.

As with all establishments, these sports bars are not monoliths. They appeal to different tastes. Some cater to young professionals, others to college students, others to tourists, and still others to no-nonsense fans who just want a television and a beer. Keep in mind that in addition to these sports bars in and around downtown Boston, the suburbs have some great places to catch games as well.

❶ THE FOUR'S

166 Canal Street
Boston, MA 02114
Phone: 617-720-4455
www.thefours.com

The stat line
Capacity: 395

BOSTON'S SPORTS BARS

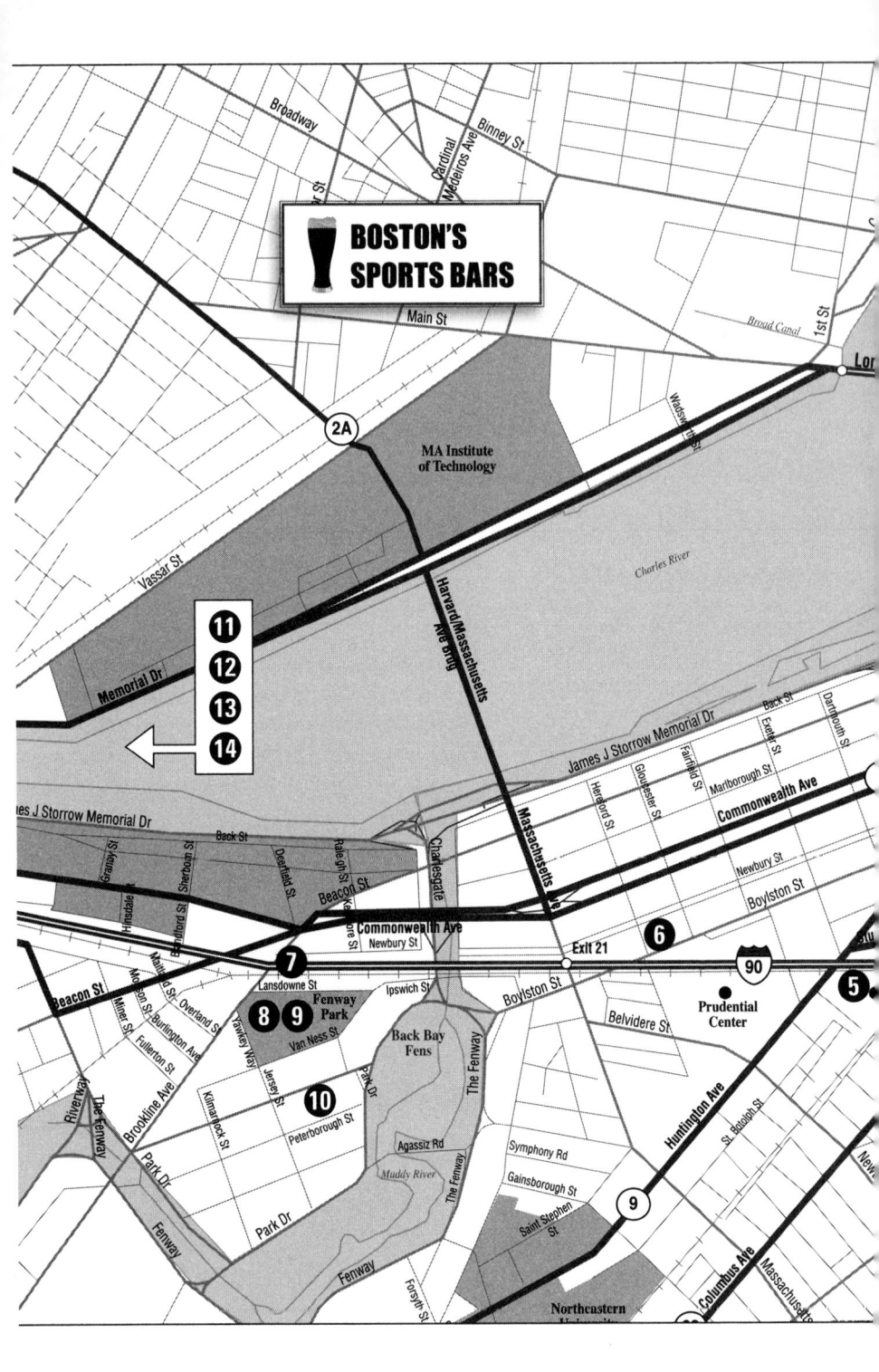

250

THE DIE★HARD SPORTS FAN'S GUIDE TO BOSTON

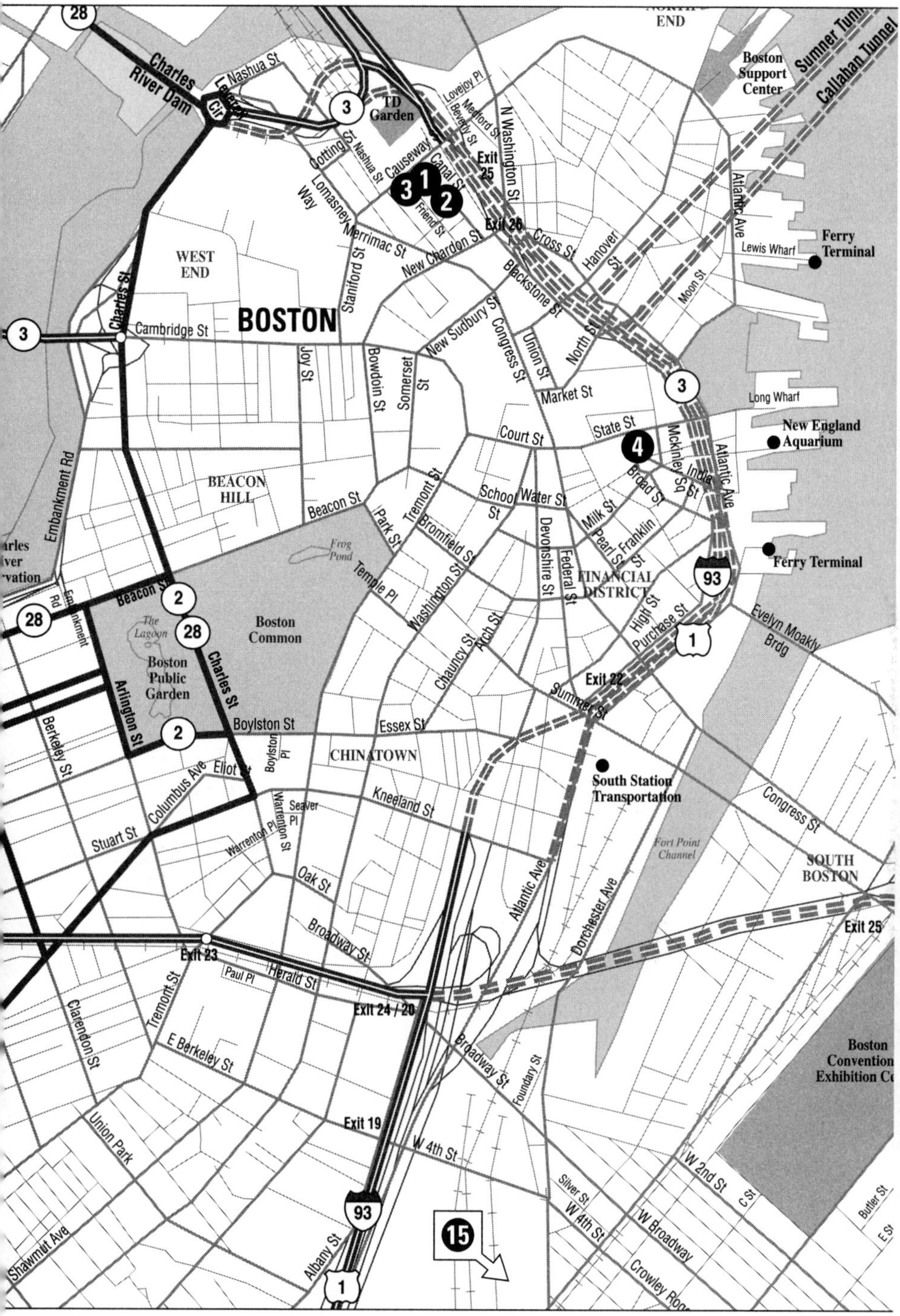

END
Boston Support Center
Sumner Tunnel
Callahan Tunnel
Charles River Dam
Leverett Cir
Nashua St
TD Garden
Lovejoy Pl
Medford St
Beverly St
N Washington St
Exit 25
Causeway
Canal St
Gotting St
Nashua St
Lomasney Way
Friend St
Exit 26
Cross St
Hanover St
Atlantic Ave
Lewis Wharf
Ferry Terminal
Merrimac St
New Chardon St
Blackstone St
Moon St
WEST END
Staniford St
BOSTON
Charles St
Cambridge St
New Sudbury St
Congress St
Union St
North St
Joy St
Bowdoin St
Somerset St
Market St
Long Wharf
Court St
State St
Mckinley Sq
India St
New England Aquarium
BEACON HILL
Beacon St
Tremont St
School St
Water St
Broad St
Embankment Rd
Frog Pond
Park St
Bromfield St
Milk St
Franklin St
Pearl St
Devonshire St
Federal St
Ferry Terminal
FINANCIAL DISTRICT
Temple Pl
Washington St
High St
Purchase St
Evelyn Moakly Brdg
Beacon St
Embankment Rd
Boston Common
The Lagoon
Boston Public Garden
Charles St
Arlington St
Chauncy St
Arch St
Exit 22
Summer St
Boylston St
Essex St
Berkeley St
Boylston Pl
CHINATOWN
Eliot St
Columbus Ave
South Station Transportation
Seaver Pl
Warrenton St
Kneeland St
Congress St
Stuart St
Warrenton Pl
Fort Point Channel
Oak St
Atlantic Ave
SOUTH BOSTON
Broadway St
Dorchester Ave
Exit 25
Exit 23
Paul Pl
Herald St
Exit 24 / 20
Tremont St
Clarendon St
E Berkeley St
Broadway St
Foundary St
Boston Convention Exhibition Ce
Union Park
Exit 19
W 4th St
W 2nd St
C St
Silver St
W 4th St
W Broadway
Butler St
E St
Shawmut Ave
Albany St
Crowley Rogers
93
1
3
2
28
4
15

Bottled beers: 10
Draft beers: 8
Televisions: 38
Sports packages: NFL Sunday Ticket, MLB Extra Innings, NBA League Pass, NHL Center Ice, ESPN GamePlan, ESPN FullCourt, NCAA Mega March Madness
Hours: Daily, 11 AM–midnight

The Four's was one of the few sports bars in Boston when it first opened its doors in the shadows of Boston Garden in 1976. Today, it's a popular spot not only for ticket holders heading to and from Garden events but for Boston sports fans all year long. It's not unusual to spy current or former sports figures grabbing a bite to eat along with families and fans of all ages. The Four's is such a draw that in 2005 it was voted the Best Sports Bar in America by *Sports Illustrated*.

The walls of the bar's two floors are plastered with sports memorabilia, including framed jerseys, magazine covers, and vintage photographs. Televisions surround the downstairs bar, although its cozy confines can quickly become a cramped and difficult place to watch a game for those not fortunate enough to grab a seat. When the weather is warm, there is outdoor seating on the sidewalk as well.

The Four's food is as well known as its sports theme. The extensive menu includes seafood, charbroiled steak tips, buffalo wings, and signature sandwiches named after Boston sporting greats. The menu—which costs a few dollars more at dinner than at lunch—includes soups, salads, and appetizers ($6.95–$10.95) such as buffalo chicken nachos, shrimp cocktail, and mushrooms stuffed with lobster, crab, and shrimp. Entrees ($7.50–$19.95) include burgers, wraps, baby back ribs, surf and turf, fresh salmon, swordfish, and baked stuffed shrimp. The Bobby Orr steak sandwich topped with melted American cheese is the house specialty, which makes sense since the bar is named in honor of the hockey legend's number with the Bruins—4. In addition to its location near the Garden, The Four's also has an outpost in Quincy.

❷ SPORTS GRILLE BOSTON
132 Canal Street
Boston, MA 02114
Phone: 617-367-9302

The stat line
Capacity: 156
Bottled beers: 20
Draft beers: 24
Televisions: 130
Sports packages: NFL Sunday Ticket, MLB Extra Innings, NBA League Pass, NHL Center Ice, ESPN GamePlan, ESPN FullCourt, NCAA Mega March Madness, MLS Direct Kick
Hours: Daily, 11 AM–11 PM

When sports fans step inside the Sports Grille Boston, they can easily mistake it for a local Best Buy. With a remarkable 130 televisions packed inside, sports fans will need eyes in the back of their heads to catch all the action. There are flat-screen TVs encircling the bar, TVs sitting on ledges around the perimeter of the dining space, even personal TVs at tables. If any pro or college game is on television in America, fans can bet it will be on at the Sports Grille Boston. Consequently, it's a popular spot with alumni groups, ticket holders heading to the Garden, and fans just looking for the basics: beer, food, and games.

The menu includes hot dogs, pizza, pasta dishes, kids' choices, and sandwiches named after athletes. There's a "Marciano Baby Rib Sub" as well as a "Larry Bird Burger"—a chicken breast with marinade. Menu items cost $6.50–$11.95. In warmer weather, there is outdoor seating on the sidewalk, presenting fans with the dilemma of either soaking in the sun or basking in the glow of 130 televisions.

❸ THE GREATEST BAR
262 Friend Street
Boston, MA 02114
Phone: 617-367-0544
www.thegreatestbar.com

The stat line
Capacity: 440
Bottled beers: 21
Draft beers: 8
Televisions: 22
Sports packages: NFL Sunday Ticket, MLB Extra Innings, NBA League Pass, NHL Center Ice, ESPN GamePlan, ESPN FullCourt, NCAA Mega March Madness, MLS Direct Kick
Hours: Monday–Friday, 4 PM–2 AM; Saturday–Sunday, noon–2 AM

The Greatest Bar is so big that it's actually composed of three different bars on four levels. The ground-floor bar has a bank of gigantic high-def televisions that rivals some sports books in Las Vegas. No need to worry about squinting to follow the action here. In addition to bar and table seating on the first floor, a second floor balcony gives patrons a bird's eye view of the television screens as well as the ceiling mural that features great moments in Boston sports history. The third and fourth floors also have bars and dining areas.

The Greatest Bar is just down the street from the Garden, and before every home game it plays a unique ninety-minute video that showcases great Boston sports highlights. The bar is also the official pick-up spot for StubHub tickets and the official sponsor of the Boston Blazers. The Greatest Bar offers DJs, live music, and dance floors for late-night entertainment with music choices ranging from Motown to contemporary Top 40 hits. Cover charges may apply for late-night entertainment.

The Greatest Bar's menu includes soups, salads, and appetizers ($6.95–$10.95), such as loaded nachos, fried calamari, jalapeno poppers, and shrimp scampi. Entrees ($8.95–$18) feature deep-dish personal pan pizzas, burgers, penne primavera, shrimp plates, grilled swordfish, and New York sirloin.

❹ THE PLACE
Two Broad Street
Boston, MA 02109
Phone: 617-523-2081
www.theplaceboston.com

The stat line
Capacity: 300
Bottled beers: 12
Draft beers: 7
Televisions: 17
Sports packages: NFL Sunday Ticket, ESPN GamePlan, ESPN FullCourt, NCAA Mega March Madness
Hours: Monday–Friday, 4 PM–2 AM; Saturday–Sunday, 11 AM–2 AM

With its location in the Financial District, The Place tends to draw a blend of college students, young professionals, and the after-work crowd. Games are shown on flat-screen plasma televisions throughout the bar. At night, The Place definitely appeals more to young, single sports fans who also enjoy the late-night club scene. Most nights after 10 PM, The Place features DJs spinning music, and space around the bar can become tight, particularly on weekends.

The Place has a straightforward menu that includes salads, appetizers ($2.95–$8.95), and sandwiches ($5.95–$8.95) such as chicken parmesan, turkey club, and a buffalo chicken wrap. The most popular menu items are pizzas and calzones ($6.95–$8.50), which are served all night.

❺ CHAMPIONS
Boston Marriott Copley Place
110 Huntington Avenue
Boston, MA 02116
Phone: 617-236-5800 x6936
www.championsboston.com

The stat line
Capacity: 300
Bottled beers: 22
Draft beers: 19
Televisions: 34
Sports packages: NFL Sunday Ticket, MLB Extra Innings, NBA League Pass, NHL Center Ice, ESPN GamePlan, ESPN FullCourt, NCAA Mega March Madness, Setanta Sports
Hours: Sunday–Thursday, 11:30 AM–1 AM; Friday–Saturday, 11:30 AM–2 AM

Champions, located on the lobby level of the Boston Marriott Copley Place, is the local outpost of the national sports bar chain. With its hotel location, Champions draws more out-of-town fans than most Boston sports bars. The good news for Boston sports fans is that means Champions has a full range of sports packages to cater to its geographically diverse clientele. In addition to televisions all around the bar, the dining area features two large projection screens for the big games of the day. Champions scores bonus points for its bubble hockey table.

The menu at Champions covers all the bases. Appetizers ($3.98–$9.50) include quesadillas, jalapeno poppers, nachos, and chicken tenders. Main dishes ($8.75–$18.50) include salads, burgers, entrees, and sandwiches. There are dessert items and a kids' menu as well. Although Champions is a chain, the menu includes a couple of nods to the local fandom with the "Larry Legend Lobster Roll" and the "Red Reuben Grilled Reuben Sandwich." The bar's signature dessert is the "Babe Ruth Sundae," which features caramel ice cream, chocolate and caramel sauces, chopped nuts, whipped cream, and a Baby Ruth bar.

❻ McGREEVY'S
911 Boylston Street
Boston, MA 02115
Phone: 617-262-0911
www.mcgreevysboston.com

The stat line
Capacity: 317
Bottled beers: 20
Draft beers: 8
Televisions: 14
Sports packages: None
Hours: Monday–Friday, 11 AM–2 AM; Saturday–Sunday, 10:30 AM–2 AM

The spirit of Michael "Nuf Ced" McGreevy's old Third Base Saloon was resurrected with the opening of this bar in 2008, across from the Prudential Center. The interior of the tavern is a replica of the original Third Base Saloon, which makes the place feel as much like a museum as a sports bar. Originals and reproductions of the saloon's pictures hang on the walls, and even its distinctive light fixtures—baseball-shaped orbs mounted on baseball bats hanging from the ceiling—have been recreated. Display cases inside the bar are filled with memorabilia relating to the Red Sox and Royal Rooters. McGreevy's is owned by Peter Nash, a baseball historian who was formerly with the hip-hop group 3rd Bass, and Ken Casey, a founding member of Boston's Dropkick Murphys. While McGreevy's is a good spot to watch the Sox and other local teams, the one downside is that the bar's lack of sports packages limits viewing choices.

In addition to being a shrine to the national pastime, McGreevy's is an Irish pub, and its menu definitely reflects that influence. (It's also known around town as one of the best places to grab a pint of Guinness.) Appetizers ($6–$9) include Guinness barbeque wings and tenders, corned beef and potato croquettes, and traditional Irish boxty, which is like a potato pancake or an Irish quesadilla. McGreevy's also serves soups, salads, sandwiches, and entrees ($7–$18) that include shepherd's pie, Guinness beef stew, and all-day Irish breakfast. On weekends, the tavern serves breakfast ($5–$12) that includes eggs, omelets, pancakes, and waffles. Fans with big appetites can try "The Big Papi," which includes pancakes, French toast, two eggs, home fries, ham, bacon, and sausage.

❼ CASK'N FLAGON

62 Brookline Avenue
Boston, MA 02215
Phone: 617-536-4840
www.casknflagon.com

The stat line
Capacity: 700
Bottled beers: 18
Draft beers: 12
Televisions: 60
Sports packages: NFL Sunday Ticket, MLB Extra Innings, NBA League Pass, NHL Center Ice, ESPN GamePlan, ESPN FullCourt, NCAA Mega March Madness
Hours: Monday–Saturday, 11:30 AM–2 AM; Sunday, 11:30 AM–1 AM

The Fenway faithful have been filling up the Cask'n Flagon before and after Red Sox games ever since it opened in 1969. But even when the Sox aren't playing at home, the Cask is still a draw for the city's sports fans. Flat-screen televisions suspended from the ceiling are everywhere. (There are even small televisions in the bathrooms.) While a 2006 renovation added considerably more space inside, the Cask still maintains a cozy tavern atmosphere with its brick walls and tile floors that mirror the ballpark across the street.

Before Sox games, large picture windows allow patrons to watch the pregame activity on Lansdowne Street and see the fans walking up Brookline Avenue. In warm weather, outdoor seating is available on the Lansdowne Street sidewalk, literally in the shadows of the Green Monster. Fans can keep watch for baseballs sailing over the wall during batting practice while having a bite to eat. In the rear of the Cask'n Flagon is Oliver's, a late-night club that includes DJs, live music, and stand-up comedy. Prior to Red Sox games, it's open to fans who can watch sporting events on big-screen projection televisions. The Cask has two big bars but stations around the bar are a bonus, allowing fans to buy a beer without having to get a bartender's attention.

The Cask's menu includes soup, salads, calzones, and pizzas ($7.99–$11.99). In addition to basic appetizers ($4.99–$12.99), the Cask offers yakitori chicken skewers—tender grilled chicken and green onions served with chili sauce—for 1,048.83 yen ($9.99). The Cask also has a special lunch menu that includes additional pasta dishes and a businessperson's lunch of a half sandwich and soup for $6.99. Entrees ($7.99–$17.99) include wraps, burgers, sandwiches, rib eye, seafood gumbo, chicken and broccoli alfredo, and meatloaf. And if fans want to get in the baseball spirit, the Cask's menu includes "Bleacher Dogs"—two all-beef hot dogs grilled and smothered in homemade chili with chopped onions and cheddar cheese ($8.99).

❽ GAME ON!

82 Lansdowne Street
Boston, MA 02215
Phone: 617-351-7001

www.gameonboston.com
The stat line
Capacity: 630
Bottled beers: 20
Draft beers: 7
Televisions: 90
Sports packages: NFL Sunday Ticket, MLB Extra Innings, NBA League Pass, NHL Center Ice, ESPN GamePlan, ESPN FullCourt, NCAA Mega March Madness, Setanta Sports
Hours: Daily, 11:30 AM–2 AM

Since Game On! opened at the corner of Brookline Avenue and Lansdowne Street in the former Kenmore Bowladrome in 2005, it has quickly become one of the city's favorite sports bars. The bar's wealth of flat-screen televisions throughout its two levels makes it a popular spot, not only for fans of the Boston sports teams, but for alumni groups and fans of out-of-town teams wanting to cheer on their favorites. Red Sox players also swing by Game On! to enjoy a pregame meal. On nice days, there are outdoor seats along the sidewalk, and the dining room's picture windows are opened.

The downstairs level has a traditional sports bar atmosphere with seven projection screens surrounding an island bar. The upstairs bar and dining room—and its upscale menu—has more of a premium seating vibe. If fans want to take the luxury amenities one step further, they can rent one of the bar's skyboxes, which seat between ten and twenty-five and include private service and televisions tuned to any games. Game On! also offers groups the unique chance to take some cuts in the visiting team's batting cage inside Fenway Park when it's not being used by the big leaguers.

The lunch and dinner menu at Game On! features twists on traditional comfort foods. The bar offers soups, salads, and appetizers ($7–$10) such as calamari, pot-stickers, fried ravioli, and cheeseburger spring rolls. Fans can build their own fries by choosing different toppings and dips. Main dishes ($8–$17) include pizzas, burgers, and sandwiches such as fish tacos, Italian panini, and baked Cajun whitefish. Entrees include macaroni and cheese and steak tips. For dessert, there is Oreo chocolate chunk cake.

❾ BLEACHER BAR
82A Lansdowne Street
Boston, MA 02215
Phone: 617-262-2424
www.bleacherbarboston.com
The stat line
Capacity: 170
Bottled beers: 23
Draft beers: 3
Televisions: 6
Sports packages: NFL Sunday Ticket, MLB Extra Innings, NBA League Pass, NHL Center Ice, ESPN GamePlan, ESPN FullCourt, NCAA Mega March Madness, Setanta Sports
Hours: Sunday–Wednesday, 11 AM–1 AM; Thursday–Saturday, 11 AM–2 AM

Other sports bars in Boston have more televisions, but TVs aren't the main attraction for patrons of the Bleacher Bar. Sports fans are too busy gazing upon Fenway Park's verdant center field to notice the action on the tube. Opened in 2008, the Bleacher Bar occupies the space underneath the center-field stands that used to be the home of the visiting team's batting cages. When the Red Sox are playing at home, fans inside the Bleacher Bar can watch batting practice and even parts of games through the bar's huge window. During winter, fans get a unique chance to see what the ballpark looks like tucked under a blanket of snow. And if fans somehow tire of the view, the Bleacher

Bar's televisions do broadcast nearly every major sports package.

Like the park itself, the Bleacher Bar has a highly irregular shape, so only a few coveted tables have field views. Those seats are limited to forty-five minutes during games, but standing patrons can also get field views. Photographers should take note that flash photography is not allowed during batting practice and games. While other sports bars have televisions in the bathrooms, the men's room in the Bleacher Bar features an eye-level window that looks out over the bar and out to the field. The walls of the Bleacher Bar are adorned with Red Sox memorabilia, and the team's retired numbers are carved in the wood along the length of the bar.

The Bleacher Bar has a limited bar menu that mostly features hot and cold sandwiches. Appetizers ($3–$9) include onion rings, pretzel sticks, and sliders. Main dishes ($6–$16) include burgers, salads, and deli sandwiches with pastrami, salami, beef brisket, and corned beef among the choices in addition to standard fare and a few desserts.

⑩ THE BASEBALL TAVERN

1270 Boylston Street
Boston, MA 02215
Phone: 617-867-6526
www.thebaseballtavern.com

The stat line
Capacity: 555
Bottled beers: 15
Draft beers: 4
Televisions: 20+
Sports packages: NFL Sunday Ticket, MLB Extra Innings, ESPN GamePlan, ESPN FullCourt, NCAA Mega March Madness
Hours: Daily, 11 AM–2 AM

Since 1963, The Baseball Tavern has been serving up suds to Red Sox fans in the shadows of Fenway Park. The Baseball Tavern is so much of a Fenway institution that after the Sox clinched the wild card in 2003, players Kevin Millar, Gabe Kapler, Derek Lowe, Lou Merloni, and Tim Wakefield—still dressed in their uniform pants—kept the celebration going at The Baseball Tavern and poured beers for the cheering fans. After the tavern's previous location was torn down to build a residential complex, it moved down Boylston Street to spacious new digs that spread over three floors.

What really makes The Baseball Tavern stand apart, however, is its roof deck, which has a view of the exterior of Fenway Park, just a lazy fly ball away. The deck is open for Red Sox home games between Memorial Day and Labor Day, and it's a great place to lounge in an Adirondack chair and soak up some summertime rays. The roof deck's décor mirrors that of its famous neighbor, down to its green paint and bank of lights that looks like the Fenway light towers. Fans who don't have tickets to the game can still hang out on the deck and, hopefully, hear the roar of the crowd. If fans want to get out of the sun, the bar on the roof deck is covered, and there are televisions airing the game.

The Baseball Tavern's menu is pretty straightforward. Appetizers ($4–$7) include clam chowder and buffalo wings. Main dishes ($7–$15) include sandwiches, salads, burgers, seafood plates, and teriyaki steak tips.

⑪ SPORTS DEPOT

353 Cambridge Street
Allston, MA 02134
Phone: 617-783-2300
www.sportsdepotboston.com

The stat line
Capacity: 330
Bottled beers: 20
Draft beers: 20

Televisions: 67

Sports packages: NFL Sunday Ticket, MLB Extra Innings, NHL Center Ice, NBA League Pass, ESPN GamePlan, ESPN FullCourt, NCAA Mega March Madness, MLS Direct Kick

Hours: Monday–Tuesday, 4 PM–1 AM; Wednesday–Friday, 11:30 AM–1 AM; Saturday–Sunday, 10 AM–1 AM

Odds are sports fans will be able to find whatever sporting event they want to watch at the Sports Depot. The Sports Depot has nearly every sports package on its televisions, and it even shows Ultimate Fighting Championship events. Tables include speakers so patrons can listen to any of the games being broadcast on the televisions, and the bathrooms feature televisions as well.

Parking in Allston is notoriously difficult, but the Sports Depot has a couple of lots reserved for its patrons. In warmer weather, it has an outdoor bar and patio seating, but the view isn't exactly picturesque. Karaoke, trivia contests, and DJs on Fridays and Saturdays, as well as other late-night entertainment, are regular features after games wind down. It also has video games, free Wi-Fi, and even a Nintendo Wii.

The Sports Depot's name harkens back to the days when the stone structure was the Allston train depot. According to legend, the depot, which dates back to the 1880s, was Babe Ruth's point of departure for New York City after he was sold to the Yankees. Fans sitting in the restaurant's alcove along the railroad tracks are regularly reminded of the building's former life whenever commuter trains whiz by just a few feet away from their chicken fingers and beer.

The Sports Depot has a huge menu with more than one hundred items. Appetizers ($4.99–$11.99) include sesame beef and Italian sausage. Main dishes ($7.99–$19.99) include Mexican meals—such as tacos, quesadillas, burritos, and fajitas—salads, pizzas, burgers, seafood, barbeque, and sandwiches. The Sports Depot also has a kids' menu and dessert choices such as key lime pie and chocolate cake. On the weekends, the Sports Depot serves breakfast and brunch.

⓬ BRIGHTON BEER GARDEN

386 Market Street
Brighton, MA 02135
Phone: 617-562-6000
www.brightonbeergarden.com

The stat line

Capacity: 600

Bottled beers: 70

Draft beers: 12

Televisions: 40

Sports packages: NFL Sunday Ticket, MLB Extra Innings, ESPN GamePlan, ESPN FullCourt, NCAA Mega March Madness, Setanta Sports

Hours: Monday–Saturday, 11 AM–1 AM; Sunday, 10 AM–1 AM

Since opening in 2008, the Brighton Beer Garden has quickly become a popular gathering spot for sports fans. The sports bar and restaurant draws a diverse clientele, from college students to business people to baby boomers. With its hardwood floors, leather booths, high bar chairs, and a plethora of flat-screen high-def televisions, the Brighton Beer Garden has an upscale atmosphere. In addition, the Brighton Beer Garden has three huge projection screens that are usually tuned to the local teams. Servers are decked out in jerseys of the Boston sports teams, while the uniforms of current and former players hang in frames on the wall.

True to its name, the Brighton Beer Garden has an extensive lineup of beers, with some imported from as far away as China and Singapore. It also features an extensive wine list and menu as well. Among the twenty appetizers ($6.99–$9.99) are more exotic choices such as smoked salmon, coconut shrimp, pot-stickers, sweet potato dumplings, and Philly cheese steak spring rolls. Sports fans not counting calories may want to try the stuffed smokehouse burger, which is filled with bacon and cheddar cheese and topped with barbeque sauce and even more cheddar cheese. Main dishes ($7.99–$23.99) include filet mignon, lobster ravioli, barbeque ribs, and salmon piccata. The Brighton Beer Garden also has a kids' menu and serves dessert. On-street parking in Brighton Center is available near the Brighton Beer Garden.

⑬ JOSHUA TREE

1316 Commonwealth Avenue
Allston, MA 02134
Phone: 617-566-6699
www.joshuatreeallston.com

The stat line
Capacity: 450
Bottled beers: 25
Draft beers: 15
Televisions: 18
Sports packages: NFL Sunday Ticket, MLB Extra Innings, NHL Center Ice, NBA League Pass, ESPN GamePlan, ESPN Full-Court, NCAA Mega March Madness
Hours: Monday–Wednesday, 5 PM–1 AM; Thursday–Friday, 5 PM–2 AM; Saturday, 10:30 AM–2 AM; Sunday, 10:30 AM–1 AM

The Joshua Tree caters to a younger crowd, which is understandable since the surrounding Allston neighborhood is filled with college students and new graduates. The interior of the Joshua Tree, which opened in 2007, has a lounge feel to it with its leather seats, dim lighting, extensive cocktail list, and futuristic-looking bar. In addition to flat-screen televisions mounted behind the bar, the upstairs walls are lined with huge projection screens, so sports fans won't have any trouble watching games no matter where they are. On Thursdays, Fridays, and Saturdays, the Joshua Tree (which has a sister location in Somerville's Davis Square) becomes more of a nightclub with DJs and dancing in its downstairs bar. That might not be a good fit for sports fans who just want to concentrate on the game, but it will appeal to those who want to go to a single place where they can watch the game and enjoy the night life.

While the Joshua Tree specializes in burgers, it also has an extensive menu. Appetizers ($7.99–$9.99) include Thai lettuce wraps and "Big Dig Fries"—waffle fries topped with monterey jack and cheddar and bacon. Entrees (5.99–$13.99) include Mexican dishes—such as fajitas, burritos, tacos, and enchiladas—salads, sandwiches, pizza, and comfort food such as macaroni and cheese, steak tips, and shepherd's pie. On weekends, the Joshua Tree opens early for breakfast and brunch. The breakfast menu includes make-your-own omelets, pancakes, and decadent cinnamon and vanilla French toast crusted with Corn Flakes and drizzled with white chocolate.

The Green Line offers the most convenient transportation option to the Joshua Tree. On-street parking is limited, but the bar offers valet parking.

⑭ COOLIDGE CORNER CLUBHOUSE

307 Harvard Street
Brookline, MA 02446
Phone: 617-566-4948

The stat line
Capacity: 90
Bottled beers: 16
Draft beers: 36
Televisions: 21
Sports packages: NFL Sunday Ticket, MLB Extra Innings, NHL Center Ice, NBA

League Pass, ESPN GamePlan, ESPN FullCourt, NCAA Mega March Madness

Hours: Monday–Friday, 11:30 AM–1:30 AM; Saturday–Sunday, 10 AM–1:30 AM

Sports fans who like choices will love the Coolidge Corner Clubhouse, which has been catering to sports fans for twenty years. The menu, which is as thick as an NFL rulebook, features more than two hundred items. There is a huge cocktail menu and so many draft beers it's difficult to spot the bartender behind all the taps. Not only is the menu huge, but so are the portions: the "Mile High Nachos" are big enough for offensive linemen.

Sandwiches and burgers are named after famous sports figures (and infamous ones, in the case of the "O. J. Simpson Buffalo Chicken Sandwich"). The "Bill Parcells," named for the Big Tuna, is naturally a tuna sandwich, and the "Rosie Ruiz," named after the woman who cheated her way to the finish line of the Boston Marathon, is a turkey sandwich. Appetizers ($5.95–$12.95) include wings, quesadillas, and a basket of soft pretzels. Entrees ($7.95–$19.95) include salads, burgers, sandwiches, Mexican fare, and an extensive range of vegetarian options. The Clubhouse also has a brunch menu on weekends.

The Coolidge Corner Clubhouse is smaller than most sports bars in Boston. The good news for sports fans is that it means the televisions encircling the bar are always in easy viewing range. The bad news is that the cozy bar area can quickly become claustrophobic when a big game is on, and big groups may have trouble sitting together. Tables are usually restricted to patrons who order food, so drinkers are confined to the bar area. Two-hour parking is usually available on the side streets around Coolidge Corner.

⓯ STADIUM SPORTS BAR & GRILL

232 Old Colony Avenue
South Boston, MA 02127
Phone: 617-269-5100
www.stadiumbars.com

The stat line
Capacity: 505
Bottled beers: 15
Draft beers: 17
Televisions: 34
Sports packages: NFL Sunday Ticket, ESPN GamePlan, ESPN FullCourt, NCAA Mega March Madness
Hours: Daily, 11 AM–2 AM

The Stadium Sports Bar & Grill, which opened in 2004, is located near Andrew Square in South Boston and is a popular place with young professionals. The downstairs area is a spacious sports bar with three giant screens and plenty of plasma televisions attached to the brick walls. Upstairs is a sports lounge that is used as a function room and for dancing on the weekends. The bathrooms have televisions, so fans don't have to miss any of the action. The Stadium, which has a sister location at the Foxwoods Resort Casino in Connecticut, features an impressive martini list for those who want an alternative to beer.

Appetizers ($7.99–$8.99) include fried macaroni and cheese and "Castle Island Sliders" (mini-burgers). The menu also includes soups and salads, and main dishes ($7.99–14.99) include melts, burgers, and sandwiches. Entrees include meatloaf, steak tips, pan-seared salmon, baby back ribs, and New York strip steak. The Stadium Sports Bar & Grill has an all-you-can-eat buffet and a Bloody Mary bar during NFL games on Sundays. There is on-street parking around the bar, or it's a short walk from the Andrew Square stop on the Red Line.

BOSTON SPORTS BARS AROUND THE WORLD

Just because you're visiting another city—or another country—doesn't mean that you can't find a sanctuary to watch the Sox, Patriots, or other home teams with fellow Boston sports fans. There are even plenty of safe houses where you can cheer on the Sox in the heart of Yankee territory in Manhattan. While you can usually find a sports bar in another city that may have the Boston game on—along with twenty others—the bars listed below extend their open arms specifically to Boston sports fans. (In many cases, the owners are Boston transplants.) So here are some places—from Sweden to Los Angeles to Japan—to catch the games with your brethren.

Baltimore
Don't Know Tavern, 1453 Light Street, Baltimore, MD 21230. 410-539-0231; www.dontknowtavern.com.

Charlotte
Beantown Tavern, 8155 Ardrey Kell Road, Suite 104, Charlotte, NC 28277. 704-841-1421; www.beantowntavern.com.

Chicago
Brendan's Pub, 3169 N. Broadway, Chicago, IL 60657. 773-929-2929; www.brendanspubchicago.com.
Nic and Dino's Tripoli Tavern, 1147 W. Armitage Avenue, Chicago, IL 60614. 773-477-4400.

Denver
The Pour House Pub, 1435 Market Street, Denver, CO 80202. 303-623-7687.

Florida
Boston Beer Garden, 2396 Immokalee Road, Naples, FL 34110. 239-596-2337; www.bostonbeergardennaples.com.
Boston's on the Beach, 40 South Ocean Boulevard (A1A), Delray Beach, FL 33483. 561-278-3364; www.bostonsonthebeach.com.
Foxboro Sports Tavern, 4420 Thomasson Drive, Naples, FL 34113. 239-530-2337; www.foxborotavern.com.
The Lazy Gecko, 203 Duval Street, Key West, FL 33040. 305-292-1903; www.thelazygecko.com.

Kyoto
Fenway Park, 408 Kawaramachi-dori (between Sanjo and Okie), KUS Building, Third Floor, Kyoto, Japan. 011-81-75-255-4633; www.fenway-park.net.

Los Angeles
Fat Face Fenner's Fishack, 53 Pier Avenue, Hermosa Beach, CA 90254. 310-379-5550.
Sonny McLean's, 2615 Wilshire Boulevard, Santa Monica, CA 90403. 310-449-1811; www.sonnymcleans.com.

New York City
The Hairy Monk, 337 Third Avenue (corner of 25th Street), New York, NY 10010. 212-532-2929; www.thehairymonknyc.com.
Lion's Head Tavern, 995 Amsterdam Avenue, New York, NY 10025. 212-866-1030.
Pat O'Brien's Bar, 1701 Second Avenue (corner of 88th Street), New York, NY 10128. 212-410-2013; www.patobriensnyc.com.
Professor Thom's, 219 Second Avenue (between 13th and 14th streets), New York, NY 10003. 212-260-9480; www.professorthoms.com.
Riviera Cafe & Sports Bar, 225 West 4th Street (corner of Seventh Avenue), New York, NY 10014. 212-929-3250; www.rivieracafe.ypguides.net.
Standings Bar, 43 East 7th Street (between Second Avenue and Cooper Square), New

York, NY 10003. 212-420-0671; www.standingsbar.com.

San Francisco
The Connecticut Yankee, 100 Connecticut Street, San Francisco, CA 94107. 415-552-4440; www.theyankee.com.

San Diego
RT's Longboard Grill, 1466 Garnet Avenue, San Diego, CA 92109. 858-270-4030; www.longboardgrill.com.

Singapore
O'Learys Sports Bar & Grill, Singapore Flyer, 30 Raffles Avenue #01-04, Singapore. 011-65-6337-6718; www.olearys.se.

Stockholm
O'Learys Sports Bar & Grill, Götgatan 11, Stockholm, Sweden. 011-46-8-644-6901; www.olearys.se. (Note: O'Learys also has more than forty locations in Sweden, Norway, and Denmark.)

Washington, DC
Murphy's Grand Irish Pub, 713 King Street, Alexandria, VA 22314. 703-548-1717; www.murphyspub.com.
Rhino Bar & Pumphouse, 3295 M Street NW, Washington, DC 20007. 202-333-3150; www.rhinobardc.com.

BOSTON SPORTS PILGRIMAGES
ROAD TRIPS FOR THE DIE-HARD FAN

Sure, there's always plenty going on around Boston to satisfy the appetite of even the most devoted die-hards, but Boston sports fans will find much to do outside New England as well—from visiting halls of fame to attending sporting events.

Road trips to away games are a great way to get out of town, especially since a game is involved. Let's face it: as much fun as it is to scream with tens of thousands of your brethren, there's something special about invading enemy turf. Plus, with so many sold-out games in Boston, you may have an easier time scoring a ticket to see the pro teams on the road.

A sports-themed vacation offers the perfect excuse to leave New England behind and travel the country. Here is a baker's dozen of road trips that die-hard Boston sports fans can take to visit some of the greatest shrines in sports in order to root, root, root for the home teams.

PRO FOOTBALL HALL OF FAME
Canton, Ohio

All pigskin fans should make at least one trip in their lifetimes to the Pro Football Hall of Fame in Canton, Ohio, an hour's drive south of Cleveland. Among the gridiron greats enshrined in the hall are Patriots Nick Buoniconti, John Hannah, Mike Haynes, and Andre Tippett. Their bronze busts are among those gracing an entire gallery of football legends. In coming years, the hall's annual enshrinement ceremony will become a regular date on the Boston sports calendar as members of the Patriots' Super Bowl championship teams join the ranks of the greats. The museum at the hall includes memorabilia and audio-video displays, and the Super Bowl Room has numerous items related to the Pats. **More information:** www.profootballhof.com.

BRUINS-CANADIENS
Montreal, Canada

The Bruins and Canadiens have been waging a fierce, cross-border battle for more than eighty years. Both members of the Original Six have a rich history, although the Canadiens have an unmatched pedigree of championship success and have gotten the better of the black-and-gold on many an occasion. Make the 300-mile (or 482-kilometer, if you want to get in the Canadian spirit) journey to Montreal for some old-school hockey between bitter foes. Just like the Bruins, the Canadiens abandoned a great old hockey barn, the Forum, for the comforts of a sterile, corporate-named rink, the Bell Centre. The new arena still thunders, however, when the Habs take the ice, and Canadiens fans are always in full throat cheering on their beloved bleu, blanc, et rouge. **More information:** canadiens.nhl.com.

HOCKEY HALL OF FAME
Toronto, Canada

The Hockey Hall of Fame's entrance in the middle of a Toronto shopping center isn't exactly awe-inspiring, but it belies the thrills hockey fans will get once inside. Dozens of Bruins are enshrined in the hall, including Ray Bourque, Cam Neely, and Bobby Orr. The highlight of a trip to the hall is the opportunity to get your picture taken with the Stanley Cup. (Lord Stanley's Mug hasn't been hoisted by the Bruins since before Watergate, so you might want a photo to jog your memory of what it looks like.) The hall is filled with hockey memorabilia, but you can also get interactive and try to get a shot past a goalie or put on the gloves and blockers to try and stone Wayne Gretzky. For a true Boston hockey pilgrimage, time a visit to the hall when the Bruins are in town to play the Maple Leafs. **More information:** www.hhof.com.

RED SOX SPRING TRAINING
Fort Myers, Florida

Legions of Red Sox make the annual trek to Fort Myers, Florida, to catch some rays (not of the Tampa Bay variety) and feel renewed by the crack of the bat and the thwack of the mitt. Fans can watch the team work out at its minor league complex in the early weeks of camp before they take on Grapefruit League opponents at City of Palms Park. (For more information on Red Sox spring training, see page 39.) **More information:** www.redsox.com.

RED SOX-YANKEES
Bronx, New York

Isn't it funny? Just when the Red Sox *finally* conquered all the ghosts that demonized them in the House that Ruth Built, the Yankees up and move into a swanky, brand new stadium across the street. While the venue for the fiercest rivalry in American sport has switched to the House that George Steinbrenner (and New York City Taxpayers) Built, the intensity of the matchup has lost none of its luster. On your way home from the Bronx, stop by Babe Ruth's grave at Gate of Heaven Cemetery in Hawthorne, New York, thirty miles north of Yankee Stadium, and offer your condolences at the loss of his old stomping ground. **More information:** www.yankees.com.

NATIONAL BASEBALL HALL OF FAME AND MUSEUM
Cooperstown, New York

There are few bigger thrills for baseball fans than a pilgrimage to the sleepy upstate New York hamlet of Cooperstown. Seamheads can easily spend an entire day in the Baseball Hall of Fame, browsing artifacts and reading the plaques honoring the pantheon of baseball deities enshrined in hardball heaven. Statues of Ted Williams and Babe Ruth grace the entrance, and the Boston connections don't end there. Inside the museum are the promissory note selling Babe Ruth to the Yankees; baseballs from no-hitters tossed by Sox hurlers Jon Lester, Clay Buchholz, Derek Lowe, and Hideo Nomo; Ted Williams' cleats and gloves; and Curt Schilling's famed bloody sock from the 2004 championship season. An exhibit on old ballparks includes a virtual tour of the South End Grounds and items from the first World Series at the Huntington Avenue Grounds. To make it a complete hall of fame road trip, check out the National Soccer Hall of Fame in nearby Oneonta, New York, and stop by the Basketball Hall of Fame in Springfield, Massachusetts, along the 240-mile trek from Boston to Cooperstown. **More information:** www.baseballhalloffame.org. For Soccer Hall of Fame and Basketball Hall of Fame: www.soccerhall.org; www.hoophall.com.

COLLEGE FOOTBALL HALL OF FAME
South Bend, Indiana

Boston College has dominated football's "Holy War" with Notre Dame in recent years, but the bad news for the Eagles is that its series with the Fighting Irish is due to end in 2010. BC will pay its last visit to South Bend in 2009, which provides a great opportunity to visit tradition-rich Notre Dame Stadium, always high on a sports fan's wish list. Even if you can't make the game, Boston sports fans would be interested in visiting downtown South Bend and the College Football Hall of Fame. Eagles fans will enjoy the exhibits related to Doug Flutie, one of the more recent inductees. Other greats from BC, Boston University, Harvard, and Northeastern are enshrined in the hall, including Harry Agganis, "the Golden Greek." In addition to the hall's exhibits, visitors can test their passing, blocking, and kicking skills or participate in a football strategy clinic. **More information:** www.collegefootball.org.

IVAN ALLEN JR. BRAVES MUSEUM & HALL OF FAME
Atlanta, Georgia

Baseball fans who remember when the Braves called Boston home will enjoy the Ivan Allen Jr. Braves Museum & Hall of Fame at Turner Field. Much of the museum focuses on the team's exploits in Atlanta, but a section devoted to the team's eighty-two seasons in Boston includes a painted mural of the South End Grounds, ten different Boston jerseys, mementos from the 1914 and 1948 World Series, and an exhibit on Babe Ruth's brief stint with the team. Even for die-hard fans of the Boston Braves, the museum itself probably doesn't warrant a separate trip to Atlanta, but the Red Sox play interleague games in Atlanta on occasion and the Celtics and Bruins make annual appearances in Georgia's capital city—so keep it in mind if you're on the road. **More information:** www.braves.mlb.com.

FROZEN FOUR
Various sites

While it doesn't capture the same national attention as college basketball's Final Four, the semifinals and finals of the men's NCAA Ice Hockey Championship often have a Boston flavor. Boston College, which won the title in 2001 and 2008, has appeared in twenty-one Frozen Fours and has been a regular entrant in recent years. Boston University has twenty-one appearances as well, and the Terriers captured the crown in 2009. Northeastern and Harvard have made sporadic appearances, but other New England teams, such as New Hampshire and Maine, have appeared with greater frequency. The Frozen Four is being played in Detroit in 2010, Saint Paul in 2011, and Tampa in 2012. **More information:** www.ncaa.com.

BOSTON COLLEGE-DUKE/BOSTON COLLEGE-NORTH CAROLINA
Durham & Chapel Hill, North Carolina

When Boston College made the jump to the Atlantic Coast Conference in 2005, they joined what might be the best men's college basketball conference in the country. The move also meant that BC plays two perennial powers, North Carolina and Duke, each year. Make a trip down to Tobacco Road and take in a game among the Cameron Crazies at Duke or a sea of Carolina blue at Chapel Hill. The fans at these two universities are as passionate about their teams as Boston fans are about the Red Sox. **More information:** www.goduke.com; tarheelblue.cstv.com.

CELTICS-LAKERS
Los Angeles, California

Even though they only play twice each year, the rivalry between the two most storied franchises in the NBA—the Celtics and the Los Angeles Lakers—is among the greatest in sports. Boston and Los Angeles could hardly be further apart in just about every measure: distance, culture, weather, walkability, history. Even the traditional styles of play between the half-court, defensive Celtics and the run-and-gun Showtime Lakers are polar opposites. The clash of cultures and styles feeds into the rivalry, which was renewed when the two teams met in the 2008 NBA Finals, twenty-one years after their last playoff matchup. Take in a game at Tinseltown and be on the lookout for noted Laker fan Jack Nicholson and the other A-list celebrities. Just don't expect them to join you in chants of "Beat LA." **More information:** www.nba.com/lakers.

PATRIOTS-DOLPHINS/PATRIOTS-BILLS
Miami, Florida/Buffalo, New York

The Orange Bowl, the former home of the Miami Dolphins, used to be a house of horrors for the Patriots, but these days the Pats have had some success in heading to Florida to "Squish the Fish." Many Patriots fans circle the date of the Miami game on the calendar and head south for some sun and fun. Tickets are usually fairly easy to get your hands on. If you're more partial to lake-effect snow and buffalo wings, skip the flight to Miami and make the trek with the Patriots to Buffalo instead. The driving directions are easy: get on the Mass Pike heading west and go straight for 460 miles until you reach the stadium. **More information:** www.miamidolphins.com; www.buffalobills.com.

TED WILLIAMS MUSEUM AND HITTERS HALL OF FAME
St. Petersburg, Florida

Ted Williams once said that when he walked down the street he wanted people to say, "There goes the greatest hitter who ever lived." In the mind of many baseball fans, the Splendid Splinter achieved that goal. Who better than Williams then to have created a hall of fame dedicated to baseball's best hitters? Located in the Tropicana Dome, home of the Tampa Bay Rays, the Ted Williams Museum and Hitters Hall of Fame includes game-used baseballs, uniforms, and bats in display cases honoring each hall of famer. Displays about Teddy Ballgame range from his days in the military to his professional playing career to his love of fishing. The museum is only open to fans attending Tampa Bay Rays games, so if you're going to visit, you might as well do it when the Sox are in town. (Fun fact: Red Sox closer Jonathan Papelbon's father is a deputy director of the museum.) **More information:** www.twmuseum.com.

RESOURCES

TICKET AGENCIES

In addition to checking with the teams, sports fans may want to contact the following ticket brokers, ticket agencies, and ticket resellers for seats. The following list is not intended to be a comprehensive directory of ticket agencies around Boston nor an endorsement of any particular company.

Ace Ticket
One Braintree Street
Allston, MA 02134
Phone: 800-MY-SEATS
www.aceticket.com

Bay State Tickets & Travel, LLC
PO Box 646
Swampscott, MA 01907
Phone: 781-599-8499
www.baystatetickets.com

Best Tickets
200 Boylston Street
Chestnut Hill, MA 02467
Phone: 617-527-2378
www.bestticketsus.com

Front Row Ticket Agency
795 Elm Street
Manchester, NH 03101
Phone: 603-668-8880
www.fronttix.com

Higs Tickets
69 Causeway Street
Boston, MA 02215
Phone: 617-722-4116
www.higstickets.com

Hub Ticket Agency
800 Boylston Street, Suite 120
Boston, MA 02199
Phone: 617-426-8340
www.hubticket.com

Hub Ticket Brokers
1011 Beacon Street
Brookline, MA 02446
Phone: 617-487-4353
www.hubticketbrokers.com

Mr. Ticket
329 Lowell Street
Wilmington, MA 01887
Phone: 978-658-4810
www.misterticket.com

Out of Town Ticket Agency
872 Massachusetts Avenue, #1-6
Cambridge, MA 02139
Phone: 617-247-1300
www.outoftowntickets.com

Primio Tickets
PO Box 1006
Tewksbury, MA 01876
Phone: 978-824-2329
www.primiotickets.com

RazorGator
Phone: 800-542-4466
www.razorgator.com

StubHub
665 Beacon Street, Suite 200
Boston, MA 02215
Phone: 866-STUBHUB
www.stubhub.com

Ticketmaster
Phone: 617-931-2000
www.ticketmaster.com

Ticketplace
1540 Bulgarmarsh Road
Tiverton, RI 02878
Phone: 800-763-3502
www.ticketplace.com

TicketsNow
Phone: 800-927-2770
www.ticketsnow.com

Top Star Tickets
225 Wales Street
Abington, MA 02351
Phone: 781-982-8046
www.topstartickets.com

BLOGS AND WEBSITES

In addition to the team websites listed throughout the book, the following blogs and websites, from both media outlets and fans, cover individual Boston sports teams and Boston sports as a whole.

Boston sports
www.newengland.comcastsportsnet.com
www.barstoolsports.com
www.bornintoit.com
www.boston.com/sports
www.bostonherald.com/sports
www.bostonsportsguide.com
www.bostonsportsmedia.com
www.bostonsportz.com
www.espnboston.com
www.nes247.com
www.nesn.com

www.newenglandsportsmag.com
www.overthemonster.com
www.realbostonsportsfans.com
www.soxanddawgs.com
www.weei.com
www.1510thezone.com

Boston Red Sox
joyofsox.blogspot.com
www.bostondirtdogs.com
www.fenwaydata.com
www.fenwayfanatics.com
www.fenwaynation.com
www.girlsoxnation.com
www.redsoxconnection.com
www.redsoxnation.net
www.sawxblog.com
www.sawxheads.com
www.sonsofsamhorn.com
www.survivinggrady.com
www.theremyreport.com

Boston Bruins
www.bostonrinkrats.com
www.hubhockey.com

Boston Celtics
www.bostoncelticsnews.com
www.celticsblog.com
www.redsarmy.com

New England Patriots
www.gopats.com
www.patriotsblog.net
www.patriotsinsider.com
www.patsfans.com
www.patspulpit.com
www.pfwonline.com

New England Revolution
revsfans.blogspot.com
www.midnightriders.com
www.soccer-new-england.com

Photo Credits

Baseball: p29, Christopher Klein; p34, Christopher Klein.

Basketball: p84, Nicole Vecchiotti.

Football: p93, Christopher Klein; p98, Christopher Klein; p104, Smongkol Teng; p115, Christopher Klein.

Hockey: p128, Christopher Klein; p144, Eric Kilby.

Soccer: p151, Keith Nordstrom/New England Revolution; p152, Keith Nordstrom/New England Revolution; p157, Kevin Hassett/Boston Breakers.

Golf: p175, Christopher Klein.

Horse Racing: p179, Christopher Klein.

Lacrosse: p188, Mark Stern; p190, Boston Cannons.

Rowing: p201, Christopher Klein; p202, Christopher Klein.

Running: p209, Jeffrey Dengate; p210, Mark Stern; p214, Alonso Nichols/Tufts University.

Tennis: p223, Karen Draymore.

Additional Spectator Sports: p227, Boston Demons Australian Rules Football Club; p228, Christopher Klein; p232, Christopher Klein; p234, Patricia King Powers.